The Trans/National Study of Culture

Also of Interest

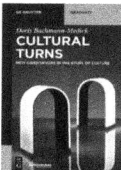

Cultural Turns: New Orientations in the Study of Culture
Doris Bachmann-Medick, 2016
ISBN 978-3-11-040297-1, e-ISBN (PDF) 978-3-11-040298-8,
Set-ISBN (EPUB) 978-3-11-040307-7

The Trans/National Study of Culture

A Translational Perspective

Edited by
Doris Bachmann-Medick

DE GRUYTER

This book was first published as a hardcover volume in 2014 in the series *Concepts for the Study of Culture*.

ISBN 978-3-11-045469-7

Library of Congress Cataloging-in-Publication Data
A CIP catalog record for this book has been applied for at the Library of Congress.

Bibliographic information published by the Deutsche Nationalbibliothek
The Deutsche Nationalbibliothek lists this publication in the Deutsche Nationalbibliografie;
detailed bibliographic data are available on the Internet at http://dnb.dnb.de.

© 2016 Walter de Gruyter GmbH, Berlin/Boston
Cover image: "Transnational Tijuana" – a design project that reconfigures the border zone
along the U.S. and Mexico border, by Nathanael Dorent (2009). © Nathanael Dorent
Printing and binding: CPI books GmbH, Leck
♾ Printed on acid-free paper
Printed in Germany

www.degruyter.com

Preface and Acknowledgements

Is there such a thing as a 'transnational study of culture?'

At present, the study of culture seems to be defined by a diversity of approaches in (Western) academe that go by the name of cultural studies, *Kulturwissenschaften*, *sciences humaines*, and other designations. These approaches differ from each other in their objects of study, research foci, internal histories, and institutionalizations. How can these differences be made productive for an emerging transnational study of culture? Before we can speak of a transnational study of culture, we are called upon to critically reflect its conditions. Exploring and estimating the diversification of nation-specific modes of approaching cultural phenomena are certainly important prerequisites for a truly trans/national study of culture that is no longer dominated by the Anglo-American model of cultural studies. But, in a wider horizon, this volume also demands critical self-positioning of the trans/national project itself – that is, reflection on its geopolitical preconditions and the often binary conceptualizations that shape our perceptions of different but entangled research cultures. The adoption of the concept of 'translation' as an analytical category offers an inspiring perspective to break open these presuppositions.

The transnationalization of the study of culture: a project of translation

The initial impetus for this book came from a conference on *The Transnational Study of Culture* at the International Graduate Centre for the Study of Culture (GCSC). This conference paved the way for continued discussion on translation as an analytical category that uncovers the pivot points of a transnational study of culture. By employing a translational perspective, this volume provides complex and critical views on the possibilities, practices, barriers, obstacles, and resistances that affect encounters between different systems of cultural research and the trans/national endeavor in general. On various levels, we are confronted with unequal conditions and power asymmetries – in terms of academic authority, the prevalence of certain analytical categories, and nation-specific differences in defining and practicing the study of culture. These frictions can and should not simply be bridged by using the category of translation in an all too smooth fashion. Beyond being a fruitful methodological impetus, a translational perspective can also serve as a critical, meta-reflective stance on interruptions in the exchange between different research systems and traditions – embedded in their histories, affected by colonial displacement. This stance can even reach the point of considering untranslatabilities.

Thinking on a global scale – acting in local networks

The effort to develop a transnational vocabulary and find common reference points transforms the project of a critical, transnational study of culture into a globally minded enterprise. Nevertheless, the transnational study of culture still accounts for local/regional and national self-positioning, which demands critical reflection of one's own categories of investigation. This entails concern for the possibilities and challenges of everyday 'small-scale communication,' which comprises a specifically translational dimension of its own in this volume and emanates from the GCSC's continuous efforts to translate between various disciplines and its culturally diverse members. I would, therefore, especially like to thank my colleagues at the GCSC, who have engaged in this transnational/translational project – both as a matter of concrete experience and in terms of wider, theoretical conceptualization. Above all, my thanks go to Ansgar Nünning, for his generous support, and to Martin Zierold. Both, together with Kirsten Zierold, provided invaluable advice and encouragement in planning the initial conference and proceeding with this volume. I am also grateful to my colleagues from different disciplines at the Justus-Liebig-Universität Giessen for their fruitful commentaries at the conference and their continuous interest in the work of the GCSC. This project would not be possible without the generous financial support of the German Research Foundation and the GCSC.

Special thanks go to the contributors of this volume for their productive endurance during the gestation period of this volume; and to Elizabeth Kovach, Kate Oden, and Robert Ryder, who, as native speakers, have polished several articles. Elizabeth Kovach, assisted by Melanie Mihm, did a marvelous job in preparing the manuscript for publication. I am also very grateful to Hans Medick and David W. Cohen for adding translational refinements and further stimulating ideas to this project, which contributes to a 'trans(n/l)ational turn' currently underway in contemporary humanities and social sciences. My hope is that the book will stimulate future debates.

Giessen, December 2013
Doris Bachmann-Medick

Contents

II. Knowledge Systems and Discursive Fields

Doris Bachmann-Medick
The Trans/National Study of Culture

A Translational Perspective

> We need new sets of translations across different
> philosophical cultures so as to rearrange the pre-
> sent segregation of discourses. Transpositions of
> ideas, norms, practices, communities and theo-
> retical genealogies have to be allowed and even
> encouraged. (Braidotti 2006: 33)

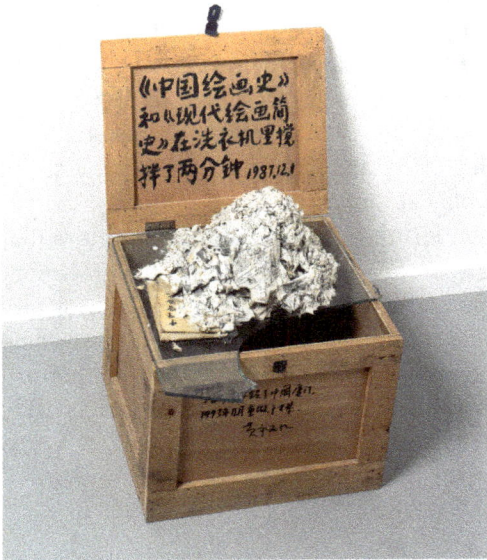

Fig. 1: Huang Yong Ping, *The History of Chinese Painting and the History of Modern Western Art Washed in the Washing Machine for Two Minutes*, 1987–1993 (Collection Walker
Art Center, Minneapolis, T. B. Walker Acquisition Fund, 2001); © VG Bild-Kunst, Bonn
2013.

The installation by the Chinese Dadaist Huang Yong Ping from 1987, *The History of Chinese Painting and the History of Modern Western Art Washed in the Washing Machine for Two Minutes,* immediately evokes the thematic scope of this book. In the front, on top of a Chinese tea caddy, lies the end product of a post-modern mélange of long-standing east-western art histories: a little heap of shredded, disintegrated texts. These were once two classical art history books – Wang Bomin's *History of Chinese Painting* (1982) and Herbert Read's *A Concise History of Modern Painting* (1959) (the first history of modern Western art to be translated into Chinese).[1] This kind of ironic critique challenges the idea of a purity of art history and cultural history as well as hierarchies of knowledge. It can be extended into a critical reflection of national traditions of knowledge, their hegemonies and the lack of entanglement in intercultural scholarly research in general.

Following up on the message of these shreds, one could ask: Does the transnationalization of the study of culture under globalized conditions lead to these kinds of hybridization of different academic histories? Does it result – in the course of going through the western laundry – only in diffuse lumps of knowledge? The danger is real. Because – as the comparatists Wang Ning and Sun Yifeng highlight from their point of view – even cultural studies is in the process of internationalizing and hybridizing itself. Yet it has, up to now, not been able to break out of its monolingual mode: "At present cultural studies is also a crisis of a monolingual mode" (Ning and Yifeng 2008: 12). Obviously, language and translation come into play at this point. Do they function as media of reproduction and dissemination for transnational studies of culture that will lead, in the end, to a common academic language? Or do they function, rather, as media of productive differentiation and separation that call for permanent negotiation, interlocution, and mediation? Perhaps we can make some progress on this question in this volume – provided, however, we neither use the washing machine (i.e. merely hybridize) nor fill up neat tea caddies (i.e. simply localize or even essentialize). Perhaps what is needed, instead, is a type

---

1 Cf. Koslow Miller 2006; and esp. the artist's own statement: "Book washing is somewhat similar to Wittgenstein's view of language. He once said: 'Now and then, some wordings should be removed from language and be sent to be washed—and after that, they can be brought back into communication.' What I do can be summed up as the following: 'washing' is both the method and the goal, because I don't believe that language can be brought back into communication after having been washed. In other words, communication is in reality a 'dirty form.' In addition, 'book washing' is not about making culture cleaner; rather, it tries to make its dirtiness more evident to the eye" ("To Beat the West with the East and to Beat the East with the West," cited in Hanru 2005).

of centrifuge in order to recapture the indispensible claims of difference and historicization from the general dynamics of a global circulation of theory.

The "crisis of a monolingual mode," to which Ning and Yifeng allude, refers to two recent developments: a crisis in American cultural studies, which remains caught up in its hegemonic position through the Anglocentric monolingualism of global English, and a crisis of the monolingual mode itself. This is a crisis, because in the framework of an established dominating language, a transnational study of culture can never be developed beyond being an Anglo-American expansionist project. However, this book hardly declares itself satisfied with the pessimistic diagnosis of the Australian Jon Stratton and the Indonesian-Australian cultural researcher Ien Ang that truly transnational studies of culture are impossible (cf. Stratton and Ang 1996). It asks, instead, a more constructive question: How can we counteract monolingualism in the study of culture?

One suggestion is to position the study of culture, in its continuing commitment to transnationalization, explicitly as a project of translation (cf. Bachmann-Medick 2011). But, then again, one could ask: Does this not just move the problem elsewhere? Do the conditions of a global circulation of knowledge really change when they are understood as relations of translation? Here I say: Yes – but on the condition that we do not get caught up in such relations of translation, in the issues of translatability and untranslatability; on the condition that we do not let ourselves be satisfied with specific local cultural translations along the lines of inventing an Arab Ramadan Burger, which, in fact, is just an American Big Mac in disguise.

All this is not about working out a menu for a transnational study of culture, with Anglo-American cultural studies as the main course offering different flavours in different places. A more fundamental approach would be to work towards truly pluralizing cultural studies itself into multi-sited courses and discourses, and thus "provincializing" it at the same time – in the sense of Dipesh Chakrabarty, who in his pathbreaking work suggested a "provincializing" of Europe, meaning that the claim that European analytical categories are universally applicable and meant to be spread over the whole world should be critically re-localized, massively questioned, and undermined (Chakrabarty 2000; see also Dipesh Chakrabarty's contribution to this volume). Thus, on the one hand, the thematic scope of a transnational study of culture should definitely be widespread.

But, on the other hand, in pursuing this goal, case studies remain a conscious starting point in this volume and we will ask: Where is concrete engagement actually possible – even when bearing in mind the more comprehensive aims to 1) break open the monolingual system of cultural studies as a whole and, in addition, 2) to "provincialize" Anglo-American cultural studies in particular.

1 The Transnational Study of Culture – A Localizing Perspective

This volume's subtitle already points towards a first starting point: The study of culture is to be pluralized and, in each case, to be analyzed for the social conditions of its emergence and the historicity of its theoretical traditions. To begin with, therefore, this means starting at the level of knowledge *production*. The different studies of culture may well be anchored in their respective Anglo-American, German, French, Eastern European, Australian or Asian academic systems. But it seems questionable whether such localizations really *precede* their transnationalization. After all, these academic systems have themselves already become internally multi-local due to translations back and forth, overlapping, friction, and transformations. The understanding of these national knowledge systems should in no way be subjugated to assumptions of a "methodological nationalism" (Beck 2000: 21–24) that takes the nation-state as a standard for academic research and analysis. Despite their assumed national location, they rather could be considered in the way that Robert Stam and Ella Shohat claim to be adequate: as being caught in a web of "a translational relationality" (Stam and Shohat 2012: 298), as a stepping stone "to perform an analytical dislocation by constructing and deconstructing, threading and unraveling the tangled webs of ideas and practices that constitute complicated national and regional formations" (Stam and Shohat 2012: 299).

A little semi-fictitious dialogue 'invented' by me here is meant to show how necessary it is to open the debate to this kind of "translational relationality:"

"Do the 'cultural turns' suggested in the context of German *Kulturwissenschaften* (cf. Bachmann-Medick 2014) really only embody a 'one-way street' from the USA to Europe" (as Hartmut Böhme has claimed in a 2008 review essay on *Cultural Turns*)?

"Not at all, because in the USA an explicit and cross-disciplinary discourse on 'cultural turns' has not yet been established."

"Then what is specifically American about the 'turns'?"

"Perhaps it is simply a projection of the idea of a superficial orientation of American cultural studies towards new trends and of the short-livedness of their concepts – which is quite the opposite to the German idea of 'disciplines working in the *longue dureé*' (cf. Böhme 2008)."

"So what then is specifically German about the 'turns'?"

"The tendency to do basic research on theoretical and conceptual developments in the study of culture seems characteristic for the German scene. Within this frame 'cultural turns' are being conceived and discussed systematically as theoretical (re)orientations – and, on top of that, they are being argued about in a historical mode."

"So the 'turns' seem to be rather a specific product of German *Kulturwissenschaften*?"

"Etc., etc."

One could ask: Does this kind of conversation really lead to fruitful insights? The answer would be: Amazingly yes, but only if it does not just result in reassertions of national ascriptions, origins and originals, if it provides new insights into entanglements and also stimulates debates "beyond the international binary" (Stratton and Ang 1996: 361), as hopefully this book will do. At any rate, this kind of dialogue points to a discursive field of highly complex interconnections. These arise precisely not just from manifest transfers of theory and corresponding processes of reception. They also imply generalized images of research attitudes as well as theoretical projections. They consist of misunderstandings, stereotyped narratives of theories and their genealogies, which feed into the self-understandings and legitimations of academic traditions, even into the developments of theory itself – not to mention the anxieties, narcissisms and competitions or even the essentializations of certain points of view (as in the 'purity' argument expressed in the widespread sceptical questions: Do the German *Kulturwissenschaften* actually need American cultural studies? Shouldn't they, after all, better concentrate on revitalizing the research approaches of their own academic tradition more strongly?).

A transnational game of ping-pong has already been going on for some time in the study of culture. And it does not just apply to the *production* of knowledge, but also to the *distribution* of knowledge: Transfers and travelling concepts have been and are the transport tracks of theory-translation. Yet here, too, one should not be overly hasty about going down the cultural mobility route. One needs to ask: How is knowledge itself gained in the first place – *before* or *through* its dissemination around the world? How one answers these questions depends on whether a "singular origin" (Abbas and Erni 2005: 5) can still be claimed for western scholarship as an assumed homogenous and hegemonic site of the production of knowledge and theories, which are then consumed in export markets outside of Europe through travelling concepts. We can expect some answers when greater attention than heretofore is directed towards internal differences – towards the slippages in transfer and breaks in translation that are already in operation between and within different European approaches themselves. By doing this, intersections might come to light from which the assumption of a European or American monolingualism could be broken-up:

The *first* point to ask then should be: What are the main sources, institutions, movements, and debates from which theories actually develop in different intellectual traditions – are these only academic practices at universities or other academic establishments? Aren't they also developed by public intellectuals, critical journalists, and the media (cf. Thomas Weber's contribution in this volume), or by the specific institutional constellations of academic systems (cf. Matthias Middell's article in this volume)? Or are social movements themselves even decisive for the development of cultural concepts and theories (as is the case with postcolonial cultural studies in Australia in its affinity towards Aboriginal people, Critical Whiteness, and "New Australian Feminism" – see Christa Knellwolf King's contribution to this volume)?

The issue, therefore, is not just about the transfers between nationally specific academic forms of cultural analysis. Focussing merely on these has the effect of diverting attention from an awareness of other, quite different, but very influential relations of exchange – such as those taking place among disciplines, intellectual spheres, practices, and even social and political movements. To name one example: In a fundamental essay, the German historian Reinhard Blänkner highlighted the far-reaching importance of this new kind of 'shift in form' ("Formwandel") through translation of one form of knowledge into another (Blänkner 2008: 366). Thus, as he states, the current post-colonially informed form of global history does not feed primarily on the questionable (European) forms of historical knowledge and history writing, but, surprisingly, rather on literary models (in particular those that originated in the context of postcolonial movements). Because – according to Blänkner's thesis – "it was only through the symbolic mode of literature that the so-called 'people without history' could finally enter the stage of world-history" (Blänkner 2008: 365, 362).

A *second* point to ask would be: Which discourses have been and are actually decisive in forming the main directions in the studies of culture? Have they developed out of historical or literary studies, or rather from the social sciences? In these specific settings, different conditions may have been created for further transnational developments, for the receptivity to or defence against specific theoretical understandings in one place as compared to those in another.

A *third* question could be posed, asking not only which theories and concepts are transferred, reviewed and transformed in each case, but also which are or have been selected by the authority and "interest" of intellectual gatekeepers (cf. Bourdieu 1999: 222–224), which are possibly denied or explicitly suppressed. Research into transfers concentrates all too easily on cases where transfer processes are or have been successful, but not on express non-transfers, on refusals of transfers or even on failures.

But how, in fact, can the complex insights into differences, breaks, and translational gains and losses between the different traditions in the studies of culture be interpreted? There is a danger of stopping short at cultural interpretation and thereby separating off the cultural sphere – for example, by making culture an "unreflectedly and thoughtlessly over-integrated" concept (Beck 2006: 71), or reducing it to just the production of meaning. How transfers and relations of transformation between studies of culture are judged also depends on the extent to which culture as a field of research itself is put under the translational x-ray: sociologically, economically, politically, and institutionally. Just by doing this, significant differences between academic traditions and systems of the study of culture become visible: the relationship between culture and power is moulded differently in each case. These kinds of translational fracture could point to how and where, *within* individual academic cultures, a 'shift in form' is taking place, as a translation between different forms of knowledge.

To what extent are social and societal relations (including social conflicts) translated into a cultural mode and to what extent, on the other hand, does the study of culture have to be translated back into other forms of knowledge, into fields of practice and spheres of analysis (cf. Bachmann-Medick 2011)? In any case, it seems no longer sufficient simply to reduce translation, transfer and travelling concepts to transmissions of meanings. What needs to be elucidated much more clearly is their involvement in institutional networks like university structures, in intellectual practices up to and including publishing, in the ways the translation market is composed, and in political-cultural fields of power (see Andreas Langenohl's contribution to this volume and new approaches to a sociology of translation, esp. Wolf and Fukari 2007). A further important differential criterion for the analysis of (uneven) transnational intellectual exchanges could be pursued with the question regarding to what extent studies of culture receive conceptual stimuli through debates outside of the university.

If we understand studies of culture as this kind of very complex intellectual, scholarly, and scientific practice, then approaches from the history of science are explicitly called for. Under these auspices, for example, British cultural studies would no longer appear as a homogeneous block. Rather, it could be seen as a succession of theory generations working with a sequence of "key concepts" from the 1960s to the 1990s.[2]

Analyses in the history of science, the question of a generation-specific approach to theory formation, to 'turns' and their historical-political contextualizations are in fact fruitful starting points for a localization of theories and concepts. Thirty years ago in his already classic essay "Traveling Theory," Edward Said took a clear stance on this. He called for theories to be inserted back into the contexts in which they arose, despite their later 'journeys.' Why this call for contextual specificity? Is this at all still necessary in times of global hybridization and migration? Should we still be searching for origins or unified theories at all, since it seems that these can no longer legitimately be claimed, and since theories develop whilst travelling and during the course of their transformations? As Johannes Angermüller recently said, theories always take shape when and where they are applied, where they operate; a telling example is the "French poststructuralism" that emerged not in France but rather later in the USA, which was then re-imported into the French "intellectual field" (cf. Angermüller 2007). Another example could be the different understandings of the concept '*transferts culturels*.' This concept was coined in France, but then travelled in shifting 'timetables' or rather met with simultaneous developments of similar concepts – in the U.S., for instance, with 'cultural encounter' in the context of new forms of writing world history and, in Germany, with 'comparative historiography' (cf. Middell's contribution in this book).

So, should we position a re-location or lack of origin of theories and concepts versus their emergence through their application (in other places)? Certainly, we should not get caught up with these binaries. Rather, we should be working out how both standpoints call for specific understandings of localization, contextualization, and translation as well as for a social and political grounding for the metaphor of 'travelling concepts.' Thus, several contributions to this volume (Nünning, Middell, as well as Langenohl and Bachmann-Medick) ask how specific frames of reference are activated in this process, how speaking positions are taken up, and to what extent theories are linked to social agency and to a cultural and social "field of production" – to formulate it in the terms of Pierre Bourdieu's theory of social and discursive fields (Bourdieu 1999: 221). To make a final point regarding the question of the necessity of localization: Even

---

2 A further example for these complex academic/institutional/political/generation-specific conditions for the different ways of developing national specific research traditions – in the field of anthropology – is offered by the volume *One Discipline, Four Ways* (Barth et al. 2005); on the question of German studies as cultural studies (USA versus Germany), see Lützeler 2013.

in times of global overlapping and mixing, processes of localization seem more important than ever – in order to stem hegemonic tendencies, in order to emphasize diversity, and in order to allow a multi-local production of theory.

What does this all mean for us as researchers in the field of a possibly transnational and transcultural study of culture? In the first instance, it calls on us to be more attentive to the close connection that already exists between theories and the particular fields of force in which they emerged and are being applied. On the level of localization itself, our task is to separate out the often interwoven threads of theory formation into translation scenarios so as to follow them as concretely as possible. These threads should be differentiated with an eye for brokers, mediations, processes of dissemination, and (often productive) misunderstanding. Only in this way can we arrive at a precise awareness of knowledge asymmetries as well as the entangled histories of knowledge formation, not least at the level of a discontinuous unfolding and elaboration of theories.

Certainly advocating a translational approach is understood here in a much broader sense than we are used to know from philological and linguistic contexts. The critical point of departure here is precisely in not taking recourse to the assumption of an 'original' or a conceptual 'origin point,' usually situated in the West. There is no 'origin point' of (western) theory. Theories are always already translated or translate themselves into new contexts. It is remarkable how dependent the concept of modernism was, for example, on African and Asian art before it, in turn, became a tremendous challenge for societies outside of Europe as an explicit European concept. In this sense, translation – as Stuart Hall emphasizes – is "a continuous process of re-articulation and re-contextualisation, without any notion of a primary origin" (Hall 1996: 393).

Translation as re-contextualization demands an endeavor to first localize cultural analyses and engage intensively with different approaches, by no means all European – something that is certainly an aim of this book. However, it is not enough to simply circulate back and forth between nationally or regionally influenced cultures of knowledge and systems in the study of culture – from the CCCS in Birmingham through to, perhaps, the GCSC in Gießen. We also should not stop at mainstream classifications. Instead, we should be asking: What are the causes and consequences, actually, of characterizing Anglophone cultural studies as more strongly politicized than German *Kulturwissenschaften*, as more strongly connected to ethnic groups and civil rights movements, as focused more on questions of power and oriented towards the analysis of popular culture (cf. Ansgar Nünning's and Rainer Winter's contributions; cf. also Musner 1999, 2001)? In contrast, to what extent and why are German *Kulturwissenschaften* characterized as interdisciplinary and systematic research efforts that, whilst less politically oriented, tend towards more fundamental kinds of research and historical reflection? And what does it mean for the study of culture if the French *Sciences Humaines* are located in a close interface with the *Sciences Sociales* and are thus closer to social analysis (Chalard-Fillaudeau 2009, 2010; Laberge 2009)? At all events, the spectrum outlined here would have to be opened up further by tracing Eastern European, Asian, and African variants, which are themselves highly complex (for cultural studies in Africa, cf. Tomaselli and Wright 2011, and Japan, cf. Schäfer 2009), as well as the Latin American *Estudios Culturales*. For their part, most of these re-articulations outside of Europe critically position "cultural studies as part of a global decolonization movement" (as Kuan-Hsing Chen put it with regard to *Trajectories: Towards a New Internationalist Cultural Studies*, a series of conferences and a key project within cultural studies in Asia; Chen 1998: 4). They understand transnationally oriented cultural studies as "attempts at decolonizing cultural studies" (Shome 2012: 6), or in general as a postcolonial-inspired, counter-hegemonic project (Berry et al. 2009; Shome 2012; Keim 2008).

Can this spectrum of different studies of culture, as sketched here, develop transnational potential? Yes, as it leaves behind a merely additive configuration and then opens itself up anew as a constellation of translation, as an emerging network of reciprocal absorptions, transmissions, interactions, but also of dominations. Such an approach may bring specific studies of culture into new 'constellations' with one another, but it may, again, produce differentiations. In doing so, national specificities will remain a decisive differential criterion for these academic traditions. Surely, we must try to go beyond this narrow mapping, following the boundaries of nation-states by studying not only differences, but also by stressing the old or new inter-weavings or blurrings of former lines of tradition or unilateral positionings. But how far will we remain caught up in this mapping of the national? It is still at work to some extent in the concept of the 'trans/national' as far as categories are concerned (see the title of this book).

Rather than focus on national identities and differences, it could be especially productive to look towards the development of transcultural "epistemic spaces" and, in doing so, focus on the "indeterminacy" of languages, knowledge systems, and people (cf. Jon Solomon's groundbreaking contribution to this volume). Epistemic spaces are – according to Stuart Hall – spaces of knowledge that are opened up tangentially to established academic systems through concepts and theoretical focuses that cross boundaries (cf. Hall 1996: 395).

But even seizing such a widened horizon should not prevent us from engaging in detailed analysis – with regard to multilateral transfers and borrowings, misunderstandings and re-interpretations – not from observing things and phenomena that seem to be or are regarded as untranslatable. Even the 'abduction' of theories and concepts among different academic systems should be kept in view. And yet we should not stop at these relations of transfer, but rather push forward to the foundations that shaped these different systems of the study of culture in the first place: in other words, consider the linguistic standardizations and classifications of which they are part and investigate how these went hand in hand with building the nation-state. These kinds of linguistic standardizations almost always imply, at the same time, territorializations. They have consequences for the positioning of research traditions within the colonial system (cf. Jon Solomon's critique in this volume), as well as in the world-wide economic and cultural division of labor.

2 The Transnational Study of Culture – A Universalizing Perspective

So far I have foregrounded the *production* and *distribution* of knowledge. A further important point in the transnationalization of the study of culture concerns the *legitimation* and *institutionalization* of knowledge, as, for instance, claimed by the Canadian cultural studies scholars Richard Cavell and Imre Szeman: "Cultural studies thus emerges as a mode of critique of forms of the legitimation of knowledge – of the creation of cultural *capital* in Bourdieu's sense – and first and foremost of the university's role in this process" (Cavell and Szeman 2007: 3).

Certainly, the extent to which, and how critically, studies of culture actually stand in relation to other forms of the legitimation of knowledge in society should be examined at a more institutional level of academic fields and of intellectual capital. But the concrete circumstances of local and global expenditure of cultural-intellectual capital are also crucial, not least when hegemonic claims to theoretical influence are being asserted and authorities or even gatekeepers of theory are being established. Just how necessary it is to carry out analysis in this field is shown by an episode, which has been related by the scholar of Latin American Studies, Daniel Mato. According to Mato, the Argentinian anthropologist Néstor García Canclini was often asked whether his concept of 'hybridization' in his book *Hybrid Cultures* had been influenced by Homi Bhabha's idea of hybridity. Canclini answered in the negative. But this was not the point, rather, says Mato: "I wondered whether Bhabha has ever been asked about the influence of García Canclini on his work. I believe it is plausible to assume that the answer is negative" (Mato 2003: 791).

Mato contends that, in the course of this kind of "passionate search for the English influence" (Mato 2003: 791), cultural studies written in Spanish always came second to cultural studies written in English. Any attempts at differentiation, localization or historicization in this context are already clearly framed by these linguistic asymmetries working hand in hand with a stabilization of intellectual hierarchies. In this case, too, the assumption predominates that Anglo-American and European concepts and theories possess universal applicability – and can, therefore, lay claim to the highest level of authority and prestige. Quite apart from this example, it can be shown that, to a large extent, legitimations of knowledge employ the universalizability of concepts and theories as an argument. On the transnational horizon, this is used at the same time as a basis for deriving claims to a universal language for 'global conversation' or 'cross-cultural dialogue.'

By taking a closer look at the institutionally and culturally specific situations of emergence and translation, these claims to universalization become highly questionable. "The 'internationalization' of cultural studies cannot mean the formation of a global, universally generalizable set of theories and objects of study" (Stratton and Ang 1996: 362). On the contrary, any internationalization of the study of culture remains necessarily referenced back to asymmetries, to relations of power and hierarchies between different cultures of knowledge and of scholarship. Instead of working towards the illusion of a unified global cosmopolitanism, the challenge of approaches working critically in fields of postcolonial asymmetries and binary divides should be brought to the fore. One, but an important, example for this can be found in the challenges of transnational feminist cultural studies. Work in this field attacks the homogenizing approach of a transnational study of culture, which does not adequately recognize differences and inequalities between gender roles and male and female positions (cf. Kaplan and Grewal 1999).

In light of assumptions about the superficial dynamics of intellectual mobility, we tend to mask such asymmetries. The critical point, however, is not to block them out, but to ask: How do things actually stand regarding access to hegemonic discourses and regarding specific positions within the geopolitics of knowledge? Here, an example: In its journey through western universities, and in particular via Latin American Studies in North America, the Indian Subaltern Studies debate has become an almost hegemonic international discourse (cf. Chakrabarty's autobiographical contribution in this volume). The *Estudios Culturales*, on the contrary, by situating research on Latin America in Latin America itself, have only gained limited access to this discourse. For them, subaltern research remains explicitly connected to a commitment towards the "local" production of theory. These kinds of epistemological differences and power gaps can be seen as productive stumbling blocks along the path of transnation-alization. They, in particular, demand critical attention. Thus, using the exam-ple of North-American Latin American Studies, the Latin America scholar Su-sanne Klengel names the main danger: the production of theory separated from the place where it arose (in this case, Latin America) and subsequently becom-ing independent and disassociated from its context as "theory politics" (Klengel 2008: 135). In following up on the argument, one could ask: Are there other theories that may be in danger of becoming independent as vehicles of a global 'theory politics?' And do they blind us to gaps existing in the global politics of translation?

Naoki Sakai has undertaken a radical effort to mark out this problematic terrain. According to him, the focus on intellectual exchange and translations between different knowledge systems might just be a sham. Since this focus always remains clouded by the "regime of translation," an "ideology that makes translators imagine their relationship to what they do in translation as the symmetrical exchange between two languages" (Sakai 1997: 51). In spite of this argument, it seems that the concept of translation is used very much as a vehi-cle of strategic universalism in the field of cultural claims toward global ex-changes. By this I do not mean the mainstream academic legitimation of trans-nationalization, i.e. its reduction to a universalizing expansion of knowledge and concepts. I rather mean the frequent strategic references to a common lan-guage, without which – according to Robert Stam and Ella Shohat – "compara-tive (multi)Cultural Studies" could not be carried out (Stam and Shohat 2005: 492). This kind of strategic universalism is seen as a corrective to cultural rela-tivism, to particularism and even to nation-based essentializations in which claims to difference often end.

By strategically extending the axis of universalization, further potential for universalizations can be recognized – the way universals connote a common language in which historically independent approaches could perhaps be artic-ulated and circulated. *Global* knowledge production in the study of culture, the creation of corresponding epistemic spaces and of "global conversations" (Tsing 2005: 3), would constitute such universal shared points of reference. It is true: For a transnational perspective, this kind of understanding of a global production of knowledge could lead away from the self-assertions of western origin points of theory. The central idea here would no longer be travelling con-cepts that journey from the 'original' to the 'translation' and are transformed in the process. Rather, communication, interaction, and media could be investi-gated more closely as productive intersections in transnational studies of cul-ture (cf. Thomas Weber's contribution). If travelling concepts are still spoken about at all in this context, then they can really only be considered as the products of academic communication – whether of assumed "global conversations," of "global encounters across difference" (Tsing 2005: 3), or of an "international cultural studies *rendez-vous*" (Stratton and Ang 1996: 367).

In any case, there is no longer a pre-given linear direction of travel, which usually runs from West to East and from North to South. These framing dichotomies are, in fact, split open (cf. Boris Buden's critical interrogation of this essentializing dichotomic framework in his contribution). And conditions and scenarios are revealed for expressly "multi-sited" studies of culture (Solomon and Sakai 2006), for a multi-origin production of theory, and for a multi-directional flow of theories, including their specific resistances and "*blocages symboliques*" (Stam and Shohat 2009: 474).

Even though we cannot cover this kind of conceptual border-crossings fully in this book, we can at least take some first steps in this direction. Above all, the translation model could be brought in and could be made productive against current suggestions for focusing on transnational forms of academic communication based on mere exchange. As Robert Stam and Ella Shohat argued in their latest book on *Race in Translation,* a translational model can be used to "criticize narratives of intellectual exchange that posit dichotomous axes of foreign/native, export/import, and original/copy, proposing instead a more fluid transnational and translational methodology appropriate to cross-border intellectual interlocution" (Stam and Shohat 2012: xviii).

3 The Transnational Study of Culture – A Translational Perspective

Finally, one should ask: How is talking about cross-cultural issues (and comparative work in a fast shrinking world) possible on the same ground? In her book *Translingual Practice* Lydia Liu suggests the following approach: "one must turn to the occurrences of historical contact, interaction, translation, and the travel of words and ideas between languages" (Liu 1995: 19). Here, translation, above all, becomes a central category of a transnational discourse. Indeed, translation can build links between universalism and particularism. Translation is both: localization, but also – as the philosopher of culture Peter Osborne puts it – "a mode of production of theoretical generality [...] that is committed to the transformation (rather than mere 'application') of basic concepts in the process of the expansion of their range of reference to new circumstances" (Osborne 2008, also 2001: 53–62, a chapter entitled "Modernism as Translation").

The basic assumption here is that "theoretical generality" is a result of translatability and translation, in particular in the sense of practical negotiation. The concern thus is not primarily with the production, distribution or legitimation of knowledge, but with intellectual cooperation. If translation is to be used as a category of practice, above and beyond a mere "trope of epistemological crossing" (Liu 1995: 1), then this level of intellectual cooperation needs to be taken seriously. Homi Bhabha's definition of translation as a negotiation of differences thus could be explicitly applied to academic practice: Conferences and books on – and originating from – intellectual exchanges could, therefore, discuss how translatability and untranslatability arise through practices of negotiation and should ask to what extent this also generates "theoretical generality."

Here, too, the starting point should not be on the level of universalistic claims and the a priori assumption of a transcultural validity of concepts, but rather with the transcultural uses and the practical working conditions of the translation of concepts. Lydia Liu, again, provides inspiration: "The study of translingual practice examines the process by which new words, meanings, discourses, and modes of representation arise, circulate, and acquire legitimacy within the host language [...] no longer [...] untouched by the contending interests of political and ideological struggles" (Liu 1995: 26). Translation, therefore, extends to "complex forms of mediations" (Liu 1995: 27), i.e. to forms of appropriation, transformation, domestication, and manipulation, and this takes place through historical contact, or even "struggles" (cf. Chakrabarty's and Buden's contributions to this volume). The dichotomy between original and translation in this perspective has long since ceased to be productive. Instead, a horizon unfolds on which translatability itself is, or has to be, created in the first place.

From this starting point, this volume could also help to collect or set out a more comprehensive range of questions in view of what is translatable, what is untranslatable, and what the existing processes of translation between the different studies of culture are. In this way, one could follow the "vehicle of translation" (Liu 1995: 21) by looking at the translation *of* concepts and categories. Going beyond this, one could also take up a different line of questioning and follow the "vehicle of concepts" instead (a translation *through* concepts). Or one could even follow an action-oriented translational path in the sense of a formulation by cultural theorist Robert Young: "Translation, the activity of the transposition of one language into another, has itself been translated by commentators into a modus operandi of our times" (Young 2011: 59). Because the processes of translation between academic cultures take place precisely *through and with the help of* concepts and categories, an important intersection for cross-cultural analyses surely lies here: taking, as a starting point, concepts and categories that develop transnationally in the first place but which are also open to translation, to rewriting and transformation, i.e. not universalized from the start.

It is precisely attention to this close connection between translation and the unfolding of concepts and categories that promises to be a particularly productive field for further inquiry. It encourages a research practice that approaches things differently: Even before "cross-cultural translation" can be discussed, attention should be focussed on what Dipesh Chakrabarty has called "cross-categorical translation" (Chakrabarty 2000: 85). By introducing this concept, Chakrabarty challenges students of culture to apply the translational perspective first to their own analytical instruments. Before, in transnational approaches, issues of content are addressed, the fundamental terms of research, and the categories themselves – be they diverse categories of work, society, family, rights, democracy, etc. – should be questioned and their applicability checked. They should, above all, be opened to analytical categories from other knowledge and research systems.

The assumption underlying this demand is that a transnationally oriented study of culture needs to refer to diverse cultural histories and classifications as well as social practices as they are reflected in the terms of analysis themselves. Even at this state, there are already decisive and critical translational intersections. Comparison, transfer research, and translation analysis, therefore, need to start at these very intersections. Only then can we head towards a shared language or a possibly common point of reference. Only then can the different studies of culture be examined for systematic possibilities of connection along overlapping categories, concepts, and, finally, perhaps also 'turns.' This book seeks to demonstrate that attention to these kinds of transnational and translational intersections can indeed lead to new "epistemic spaces." It thus hopes to open up a new horizon for a translational conception of the humanities. In this conception, as Emily Apter claimed in her article on "Untranslatables," the leading question should address: "How to build a translational humanities responsive to fluctuations in geopolitics, and which intersects with but is not confined to national language frontiers" (Apter 2008: 597). The answer, according to Apter, can only be given with a new acknowledgement of the "untranslatable" (for an elaboration of this category in the context of a transformed transnational study of comparative literature, cf. Apter 2013).

In a similar sense, but perhaps more radically, is the position taken by Jon Solomon in his contribution to this volume: any effort to build a transnational study of culture has to critically consider the condition of the possibility of such a transnational project, i.e. the asymmetry of languages, cultures, and knowledge systems – which can only lead beyond the constraints of a "homolingual system" by acknowledging the "indeterminacy" of peoples and languages (cf. Sakai 1997). With critical meta-reflections like these in mind, we should finally ask: What does this mean, in concrete terms, for the focus of this volume?

By returning to the image used at the beginning of this introduction, one could answer: The so-called western studies of culture could subject their own academic traditions to a "centrifuge" and, in doing so, disconnect themselves from both a universalistic top-down approach as well as from monolingualism. Instead, they could strengthen a bottom-up approach via increased attention to local knowledge and to specific traditions in the history of science. In this sense, the study of culture should be understood as a translation discipline and continue to elaborate the category of translation in this way: as a category that expressly throws light on the smaller units of communication – on concrete situations of interaction. To follow the study of culture along these lines would then also mean: bringing processes of translation in their intermediary steps into focus – steps that are force-fields too easily masked by a hazy view of the longer arcs of transition and transfer. What is advocated here is the attempt to really engage more with concrete actions and situations of translation, with all their breaks and non-simultaneities, even with untranslatabilities or failed translations.

Last but not least, at such intersections as those addressed in this book one could push forward to a level at which the course is also set for future transnational (academic) encounter: through world-crossing efforts of translations (instead of mere global dialogues). This could lead to examinations of the constellations and configurations of different 'studies of culture' much more strongly than ever, with regard to their zones of contact and confrontation. In particular, the relations of tension and differences among these various approaches could be developed as a 'third space' of academic communication. From this perspective, the transnational production of knowledge can then be thought of – according to Anna Lowenhaupt Tsing's category – as global co-operation through "friction," relying on translations as appropriations and transformations (cf. Tsing 2005).

Perhaps here, at the end of this introductory essay, we can be inspired by another provocative piece of art by the famous contemporary Chinese conceptual artist and political activist Ai Weiwei – by his revision of a richly traditional, truly antique, de facto thousand-year-old Chinese Han dynasty urn, on which there is an ostentatious, hand-painted Coca-Cola logo. Following the message of Ai Weiwei's provocative piece of art, one could ask: Are the respective theoretical traditions in the studies of culture also 'overwritten' by global points of reference that newly inscribe themselves as theory icons, as 'Coca-Cola-Theories' so to speak? Or do completely new, historically reflected forms of theory grow out of these 'over-writings' through independent and changed forms of appropriation and transformation?

Fig. 2: Ai Weiwei, *Han Dynasty Urn with Coca-Cola Logo*, 1994; Urn, Western Han Dynasty, 206 BC–24 AD (Photo credit: Ai Weiwei).

At any rate, the Coca-Cola urn provides one possible answer to the question posed at the start: How is knowledge gained – *before* or *through* its dissemination around the world? The answer could be: Knowledge is gained through translation – not through dissemination from an original, but through ongoing translations as negotiations, appropriations, and transformations.

References

Abbas, Ackbar, and John Nguyet Erni. "General Introduction." *Internationalizing Cultural Studies: An Anthology.* Eds. Ackbar Abbas and John Nguyet Erni. Oxford/Malden, MA: Blackwell, 2005. 1–12.

Allerkamp, Andrea, and Gérard Raulet, eds. *Kulturwissenschaften in Europa – eine grenzüberschreitende Disziplin?* Münster: Westfälisches Dampfboot, 2010.

Amelung, Iwo, and Anett Dippner, eds. *Kritische Verhältnisse. Die Rezeption der Frankfurter Schule in China.* Frankfurt a.m./New York: Campus, 2009.

Angermüller, Johannes. "Institutionelle Kontexte geisteswissenschaftlicher Theorieproduktion: Frankreich und USA im Vergleich." *Wissenschaftskulturen, Experimentalkulturen, Gelehrtenkulturen.* Eds. Markus Arnold and Gert Dressel. Wien: Turia & Kant, 2004. 69–85.

Angermüller, Johannes. *Nach dem Strukturalismus. Theoriediskurs und intellektuelles Feld in Frankreich.* Bielefeld: transcript, 2007.

Apter, Emily. "Untranslatables: A World System." *New Literary History* 39.3 (2008): 581–598.

Apter, Emily. *Against World Literature: On the Politics of Untranslatability.* New York: Verso, 2013.

Bachmann-Medick, Doris (Interview by Boris Buden). "Cultural Studies – a Translational Perspective." *Transversal* 6 (2008). http://eipcp.net/transversal/0908/bachmannmedick-buden/en (11 August 2013).

Bachmann-Medick, Doris. "Transnationale Kulturwissenschaften: Ein Übersetzungskonzept." *Lost or Found in Translation? Interkulturelle/Internationale Perspektiven der Geistes- und Kulturwissenschaften.* Eds. René Dietrich, Daniel Smilovski, and Ansgar Nünning. Trier: WVT, 2011. 53–72.

Bachmann-Medick, Doris. *Cultural Turns. Neuorientierungen in den Kulturwissenschaften.* 5th edition. Reinbek: Rowohlt, 2014 [2006] (English translation: *Cultural Turns: New Orientations in the Study of Culture.* Berlin/Boston: De Gruyter, 2016).

Barth, Fredrik, Andre Gingrich, Robert Parkin, and Sydel Silverman. *One Discipline, Four Ways: British, German, French, and American Anthropology.* Chicago/London: University of Chicago Press, 2005.

Beck, Ulrich. *What is Globalization?* Cambridge/Malden, MA: Polity Press, 2000.

Beck, Ulrich. *The Cosmopolitan Vision.* Cambridge/Malden, MA: Polity Press, 2006.

Berry, Chris, Nicola Liscutin, and Jonathan D. Mackintosh, eds. *Cultural Studies and Cultural Industries in Northeast Asia: What a Difference a Region Makes.* Hong Kong: Hong Kong University Press, 2009.

Bielsa, Esperança. "Beyond Hybridity and Authenticity: Globalisation, Translation and the Cosmopolitan Turn in the Social Sciences." *Synthesis* 4 (Summer 2012). 17–35.

Blänkner, Reinhard. "Historische Kulturwissenschaften im Zeichen der Globalisierung." *Historische Anthropologie* 16.3 (2008): 341–372.

Böhme, Hartmut. "Vom 'turn' zum 'vertigo.' Wohin drehen sich die Kulturwissenschaften?" (Review of *Cultural Turns: Neuorientierungen in den Kulturwissenschaften* by Doris Bachmann-Medick). *Journal of Literary Theory Online* 2 (2008). http://www.culture.hu-berlin.de/hb/files/RezHB_BachmannMedick_240408.pdf (11 August 2013).

Bourdieu, Pierre. "The Social Conditions of the International Circulation of Ideas." *Bourdieu: A Critical Reader.* Ed. Richard Shusterman. Oxford/Malden, MA: Blackwell, 1999. 220–228.

Braidotti, Rosi. *Transpositions: On Nomadic Ethics*. Malden, MA/Cambridge: Polity Press, 2006.

Braidotti, Rosi. *Nomadic Subjects: Embodiment and Sexual Difference in Contemporary Feminist Theory*. 2nd edition. New York: Columbia University Press, 2011.

Cavell, Richard, and Imre Szeman. "Introduction: New Cultural Spaces: Cultural Studies in Canada Today." *The Review of Education, Pedagogy, and Cultural Studies* 29 (2007): 1–20.

Chakrabarty, Dipesh. *Provincializing Europe: Postcolonial Thought and Historical Difference*. Princeton/Oxford: Princeton University Press, 2000.

Chalard-Fillaudeau, Anne. "From Cultural Studies to Études Culturelles, Études de la Culture, and Sciences de la Culture in France: Questions of Singularity." *Cultural Studies* 23.5/6 (special issue *Transnationalism and Cultural Studies*) (2009): 831–854.

Chalard-Fillaudeau, Anne. "Kulturwissenschaften *à la française?*" *Kulturwissenschaften in Europa – eine grenzüberschreitende Disziplin?* Eds. Andrea Allerkamp and Gérard Raulet. Münster: Westfälisches Dampfboot, 2010. 159–173.

Chen, Kuan-Hsing, ed. *Trajectories: Inter-Asia Cultural Studies*. London/New York: Routledge, 1998.

Chen, Kuan-Hsing, and Chua Beng Huat, eds. *The Inter-Asia Cultural Studies Reader*. Abingdon/New York: Routledge, 2007.

Cornut-Gentille D'Arcy, Chantal. "Cultural Studies' Relationship to Institutionalization and Disciplinarity in Spain." *Cultural Studies* 23.5/6 (2009): 855–872.

Hall, Gary, and Clare Birchall, eds. *New Cultural Studies: Adventures in Theory*. Edinburgh: Edinburgh University Press, 2006.

Hall, Stuart. "Cultural Studies and the Politics of Internationalization: An Interview with Stuart Hall by Kuan-Hsing Chen." *Stuart Hall: Critical Dialogues in Cultural Studies*. Eds. David Morley and Kuan-Hsing Chen. London/New York: Routledge, 1996. 393–409.

Hanru, Hou. "Change is the Rule." http://visualarts.walkerart.org/oracles/details.wac?id=2232&title=Writings. 2005 (21 October 2013).

Kaplan, Caren, and Inderpal Grewal. "Transnational Feminist Cultural Studies: Beyond the Marxism/Poststructuralism/Feminism Divides." *Between Woman and Nation: Nationalisms, Transnational Feminisms, and the State*. Eds. Caren Kaplan, Norma Alarcón, and Minoo Moallem. Durham, NC/London: Duke University Press, 1999. 349–363.

Keim, Wiebke. *Vermessene Disziplin. Zum konterhegemonialen Potential afrikanischer und lateinamerikanischer Soziologien*. Bielefeld: transcript, 2008.

Klengel, Susanne. "Vom transatlantischen Reich der Kulturwissenschaft. Konjunkturen und 'keywords' in der internationalen Lateinamerikaforschung." *Kultur, Übersetzung, Lebenswelten. Beiträge zu aktuellen Paradigmen der Kulturwissenschaften*. Eds. Andreas Gipper and Susanne Klengel. Würzburg: Königshausen & Neumann, 2008. 121–137.

Koslow Miller, Francine. "Huang Yong Ping." *Frieze Magazine* 100 (June-August 2006). http://www.frieze.com/issue/review/huang_yong_ping/ (11 August 2013).

Kuhn, Michael, and Doris Weidemann, eds. *Internationalization of the Social Sciences: Asia – Latin America – Middle East – Africa – Eurasia*. Bielefeld: transcript, 2009.

Laberge, Yves. "Are Cultural Studies an Anglo-Saxon Paradigm? Reflections on Cultural Studies in Francophone Networks." *Canadian Cultural Studies: A Reader*. Eds. Sourayan Mookerjea, Imre Szeman, and Gail Faurschou. Durham, NC/London: Duke University Press, 2009. 561–580.

Levitt, Peggy, and Sanjeev Khagram, eds. *The Transnational Studies Reader: Intersections and Innovations*. London: Routledge, 2007.

Liu, Lydia H. *Translingual Practice: Literature, National Culture, and Translated Modernity. China, 1900–1937*. Stanford: Stanford University Press, 1995.

Lützeler, Paul Michael. *Transatlantische Germanistik. Kontakt, Transfer, Dialogik*. Berlin/Boston: de Gruyter, 2013.

Mato, Daniel. "Latin American Intellectual Practices in Culture and Power: Experiences and Debates." *Cultural Studies* 17.6 (2003): 783–804.

Mookerjea, Sourayan, Imre Szeman, and Gail Faurschou, eds. *Canadian Cultural Studies: A Reader*. Durham, NC: Duke University Press, 2009.

Musner, Lutz. "Locating Culture in the US and Central Europe – a Transatlantic Perspective on Cultural Studies." *Cultural Studies* 14.4 (1999): 577–590.

Musner, Lutz. "Kulturwissenschaften und Cultural Studies: Zwei ungleiche Geschwister?" *Kulturpoetik* 1.2 (2001): 261–271.

Ning, Wang, and Sun Yifeng, eds. *Translation, Globalisation and Localisation: A Chinese Perspective*. Clevedon: Multilingual Matters, 2008.

Osborne, Peter. *Philosophy in Cultural Theory*. London/New York: Routledge, 2001.

Osborne, Peter (Interview by Boris Buden). "Translation – between Philosophy and Cultural Theory." *Transversal* 8 (2008).
http://translate.eipcp.net/transversal/0908/osbornebuden/en (11 August 2013).

Said, Edward W. "Traveling Theory." *The World, the Text, and the Critic*. Cambridge, MA: Harvard University Press, 1983. 226–247.

Sakai, Naoki. *Translation and Subjectivity: On "Japan" and Cultural Nationalism*. Minneapolis/London: University of Minnesota Press, 1997.

Schäfer, Fabian. "The Re-Articulation of Cultural Studies in Japan and Its Consequences for Japanese Studies." *International Journal of Cultural Studies* 12.1 (2009): 23–41.

Shome, Raka. "Post-Colonial Reflections on the 'Internationalization' of Cultural Studies." *Cultural Studies of Transnationalism*. Eds. Handel Kashope Wright and Meaghan Morris. London/New York: Routledge, 2012. 6–31.

Solomon, Jon, and Naoki Sakai, eds. *Translation, Biopolitics, Colonial Difference. Traces: A Multilingual Series of Cultural Theory and Translation*, 4. Hong Kong: Hong Kong University Press, 2006.

Stam, Robert, and Ella Shohat. "De-Eurocentricizing Cultural Studies: Some Proposals." *Internationalizing Cultural Studies: An Anthology*. Eds. Ackbar Abbas and John Nguyet Erni. Oxford/Malden, MA: Blackwell, 2005. 481–498.

Stam, Robert, and Ella Shohat. "Transnationalizing Comparison: The Uses and Abuses of Cross-Cultural Analogy." *New Literary History* 40.3 (2009): 473–499.

Stam, Robert, and Ella Shohat. *Race in Translation: Culture Wars around the Postcolonial Atlantic*. New York/London: New York University Press, 2012.

Stratton, Jon, and Ien Ang. "On the Impossibility of a Global Cultural Studies: 'British' Cultural Studies in an 'International' Frame." *Stuart Hall: Critical Dialogues in Cultural Studies*. Eds. David Morley and Kuan-Hsing Chen. London/New York: Routledge, 1996. 362–390.

Szeman, Imre. "Cultural Studies and the Transnational." *New Cultural Studies: Adventures in Theory*. Eds. Gary Hall and Clare Birchall. Edinburgh: Edinburgh University Press, 2006. 200–219.

Tomaselli, Keyan G., and Handel Kashope Wright, eds. *Africa, Cultural Studies and Difference*. London/New York: Routledge, 2011.

Tsing, Anna Lowenhaupt. *Friction: An Ethnography of Global Connection*. Princeton: Princeton University Press, 2005.

Vatanabadi, Shouleh. "Translating the Transnational: Teaching the 'Other' in Translation." *Cultural Studies of Transnationalism*. Eds. Handel Kashope Wright and Meaghan Morris. London/New York: Routledge, 2012. 107–121.

Wolf, Michaela, and Alexandra Fukari, eds. *Constructing a Sociology of Translation*. Amsterdam/Philadelphia: John Benjamins, 2007.

Wright, Handel Kashope, and Meaghan Morris, eds. *Cultural Studies of Transnationalism*. London/New York: Routledge, 2012.

Young, Robert J.C. "Some Questions about Translation and the Production of Knowledge." *Translation: A Transdisciplinary Journal* (2011): 59–61.

Ansgar Nünning
Towards Transnational Approaches to the Study of Culture

From Cultural Studies and *Kulturwissenschaften* to a Transnational Study of Culture*

1 On the Cultural and National Specificity of Approaches to the Study of Literature and Culture

Although the development of literary and cultural studies, just like that of other disciplines in the humanities, has been characterized by an ongoing trend towards internationalization and globalization, there are still marked differences between various national research cultures and traditions. These differences can hardly be overlooked when comparing, for instance, the ways in which literary criticism as practiced in American and British universities differs from the German tradition of *Literaturwissenschaften*. As Peter Zima has convincingly shown, the German notion of *Literaturwissenschaften* and the very term itself do not readily lend themselves to being used internationally; in fact, they are so closely tied up with a particular notion of scientificity that they tend to get lost in translation (cf. Zima 2002; Nünning and Nünning 2011).

Similar differences can be observed when pitting British cultural studies against German *Kulturwissenschaften*, both of which are also characterized by cultural and national specificity. As any comparison of a random selection of introductory text books from different countries will confirm, approaches to the

* This article is based on a revised and expanded version of ideas and formulations first published in an essay that originally appeared in a German volume devoted to providing an introduction to *English and American Studies* (see Nünning 2012). I would like to thank Rose Lawson and Elizabeth Kovach for their thorough proofreading of this article, and my colleague and friend Roy Sommer for a number of critical and cautionary comments as well as valuable suggestions, from which the article has greatly benefitted. All the translations of quotations from German publications are by the author unless otherwise stated.

study of culture differ considerably from one national tradition to the next. Although British cultural studies and German *Kulturwissenschaften* are both concerned with the domain of culture, the differences between their respective research traditions and methodologies by far outweigh the similarities (see section 2 below).

Such differences between national approaches testify to the fact that the study of culture – and of literature, one might add – is itself very much a cultural practice that is characterized by cultural and national specificity. Different approaches to the study of culture are themselves culturally and historically conditioned and, thus, subject to change and cultural variation. Though this is seldom acknowledged, let alone subjected to self-reflexive research, anyone who has experienced university life in more than one country will have noticed such differences. The latter can pose serious obstacles to both the transfer of approaches and concepts from one national research culture to the other and the development of genuinely transnational approaches to the study of culture.

There are several reasons why approaches to the study of culture as developed and practiced in different countries still display considerable differences, even in an age of globalization and worldwide mobility, especially among academics. Among the most important reasons that can explain such cultural and national differences are language, intellectual styles (cf. Galtung 1981; Nünning 2011), the cultural contexts and historical development of disciplines, and approaches and institutional differences between research cultures and their traditions.

As the comparison between German *Kulturwissenschaften* and British cultural studies in section 2 below will serve to show, the differences between these national traditions of studying culture are still so big that it would be unwarranted to speak of transnational approaches as though they actually existed. While there is a broad range of different national traditions of studying culture, including various kinds of British cultural studies (cf. Huck 2012), American cultural studies (cf. Fluck 2011), and, more recently, Latino/a cultural studies (cf. Allatson 2007), the development of genuinely transnational, or even trans-European, approaches to the study of culture is still a desideratum for future research rather than an established fact. Since separate chapters in this volume are devoted to the delineation of British cultural studies and other variants of cultural studies, this article will focus on approaches not primarily associated with either Britain or the U.S.

The present outline of transnational approaches to the study of culture refers to a project that does not yet exist as a fully fledged theoretical or analytical framework. Therefore, this chapter can speak of the study of culture only in a largely programmatic manner, outlining how it could be fostered and what it could be. In addition to exploring some of the differences between national research traditions to the study of culture, it will provide an overview of recent contributions to research that have fostered, or are fostering, the development of transnational approaches to the study of culture. These include approaches that either cut across national traditions or have successfully travelled from one research culture to others; a number of influential 'cultural turns' (cf. Bachmann-Medick 2006) in the humanities or 'cultural sciences' (*Kulturwissenschaften*); and the notions of 'travelling concepts' (cf. Bal 2002) and 'translation' as promising ways of overcoming boundaries between different research cultures and national traditions. This chapter, thus, outlines possible trajectories for how Anglo-American varieties of cultural studies, German *Kulturwissenschaften*, and other approaches associated with particular national research cultures and traditions could be transformed into a truly transnational study of culture.

2 Cultural Studies and the Study of Culture in an International Context: Differences between British Cultural Studies and German *Kulturwissenschaften*

Although British and American varieties of cultural studies and their rough equivalent of German *Kulturwissenschaften* are all concerned with the study of culture in the widest possible sense, they nonetheless display considerable differences. For anyone interested in the development of transnational approaches to the study of culture, it is important to be aware of such differences and to be able to assess and deploy different theoretical and methodological frameworks. Rather than taking a particular approach for granted or uncritically trying to adopt or emulate either British cultural studies or American cultural studies, one should first of all regard them as objects of inquiry in their own rights that represent complex manifestations of Englishness (or Britishness) and Americanness, respectively. Just as there is arguably a 'national style' of English literary criticism, historiography, and cultural studies (cf. Nünning 2001), German *Kulturwissenschaften* also share a number of epistemological claims, discursive strategies, and institutional practices that set them apart from their American and British counterparts.

To begin with, the German term *Kulturwissenschaften*, just like *Literaturwissenschaften*, gets lost in translation. It serves to emphasize the scientificity of the discipline that it designates, implicitly claiming that the study of culture can be as scientific (*wissenschaftlich*) as any discipline in the hard sciences. As Peter Zima has shown in a pioneering article, the term *Literaturwissenschaften* in the German sense is very much "a language- and culture-bound phenomenon" that "becomes questionable as soon as it is projected into an intercultural context" (2002: 26). The same holds true for the term *Kulturwissenschaften*, which should not be confused with the English term 'cultural studies.' What is at stake here is much more than just a question of terminology, in that there is a semantic rupture between the German and English sociolinguistic contexts that concerns the constitution and traditions of the respective disciplines and research cultures as wholes, including the ways in which they construct their objects, define their objectives, develop their methodologies, select their subject matter, and practice the study of culture.

In spite of some similarities with regard to subject matter and methods, the German version of *Kulturwissenschaften* should be distinguished from the special brand of cultural studies developed in Britain. At the risk of oversimplification, the main differences between British (and American) cultural studies and German *Kulturwissenschaften* can be located on at least five levels (cf. Sommer 2003; Assmann 2006: 16–26):

- Firstly, British cultural studies were developed as a response to concrete social and political challenges of the British class system and as a politically motivated project aimed at producing changes in society and strategies of resistance; in this research tradition, culture and politics have been inextricably intertwined. By contrast, the German tradition of *Kulturwissenschaften*, which can be traced back to the late 19th and early 20th centuries (cf. Böhme et al. 2000), has quite a different genealogy, lineage, and nonpolitical agenda, as it is largely an academic enterprise that explores cultural phenomena as objects of academic research, not with an eye on engendering political change.
- Secondly, while British cultural studies is characterized by an ideological position and marked by a Marxist approach, German *Kulturwissenschaften* display a more pluralistic, multiperspectival theoretical orientation, exploring symbolic forms (cf. Cassirer 1965) and ways of worldmaking (cf. Goodman 1992).
- Thirdly, as the term *Kulturwissenschaften* already indicates, there is a strong emphasis and methodological insistence on the scientific quality of the discipline in the German tradition in which the study of culture has been characterized as a form of textual science (cf. Grabes 1996). This has far-reaching implications for the scholar's position and self-understanding, which is quite different from that of scholars working in the British tradition of cul-

tural studies: "Cultural studies practitioners [...] think that they are doing one thing and something else, namely academic work which is also cultural, that is, work which is reflexively and democratically situated within the conditions of all types of cultural practice" (Quinn 2002: 74). In a similar but less polemical vein, Demoor and Pieters point at the "critical and political ethos of prominent theorists of cultural studies" (2003: 102). In contrast, the German position is primarily defined by its external, scholarly perspective on British culture (which, it goes without saying, is not necessarily more objective but involves its own, slightly different premises and blind spots).

– Fourthly, as the very name of its most renowned and important institution, The Birmingham Centre for Contemporary Cultural Studies, already indicates, British cultural studies has tended to expand the concept of culture from high-brow culture to popular culture, paving the way for a new approach to contemporary forms of popular culture, on which the Birmingham school largely focused. By way of contrast, German *Kulturwissenschaften* has favored a broader anthropological and semiotic concept of culture (see section 3 below), taking a wider range of cultural objects and a broader diachronic perspective into consideration. While British cultural studies and *Kulturwissenschaften* are both characterized by the "non-priorization of the written" and the "non-differentiation between types of texts," the "emphasis on the contemporary" distinguishes the British approach from the German tradition (Bassnett 1994: 64).

– Being an integral part of the respective national, institutional, and academic cultures from which they have emerged, British cultural studies and German *Kulturwissenschaften* have, fifthly, developed different research questions, topics, and methods (cf. Assmann 2006: 16).

Although this brief outline of some of the most important differences between German *Kulturwissenschaften* and British cultural studies makes no claim to have exhaustively covered this complex topic, it should have become clear that the different national practices of studying culture are characterized by a number of distinctive features. The same holds true for other variants of doing cultural studies, for example, American cultural studies (cf. Fluck 2011) and Latino/a cultural studies (cf. Allatson 2007). This underscores that the study of culture is itself very much culture-bound.

One should hasten to add, however, that research cultures are themselves subject to historical change, and both cultural studies and German *Kulturwissenschaften* have undergone far-reaching developments and seen important innovations in recent years. In comparison to the programmatic mission encapsulated in the name of The Birmingham Centre for Contemporary Cultural Studies, which suggests that cultural studies "is a field devoted entirely to the immediate present" (Felski 2003: 501), from today's point of view the "rationale for isolating the study of popular, contemporary culture from high culture and the culture of the past now seems purely historical" (Belsey 2003: 91). In an article entitled "Beyond Literature and Cultural Studies," Catherine Belsey made a programmatic proposal that calls for "a new discipline [...], beyond literature and Cultural Studies, that would explicitly treat all culture as its province, and would take full advantage of the attention French theory pays to the signifier" (2003: 99). Moreover, recent international developments in cultural studies have considerably broadened the aims and scope of what falls under the purview of the study of culture, both historically and as far as the synchronic range of forms of art and culture are concerned. During the last decade there have also been sustained attempts at *Internationalizing Cultural Studies*, as the title of an anthology edited by Ackbar Abbas and John Nguyet Erni (2005) indicates.

Nonetheless, the differences between British cultural studies and German *Kulturwissenschaften* outlined above show that national traditions in the study of literature and culture are shaped by the – to use Johan Galtung's felicitous term – 'intellectual style' that is predominant in a culture and colors the research process. According to Galtung, intellectual style is located on a "level between the individual and the universal": "In the broadest sense it is the level of the civilisations or sub-civilisations – in other words, the macro-cultural level" (1981: 304). It is no coincidence that most of what Galtung writes about the Saxon style is also true for English literary criticism, historiography, and forms of doing cultural studies, just as his observations on the 'teutonic' intellectual style pertain to the German traditions of *Literaturwissenschaften* and *Kulturwissenschaften*.

Such differences in intellectual style manifest themselves in a number of concrete and tangible ways, shaping both prevalent research agendas and practices. While German *Kulturwissenschaften* display a predilection for theorizing, what constitutes the lowest common denominator of most of the features specific to British cultural studies is a much more pragmatic and empirical orientation, a clear preference for particulars and concrete 'facts,' and a concomitant distrust of generalities and abstractions. The national style of English literary history and cultural studies is not only marked by a number of prominent stylistic traits (e.g., a strong dislike of theory, a focus on individual writers and their works as well as on facts and figures, a preference for the tradition of empiricist discourse) and by ideas of Englishness (cf. Easthope 1999), but it also simultaneously serves to reinforce such collectively held concepts (cf. Nünning 2001).

One of the problems and impediments for the development of transnational approaches to the study of culture results from the prevailing tendency to 'import' British (or American) cultural studies into other (e.g., German) academic and institutional contexts and merely emulate or imitate the imported model(s). The main problem with such a transfer, however, is that while British cultural studies must be seen against the background of Britain's class system, the American debates about race, class, and gender, or the revision of the Western canon, only make sense in the context of the multicultural society of the U.S. The strength of the study of culture as practiced in, e.g., Germany, the Netherlands, or Scandinavian countries for that matter resides precisely in the fact that they can apply the differences between their own and foreign culture(s) in a fruitful manner. Both the canon debates (and revisions), with their focus on race, class, and gender, and the British and American forms of cultural studies can, thus, be seen as (highly interesting!) objects of inquiry in themselves, both from the point of view of English and American studies as practiced in Germany and other countries and in a broader, transnational framework for the study of culture(s). It is also important not to forget or ignore the indigenous research tradition developed for the study of culture in Germany, *Kulturwissenschaft* or *Kulturwissenschaften*.

Despite many attempts, the term *Kulturwissenschaft(en)*, just like the term 'cultural studies,' is used as a catchphrase for a wide range of different approaches and concepts (cf. Nünning and Nünning 2008). Many scholars have acknowledged that it is notoriously hard to define and that it does not exist as an independent and clearly circumscribed discipline (cf. Bollenbeck and Kaiser 2004: 617). The main difficulty of any attempt at a definition has to do with the fact that the term is used to cover a multiplicity of different fields of research and trends in the humanities, that it functions as an umbrella term for open and interdisciplinary discussions, and that the scope of its application and extension is subject to debate. Like the term 'cultural studies,' the terms *Kulturwissenschaft* and *Kulturwissenschaften* have become a catch-all, used in at least four different senses:

- Firstly, in a very broad sense, *Kulturwissenschaft(en)* stands for an interdisciplinary frame of reference, which is supposed to integrate the whole spectrum of traditional disciplines in the humanities.
- Secondly, the term *Kulturwissenschaft* is also used as a key concept for calls for change and an opening of traditional philologies, especially literary studies but also of the humanities at large.
- Thirdly, in a more narrow and specialized sense, *Kulturwissenschaft* denotes a special subdiscipline within the individual philologies. A closer look reveals that this often amounts to little more than a new label for a traditional

approach that is often denounced as old-fashioned: the study of the geo-graphical, social, economical, and cultural characteristics of individual countries, known as *Landeskunde* at German universities.

– Fourthly, the discipline that used to be called *Volkskunde* ('folklore studies') or *Europäische Ethnologie* ('European ethnology') is now also sometimes re-ferred to as *Kulturwissenschaft*.

There are, however, also trends and forces that have contributed to the interna-tionalization of academic and scholarly practices in the broad field(s) of the study of culture, and these trends pertain both to German *Kulturwissenschaften* and innovative directions in cultural studies. Recent developments in German *Kulturwissenschaften*, for instance, include a less theory-driven kind of research of culture, termed *Kulturforschung* by Uwe Wirth, one of its major proponents. The logic and practice of this innovative form of *Kulturforschung* is mainly geared toward a bottom-up approach that focuses on 'thick description' (cf. Geertz 1973) of significant details (cf. Wirth 2008). On the other hand, theory has assumed a more prominent role in new forms of cultural studies, as the volume edited by Gary Hall and Clare Birchall (2007), for instance, serves to show.

3 The Study of Culture as an Interdisciplinary and International Field of Research: Premises, Concepts, and Approaches

As both the interest that various disciplines in the humanities and social scienc-es have paid to culture, and the co-existence of various kinds of British cultural studies, American cultural studies, German *Kulturwissenschaften*, and other national traditions already demonstrate, the study of culture is essentially an interdisciplinary and an international field of research. With regard to both the range of disciplines that are concerned with culture and its international di-mensions, the study of culture is characterized by theoretical and methodologi-cal pluralism as well as multiperspectivism (cf. Nünning and Nünning 2011). The study of such a broad research domain as culture demands novel forms of interdisciplinary research, the crossing of the boundaries between disciplines and different academic cultures of knowledge.

During the last three decades, the study of culture has been one of the most rapidly developing research fields in not only European and American but in-creasingly also Asian and Australian scholarship (see the contribution on Australian cultural studies by Knellwolf King in this volume). The development of theories, methods, and models that envisage texts, social structures, and human actions (the classical research objects of the humanities and the social sciences) as 'cultural phenomena' and, thus, provide common ground for dialogue among various disciplines, has also been one of the recent significant advances in German humanities, particularly in *Kulturwissenschaften* (see section 2 above). As a newly emerging interdisciplinary field, the study of culture not only forges new relations between, e.g., literary studies, film studies, media studies, theater and performance studies, and musicology, but it also engages in dialogue with neighboring disciplines such as anthropology, architecture, art history, cultural geography, cultural psychology, political science, and sociology.

In addition to interdisciplinary cooperation, research into the broad range of domains that fall under the purview of the study of culture also presupposes theoretical and methodological pluralism. The development of transnational approaches to the study of culture does not privilege any one approach to the study of culture but must display a commitment to diversity, including empirical approaches, quantitative analysis, and thick description. Such a pluralistic approach resulting from an anthropological, semiotic, and constructivist understanding of culture that characterizes many recent approaches is a prerequisite for the rich exchange that takes place in transdisciplinary and international research undertakings. Approaches that have cut across disciplinary and national research traditions include, e.g., cultural semiotics (*Kultursemiotik*, cf. Posner 2008), cultural anthropology, historical anthropology, literary anthropology, the new cultural history, cultural ecology, and area studies (for an overview, cf. Nünning and Nünning 2011). Although the traditions, research foci and methodologies of these different ways of studying culture differ quite substantially, all of these approaches embrace both inter- or transdisciplinary collaboration and an international, or even global, orientation.

Across disciplinary borders, it has become clear that approaches to culture – historical and synchronic, contextual and systematic, interpretive and empirical – are not mutually exclusive but can, instead, profit from cross-disciplinary collaboration. In fields like 'cultural memory studies' (cf. Erll and Nünning 2008), for instance, disciplinary areas of competence converge in interdisciplinary research areas in a lively and productive exchange. The term 'study of culture,' thus, does not refer to any narrow definition or the understanding of the object of study, or to a particular theoretical approach or school of thought, as is the case with, for example, 'cultural studies,' 'cultural analysis' (Bal 2002: 6–8), 'cultural materialism,' or 'cultural criticism' (Belsey 2003). Instead, the goal is to enhance dialogue among disciplines and different cultures of research, fostering self-reflexive, interdisciplinary, international, and potentially even transnational approaches to the study of culture. Such a project also involves a sustained dialogue about the key concepts used to define the subject-matter, research areas, or domains and the theoretical and methodological frameworks deployed.

4 Trans/national Concepts of Culture: The Subject-Matter and Domains of the Study of Culture

While there are still many differences between the research traditions that prevail in the study of culture in different countries and academic disciplines, some concepts of culture, which were originally developed in particular fields, disciplines, or national contexts, have increasingly been used across several disciplines as well as internationally. A brief survey of some of the most widely used concepts of culture can, thus, be helpful for any attempt to develop and promote transnational approaches to the study of culture.

Already in 1952, the anthropologists Kroeber and Kluckhohn provided a systematic overview of no fewer than 175 different definitions of the word 'culture.' Since then, the number of competing concepts of culture has increased significantly, because many disciplines, including anthropology, ethnology, history, psychology, and sociology, have developed a plethora of new concepts of culture (cf. Ort 2008). Andreas Reckwitz has developed a useful typology of concepts of culture, according to which one can distinguish between four basic kinds or types:
1. the normative concept of culture ("der normative Kulturbegriff");
2. the totalizing concept of culture ("der totalitätsorientierte Kulturbegriff");
3. the difference- or systems-theoretical concept of culture ("der differenztheoretische Kulturbegriff");
4. the semiotic or meaning-oriented concept of culture ("der bedeutungs- und wissensorientierte Kulturbegriff" [Reckwitz 2000: 64]).

The normative concept of culture is based on an evaluative definition of aesthetic phenomena and objects that are considered to belong to 'high' culture and regarded as worth including in the canon of great works of art that are preserved by institutions and cultural memory. Since such a normative definition is relatively narrow and restrictive, it has been challenged by proponents of cultural studies more interested in the products of popular culture that such a narrow view tends to exclude.

In contrast to such a normative definition, the totalizing concept of culture refrains from any aesthetic value judgments, taking 'the whole way of life' into consideration (cf. Williams 1989). According to such a non-normative understanding, which has dominated in, for example, anthropology and ethnology, the concept of culture is used as an umbrella term that subsumes all the collectively shared ways of thinking, feeling, and believing, the structures of attitudes and the hierarchies of norms and values that are characteristic of and differentiate given communities, groups, or nations. Accepting the basic equality of different cultures and cultural manifestations, such a broad, holistic, and totalizing concept of culture draws attention to a full range of cultural expressions, objects, and practices, including, e.g., institutions, rituals, and other social practices.

The difference-theoretical concept of culture is much more restrictive again, focusing solely on the "narrow field of art, education, science, and other intellectual activities" (Reckwitz 2000: 6). Originating from sociology and systems theory, this concept of culture is based on the notion that culture is a particular sub-system of modern society, viz., the system that is specialized in intellectual and aesthetic ways of worldmaking.

According to the semiotic and constructivist understanding of culture adopted by many scholars today, culture is understood as the entire complex of discursive formations, ideas, values, and meanings created by humans and materialized in symbolic systems. In this definition of culture, not only material forms of expression (for example, artistic artifacts) but also social institutions and mentalities are part of culture, and, without them, the creation of such artifacts would not even be possible. Cultures possess not only a material aspect – the cultural assets/goods/treasures of a nation – but also social, emotional, and cognitive components.

- The material dimension of culture is evident primarily in the wide variety of media studies (from language and literary texts to historical sources, texts of any kind, interviews, photography, film, and new media). Yet elements of material culture or performative acts of a transitory nature (such as theater, rituals, and festivals) are also regarded as material objects of study.
- The social dimension of culture is studied in the form of institutions, political organizations, and social hierarchies and roles, as well as in the social components of media systems.
- The cognitive dimension of culture – mentalities, systems of values and norms, taboos, and concepts of identity – is at the center of almost all re-

search projects, although it is only indirectly observable via its material and social dimensions.

These three dimensions are not isolated phenomena but rather interdependent and complementary elements within the study of culture. Research in these fields revolves around the synchronic and diachronic plurality of cultural formations through a broad spectrum of areas of study, which range historically from Antiquity through the Middle Ages to the postmodern era, and geographically from Anglo-American to Latin American, Asian, African, and Eastern European contexts.

Proceeding from an anthropological, semiotic, and constructivist understanding of culture, the project of developing transnational approaches to the study of culture attempts to foster a sustained dialogue between different research traditions and conceptualizations of culture. Moving beyond a narrow and normative concept of culture, solely understood as the field of artistic and intellectual creation, the study of culture is concerned with both cultural expressions, discourses, cultural heritage, and artistic objects, and a wider anthropological notion of culture, understood as the broad realm of whole ways of life, or human life forms, including material manifestations, collective habits, and mentalities, social institutions, practices, and rituals, as well as shared values and social norms. Instead of privileging a particular domain, interdisciplinary and transnational approaches tend to conceive of culture as the totality of discourses, texts, images, performances, and other products of media culture, while they also take political culture, institutions, rituals, mentalities, as well as norms and values into consideration. A semiotic approach to culture explores how artistic and literary creation is embedded in, and shaped by, social conditions and prefigured by cultural heritage. Culture is, in turn, considered to have performative power, act as an active force in its own right and intervene in its context.

Methodologically, the project of initiating and developing transnational approaches to the study of culture is also informed by pluralism, which begins by taking stock of the wide ranges of methods and practices that have been developed in different research traditions like British cultural studies and *Kulturwissenschaften*. In his informative overview of semiotic and narratological approaches, Roy Sommer deliberately violates what he calls "cherished conventions: Instead of celebrating heterogeneity, they try to map the common ground that has emerged in cultural theory and critical practice in recent years" (2007: 179). According to Sommer, semiotic and narratological approaches are particularly fruitful ways for studying cultural representations, providing the scholar with a broad range of clearly-defined concepts and analytical tools. An additional advantage of these approaches can be seen in the fact that they are not associated with specific national research traditions, thus lending themselves particularly well to the ongoing projects concerned with transnationalizing the study of culture, which will be delineated in the next two sections.

5 Transnationalizing the Study of Culture: Cultural Turns in the Humanities

Since the sustained development of transnational approaches to the study of culture involves, and even presupposes, an exchange and a sharing of concepts, methods, and research agendas across the broad range of different disciplines that partake in this project, it can profit from the dynamic force fields that have emerged in the humanities. As Doris Bachmann-Medick has shown in her wide-ranging and sophisticated monograph *Cultural Turns* (2006), in addition to the approaches mentioned in the sections above, there have also been a number of 'cultural turns' in the humanities that cut across disciplinary and national boundaries and that have significantly changed the ways in which research agendas have developed. Though many of these developments can arguably be traced back to the 'linguistic turn' and the 'interpretive turn,' all of the turns covered in Bachmann-Medick's book have helped foster a move beyond the boundaries of disciplines and national borders. Devoting a chapter to each turn, she explores in systematic detail the research questions, epistemic ruptures, theoretical frameworks, and possibilities of application offered by the following cultural turns, all of which not only provide important concepts for the study of culture but have also been, and continue to be, instrumental in transnationalizing it:

- the interpretive turn, i.e. the redirection of attention towards cultural meanings, negotiations, and interpretations that was ushered in by cultural anthropology and that initiated both an understanding of culture as a huge repertoire of texts and an anthropological turn within literary studies (cf. Bachmann-Medick 2004, 2006);
- the performative turn, i.e. the complementary as well as corrective move to an understanding of 'culture as performance,' a view that takes into consideration all the factors, institutions, social processes, and practices that are involved in the practical production of cultural meanings;
- the reflexive/literary/rhetorical turn, i.e. an enhanced critical and self-conscious exploration of the complex issues involved in the representation

and writing of culture as well as of the forms and structures of texts and other cultural ways of worldmaking;
- the postcolonial turn;
- the translational turn, i.e. an explicit focus on translation processes across the humanities and a sustained analysis of the mediation processes and problems of transfer involved in cultural exchanges conceived of as translations (see section 6);
- the spatial turn, i.e. a cross-disciplinary focus on, and analysis of, the categories of space, place, borders, and border-crossings based on a new understanding of space as a relational category and as a result of social relations, practices, and orders of knowledge;
- the iconic/pictorial turn, i.e. the immense importance of, and the widespread cross-disciplinary interest in, the functions of images and visualization in today's media culture.

In addition to the turns surveyed in Bachmann-Medick's book, one could mention a number of other key concepts for the study of culture that have arguably also initiated wide-ranging new developments, or even turns, in the humanities. These complex changes in the theoretical and critical climate have been dubbed, respectively, as the 'historical turn,' 'anthropological turn,' 'ethical turn,' and 'narrative turn,' or 'narrativist turn.' There has also been so much cross-disciplinary interest in the concepts of transnationalism and transculturality that one may even speak of a 'transnational turn' and a 'transcultural turn.' While all of these turns, just like the cultural turns discussed by Bachmann-Medick, have greatly increased interest in what Jerome Bruner calls "The Narrative Construction of Reality" and in what the philosopher Nelson Goodman felicitously christened "Ways of Worldmaking," the transnational study of culture is, of course, interested in cultural ways of worldmaking like those of the media and narratives (cf. Nünning et al. 2010).

All of these turns have been conducive to transcending the limitations of national research traditions, in fostering transnational as well as transcultural approaches to the study of culture and to foregrounding both global and transnational cultural issues and the concept of transnationalism itself. The latter has mainly been explored by global historians, but cultural theory has also developed a keen interest in the concepts of transnationalism and transculturality (cf. Welsch 1997), as recent developments in American cultural studies (cf. Fluck et al. 2011; Fluck 2012) and postcolonial studies, for instance, demonstrate. There has been such great and widespread interest in transnational issues across disciplinary boundaries that one could even posit a transnational turn itself.

In what is arguably the most sophisticated and stimulating article on the topic of "Cultural Studies and the Transnational" to date, Imre Szeman has convincingly shown that the notion, or indeed the "concept-metaphor" (Szeman 2007: 200), of the transnational cannot only open up interesting new conceptual and theoretical directions for the study of culture, but it also "forces us to consider seriously that the very object of cultural studies – culture – has been radically changed in ways that require the activity of the field to shift from what has remained its basic orientation: the study of cultural objects and practices of everyday life in relation to power" (Szeman 2007: 202). What is more, Szeman carefully delineates and discusses various levels on which the transnational functions within cultural studies, distinguishing three distinct levels: the transnational spread of cultural studies as a discipline; the exploration of transnational contexts, issues, and sites of cultural analysis; and the political and epistemological challenges involved in the transfer of British and American cultural studies to other contexts. The most obvious way in which the transnational impinges on the study of culture concerns "the spread of cultural studies beyond the national sites and spaces with which it has been typically identified – beyond that familiar trajectory that begins with Birmingham, before splintering off to the United States, Australia and Canada" (Szeman 2007: 202–203). What needs to be emphasized in this context, however, is that this spread of cultural studies concerns "the emergence of cultural studies as a globalised academic practice" (Szeman 2007: 203) rather than the development of truly transnational approaches to the study of culture. While it may well be "apparent that cultural studies as a professional practice is now truly transnational" (Szeman 2007), what is much less apparent or clear is whether there have been any sustained attempts at inter- or transnationalizing research traditions and practices themselves.

Moreover, the notion of transnationalization challenges established and especially Eurocentric (and American) concepts denoting modern cultures and collectivities such as the nation-state and the polity. At the same time, it draws attention to the interconnections between polity, nation, and culture in its various manifestations in language, media, memory, and identity. Itself a major mode of the diffusion, transfer, and problematization of key concepts, the transnational perspective epitomizes the emergent character of concepts and the necessity of greater self-reflexivity. The concept of transnationalism draws attention not only to transnational cultural phenomena (e.g., Hollywood and Bollywood movies, popular music and MTV, a new understanding of world literature) that have proliferated in the age of globalization but also to the far-reaching effects transnationalization has had on the historical and heuristic reconfiguration of the interdependence of culture, society, and the polity. Both

such transnational cultural phenomena and various transnationalization processes underline the fact that the development of transnational approaches to
the study of culture is a great desideratum, especially in the present age of
globalization and world-wide migration. Although the process of internationalizing cultural studies has been underway for almost two decades (cf., e.g.,
Stratton and Ang 1996; Cvetkovich and Kellner 1996; Abbas and Erni 2005;
Connery and Wilson 2007; Szeman 2007, 2011), it has mainly consisted of
spreading the dominant models of British and American cultural studies across
the globe rather than transnationalizing the study of culture itself or exploring
the biases and limitations of cultural studies: "Consequently, an interrogation
of the potential cultural parochialisms and conceptual blind spots of cultural
studies constitutes, for me, one of the most important and compelling 'theoretical' projects in the field today" (Szeman 2007: 206).

6 Travelling Concepts and Translation as Ways of Fostering Transnational Approaches to the Study of Culture

Several key concepts, or meta-concepts, present themselves as possible models
for framing and fostering the development of transnational approaches to the
study of culture. They include the notions of 'travelling concepts' (cf. Bal 2002),
translation (Bachmann-Medick 2006: Ch. 5), cultural exchange, or cultural
transfer and emergence. Though the focus in this section will be on the potential of 'travelling concepts' as a metatheoretical framework for developing a
transnational perspective for the study of culture, recent insights of the other
fields and approaches, i.e., translation studies, cultural exchange, and cultural
transfer, converge in a number of ways that impinge on any attempt to develop
transnational approaches to the study of culture.

Though all of these approaches are concerned with the dynamic processes
involved in the traffic between cultures and disciplines, and are, thus, intertwined in a number of ways, they focus on different aspects. Bal's cross-disciplinary project of 'travelling concepts' is mainly concerned with the development of a "concept-based methodology" and with fostering interdisciplinary
research projects in the humanities (Bal 2002: 5). The approaches developed in
translation studies, cultural exchange, and cultural transfer look much more
closely at the historical and social contexts, actual people, and institutions that
adapt concepts, goods, or practices from other countries; multilayered process-

es involved in the acts of translation or appropriation; and the transformations that theories, concepts, or other cultural phenomena undergo as they are transferred from one (e.g., academic) context into another.

What the notions of travelling concepts, translation, cultural exchange, and cultural transfer have in common is that they share at least two central epistemological assumptions: firstly, the assumption that concepts are 'operative terms' (Welsch 1997), i.e. that they are never merely descriptive but "also programmatic and normative" (Bal 2002: 28) and that they construct and change the very objects they analyze (cf. Welsch 1997: 20), "entailing new emphases and a new ordering of the phenomena within the complex objects constituting the cultural field" (Bal 2002: 33); secondly, the assumption that there are no universal concepts for the study of culture, society, or politics and that no approach or theory can ever claim any universal validity.

Approaches and concepts in the humanities are not only heavily imbued with, and shaped by, very particular historical, intellectual, and national traditions, but they also come with ideological freight and unconscious biases, as the insights of postcolonial theory and globalization studies have demonstrated. As Dipesh Chakrabarty has shown in his influential book *Provincializing Europe*, every case of transferring a cultural, economic, or political model or theory from one context to another is always "a problem of translation" (2008: 17) as well – a translation of existing worlds, their "conceptual horizons" and their thought-categories into the context, concepts, and horizons of another life-world (2008: 71). He draws attention to the fact that any seemingly "abstract and universal idea" can "look utterly different in different historical contexts," that no country is "a model to another country," that "historical differences actually make a difference," and that "no human society is a *tabula rasa*" (2008: xii). What Chakrabarty observes about the "universal concepts of political modernity" is also true of every approach and concept for the study of culture that is transferred from one academic context to another: such travelling concepts "encounter pre-existing concepts, categories, institutions, and practices through which they get translated and configured differently" (2008: xii). All of this should be kept in mind when trying to gauge the challenges and possibilities offered by the notion of travelling concepts, as well as of translation, cultural exchange, and cultural transfer, for the development of transnational approaches to the study of culture.

One of the most promising ways of fostering the development of transnational approaches to the study of culture was suggested by the Dutch narratologist and cultural theorist Mieke Bal in her book *Travelling Concepts in the Humanities: A Rough Guide* (2002). Her project proceeds from the assumption that concepts are indispensable for the study of culture because they are "the tools of intersubjectivity" in that "they facilitate discussion on the basis of a common language" and "offer miniature theories" (Bal 2002: 22). More often than not, however, the "meaning, reach, and operational value" of concepts differ between diverse disciplines, different academic cultures, and historical periods (Bal 2002: 24). Though various key concepts are at the core of many disciplines in the social sciences and humanities concerned with the study of culture, they are usually not univocal and firmly established terms. Rather, they are dynamic and flexible, undergoing semantic changes as they travel back and forth "between disciplines, between individual scholars, between historical periods, and between geographically dispersed academic communities," which are often shaped by different national research cultures (Bal: 2002: 24). Some concepts and theories tend to travel better than others: while some concepts are roughly translatable, others may contain cultural connotations or implications that defy translation. The travelling of concepts, thus, serves to show that the very assumption of translatability, in general, and the "translatability of cultures" (cf. Budick and Iser 1996), in particular, may not quite hold (cf. Chakrabarty 2008: 74).

With the move towards greater interdisciplinarity, the dynamic exchange of concepts, as well as metaphors and narratives, between different disciplines has intensified considerably (cf. Neumann and Tygstrup 2009), with concepts and metaphors not only being shaped by cultures and theories but also, in turn, shaping the latter (cf. Grabes et al. 2009). Through constant appropriation, translation and reassessment across various fields, approaches to, and concepts of cultural phenomena have acquired new meanings, triggering a reorganization of prevalent orders of knowledge and opening up new horizons of research in the social sciences as well as the humanities. To the extent that the meaning of such travelling concepts must, therefore, be constantly renegotiated, a sustained inquiry into the dynamics of such travelling, the "'translational' processes" (Chakrabarty 2008: 19), the politics involved, and the genealogies of the concepts in question is a prerequisite for both the development of transnational approaches to the study of culture and a higher degree of self-reflexivity in any approach to this blossoming and increasingly diverse field.

In order to provide theoretical, conceptual, and methodological backbones to any project concerned with either the travelling and translation of concepts or the development of transnational approaches to the study of culture, four axes along which approaches, theories, concepts, metaphors, and narratives can travel can be distinguished:

1. travelling between academic disciplines: crossing disciplinary boundaries;
2. travelling between academic and national cultures and cultures of research: crossing national borders;

3. travelling diachronically across time: crossing the boundaries between historical periods;
4. travelling synchronically between functionally defined subsystems: travelling between academia and society.

The complexity of such theoretical and conceptual transfers resides in the fact that concepts are always embedded in their respective co-texts and in various contexts. The latter include the theories, frameworks, or paradigms in which a given concept develops, the discipline from which it originates as well as the respective disciplinary discourses associated with it and the academic research culture with its concomitant institutional practices, national traditions, and intellectual styles. Therefore, concepts always have a number of disciplinary, formal, and functional features that can be derived either from their position and role in a particular theory, conceptual system, or discipline, or from the traditions and intellectual styles from which they originate. Whenever a concept is transferred from its original context(s), it is never innocent, nor does it travel alone; it always comes with theoretical baggage and, possibly, even ideological freight, both of which may, however, be lost in transit or translation. The incorporation of concepts adapted from other disciplines or research cultures, therefore, always entails acts of recontextualization, i.e., relating the adapted concepts to established frameworks and theories in the new disciplinary and institutional context.

Although such conceptual transfers across any of the axes identified above constitute a promising way for the development of interdisciplinary and transnational approaches to the study of culture, they are also inevitably fraught with some challenges and risks. Important challenges are arguably the tasks of paying critical attention to the processes of translation and of successfully mediating between different cultural traditions as well as between academic and theoretical differences. In doing so, one has to avoid the danger that the travelling of concepts can result in bringing together two incommensurable cultural or theoretical frameworks. The most obvious risks include the danger of oversimplification and loss of terminological precision, theoretical consistency, analytical insight, and epistemological and heuristic power. When concepts travel they may also become mere commonplaces or metaphors, which can result in the dissolution of a concept as a whole. On the other hand, the importation of concepts from other fields can be an important heuristic move and tremendously productive, yielding new combinations of insights and leading to the revision of established disciplinary theories or the discovery of unknown phenomena. Moreover, it can "trigger and facilitate reflection and debate on all levels of methodology" (Bal 2002: 29), enhance disciplinary innovation and even redefine a discipline and its boundaries, generating new theoretical frameworks, disciplinary research domains, or even new fields of interdisciplinary research.

The most important gain that can result from concepts travelling across disciplinary and national boundaries is, thus, arguably the emergence of new areas or fields of research for the transnational study of culture, or even of new and truly interdisciplinary academic fields that cut across traditional disciplines. The quite well-established field known as 'cultural memory studies' (cf. Erll and Nünning 2008) provides a typical case in point of such an emergent transnational approach to the study of culture and transdisciplinary field of research, though there are a number of equally pertinent examples, including, e.g., postcolonial studies, ritual studies (cf. Dücker 2007), visual studies, cross-disciplinary narrative research (cf. Heinen and Sommer 2009; Müller-Funk 2008), as well as performance studies and cultures of performativity. Already in 1992, the Egyptologist Jan Assmann suggested that a new paradigm of *Kulturwissenschaften* was emerging around the concept of memory (cf. the 1992 "Foreword" reprinted in Assmann 2011: vii-viii), which actually dates back even further to the works of Maurice Halbwachs on *mémoire collective* at the beginning of the twentieth century. In the course of the last two decades, this area of research has witnessed a veritable boom in various countries and disciplines.

As a consequence, the study of the relations between culture, media, and memory has diversified into a broad range of approaches, culminating in the field of cultural memory studies (cf. Erll and Nünning 2008), which can serve as an example of what an interdisciplinary and transnational approach to the study of culture can look like. Concepts of cultural memory have circulated in history, the social and political sciences, philosophy and theology, psychology, the neurosciences and psychoanalysis, as well as in literary and media studies. Sometimes the concepts of memory developed and used by different disciplines converge; at other times, they seem to diverge or even exclude one another. All too often, researchers in one discipline or research culture seem to take only little notice of the work done in neighboring disciplines, and the same holds true, albeit to a lesser extent, for research done in different countries. Nonetheless, cultural memory studies has become a decidedly inter- and even transnational field. Important concepts have been generated in France, Germany, Great Britain, Italy, Canada, the United States, and the Netherlands, as well as in China and other countries in Asia. At the same time, however, cultural memory studies testify to the claim made above: nationally specific academic traditions and language barriers have tended to impede the transfer of knowledge about cultural memory in particular and different approaches to the study of culture in general, thus, posing a challenge to the development of genuinely transnational approaches to the study of cultural phenomena.

7 From Cultural Studies to the Transnational Study of Culture

Much more work needs to be done in order to gauge the complex differences between national research cultures, to reconfigure and re-conceive of particular national kinds of 'cultural studies' as a transnational study of culture, and, even more so, to develop full-fledged transnational approaches and concepts for the study of culture. It, therefore, seems apt to conclude by making a modest plea for further research into, and debate on, a key issue for the trans/national dimension of the study of culture: the different national approaches, styles, and traditions that have emerged in different institutional contexts and research cultures. Anyone interested in fostering the development of transcultural and transnational approaches to the study of culture can profit considerably from comparing different national approaches and considering the ways in which such influential, invented traditions are discursively constructed and institutionally implemented.

What is needed for the development of transnational approaches to the study of culture is an enhanced degree of self-reflection about, and much more detailed and comprehensive investigations of, the different national traditions and styles of 'doing' cultural studies, or the study of culture; the promotion of greater "transnational literacy" (Bal 2002: 291); and a willingness to endorse interdisciplinarity – to question one's own academic routines and negotiate between different national research traditions and intellectual styles. In this day and age, in which "there is increased awareness that a particular national literature can look quite different from a different national perspective" (Thomas 1998: 10), there is also an increased need to compare not just the literatures and cultures of different countries but also the various national traditions of studying literature and culture; it is time to move beyond the epistemological limitations of national boundaries, institutionally driven conceptual frameworks, and particular intellectual styles (cf. Galtung 1981).

To be able to gauge the complex problems of developing transnational and transcultural approaches to the study of culture, one needs to get to grips with, and transcend, the different national traditions that have emerged and become institutionalized. Worldwide migration and the global interfacing of cultures require different approaches than those championed by British (or American) cultural studies, approaches that are no longer limited to national research traditions and concepts of culture. Yet, it is difficult to actually devise new models for a transnational study of culture freed from the shackles of the hitherto dominant British or American approaches.

As already mentioned above, however, a number of promising new departures have served to internationalize, and even transnationalize, approaches to the study of culture. These include valuable volumes and anthologies like *Internationalizing Cultural Studies: An Anthology* (Abbas and Erni 2005), *The Worlding Project: Doing Cultural Studies in the Era of Globalization* (Connery and Wilson 2007), and *New Cultural Studies: Adventures in Theory* (Hall and Birchall 2007), all of which, despite their heterogeneous nature, delineate interesting new departures and trajectories for developing innovative approaches for a transnational study of culture in an age of globalization. Moreover, we have not only recently witnessed a "transnational turn in American Studies" (cf. Fluck et al. 2011) but also sustained attempts to develop new forms of 'global' cultural studies. Though an Institute for Global Cultural Studies (IGCS) was founded as early as 1991 at Binghampton University, with other universities offering programs on global cultural studies following suit (e.g., Point Park University and, most recently, Université Jean Moulin Lyon 3), critical voices have also expressed skepticism about the very notion of a 'global cultural studies,' even calling it an "impossibility" (cf. Stratton and Ang 1996). Jon Stratton and Ien Ang's warning that the "'internationalization' of cultural studies cannot mean the formation of a global, universally generalizable set of theories and objects of study" (Stratton and Ang 1996: 363) may still serve as a timely reminder that the field of the study of culture may not lend itself particularly well to universalizing or transnationalizing gestures. In a particularly stimulating and thought-provoking review-essay, Imre Szeman has provided a balanced assessment of the notion of "*Global* Cultural Studies?" (cf. Szeman 2011), carefully gauging both the risks and promises of such an ambitious project, and the political and epistemological problems that it entails. What we are actually faced with today are both "national-cultural situations, events, and circumstances" and a more or less "shared global critico-theoretical discourse" (Szeman 2011: 148), though the latter indeed tends to be "heavily weighted towards ideas emerging from Anglo-American and European traditions" (Szeman 2011: 148).

In order to move beyond nationally based boundaries and academic styles, transnational approaches to the study of culture need to investigate the (usually unacknowledged) presuppositions, discursive practices, and structural features of its own research traditions, which have so far been largely unacknowledged and have tended to become naturalized, in detail. Therefore, transnational and transcultural approaches to the study of culture require the development of a new set of guiding principles, travelling concepts and other ways of academic worldmaking that expand the limited horizons of British cultural studies, American cultural studies, German *Kulturwissenschaften*, and other nationally specific research traditions. While cultural studies may have gone international or even transnational, there is still a great "need to pluralize cultural studies" (Szeman 2007: 208) and develop innovative, truly transnational approaches to the study of culture.

References

Abbas, Ackbar, and John Nguyet Erni, eds. *Internationalizing Cultural Studies: An Anthology.* Malden, MA/Oxford/Carlton: Blackwell, 2005.
Achilles, Jochen, Horst W. Drescher, and Christopher Harvie. "The Study of the British Regions from Germany." *Journal for the Study of British Cultures* 2.2 (1995): 201–217.
Allatson, Paul. *Key Terms in Latino/a Cultural and Literary Studies.* Malden, MA/Oxford/Carlton: Blackwell, 2007.
Appelsmeyer, Heide, and Elfriede Billmann-Mahecha, eds. *Kulturwissenschaft. Felder einer prozeßorientierten wissenschaftlichen Praxis.* Weilerswist: Velbrück, 2001.
Assmann, Aleida. *Einführung in die Kulturwissenschaften. Grundbegriffe, Themen, Fragestellungen.* Berlin: Erich Schmidt, 2006.
Assmann, Jan. *Cultural Memory and Early Civilization: Writing, Remembrance, and Political Imagination.* Cambridge: Cambridge University Press, 2011. vii–x.
Bachmann-Medick, Doris, ed. *Kultur als Text. Die anthropologische Wende in der Literaturwissenschaft.* 2nd edition. Tübingen/Basel: Francke, 2004.
Bachmann-Medick, Doris. *Cultural Turns. Neuorientierungen in den Kulturwissenschaften.* Reinbek: Rowohlt, 2006.
Bal, Mieke. *Narratology: Introduction to the Theory of Narrative.* Toronto: University of Toronto Press, 1997 [1985].
Bal, Mieke. "Introduction." *Acts of Memory: Cultural Recall in the Present.* Eds. Mieke Bal, Jonathan Crewe, and Leo Spitzer. Hanover/London: University Press of New England, 1999. vii–xvii.
Bal, Mieke. *Travelling Concepts in the Humanities: A Rough Guide.* Toronto: University of Toronto Press, 2002.
Bal, Mieke, Jonathan Crewe, and Leo Spitzer, eds. *Acts of Memory: Cultural Recall in the Present.* Hanover/London: University Press of New England, 1999.
Bassnett, Susan. "Teaching British Cultural Studies: Reflections on the Why and the How." *Journal for the Study of British Cultures* 1.1 (1994): 63–74.
Belsey, Catherine. "Towards Cultural History – In Theory and Practice." *Textual Practice* 3.2 (1989): 159–172.
Belsey, Catherine. *Shakespeare and the Loss of Eden: The Construction of Family Values in Early Modern Culture.* Basingstoke: Macmillan, 1999.

Belsey, Catherine. "Beyond Literature and Cultural Studies: The Case for Cultural Criticism." *Belgian Journal of English Language and Literatures*. New Series 1, Thematic Issue (2003): 91–100.

Böhme, Hartmut, Peter Matussek, and Lothar Müller. *Orientierung Kulturwissenschaft. Was sie kann, was sie will*. Reinbek: Rowohlt, 2000.

Bollenbeck, Georg, and Gerhard Kaiser. "Kulturwissenschaftliche Ansätze in den Literaturwissenschaften." *Handbuch der Kulturwissenschaften. Band 2: Paradigmen und Disziplinen*. Eds. Friedrich Jaeger and Jürgen Straub. Stuttgart/Weimar: Metzler, 2004. 615–637.

Bromley, Roger, Udo Göttlich, and Carsten Winter, eds. *Cultural Studies. Grundlagentexte zur Einführung*. Lüneburg: zu Klampen, 1999.

Brottman, Mikita. *High Theory/Low Culture*. New York/Houndmills: Palgrave Macmillan, 2005.

Bruner, Jerome. "The Narrative Construction of Reality." *Critical Inquiry* 18 (1991): 1–21.

Budick, Sanford, and Wolfgang Iser, eds. *The Translatability of Cultures: Figurations of the Space Between*. Stanford: Stanford University Press, 1996.

Bundesministerium für Wissenschaft und Verkehr/Internationales Forschungszentrum Kulturwissenschaften, eds. *The Contemporary Study of Culture*. Wien: Turia + Kant, 1999.

Burgett, Bruce, and Glenn Hendler, eds. *Keywords for American Cultural Studies*. New York: New York University Press, 2007.

Cassirer, Ernst. *The Philosophy of Symbolic Forms*. Volumes 1–3. New Haven/London: Yale University Press, 1965 [1955].

Chakrabarty, Dipesh. *Provincializing Europe: Postcolonial Thought and Historical Difference*. Reissue, with a new preface by the author. Princeton/Oxford: Princeton University Press, 2008 [2000].

Childs, Peter, and Mike Storry, eds. *Encyclopedia of Contemporary British Culture*. London/New York: Routledge, 1999.

Connery, Christopher Leigh, and Rob Wilson, eds. *The Worlding Project: Doing Cultural Studies in the Era of Globalization*. Santa Cruz: New Pacific, 2007.

Cvetkovich, Ann, and Douglas Kellner, eds. *Articulating the Global and the Local: Globalization and Cultural Studies*. Boulder: Westview, 1996.

Del Sarto, Ana, Alicia Ríos, and Abril Trigo, eds. *The Latin American Cultural Studies Reader*. Durham, MA/London: Duke University Press, 2004.

Demoor, Marysa, and Jürgen Pieters. "The Critic as Acrobat: Walking the Tightrope between Cultural Studies and Cultural History." *Belgian Journal of English Language and Literatures*. New Series 1, Thematic Issue (2003): 101–109.

Denning, Michael. *Culture in the Age of Three Worlds*. London/New York: Verso, 2004.

Dietrich, René, Daniel Smilovski, and Ansgar Nünning, eds. *Lost or Found in Translation? Interkulturelle/Internationale Perspektiven der Geistes- und Kulturwissenschaften*. Trier: WVT, 2011.

Dücker, Burckhard. *Rituale: Formen – Funktionen – Geschichte. Eine Einführung in die Ritualwissenschaft*. Stuttgart/Weimar: Metzler, 2007.

Easthope, Antony. *Englishness and National Culture*. London/New York: Routledge, 1999.

Erll, Astrid, and Ansgar Nünning, eds. *Cultural Memory Studies: An International and Interdisciplinary Handbook*. MCM: Media & Cultural Memory, 7. Berlin/New York: de Gruyter, 2008.

Felski, Rita. "Modernist Studies and Cultural Studies: Reflections on Method." *Modernism/Modernity* 10.3 (2003): 501–517.

Fluck, Winfried. "American Cultural Studies." *English and American Studies: Theory and Practice*. Eds. Martin Middeke, Timo Müller, Christina Wald, and Hubert Zapf. Stuttgart/Weimar: Metzler, 2012. 287–300.

Fluck, Winfried, Donald Pease, and John Carlos Rowe, eds. *Re-framing the Transnational Turn in American Studies*. Hanover: Dartmouth College Press, 2011.

Galtung, Johan. "Structure, Culture, and Intellectual Style: An Essay Comparing Saxonic, Teutonic, Gallic and Nipponic Approaches." *Social Science Information* 20.6 (1981): 817–856.

Geertz, Clifford. "Thick Description: Toward an Interpretive Theory of Culture." *The Interpretation of Cultures: Selected Essays*. New York: Basic Books, 1973. 3–30.

Goodman, Nelson. *Ways of Worldmaking*. Indianapolis: Hackett, 1992 [1978].

Grabes, Herbert. "Textwissenschaftlich fundierte Kulturwissenschaft/Landeskunde." *Anglistik* 7.1 (1996): 35–40.

Grabes, Herbert, ed. *Literary History/Cultural History: Force-Fields and Tensions*. Tübingen: Narr, 2001.

Grabes, Herbert. "Literary History and Cultural History: Relations and Difference." *Literary History/Cultural History: Force Fields and Tensions*. Tübingen: Narr, 2001. 1–34.

Grabes, Herbert, Ansgar Nünning, and Sibylle Baumbach, eds. *Metaphors Shaping Culture and Theory*. (*REAL: Yearbook of Research in English and American Literature* 25). Tübingen: Narr, 2009.

Gray, Ann. "Cultural Studies at Birmingham: The Impossibility of Critical Pedagogy?" *Cultural Studies* 17.6 (2003): 767–782.

Hall, Catherine. "British Cultural Identities and the Legacy of the Empire." *British Cultural Studies: Geography, Nationality, and Identity*. Eds. David Morley and Kevin Robins. Oxford/New York: Oxford University Press, 2001. 27–40.

Hall, Gary, and Clare Birchall, eds. *New Cultural Studies: Adventures in Theory*. Athens: University of Georgia Press, 2007.

Heinen, Sandra, and Roy Sommer, eds. *Narratology in the Age of Cross-Disciplinary Narrative Research*. *Narratologia* 20. Berlin/New York: de Gruyter, 2009.

Herman, David, Manfred Jahn, and Marie-Laure Ryan, eds. *Routledge Encyclopedia of Narrative Theory*. London/New York: Routledge, 2005.

Hitchcock, Peter. *Imaginary States: Studies in Cultural Transnationalism*. Champaign: University of Illinois Press, 2003.

Hoggart, Richard. *The Uses of Literacy: Aspects of Working Class Life with Special Reference to Publications and Entertainments*. Harmondsworth: Penguin, 1957.

Huck, Christian. "British Cultural Studies." *English and American Studies: Theory and Practice*. Eds. Martin Middeke, Timo Müller, Christina Wald, and Hubert Zapf. Stuttgart/Weimar: Metzler, 2012. 271–286.

Hütig, Andreas. "Dimensionen des Kulturbegriffs." *Historische Kulturwissenschaften. Positionen, Praktiken und Perspektiven*. Eds. Jan Kusber, Mechthild Dreyer, Jörg Rogge, and Andreas Hütig. Bielefeld: transcript, 2010. 105–124.

Iser, Wolfgang. *How to Do Theory*. Malden, MA/Oxford/Carlton: Blackwell, 2006.

Jaeger, Friedrich, and Burkhard Liebsch, eds. *Handbuch der Kulturwissenschaften. Band 1: Grundlagen und Schlüsselbegriffe*. Stuttgart/Weimar: Metzler, 2004.

Jaeger, Friedrich, and Jürgen Straub, eds. *Handbuch der Kulturwissenschaften. Band 2: Paradigmen und Disziplinen*. Stuttgart/Weimar: Metzler, 2004.

Koschorke, Albrecht. *Wahrheit und Erfindung. Grundzüge einer Allgemeinen Erzähltheorie*. Frankfurt a.M.: Fischer, 2012.

Kramer, Jürgen. *British Cultural Studies*. Munich: Fink, 1997.

Kroeber, Alfred L., and Clyde Kluckhohn. *Culture: A Critical Review of Concepts and Definitions*. New York: Vintage Books, 1952.

Morley, David, and Kevin Robins, eds. *British Cultural Studies: Geography, Nationality, and Identity*. Oxford/New York: Oxford University Press, 2001.

Müller-Funk, Wolfgang. *Die Kultur und ihre Narrative. Eine Einführung*. Wien/New York: Springer, 2008 [2002].

Neumann, Birgit, and Frederik Tygstrup, eds. *Travelling Concepts in English Studies. EJES: European Journal of English Studies* 13.1 (2009).

Neumann, Birgit, and Frederik Tygstrup. "Travelling Concepts in English Studies." *Travelling Concepts in English Studies. EJES: European Journal of English Studies* 13.1 (2009): 1–12.

Neumann, Birgit, and Ansgar Nünning, eds. *Travelling Concepts for the Study of Culture*. Berlin/Boston: de Gruyter, 2012.

Nünning, Ansgar. "On the Englishness of English Literary Histories: Where Literature, Philosophy and Nationalism Meet Cultural History." *Critical Interfaces: Contributions on Philosophy, Literary Theory and Culture in Honour of Herbert Grabes*. Eds. Gordon Collier, Klaus Schwank, and Franz Wieselhuber. Trier: WVT, 2001. 55–83.

Nünning, Ansgar. "Literatur, Mentalitäten und kulturelles Gedächtnis. Grundriß, Leitbegriffe und Perspektiven einer anglistischen Kulturwissenschaft." *Literaturwissenschaftliche Theorien, Modelle und Methoden. Eine Einführung*. Ed. Ansgar Nünning. Trier: WVT, 2004 [1995]. 173–197.

Nünning, Ansgar. "Wissenschaftsstile und kollektive Identitäten von Literaturwissenschaftlern. Teutonische Thesen zur *Englishness* der englischen Literaturgeschichtsschreibung." *Lost or Found in Translation? Interkulturelle/Internationale Perspektiven der Geistes- und Kulturwissenschaften*. Eds. René Dietrich, Daniel Smilovski, and Ansgar Nünning. Trier: WVT, 2011. 133–157.

Nünning, Ansgar. "Transnational Approaches to the Study of Culture." *English and American Studies: Theory and Practice*. Eds. Martin Middeke, Timo Müller, Christina Wald, and Hubert Zapf. Stuttgart/Weimar: Metzler, 2012. 261–270.

Nünning, Ansgar, and Jürgen Schlaeger. "Quo vadis, *Anglistik*? Recent Trends in and Challenges for English Studies." *English Studies Today: Recent Developments and New Directions*. Eds. Ansgar Nünning and Jürgen Schlaeger. Trier: WVT, 2007. 7–22.

Nünning, Ansgar, and Vera Nünning. "Literatur- und Kulturwissenschaften im interkulturellen und internationalen Kontext. Selbstverständnis, Wissenschaftstraditionen, Methoden und Forschungsschwerpunkte." *Lost or Found in Translation? Interkulturelle/Internationale Perspektiven der Geistes- und Kulturwissenschaften*. Eds. René Dietrich, Daniel Smilovski, and Ansgar Nünning. Trier: WVT, 2011. 83–101.

Nünning, Ansgar, ed. *Metzler Lexikon Literatur- und Kulturtheorie*. 5th edition. Stuttgart/Weimar: Metzler, 2013 [1998].

Nünning, Ansgar, and Vera Nünning, eds. *Einführung in die Kulturwissenschaften. Theoretische Grundlagen – Ansätze – Perspektiven*. Stuttgart/Weimar: Metzler, 2008.

Nünning, Vera, Ansgar Nünning, and Birgit Neumann, eds. *Cultural Ways of Worldmaking: Media and Narratives*. Berlin/New York: de Gruyter, 2010.

Ort, Claus-Michael. "Kulturbegriffe und Kulturtheorien." *Einführung in die Kulturwissenschaften. Theoretische Grundlagen – Ansätze – Perspektiven*. Eds. Ansgar Nünning and Vera Nünning. Stuttgart/Weimar: Metzler, 2008. 19–38.

Posner, Roland. "Kultursemiotik." *Einführung in die Kulturwissenschaften. Theoretische Grundlagen – Ansätze – Perspektiven*. Eds. Ansgar Nünning and Vera Nünning. Stuttgart/ Weimar: Metzler, 2008. 39–72.

Quinn, Malcolm. "'Theor-ese', or the Protocols of the Elders of Cultural Studies." *Cultural Studies – Interdisciplinarity and Translation*. Ed. Stefan Herbrechter. Amsterdam et al.: Rodopi, 2002. 73–80.

Reckwitz, Andreas. *Die Transformation der Kulturtheorien. Zur Entwicklung eines Theoriepro-gramms*. Weilerswist: Velbrück, 2000.

Said, Edward. "Traveling Theory." *The World, the Text, and the Critic*. Cambridge, MA: Harvard University Press, 1983. 226–247.

Sommer, Roy. *Grundkurs Cultural Studies/Kulturwissenschaft Großbritannien*. Stuttgart: Klett, 2003.

Sommer, Roy. "From Cultural Studies to the Study of Culture: Key Concepts and Methods." *English Studies Today: Recent Developments and New Directions*. Eds. Ansgar Nünning and Jürgen Schlaeger. Trier: WVT, 2007. 165–191.

Storry, Mike, and Peter Childs, eds. *British Cultural Identities*. London/New York: Routledge, 2002 [1997].

Stratton, Jon, and Ien Ang. "On the Impossibility of a Global Cultural Studies. 'British' Cultural Studies in an 'International' Frame." *Stuart Hall: Critical Dialogues in Cultural Studies*. Eds. David Morley and Kuan-Hsing Chen. New York: Routledge, 1996. 361–391.

Szeman, Imre. "Cultural Studies and the Transnational." *New Cultural Studies: Adventures in Theory*. Eds. Gary Hall and Clare Birchall. Athens: University of Georgia Press, 2007. 200–218.

Szeman, Imre. "*Global* Cultural Studies?" *The Minnesota Review* 76 (2011): 147–161.

Thomas, Brook. "Placing Literature Written in English." *Literature and the Nation (REAL: Year-book of Research in English and American Literature* 14). Ed. Brook Thomas. Tübingen: Narr, 1998. 1–31.

Welsch, Wolfgang. "Transkulturalität." *Universitas* 52, 607 (1997): 16–24.

Williams, Raymond. "Culture is Ordinary." *Resources of Hope: Culture, Democracy, Socialism*. London: Verso, 1989 [1958]. 3–14.

Winter, Rainer. *Die Kunst des Eigensinns. Cultural Studies als Kritik der Macht*. Weilerswist: Velbrück, 2001.

Wirth, Uwe, ed. *Logiken und Praktiken der Kulturforschung*. Berlin: Kadmos, 2008.

Zima, Peter V. "Die Stellung der Literaturwissenschaft zwischen den Kulturen. Eine textsozio-logische Betrachtung." *Literaturwissenschaft: intermedial – interdisziplinär*. Eds. Herbert Foltinek and Christoph Leitgeb. Wien: Verlag der Österreichischen Akademie der Wissen-schaften, 2002. 25–38.

I. Conceptualizations and Histories

Dipesh Chakrabarty
Place and Displaced Categories, or How We Translate Ourselves into Global Histories of the Modern·

This essay elaborates on the related ideas of translation and displacement to show how one could use them in understanding the historical processes through which particular histories – in this case, that of India – blend into the global history of capitalism.

A ubiquitous theme of modern history – indeed, a theme that often makes a particular piece of history belong to the so-called 'modern' period – is how and why different parts of the world come to embrace capitalist relations. This is the process that, in the past, has given rise to debates about the 'transition to capitalism' in the history of the modern West. It has its echoes in the history of the non-West. Narratives of transition have usually concerned themselves with sociological questions: Was trade the real motor of capitalist growth in Europe? Or was it class struggle? Or proto-industrialization? What weakened the social bonds of pre-capitalist societies? And so on. In my book, *Provincializing Europe* (2007, hereafter *PE*), I argued that models drawn from sociological theories do not sufficiently explain how the transition to the rule of capital comes about. They need to be supplemented by linguistic models, particularly those that have to do with translation. I am concerned with translation not only in the literal sense but also in some larger, spatial sense. However, I elaborated more on the literal side in the book. Here, I want to turn to the idea of displacement-as-translation as an explanatory trope in discussions of modernity.

My argument in *PE* had to do with the fact that, for people to behave as subjects of a capitalist order, they need to learn to think of themselves and the world through categories relevant to the capitalist mode of production. But, because societies that embraced capitalist rules had histories that were longer and deeper than the history of capitalism, no society acted as a *tabula rasa* in coming under the hegemony or dominance of capital. They had other categories

· This essay draws on my article "Subaltern History as Political Thought" and my introduction to *Provincializing Europe*. I am grateful to Doris Bachmann-Medick for helpful comments on an earlier draft.

that needed to be translated into the categories of capital, such as 'labor' or 'land,' to give but two examples. The way these abstract categories came to have reality in people's lives, I argued, was through a process that involved two very different processes of translation that were contradictory and yet complementary to each other. One could call them, respectively, a sociological or scientific model of translation and a quotidian, practical model. In the sociological model, the sociological term (such as 'capital' or 'labor') assimilates or sublates all other vernacular terms that may be used in different societies to designate it into itself. This is a model in which a third and higher category – as in Hegelian dialectic – mediates and subsumes other words both similar to and different from itself, thereby rendering all differences neutral. To explain this model, I gave the example of the technical/scientific expression 'H_2O' subsuming into itself both the English word *water* and the Hindi word *pani*, thus, making their difference immaterial to the process of translation (2007: 83). Here, the assumption is that the "higher" category has a superior descriptive capacity; it can see into the real better than the "lower" categories can. This superiority is what gives it analytical value and status. Such a model underlies much sociological writing that assumes that the categories 'capital' or 'labor' simply describe the reality of a society, irrespective of the history, which the society in question may have had before the arrival of these terms.

I did not, in any absolute sense, question the veracity of this mode of thinking but rather tried to suggest that what made categories like 'capital' or 'labor' plausible in real history and to real historical actors was another mode of translation that could be compared to barter and that, in any historical process of transition to capitalism, accompanies and supplements the sociological model of translation. In the same way that, as in barter, one article is exchanged for another without the exchange being routed or measured by a third and higher category ('money,' for instance) and with some equivalence between the objects posited, a new and old concept could also swap places through a direct interaction between them, thanks to their linguistic properties – their alliterative, associational, or analogical values – without the intervention of any third, generalizing and supervening terms. Consider the case of the expression 'horsepower' coming to be a measure of the power of an engine – surely the word 'horse,' here, has no scientific status and only celebrates the associational and analogical functions of historical memory. My discussion in *PE* turned around these and related questions.

One point I did not emphasize enough in *PE* was that the linguistic model of translation is a spatial model as well. For displacement is, indeed, a major meaning of the English word 'translation.' The *Oxford English Dictionary* says as much in explaining the word: "removal or conveyance from one person, place or condition to another" is a sense that is inherent in the word.[1] I want to make the case that postcolonial criticism arises from displacement of both persons and categories. For the first point – ideas and their relationship to displacement of people – I want to offer *PE* (both as a book and an intellectual project) as an example. And, for the second point, I want to examine the global career of the category 'revolutionary class' in Marxist theory and show how it has survived precisely through a process of intellectual displacement. Here, my particular example is derived from the experience of the well-known Indian series *Subaltern Studies*.

Since I speak of global history and the history of capitalism by deploying ideas about cross-categorical translation and translation-as-displacement – and they often work together – I need to make it clear that translation between different cultures and places often works as two-way traffic. This essay mainly concerns categories of political modernity. In *PE*, I explain political modernity and its attendant formulations along the following lines:

> The phenomenon of "political modernity" – namely, the rule by modern institutions of the state, bureaucracy, and capitalist enterprise – is impossible to *think* of anywhere in the world without invoking certain categories and concepts, the genealogies of which go deep into the intellectual and even theological traditions of Europe. Concepts such as citizenship, the state, civil society, public sphere, human rights, equality before the law, the individual, distinctions between public and private, the idea of the subject, democracy [...] and so on all bear the burden of European thought and history. (Chakrabarty 2007: 4)

This contention may give the impression that, in speaking of translation and displacement, my focus is only on the transmission of European categories outside of Europe. However, translation is never a one-way street. True, I focus on what happens in Indian sites of translation as India modernizes and borrows some categories and practices from Europe that Indians will make their own. But one only has to read histories of political economy to see how terms like 'labor' accommodate into themselves the world-history of capitalism, a history that is always a place of encounter between different parts of the world. The so-called European categories also have deep genealogies that stretch far beyond the boundaries of geographical Europe – a fact I acknowledged in *PE*. Also, think of words like 'caste,' 'mana,' or 'ashram' that have passed into European languages. How could this have happened if translation did not work both ways? At the same time, however, the simple fact that *translation* is a two-way street should not blind us to questions of domination and power in global histo-

---

1 See the *Oxford English Dictionary* website's definition ("Translation" 2013).

ry. Modern Europe or America may have borrowed many of their operative categories from other cultures. That borrowing actually speaks of their power in the same way that credit-worthiness is something that belongs to the privileged. The less powerful cannot borrow, either in symbolic or substantial ways, as much as the powerful can. With these qualifications out of the way, let me get on with the argument at hand.

1 *Provincializing Europe*: A Project Born out of Displacement and Translation

'Europe' was not a word that ever bothered me in my middle-class Bengali childhood or youth, as I was growing up in postcolonial Calcutta. The legacy of Europe – or British colonial rule, for that is how Europe came into our lives – was everywhere: in traffic rules, in grown-ups' regrets that Indians had no civic sense, in the games of soccer and cricket, in my school uniform, in Bengali-nationalist essays and poems critical of social inequality (especially the so-called "caste-system"), in implicit and explicit debates about love-match versus arranged marriages, in literary societies and film clubs. In practical, everyday life, 'Europe' was not a problem to be consciously named or discussed. Categories or words borrowed from European histories had found new homes in our practices. It made perfect sense, for instance, when radical friends in college would refer to someone – say, an obstructionist father-in-law-to-be – as being full of "feudal" attitudes or when we debated – for interminable hours over cheap cups of coffee or tea in inexpensive restaurants or tea-shops in which we generally overstayed our welcome – whether the Indian capitalists were a "national bourgeoisie" or a "comprador" class playing second fiddle to foreign capital. We all knew, practically, what these words meant without having to put them under any kind of analytic microscope. Their meanings did not travel beyond the immediate environment in which they were used.

What was the need, then, for "provincializing" this Europe? The answer to this question has to do with the story of my own dislodgement from this everyday life in ways that were both metaphorical and physical. I will recount the story briefly, for the implications of it go, I think, beyond the merely autobiographical. My metaphorical displacement from my everyday middle-class life happened as I trained, in Marxist circles in the city of Calcutta, to be a professional historian for whom Marx's ideas were to be a conscious analytical tool. Words familiar from their everyday use (I should explain that I had been a student of science and business management before) now grew analytical wings, soaring to the level of what Roland Barthes would have called "second or third-order" metalanguages. Marxism, even more than liberalism, was the most concentrated form in which one encountered the intellectual pasts of Europe in Indian social-science circles.

It was about two decades ago, as I completed the manuscript for my book *Rethinking Working-Class History: Bengal 1890–1940* (2000), that the question *PE* addresses began to formulate itself. The roots of my effort in labor history went back to some of the passionate debates in Bengali and Indian Marxism of my youth about the world-historical role the proletariat might play in a country such as India that was still predominantly rural. There were obvious things to be learned from the Chinese and the Vietnamese revolutions. Yet, the more I tried to imagine relations in Indian factories through categories made available by Marx and his followers, the more I became aware of a tension that arose from the profoundly – and, one might say, parochially – European origins of Marx's thoughts and their undoubted international significance. To call historical characters, whose analogues I knew in everyday life as familiar types, by names or categories derived from the revolutions in Europe of 1789 or 1848 or 1871 or 1917 felt increasingly like a doubly distancing activity. There was, first of all, the distance of historical objectivity that I was trying to enact. But there was also the distance of comical misrecognition similar to what I had often experienced watching performances of Bengali plays in which Bengali actors, cast as colonial Europeans, acted out their heavily Bengali-accented imitations of how Europeans might have spoken Bengali, that is to say, their own stereotypes of how Europeans may have stereotyped us! Something similar was happening to my characters from Bengali and Indian history, now clad, in my text, in the European costumes lent by the Marxist drama of history. There was a sense of comicality in my own earnestness that I could not ignore.

Yet, in this discussion of Marx to which I was heir in Calcutta – the discussion was always mediated, for historical reasons, by the available English-language literature on the subject – there was no room for thinking about Marx as someone belonging to certain European traditions of thought that he may even have shared with other intellectuals whom we usually pitted against Marx. This was not something that arose from a deficiency of reading. Calcutta had no dearth of bibliophiles. People knew nooks and crannies of European scholarship. But there was no sense of academic practices being part of living, disputed intellectual traditions in Europe. No idea that a living intellectual tradition never furnished final solutions to questions that arose within it. Marxism, as far as we were concerned, was simply true. The idea of 'uneven development,' for example, so central to much of Marxist historiography, was treated as a piece of truth, at most an analytical tool, but never as a provisional way of organizing information or even as something that was originally forged in the workshop of the Scottish Enlightenment. Marx was right (though he needed updating) and anti-Marxists were plain wrong, if not immoral; such were the stark political antinomies through which we thought. Even Max Weber did not get much of a serious look in the passionate scholarship of Indian historians of Marxist persuasion of the 1970s. There were, indeed, some gifted non-Marxist social scientists and historians in India. The names of Ashis Nandy and the late Ashin Das Gupta or Dharma Kumar easily come to mind. But in the heady and troubled days of a political and cultural *entente* between Mrs. Gandhi's India and the then Soviet Union, it was the Marxists who wielded prestige and power in the academic institutions of India.

My early unease, which later became a matter of intellectual curiosity about the tension between the European roots of Marx's thoughts and their global significance, did not have many takers among my Marxist friends in India – not then. The only significant dissident voice within the Marxist camp was that of Indian Maoism. The Maoist movement, known as the *Naxalite* movement (1967–1971) after a peasant revolt in the village of Naxalbari in West Bengal, suffered a catastrophic political defeat in the early 1970s, when the government ruthlessly crushed the rebellion with an iron hand.[2] Maoism, it is true, had a vibrant intellectual presence in the early work of *Subaltern Studies*, a group with which I came to be identified in the 1980s and later. But Maoism itself had become a soteriological formation by the time I began to train as a social scientist, and its 'corrections' or 'modifications' of Marx's thoughts were practical. On the question of Marx's Europeanness, Maoists were incurious.

My theoretical unease was made more acute by my experience of physical displacement from my everyday life in India. That experience was another important influence on this project. I left India in December 1976 to pursue a doctoral degree in History at the Australian National University and have lived outside India ever since, though I have been involved in discussions with my Indian friends through annual visits, lectures, and regular publications in India, both in English and my first language, Bangla. Without the experience of migration, however – a profound combination of loss and gain, the opening up of new possibilities that do not necessarily compensate for the ones that get closed – I doubt that I would have written *Provincializing Europe*.

Until I arrived in Australia, I had never seriously entertained the implications of the fact that an abstract and universal idea characteristic of political modernity everywhere – the idea of equality, say, or of democracy, or even of

---

2 For a history of this movement, see Banerjee 1984.

the dignity of the human being – could look utterly different according to historical context. Australia, like India, is a thriving electoral democracy, but election-day does not have anything of the atmosphere of festivity that I was used to in India. Things that, in everyday life, Australians assume to be essential to preserving the dignity of the individual – their personal space, for instance – are simply impracticable in my poor and crowded India. Besides, the structures of sentiment and emotion underlying specific practices in Australia were things from which I felt somewhat foreign until, over time, I myself came to inhabit many of them.

Being a migrant made me see the necessarily unstable relationship between any abstract idea and its concrete instantiation more clearly. No concrete example of an abstract can claim to be an embodiment of the abstract alone. Thus, no country is a model for another country, though the discussion of modernity that thinks in terms of "catching up" posits precisely such models. There is nothing like the cunning of reason that ensures that we all converge at the same terminal point in history in spite of our apparent, historical differences. Our historical differences actually make a difference. This difference exists because no human society is a *tabula rasa*. The universal concepts of political modernity encounter pre-existing concepts, categories, institutions, and practices through which they are translated and newly configured.

If this argument is true of India, then it is true of any other place as well, including, of course, Europe or, broadly, the West. This proposition has interesting consequences. It means, firstly, that the distinction I have drawn between the figurative – how a concept is *visualized* in practice – and the discursive sides of a concept – its abstract purity, as it were – is, itself, a partial and overdrawn distinction. As Ferdinand de Saussure taught us a long time ago, one can distinguish between the "sound-image" of an idea and its "concept-image" only in an artificial manner. The two sides merge into each other (Saussure 1966: 65–67). If this is true, as I think it is, a second important conclusion follows. It is that the so-called "universal" ideas that European thinkers produced in the period from the Renaissance to the Enlightenment, and that have since influenced projects of modernity and modernization all over the world, could never be completely universal and pure concepts (so long as they were expressible in prose – I am not concerned here with symbolic language like algebra). The very languages and the circumstances of their formulation must have imported intimations of pre-existing histories that were singular and unique, histories that belonged to the multiple pasts of Europe, into them. Irreducible elements of these parochial histories must have lingered in concepts that otherwise seem to be meant for all.

To provincialize Europe is precisely to find out how and in what sense European ideas that were universal were also, at one and the same time, drawn from very particular intellectual and historical traditions that cannot claim any universal validity. It is to ask a question about how thought is related to place. Can thoughts transcend the places of their origin? Or do places leave their imprint on thought in such a way as to call the idea of purely abstract categories into question? My starting point in all this questioning, as I have said before, was the silent and everyday presence of European thought in Indian life and practices. The Enlightenment was part of my sentiments. But I did not know it as such. Marx was a household Bengali name. His German upbringing was never commented upon. Bengali scholars translated *Das Kapital* without the slightest hint of any philological concerns. This recognition of a deep – and often unknown – debt to European thought was my point of departure; without that, there could be no "provincializing Europe." One aim of the project was, precisely, to be aware of the specific nature of this debt.

The global relevance of European thought, then, was something I took for granted. Nor did I question the need for universalistic thinking. It was never, for instance, an aim of *Provincializing Europe* to "pluralize reason," as a serious reviewer suggested in a somewhat mistaken – I use this word with respect – reading of the project.[3] As my chapter on Marx in *PE* shows, I argue not against the idea of universals as such but emphasize that the universal is a highly unstable figure, a necessary place-holder in our attempt to think through questions of modernity. We glimpse its outlines only when a particular usurps its place. Yet nothing concrete or particular could ever be the universal itself, for concept-images are intertwined with the sound-values of words like 'right' or 'democracy' that, while (roughly) translatable from one place to another, also contain elements that defy translation. Such defiance of translation is, of course, part of the everyday process of translation. Once put into prose, a universal concept carries traces of what Hans-Georg Gadamer would call "prejudice," not a conscious bias but a sign that we think out of particular accretions of histories that are not always transparent to us.[4] To provincialize Europe is, then, to know how universalistic thought is always and already modified by the

---

3 See Jacques Pouchepadass' review of *PE* published under the title "Pluralizing Reason" (2002).
4 The "recognition," writes Gadamer, "that all understanding inevitably involves some prejudice gives the hermeneutic problem its real thrust" (Gadamer 1979: 239). See the discussion in Gadamer between pages 235–258; Gadamer generally sees prejudices as "conditions of understanding" (Gadamer 1979: 239).

accretion of histories in particular places, whether or not we can fully excavate such pasts.

2 *Subaltern Studies*: The Displacement/ Translation of the Revolutionary Subject

Subaltern Studies, the series with which I have been associated since 1982, was an instance of politically motivated historiography. It came out of a Marxist tradition of history-writing in South Asia and was markedly indebted to Mao and Gramsci in the initial formulations that guided the series. The tradition of history-writing on the Left in India is deeply, though perhaps unsurprisingly, influenced by English Marxist or socialist historiography, the so-called "history from below" tradition pioneered by the likes of Edward Thompson, Eric Hobsbawm, Christopher Hill, George Rudé, and others. Just as Thompson's work on English popular history is predicated on the question: What did the lower orders of society contribute to the history of English democracy, so, too, did historians in the *Subaltern Studies*-series begin by asking a similar question: What contributions did the subaltern classes make, on their own, to the politics of nationalism in India and, hence, to Indian democracy as well (cf. Thompson 1975)? But the similarity ends here. English Marxist narratives of popular histories are molded on a developmental idea of time: the peasant, in that story, either became extinct or was superseded by the rise of the worker who, through machine-breaking, Chartism, and other struggles for rights, metamorphosed into the figure of the citizen or the revolutionary proletariat. The peasant or tribals of the third world, who – as if through a process of telescoping centuries – suddenly had the colonial state and its modern bureaucratic and repressive apparatus thrust in his or her face, was, in this mode of thinking, a pre-political person. He or she was someone who does not, as it were, understand the operative languages of modern, governing institutions, while having to deal with them. In terms of the English "history from below" propositions, it was only over time and a process of intellectual development that the subaltern classes could mature into a modern political force.

Subaltern Studies began by repudiating this developmental idea of "becoming political." The peasant or the subaltern, it was claimed, was *political* from the very instant he or she rose up in rebellion against the institutions of the Raj.[5] Their actions were political in the sense that they responded to and impacted the institutional bases of colonial governance: the Raj, the moneylender, and the landlord. We did not then think much about the implications of our claim that the subaltern could be political without undergoing a process of "political development." Yet, the implications of that claim were writ large on our historiography.[6]

I should explain that the legacies of both imperialism and anti-colonialism speak to each other in this implicit debate about whether the subaltern became political over time (through some kind of pedagogic practice) or whether the figure of the subaltern was constitutionally political. Developmental time, or the sense of time underlying a stadial view of history, is indeed a legacy bequeathed by imperial rule in India. This is the time of the "not yet," as I called it in *PE*. European political thinkers, such as Mill (or even Marx), employed this temporal structure in the way that they thought history. Nationalists and anti-colonialists, on the other hand, repudiated this imagination of time in the twentieth century by asking for self-rule to be granted right away, without a period of waiting or preparation, without delay – "now." What replaced the structure of the "not yet" in their imagination was the horizon of the "now."[7]

The British argued against giving self-rule to educated Indians in the nineteenth century by saying that they were not representative of the larger masses of the Indian "people." The answer came from Gandhi who, following his entry into Indian politics during the First World War, turned the main nationalist party, the Indian National Congress, into a mass organization. He did so by enlisting peasants as ordinary, so-called "four-anna" members – an anna being one-sixteenth of a rupee – with voting rights within the party. The "mass base" of the Congress enabled its leaders to claim to be "representative" of the nation, even if the poor and the non-literate did not formally have any electoral power under the Raj. The educational gap that separated the peasant from educated leaders was never considered a problem in this idea of representation. The peasant, it was assumed, was fully capable of making citizenly choices that

---

5 I discuss this in some detail in my essay "A Small History of Subaltern Studies" in *Habitations of Modernity: Essays in the Wake of Subaltern Studies* (2002).

6 This claim has sometimes provided starting points for younger historians of peasant-nationalism India who have developed – historiographically speaking – productive but critical relationship to *Subaltern Studies*. See, for example, Vinayak Chaturvedi's fascinating book, *Peasant Pasts: History and Memory in Western India* (2007).

7 See the discussion in the introduction to my book *Provincializing Europe: Postcolonial Thought and Historical Difference* (2007).

colonial rule withheld from him or her. From the very beginning of the 1920s, Gandhi spoke in favor of universal adult franchise in a future, independent India. The peasant would, thus, be made a citizen overnight (at least with respect to voting), without having to live out the developmental time of formal or informal education – that was the "now" the nationalists demanded. In the constitutional debates that took place in the Constituent Assembly right after independence, the philosopher, and later statesman, Radhakrishnan argued for a republican form of government by claiming that thousands of years of civilization had – even in the absence of formal education – already prepared the peasant for such a state (for details, see the introduction to Chakrabarty 2007).

What underwrote this anti-colonial but populist faith in the modern political capacity of the masses was another European inheritance: romanticism. It is, of course, true that the middle-class leaders of anti-colonial movements involving peasants and workers never quite abandoned the idea of developmental time and a pedagogical project of educating the peasant. Gandhi's writings and those of other nationalist leaders often express a fear of the lawless mob and see education as a solution to the problem.[8] But this fear was qualified by its opposite, a political faith in the masses. In the 1920s and 30s, this romanticism marked Indian nationalism generally – many nationalists who were not Communist or of the Left, for instance, would express this faith. Francesca Orsini, of Cambridge University, who works on Hindi literature, recently excavated a body of evidence documenting this tendency. To take but stray examples from her selection, here is Ganesh Shankar Vidyarthi (1890–1931), the editor of the Hindi paper *Pratap*, editorializing on 31 May 1915:

> The much-despised peasants are our true bread-givers [*annadata*], not those who consider themselves special and look down upon the people who must live in toil and poverty as lowly beings. (Orsini 2003)

Here is Vidyarthi, again, on 11 January 1915:

> Now the time has come for our political ideology and our movement not [to] be restricted to the English-educated and to spread among the common people [*samanya janta*], and for Indian public opinion [*lokmat*] to be not the opinion of those few educated individuals but to mirror the thoughts of all the classes of the country [...] democratic rule is actually the rule of public opinion. (Orsini 2003)[9]

---

8 See Gyanendra Pandey's essay on the topic in *Selected Subaltern Studies* (1988).

9 Unfortunately, I have not been able to chase down a published version of Orsini's essay, but the general point about the emergence of "the peasant as the subject" of Indian nationalism in

One should note that this romantic-political faith in the masses is populist in a classical sense of the term as well. Like Russian populism of the late nineteenth century, this mode of thought not only sought a "good" political quality in the peasant, but also, by that step, worked to convert the so-called "backwardness" of the peasant into a historical advantage. The peasant, "uncorrupted" by the self-tending individualism of the bourgeoisie and oriented to the needs of his or her community, was imagined as already endowed with the capacity to usher in a modernity different and more communitarian than what was prevalent in the West.[10] The contradiction entailed in the very restricted nature of the franchise under colonial rule and the simultaneous induction of the peasant and the urban poor into the nationalist movement had one important consequence. The very restrictions put on constitutional politics meant that the field, the factory, the bazaar, the fair, and the street became major arenas for the struggle for independence and self-rule. And it is in these arenas that subaltern subjects, with their characteristic mode of politics (that included practices of public violence), entered public life.

The inauguration of the age of mass politics in India was, thus, enabled by ideologies that display some of the key global characteristics of populist thought. There was, firstly, the tendency to see a certain political goodness in the peasant or in the masses. And there was, in addition, the tendency also to see historical advantage wherein, by colonial judgment, there was only backwardness and disadvantage. To see advantage in backwardness meant also to challenge the time of stadial history; it was to twist the time of the colonial "not yet" into the structure of the democratic and anti-colonial "now."

I give this potted history of the romantic-populist origins of Indian democratic thought – though not of Indian democracy as such, and the distinction is important – to suggest a point fundamental to my exposition. The insistence, in the early volumes of *Subaltern Studies* (first published in 1982) and in Ranajit Guha's *Elementary Aspects of Peasant Insurgency in Colonial India* (1983), that the peasant or the subaltern was always already political – and not pre-political in any developmental sense – is, in some ways, a recapitulation of a populist premise that was implicit, in any case, in the anti-colonial mass movements in British India (Guha 1983: Ch. 1). But there is, in my sense, a displacement, as well, of this term. The populism in *Subaltern Studies* is more intense and explic-

---

the 1920s and 30s is covered well in her book *The Hindi Public Sphere 1920–1940: Language and Literature in the Age of Nationalism* (2002); see in particular 322–346.

10 For an excellent discussion of this point, see Andrzej Walicki's *The Controversy over Capitalism: Studies in the Social Philosophy of the Russian Populists* (1989), chapters 1 and 2, and in particular the section on "The Privilege of Backwardness."

it. There is, first of all, no "fear of the masses" in *Subaltern Studies* analysis. Absent also – and this goes against the grain of classically Marxist or Leninist analysis – is any discussion of the need for organization or a party. Guha and his colleagues drew inspiration from Mao (particularly his 1927 report on the peasant movement in the Hunan district) and Gramsci (mainly his *Prison Notebooks*). But their use of Mao and Gramsci speaks of the time when *Subaltern Studies* was born. It was, after all, the 1970s: a period of global Maoism that Althusser and others had made respectable. Excerpts from Gramsci's notebooks had come out in English in 1971. Both Gramsci and Mao were celebrated as a way out of Stalinist or Soviet Marxism after Czechoslovakia of 1968. Many of the historians in *Subaltern Studies* were participants in or sympathizers with the Maoist movement that shook parts of India between 1969 and 1971.[11]

Yet, significantly, neither Mao's references to the need for "leadership of the Party" nor Gramsci's strictures against "spontaneity" feature with any degree of prominence in *Elementary Aspects* or *Subaltern Studies*. Guha's focus remains firmly on understanding the nature of the practices that made up peasant revolts in a phase of colonial rule preceding the times when peasants became part of the politics of nationalism led by leaders from the middle classes. Guha wanted to understand the peasant as a collective author of these uprisings by conducting a structuralist analysis of the space- and time-creating practices of mobilization, communication, and public violence that constituted rebellion (and, thus, in Guha's terms, a subaltern domain of politics). There were limitations, from Guha's socialist point of view, as to what the peasants could achieve on their own, but these limitations did not call for the mediation of a party. A cult of rebellion marks the early efforts of *Subaltern Studies*, reminiscent of one of Mao's sayings, popular during the Cultural Revolution: "To rebel is justified." Rebellion was not a technique for achieving something; it was its own end. Indeed, from a global perspective, one might say that *Subaltern Studies* was the last – or the latest – instance of a long global history of the Left: the romantic-popular search for a non-industrial revolutionary subject that was initiated in Russia, among other places, in the nineteenth century. This romantic populism has shaped much of Maoism in the twentieth century and has left its imprint on the antinomies and ambiguities of Antonio Gramsci's thoughts on the Party as the Modern Prince.

---

11 See Shahid Amin's "De-Ghettoising the Histories of the non-West," Gyan Prakash's "The Location of Scholarship" and my "Globalization, Democracy, and the Evacuation of History?" in *At Home in Diaspora: South Asian Scholars and the West* (Eds. Assayag and Bénéï 2003).

The once global and inherently romantic search for a revolutionary subject outside of the industrialized West has, thus, had a long history, travelling from Russia in the late nineteenth century to the colonial and semi-colonial (to use a Maoist expression) "third" world in the twentieth. The political potential of this romanticism is exhausted today. But, looking back, one can see what plagued this history of a search for a revolutionary subject in the relatively non-industrialized countries of the world. Such a subject, by definition, could not be the proletariat. Yet it was difficult to define a world-historical subject that would take the place of the industrial working classes that did not exist, not in great numbers anyway, in the peasant-based economies drawn into the gravitational pull of the capitalist world. Would the revolution, as Trotsky said, be an act of substitution? Would the Party stand in for the working classes? Could the peasantry, under the guidance of the Party, be the revolutionary class? Would it be the category 'subaltern' or Fanon's "the wretched of the earth?"

When the young, left-Hegelian Marx thought up the category of the proletariat as the new revolutionary subject of history that would replace the bourgeoisie – and he did this before Engels wrote his book on the Manchester working class in 1844 – there was a philosophical precision to the category. It also seemed to find a sociological correlate in the working classes born of the industrial revolution. But names like "peasants" (Mao), "subaltern" (Gramsci), "the wretched of the earth" (Fanon) and "the party as the subject" (Lenin/Lukács) have neither philosophical nor sociological precision. It is as if the search for a revolutionary subject that is *not-the-proletariat* (in the absence of a large working class) was itself an exercise in a series of displacements of the original term. A telling case in point is Frantz Fanon himself. The expression "the wretched of the earth," as Fanon's biographer David Macey has pointed out, alludes to the Communist Internationale, the song – "'Debout, les damnés de la terrre'/ Arise, ye wretched of the earth" – where it clearly refers to the proletariat (Macey 2000: 177). Yet Fanon uses it to mean something else. He cannot quite define this other subject, but he is clear that, in the colony, it cannot be the proletariat. One only has to recall how, quite early on in his book, he cautions: "Marxist analysis should always be slightly stretched every time we have to do with the colonial problem" (Fanon 1963: 40).

A collective subject with no proper name, a subject who can be named only through a series of displacements of the original European term 'the proletariat' – this is a condition both of failure and new beginning. The failure is easy to see. It lies in the lack of specificity or definition. Where is the beginning? This very imprecision points to the inadequacy of Eurocentric thought in the context of global striving for a socialist transformation of the world. Outside of the industrialized countries, the revolutionary subject was even theoretically undefined. The history of this imprecision amounts to the acknowledgment that, if we want to understand the nature of popular political practices globally, with names of subjects invented in Europe, we can only resort to a series of stand-ins (never mind the fact that the original may have been a simulacrum as well). Why? Because we are working at and on the limits of European political thought even as we admit an affiliation with nineteenth-century European revolutionary romanticism.

Recognizing the stand-in nature of categories like "the masses," "the subaltern," or "the peasant" is, I suggest, the first step towards writing histories of democracies that have emerged through the mass politics of anticolonial nationalism. There is a mass subject here, no doubt. But it can only be apprehended by consciously working through the limits of European thought. A straightforward search for a revolutionary world-historical subject only leads to stand-ins. The latest in the series, I may add in parenthesis, is Michael Hardt and Antonio Negri's "multitude," a category that, I fear, is, for all the brilliance of their analysis of global capitalism, another stand-in. Yet, in their use of the category "multitude," an insistent question of our times returns: How do we name and write histories of the mass subject of politics today (Hardt and Negri 2000: Part 4)? And it perhaps stands to reason that one encounters this "mass subject" more frequently in the restless politics of developing countries than in the "orderliness" of prosperous and liberal democracies.[12] The global and theoretical failure to find a proper name for the revolutionary-subject-that-is-not-the-proletariat, thus, inaugurates the need for new thought and research outside the West, resulting in a series of displacements of the once-European category, the proletariat.

3 Conclusion

My conclusion, then, is simple: taking the examples of *Provincializing Europe* and *Subaltern Studies*, I have sought to show that these postcolonial projects of political historiography simply would have been impossible without the enactment of a process of translation/displacement of European categories. It is through such a relay network of translation of certain key categories of modernity that we all, whether in or outside of Europe, become the modern subjects of global histories.

---

12 Even the secret, avant-gardist politics of so-called Islamic extremism is often backed by mass mobilization on the streets of Palestine or Pakistan.

References

Amin, Shahid. "De-Ghettoising the Histories of the non-West." *At Home in Diaspora: South Asian Scholars and the West*. Eds. Jackie Assayag and Veronique Bénéï. Bloomington: Indiana University Press, 2003. 91–100.
Banerjee, Sumanta. *India's Simmering Revolution: The Naxalite Uprising*. London: Zed, 1984.
Chakrabarty, Dipesh. *Rethinking Working-Class History: Bengal 1890–1940*. Princeton: Princeton University Press, 2000.
Chakrabarty, Dipesh. "A Small History of Subaltern Studies." *Habitations of Modernity: Essays in the Wake of Subaltern Studies*. Chicago: University of Chicago Press, 2002. 3–19.
Chakrabarty, Dipesh. "Globalization, Democracy, and the Evacuation of History?" *At Home in Diaspora: South Asian Scholars and the West*. Eds. Jackie Assayag and Veronique Bénéï. Bloomington: Indiana University Press, 2003. 127–147.
Chakrabarty, Dipesh. "Subaltern History as Political Thought." 2006.
http://abahlali.org/files/Chakrabarty.pdf (8 October 2013).
Chakrabarty, Dipesh. *Provincializing Europe: Postcolonial Thought and Historical Difference*. Princeton: Princeton University Press, 2007 [2000].
Chaturvedi, Vinayak. *Peasant Pasts: History and Memory in Western India*. Berkeley: University of California Press, 2007.
Fanon, Frantz. *The Wretched of the Earth*. Trans. Constance Farrington. New York: Grove Press, 1963.
Gadamer, Hans-Georg. *Truth and Method*. London: Sheed and Ward, 1979.
Guha, Ranajit. *Elementary Aspects of Peasant Insurgency in Colonial India*. Delhi: Oxford University Press, 1983.
Hardt, Michael, and Antonio Negri. *Empire*. Cambridge, MA: Harvard University Press, 2000.
Macey, David. *Frantz Fanon: A Biography*. New York: Picador, 2000.
Orsini, Francesca. *The Hindi Public Sphere 1920–1940: Language and Literature in the Age of Nationalism*. New Delhi: Oxford University Press, 2002.
Orsini, Francesca. "The Hindi Public Sphere and Political Discourse in the Twentieth Century." Unpublished paper presented at a conference on "The Sites of the Political in South Asia" (Berlin, October 2003).
Pandey, Gyanendra. "Encounters and Calamities: The History of a North Indian *Qasba* in the Nineteenth Century." *Selected Subaltern Studies*. Eds. Ranajit Guha and Gayatri Chakravorty Spivak. New York: Oxford University Press, 1988. 89–128.
Pouchepadass, Jacques. "Pluralizing Reason." *History and Theory* 41.3 (2002): 381–391.
Prakash, Gyan. "The Location of Scholarship." *At Home in Diaspora: South Asian Scholars and the West*. Eds. Jackie Assayag and Veronique Bénéï. Bloomington: Indiana University Press, 2003. 115–126.
Saussure, Ferdinand de. *Course in General Linguistics*. Eds. Charles Bally and Albert Sechehaye. New York: McGraw Hill, 1966.
Thompson, E.P. *Whigs and Hunters: The Origin of the Black Act*. London: Allen Lane, 1975.
"Translation." *Oxford English Dictionary*.
http://www.oed.com/view/Entry/204844?redirectedFrom=translation#eid (25 September 2013).
Walicki, Andrzej. *The Controversy over Capitalism: Studies in the Social Philosophy of the Russian Populists*. Notre Dame: University of Notre Dame Press, 1989.

Jon Solomon
The Transnational Study of Culture and the Indeterminacy of People(s) and Language(s)

A recent collection of essays on transnational literary studies asserts: "the inter-rogation of national narratives characteristic of transnational studies entails the putting forth of a different set of coordinates whereby to understand global configurations" (Frassinelli et al. 2011: 6). Taking our cue from this statement, the "coordinates" that we would like to advance here amount to a single word: *indeterminacy*. To convey what is meant by this word, it might be helpful at the outset to distinguish it from what has been described as "the massive economic and political diaspora of the modern world" (Bhabha 1994: 8); although migra-tion is intrinsically related to the indeterminacy of people(s) and language(s), it is not an exhaustive condition – particularly with regard to language. It is also crucially important to remember that the modern forms of diaspora occur within the context of the dominant form of social homogenization: the nation-state. Our understanding of the nation-state follows the description provided by Bruno Latour when he speaks about the work of the modern, which creates new forms of separation (for our purposes, nation-states) and then conceals those fictive productions behind naturalizing narratives (cf. Latour 1993). The themes of 'hybridity' and 'diaspora' are as much a part of those naturalizing narratives as those of origin and purity. Although transnationalism does indeed ask us to look beyond the separations instituted by the ideology of nationalism, the nar-ratives of 'massive diaspora' and 'overlapping histories' that are used to justify such moves may, in fact, serve to naturalize those separations – not just in the past but, perhaps most importantly, also through the terms of cultural compari-son.

Hence, by remembering the indeterminacy of people(s) and language(s), we are called upon to develop not just a non-national understanding of the present conjuncture but also a non-national, non-normative, and, finally, non-anthro-pological understanding of the past as well as the present and future. What we intend here is a critique not just of national narratives but also of the fundamen-tal assumptions about human collectivity (species-being) and knowledge that have sustained the normativity of the nationalist project in all its forms. It is a critique that must be pursued on several levels at once: with regard to philo-sophical ontology, it is a critique of hylomorphism; epistemologically, it is a complete reorganization of the disciplinary divisions of the humanities; politically, it is a critique of the ways in which anthropological difference is posited and mobilized in the name of population management for the benefit of capital accumulation (i.e., a critique of the state form). The changes, thus, envisioned take us so far away from the national that it would really be better to place them under a non-national, rather than simply trans-national, heading. Otherwise, it is quite likely that our critique would simply serve the interests of the current 'great transformation' from an international system (based on nation-states) of industrial capitalism to an equally constricting transnational system (based on a global state) of cognitive capitalism.

1 The Institutions of Human Speciation

The teleology of post-Enlightenment thought – here it matters little whether we call it humanism or the human sciences – can be understood in its archaeological totality as a massive and highly varied effort to comprehend, in a scientific way, the staggering diversity of anthropological difference. The roots of this project lie in the early modern sciences of biology, philology, and political economy. Its goal is to create an exhaustive taxonomy that would at once be the ultimate compendium of the various types, models, and images of human individuals, communities, and their species, and an explanatory model for their respective internal differences. Needless to say, the discovery of such an 'anthropological matrix' would have profound implications not just for knowledge but also, and especially, for the organization and governance of human individuals and the societies in which they live in real time. Knowledge about anthropological difference can never be, for this reason, 'disinterested'; it is always already implicated in the technologies of population management.

In view of this post-Enlightenment teleology, the modern era is to be distinguished by this one singular trait: the bureaucratically organized, institutional study of geocultural regions. The default question for this singularly modern type of knowledge production is: "What kind of model for human being does one find in culture X?" This mode of questioning is essentially indebted to the discipline of modern philology and the objects it creates. As Michel Foucault observed in *The Order of Things* (2002), the modern understanding of language in a philological mode finds that it is rooted not in things but in the subject that apprehends and does things to objects. Language is, thus, not a manifestation of a representative order that governs the relations between things, but rather of the *will* of a certain people. Yet this will, as Foucault underlines, is not on the order of conscious volition; it is something that, in fact, can only be brought to awareness by the representational practices of a subject.

Under the regime of the philological notion of collective (yet unconscious) volition, representation is incorporated into the model of linguistic communication at the point of pronominal invocation. The assumption that you and I are capable of communicating exactly what we mean in a way that is understandable to us both, without risk of failure or need for repetition, can be accomplished only through a moment of representation that confuses 'we' as a case of the vocative designation with a specific group of people for whom repetition of the original enunciation is thought to be unnecessary. When repetition is required, it is called 'translation;' where failure is present, it is attributed to exteriority. Today, the historicity of these assumptions is becoming ever clearer: in fact, repetition and failure are integral parts of every linguistic encounter. Needless to say, the fact that human beings are disposed to share signs does not guarantee successful communication anymore than sharing itself produces or requires homogeneous community; neither can such sharing be reduced or equated to the notion of an individuated collective intentionality. Yet this is precisely what forms the basic presupposition for the modern thought of community, crystallized in the nation-state.

What had been a philological presupposition has, thus, established what must be considered one of the founding obfuscations of modern thought: the presumed equivalence between a people and a language. Giorgio Agamben writes:

> Romantic ideology – which consciously created this connection, thereby influencing extensively modern linguistic theory as well as the political theory that is still dominant nowadays – tried to clarify something that was already obscure (the concept of people) with the help of something even more obscure (the concept of language). Thanks to the symbiotic correspondence thus instituted, two contingent and indefinite cultural entities transform themselves into almost natural organisms endowed with their own necessary laws and characteristics. (Agamben 2000: 66)

What is the "transformation" described by Agamben that turns the "contingent and indefinite" into "organisms" that are "almost natural" yet governed by "necessary laws" and endowed with "characteristics?" For Foucault, it is not simply the case that objectification can define the 'turn' of the modern. *The specificity of the human lies in the peculiar fact that, unlike any other species, human beings participate in their own speciation through the acts of speaking, working, and reproduction.* Foucault's later work on biopolitics, which he famously describes as the "entry of life into history," suggests that the "transformation" of which Agamben speaks must be sought in the institutional loci that attempt to regulate language, labor, and life through normalization.

The ironic punch-line of Darwin's *Origin of Species* – that there is neither origin nor species[1] – was lost upon the normalizing institutions created, contingently, out of colonial encounter to codify "contingent and indefinite" anthropological difference. Two forms are salient: 1) the disciplinary divisions of the human sciences, which maintain an anthropological distribution of bodies, tongues, and minds inherited from the colonial/imperial modernity; and 2) the organization of human populations according to the spatial and epistemological logic of sovereignty and the exclusion of practico-temporal forms of relationship. In their universality, these are the institutional forms dedicated not to this or that concrete identity or definite knowledge but simply to *the principle of the speciation of the human* – the transposition of the biological notion of species difference into the domain of human social ontology. Let us henceforth refer to them as *the institutions of speciation*.

2 The Plasticity and Indeterminacy Liberation Front (PILF)

Given the historicity of our position, nothing is more important to the study of culture today than to militate for the liberation of people(s) and language(s) from their historical determination under the "Romantic Ideology." It may be necessary to explain that this call for the liberation of human plasticity[2] from the "Romantic Ideology" is not the product of some formalistic exercise undertaken by the philosophical initiate at "DECON Level 1,"[3] but is rather a practical necessity imposed by the amnesia of national history and all the other forms of knowledge produced under the influence of the "Romantic Ideology" identified by Giorgio Agamben. We simply lack the vocabulary to talk about people(s) and language(s) in a way that recognizes their essentially fluid and unbounded

---

1 Darwin rejects specific difference, yet not species, in favor of a genealogical system that has neither top nor bottom, higher nor lower parts (cf. Neyrat 2009–2010). See Parisi 2007 and Parisi and Marek 2006 for an interesting account of changes to the biological concept of species, contra Darwin, in light of research on endosymbiosis.
2 See Malabou 2008 for an excellent introduction to human plasticity.
3 A reference to the 'DEFCON' early warning system of the United States military; 'DECON' in this context refers to the philosophies of difference internationally known under the name of 'deconstruction.'

nature – not to mention the long history of repression of difference, homogenization, and normalization undertaken by the nation-state. We have inherited the historical problem, charted by Naoki Sakai, of treating language(s) and people(s) as if they were countable nouns (cf. Sakai 2009). *The study of culture, as it has been institutionally practiced until now, is complicitous with a racism that is broader, and no less profound for being subtle, than any phenomenon known under that name today.* It might be called an anthropologism, with all the negative connotations of the word 'racism' attached. In the face of such anthropologism, the only form of study that would make any sense would be devoted, in accordance with the indeterminacy of language(s) and people(s) and the plasticity of the human, to subjective formation.

Institutional opposition to the liberation of people(s) and language(s) through deterministic closure and the corollary liberation of human plasticity it implies is so deeply and subtly entrenched, often by default, I am convinced that nothing short of a militant social movement in the order of knowledge can redress the situation. As is the case in every social movement for historical justice, the 'recognition' of plasticity called for above means undertaking a detailed inventory of all the ways in which our *historical repression* of the indeterminacy of people(s) and language(s) is insinuated in all forms of social organization, personal identity, and divisions of knowledge. *The focus of this activity is not to produce knowledge, per se, but rather to transform the social relations that are expressed in and mystified by knowledge.*[4]

Taking a cue from Naoki Sakai, the starting exercise that I have found most helpful lies in redirecting our desire beyond the closure of cultural objects and the institutions of speciation consecrated to their maintenance and legitimation. Nothing bears witness to the importance of this challenge more than the way in which both knowledge and social relations today are funneled through the historically-determined categories and practices associated with the nation-state, such as the national language and the 'area studies' divisions in the humanities. It is precisely in these instances that desire, both the desire-to-know

---

4 My tentative partial list includes: LGBT gender issues (Lesbian, Gay, Bi-, and Trans-), Nationalism, Aboriginal Sovereignty, 'Race,' Plasticity and Neurobiology, Biotech, IT (information technologies), IPR (intellectual property rights), Molecular Biology (particularly research on bacteria and species difference), Genetic Engineering, Migrant Policy, Liberty and Security, the Valorization of Labor, Minority Issues, Western Hegemony and Eurocentrism, Translation Studies and National Language, Colonialism, Imperialism, Hylomorphism and Ontology, Posthumanism, Animal Rights, Human Rights, Feminism, Education, Eugenics, Biopolitics, and Biocultural Diversity.

and the desire-to-act, becomes hopelessly enmeshed, or enamored, with objects whose status is defined *a priori* by means of the "Romantic Ideology."

In order to pierce this closure and redirect desire towards indeterminacy, the student of culture needs to embark on a critical reevaluation of the legacy of modern thought. Although post-Enlightenment modern thought is usually associated with the attempt to dispel prejudice and myth through the public use of reason in order to establish human society on the basis of freedom and equality, it is time to admit that, in its most fundamental form, post-Enlightenment thought is really all about establishing anthropological knowledge on a scientific basis. Posing as the exercise of reason in the pursuit of liberty and equality normally associated with post-Enlightenment, modern thought, in fact, simply assumes such anthropological knowledge as its basis. It (anthropological knowledge) is the ground for 'decisions' to be made about the forms of organization deemed most appropriate to those ends. *Far from dispelling prejudice and 'stereotyping,' post-Enlightenment thought is devoted to securing the conditions of possibility for the institutionalization of anthropological difference.*

In order to understand the implications of this global underpinning, it is necessary to distinguish two distinct ways, or levels, in which the anthropological project of post-Enlightenment modern thought has developed. The first is an epistemological component that uses scientific methods to realize an exhaustive classificatory system for all biological life forms. Needless to say, the classification of all life includes the agents of classification themselves – human beings. Inevitably, the project of biological classification, inasmuch as it is undertaken by a species whose activities, particularly with regard to knowledge, are themselves directly involved in speciation, is automatically doubled by a project of anthropological classification. Applied to the human species by the human species, the quest for exhaustive classificatory knowledge, thus, includes an anthropological component that encompasses all the known and perhaps possible forms of human social organization – past, present, and future.

It is precisely at this point that the epistemological project of the classification of anthropological difference diverges into a political project of population management. The methods deemed 'most appropriate' for the realization of equality and freedom must take the specificities of anthropological difference in all of its many forms into account. This very same difference can also serve as a justification, or source of legitimacy, for actually existing social differences, such as gender, race, and class, that seemingly contradict the enlightenment principles upheld by all modern constitutions. Anibal Quijano's much-discussed elaboration of the "coloniality of power" (Quijano 2000) constitutes a very interesting example of the attempt to re-narrate modern history – i.e., the history of the single world born out of the colonial encounter – by showing how capitalism, with its uneven development and violent transitions, was elaborated on the basis of a grand project of anthropological classification.

The crux point at which the epistemological project fuses together with the anthropological project lies in the modern concept of sovereignty. Although it undoubtedly offers (some) protection against the worst depredations of capitalist deterritorialization and expropriation, the national sovereignty is precisely the form of socio-political organization in which the historical alliance between capitalism and anthropological difference described so powerfully by Quijano is ultimately crystallized – and normalized, to boot. I do not think the critique of the nation-state today has much, if anything, to do with political anarchism. Rather, *it is because, on the one hand, that nationalism is not dissociable from racism* (cf. Balibar 2004), *and, on the other hand, that the nation-state is the form of political organization that has evolved, through a contingent series of encounters, to become the most favorable to capitalist accumulation, that we must reject the normativity of sovereignty today and undertake a thorough review of all the social practices of the nation-state – including, especially, the production of knowledge in nationalized tongues – in order to (re)discover and correct their complicity with the history of racism in its most general form, the project of anthropological classification.* We need, in other words, social practices of knowledge that are a critique of the institutions of speciation.

3 Translation

The responsibility often falls, in the study of culture, to the linguistic realm to provide a bridgehead in the campaign for peaceful understanding. The name of this hopeful bridge is, typically, 'translation.' Presupposing equivalency, translation seems to promise, beyond equivalency, symmetry and its near relative, equality. Yet when we consider, as Sandro Mezzadra does, the association between equivalency and exchange in light of capitalism's historical development, we discover that 'translation' has also become the name for a great number of institutionalized asymmetries hiding behind a façade of symmetry (cf. Mezzadra 2007).

These asymmetries cannot be limited to the gross imbalance of translational flows (cf. Cronin 2003) but must also include the creation of mutually codependent forms of identity on both sides of the divide, according to what Naoki Sakai has termed "the schema of co-figuration" (Sakai 1997: 59). In the translational exchange between two officially recognized state languages on either side of the colonial/imperial divide, many will forget the asymmetries that went into producing the assumed unity of each language: the historical and/or contemporary repression of 'dialects' and 'minority' languages and the roles played by hybrid, 'exceptional' forms of address such as translation and infant aphasia. The intervention of the state into the linguistic realm of everyday life and the reorganization of linguistic being according to the principles of normalized state language serving a homogeneous sphere of exchange have had an enormous effect upon the speciation of the human. Within what I have previously characterized as the post-catastrophic terrain of the global system of nation-states (cf. Solomon 2008), linguistic asymmetries flourish behind the façade of imposed homogenization and nominal equivalency.

One form of contemporary asymmetry particularly germane to the theme of this volume can be seen in the distribution of tongues and bodies within postimperial universities. In spite of the current restructuring of national institutions of culture and technology into globalized centers of 'innovation,' virtually the only part of the research corps with professional access to authoritative knowledge in so-called 'local' languages on the other side of the colonial/imperial divide are those 'ethnic scholars' and 'elite specialists' working in domains of research and teaching that, in North America, are called 'area studies.' We are talking here only about the relatively passive form of access that does not involve active production, much less subjection to the disciplinary and market constraints under which intellectuals in the postcolonial state operate. Above and beyond their role in the production of knowledge, the 'area studies' in postimperial institutions are a technology for managing the distribution of bodies, tongues, and minds in such a way that the asymmetries of the colonial/imperial divide appear to correspond to a more or less normalized distribution of knowledge and experience that can be safely called 'cultural difference.' Naoki Sakai, in an essay that I would consider to be required reading for all those involved in the transnational study of culture, entitled "The Problem of Japanese Thought," has charted out this relationship and the role played by translation (cf. Sakai 1997). *That which distinguishes Sakai's approach from others is an admirably consistent and thorough adherence to the indeterminacy of language(s) and people(s) without hiding behind the complicity that exists between universalism and particularism.*

In this essay essentially devoted to mapping the imaginary symmetries generated by the institutions of speciation, Sakai describes how the modern regime of translation not only enables the representational schema essential to the imaginary of national language but also is vital to the institutionalization of both a disciplinary division in the heart of the human sciences and a practical division in the social relations that emerge across the colonial/imperial divide. What results from this series of mutually-related institutional instances are complicitous forms of identity – typically related to the homogeneous form of sociality favored by the nation-state – on both sides of the colonial/imperial divide.

In the introduction to *Translation and Subjectivity*, the collection in which "The Problem of Japanese Thought" was finalized (after having been published previously in English in the *Tamkang Review* and in Japanese in *Shisô*) and re-published, Sakai deftly shows how an analysis of the position of the translator offers a path for understanding the cultural encounter in a different way. Classic modern theories of translation see the translator as a member of one community who helps mediate communicational exchange with members of another community. Sakai shows how this understanding of the position of the translator is indebted to a representational schema, the "schema of configuration," that can only be established *ex post facto* and, thus, betrays the actual practice of translational encounter:

> Through the labor of the translator, the incommensurability as difference that calls for the service of the translator in the first place is negotiated and worked on. In other words, the work of translation is a practice by which the initial discontinuity between the addresser and the addressee is made continuous and recognizable. In this respect, translation is just like other social practices that render the points of discontinuity in social formation continuous. Only retrospectively and after translation, therefore, can we recognize the initial incommensurability as a gap, crevice, or border between fully constituted entities, spheres, or domains. But, when represented as a gap, crevice or border, it is no longer incommensurate. As I discuss in chapter 4, incommensurability or difference is more like "feeling" that is prior to the explanation of how incommensurability is given rise to and cannot be determined as a represented difference (or species difference in the arborescent schemata of the species and the genus) between two subjects or entities. What makes it possible to represent the initial difference as an already determined difference between one language unity and another is the work of translation itself. (Sakai 1997: 14)

In Sakai's account, the translator occupies a crucial pivot point. According to different regimes of address, which Sakai names *homolingual* and *heterolingual*, the translator can be assumed to occupy either an exceptional position or a hybrid and indeterminate one. The homolingual regime is not homolingual on account of the absence of other languages; on the contrary, it relies on plurality that has been organized in symmetrical fashion. It is considered homolingual simply on the basis of the founding exceptions that enable its fictive representation of the symmetrical relation between linguistic unities. Seen from the homolingual regime, the translator is the figure who mediates not just between addresser and addressee but also between two different linguistic communities. Yet he is excepted from the instances of pronominal invocation seen in the translational exchange; the constitution of the personal relations between addresser and addressee; and the linguistic hybridity seen in his own position. The operation of exception is accompanied by a representational schema based on anaphora: the confusion between the translator and the addresser, on the one hand, and the confusion between the languages of translation and the formation of a collective 'we' on the other. When seen from the point of view of heterolingual address, however, the translator reveals an essential indeterminacy, without exception, in the constitution of subjectivity, both at an individual and at a collective level. *The position of the translator, thus, re-presents for Sakai the concrete, practical social relation in which the indeterminacy of social relations is unfailingly present.*

Significantly, the critique of exceptionality at the heart of the homolingual address parallels the critique of exceptionality in the logic of sovereignty discussed by Giorgio Agamben (1998). It is precisely at this point that the disparate institutions of speciation converge. Both the principle of sovereignty that organizes population according to geocultural space and the notion of cultural unity that organizes the disciplines of the human sciences share a similar logic of exceptionalism that sustains the appropriation of cultural forms by specific difference. If the human species is, as Foucault says, distinguished from other species by practices of language, labor, and life that actively participate in the speciation of the human,[5] it is clear that the current historically determined conditions under which we live rely upon a discipline of language as the crucial point of articulation. *For this reason, even those intellectuals whose work is devoted exclusively to 'their own' culture or civilization are inescapably implicated.*

What Sakai is telling us is that the apparent symmetry ostensibly seen in the schema of cofiguration is, essentially, an optical illusion of representation masking the deeper asymmetries that masquerade under the normalized oppositions of cultural difference. Hence, Sakai reserves the term "cultural difference" to describe the encounter of alterity and indeterminacy in the social situation in general; what is usually called cultural difference today ought instead to be termed, asserts Sakai, "specific difference." The asymmetries lurking behind the symmetry of normalized "specific difference" are seen most clearly in the exclusions and exceptions that delineate each of the respective positions and authorize their formal equivalence. The "extremely ambiguous and unstable position the translator has to occupy" (Sakai 1997: 11) presents symmetry of a

---

5 The convergence of biotechnology, information technology, and nanotechnology is simply the most visible, recent development in a process whose archaeology traces the foundation of the modern era.

different order: it is open in the same fashion from any point of entry and does not admit any exceptions.

4 Transformations

Because the hybridity of the translator is inherent to the formation of subjectivity, one can no more pretend that it is a utopian possibility than imagine that it is a fictional chimera. Herein lies a genuine opportunity for us to transform the terms in which social practices such as the study of culture are represented. The first step in such a transformation lies for Sakai in what may be termed an ethical gesture. In place of inevitably comparative frameworks that boil down to "what kind of model for human being does one find in culture X?" – i.e., in place of frameworks that actively participate in the speciation of the human, the new transnational study of culture implicitly envisaged by Sakai proposes to ask questions about the historical, ontological, and political mechanisms that produce this kind of speciation in the first place. The question to be asked now becomes not "what kind of model?" but how can *our* engagement with the social practice of knowledge reveal how 'models' are the product of the contingent meeting between modes of production and modes of subjection? In relation to the formation of Japanese thought, Sakai urges:

> we must develop the problem of Japanese thought from perspectives that are not entirely in accord with the desire conjured up by the question "What is Japanese thought?"; instead of submitting ourselves to that desire to want to know "what Japanese thought is," we must rather analyze the apparatus whereby the desire itself is reproduced, by always shifting our focus away from it. (Sakai 1997: 42)

In response to the question, "What Is Japanese Thought?", Sakai shows: 1) the production of an identity between text and geocultural region is historically inseparable from the homogenizing role of the modern state (hence opening the way for analyses that chart the position of the state between modes of production and modes of subjection); 2) while the identity itself can never be established in a foundational mode – i.e., it is always open to contestation and negation – what *can* be instituted is the production of desire for an identity; 3) the politically-engaged researcher (i.e., the one who is concerned with relations of both exploitation and domination) must commit to a process of subjective transformation.

The questions that we need to ask, in other words, are questions resolutely focused on the production of subjectivity, rather than the supposed anteriority of cultural objects. To bring this insight into the context of a transnational study of culture, we need to undertake a complete overhaul and redefinition of the terms of 'comparison' so that they are no longer focused on the relation between supposedly independent and autonomous objects that represent unities and pluralities in the speciation of the human. Instead, the focus needs to be moved to the relations that comprise the constitution of singular subjects – indifferent to speciation, but not to each other – and the play of difference between and within each. The 'X'-factor in the study of culture, thus, moves from the 'model-of-Culture X' to the indeterminacy of human plasticity summed up in the equation, 'the Human=X.'[6]

Yet the question remains, at a pedagogical level: how can the desire of the student pursuing the study of culture be transformed? Can the teacher foster this transformation? Are the institutions of higher education currently designed to aid or prevent it? Sakai does not really answer these questions, except to say that 'desire' must be replaced by 'analysis' of the 'apparatus by which desire itself is reproduced.' Yet how might this turning away from desire, which is really the construction of a new desire ("to analyze"), be accomplished?

My answer to this constellation of questions currently revolves around displacing the foundational opposition between experience and knowledge. The reasons why this deconstruction started to appear necessary lie in my encounter, across the colonial/imperial divides in North America, Western Europe, and East Asia, with a link between the apparatus of anthropological difference and the differential attribution of experience/knowledge. Simple examples would include: the assumption that my 'identity' as a 'Westerner' or as an 'American' means that my relation to the entirety of 'Western thought' is of a different order,[7] more 'organic,' than, say, that of 'Taiwanese,' in spite of the fact that many peoples 'outside' of the 'West,' such as 'Taiwanese,' have been reading such texts for centuries (not to mention that the definition of the West is impossibly problematic and inextricably linked to exploitation and domination, capitalism and colonialism); or the assumption that I could never truly understand 'Taiwanese' suffering (from colonial trauma) and the longing for national recognition, even though I have spent more time living in Taiwan than in any other

---

6 This formula, in modified form ("the stranger = X"), is at the basis of François Laruelle's "non-philosophy" (see Laruelle 1998).

7 James Baldwin's "Stranger in the Village" sums up this assumption: "The most illiterate among them is related, in a way that I am not, to Dante, Shakespeare, Michelangelo, Aeschylus, Da Vinci, Rembrandt, and Racine; the cathedral at Chartres says something to them which it cannot say to me, as indeed would New York's Empire State Building, should anyone here ever see it" (Baldwin 1955: 166).

country in the world. The observation of such absurdities led me to start asking questions about the relation between experience and knowledge. Without retracing this path fully, let me summarize a conclusion: modern political subjects, formed in relation to the nation-state, are possessed by a *deficit of experience* that is constitutive.

It is often assumed that 'shared experience' is the basis of the national community. Yet the sharing of our experience would be unverifiable unless it were to first pass through the mediation of address. Sakai's work on translation destroys the pretended basis of *this* sharing, revealing it to be the charlatan product of a historically dominant regime of representation. In return, Sakai's approach gives us, in the heterolingual address, a sharing that is virtually unlimited. Otherwise, we are left, finally, with the numerous historical examples of nationals, both native and naturalized, suddenly expelled from the national community, no matter what their 'level of experience.' In fact, no amount of experience will ever be enough to guarantee beyond all possibility of repeal the citizen's membership in a national community nor the individual's belonging to social categories such as a people or a race (not to mention gender). The essential racism of nationalism, from which ostensibly pluralist, imperial nationalisms such as the United States of America cannot be excluded, lies in the exclusion not of this or that particular group (which is also surely a manifestation of racism) but in the possibility that anybody could be excluded by the state at any time under the right political conditions just for falling into a certain, provisionally defined social category.

5 Are you Experienced?

It is no surprise that Foucault's efforts to create the innovative 'archaeological method' in the human sciences by abandoning the concepts of origin and influence (and, hence, continuity) dominant in the historical study of culture had to be linked to a critique not just of experience (Foucault was focused particularly on rejecting the phenomenological understanding of the term), but also of the relation between experience and knowledge in the production of the individual. Foucault's work from the archaeological period was devoted to showing how the dialectical relation between experience and knowledge is consummated by the figure of Man – precisely the point where this dialectic achieves its greatest synthetic height and its fatal instability (cf. Solomon 2010). This dialectic radicalizes the trajectory of anthropological knowledge between epistemology and governance that we have been charting. Foucault is probably the one thinker

82 — Jon Solomon

who has gone the furthest in charting out the genesis of this split, which he attributes to the emergence of a new anthropological figure conscious of itself as a talking, laboring, and reproductive *species*. In *The Order of Things*, Foucault unearths and makes visible the epistemological and ontological assumptions behind the speciation of the human at the precise historical moment when 'the human' becomes both a species in biological taxonomy and an agent of speciation through the technological application of scientific knowledge. At the crux of these assumptions lies a split between the transcendental and the empirical, each of which is internally cut, divided, and finally mapped onto the difference between experience and knowledge. The human sciences in their modern declension impose upon us a quest to find ever-more effective methodologies that would explain and reduce the gap between the two – this is what is called 'rationality.' 'Man' is, for Foucault, precisely the 'effect' or 'result' of the ratio or oscillation between the empirical and the transcendental set in motion by this species that effects its own 'internal speciation' through the rationalities of talking, working, and reproducing. Precisely because the methodologies of the human sciences in all their various forms are themselves part of the subjective technologies that produce the anthropological figure of Man in the first place, they can, according to Foucault, never actually resolve the fundamental problem, only exacerbate it.

This problem or fissure at the heart of the human sciences produces considerable difficulty for our goal of expanding relationships beyond speciation in the temporality of transnational cultural study. What is particularly interesting is the way in which 'area studies'[8] implements the project of the human sciences as described by Foucault in an especially acute fashion. While the human sciences in general establish the figure of Man as a species that creates its own speciation through language, labor, and life, area studies, by exploring the epistemological representation of so-called 'actual experience' of human communities distinguished according to the discipline of specific difference, is

---

8 'Area studies' has long been a concern of ours, and a point for generalization. The rationale for this generalization comes out of the critique itself, which recognizes that 'area studies' would be impossible without the 'support' of other humanistic fields that institutionalize their mode of self-referentiality either through the universal or through the favorite straw-person of philosophical thought in an anthropological mode, 'self' and 'other.' Gavin Walker has an excellent description of this operation: "[A]rea studies operates in a logical circuit which always refers back to itself, short-circuiting the dilemma of the articulation between the nation-form and state-form with the rhetoric of the given and identitary. As is well-known and obvious, this explains nothing whatsoever, yet it remains today the decisive popular mode of 'explanation' for the alterity of the other" (Walker 2014: forthcoming).

where the human sciences reach their apogee. It is, in other words, the place where the oscillation between knowledge and experience overtly resolves into the institutions of speciation.

What I would like to draw attention to are the disciplinary-institutional aspects of the speciation of the human – bodies and tongues, rather than minds. Compared to the overtly programmatic nature of previous forms of knowledge in the mode of speciation (such as eugenics, climate studies, social pathology, national character studies, etc.) that enjoyed enormous mainstream legitimacy prior to World War Two but were ostensibly discredited by the revelation of Nazi horror, the disciplinary-institutional forms of speciation lodged in linguistically communicable experience have enjoyed much greater durability and acceptance. The notion of "non-representational geography" espoused recently by contemporary geographers such as Nigel Thrift can be seen as a critical response to the inadequacy of the cultural geography premised upon the "Romantic Ideology" (cf. Thrift 2008). Similarly, Naoki Sakai's critique of area studies' role in the maintenance of the division of labor that maintains the equivalency between thought and region expressed by the term 'Western theory' (cf. Sakai 2010) calls our attention to the way in which knowledge is continually mapped onto geography in a move that substantiates the epistemological and political legacy of post-Enlightenment thought's anthropological project.

6 Exodus or Reform?

For Ivan Illich, whose critique of the modern school as an elementary apparatus of capitalist domination has won wide critical attention since the 1970s, the educational institutions of the capitalist nation-state seem to offer no possibility for positive transformation. Hence, he favors exodus. The fundamental reason for this impossibility ultimately lies in the way in which experience has been banished from the university: "The modern university has forfeited its chance to provide a simple setting for encounters which are both autonomous and anarchic, focused yet unplanned and ebullient, and has chosen instead to manage the process by which so-called research and instruction are produced" (Illich 1971: 18). Writing in the 1970s, Illich could have barely imagined the forms of audit bureaucracy introduced into Anglophone universities – starting in the 1980s – that have rapidly established the rules of the globalized market in higher education under the WTO (cf. Ross 2009). Within this emerging global system, the aleatory possibilities for "unmeasured experience" (Illich 1971: 20) seem even more remote today than they did in Illich's time.

In their writings on the transformation of society since the advent of the postfordist economy of 'cognitive capitalism,' the Italian and French writers of the 'autonomist' school have highlighted the way in which Illich's "unmeasured experience" has become an essential component of the 'immaterial labor' that characterizes the current era. By a blurring of the distinctions between labor time and leisure time, consumption and production, contemporary capitalism has successfully incorporated many forms of experience that were formerly outside the realm of production. Indeed, experience is now a central component of the creative industries and the knowledge economy. Illich's appeal to "unmeasured experience" thus becomes yet another instance of the way in which many of his positions, such as the call for a withdrawal of the state from education, have, like so many other 'conclusions' coming out of the radicalism of the 1960s, been essentially co-opted by contemporary neo-liberalism (cf. Holmes 2002). In view of Foucault's work on the human sciences, we can safely conclude that any attempt to pit experience against knowledge is destined to expose itself to such recuperation.

Nevertheless, this does not mean that we can abandon the category of experience, or knowledge, altogether. Sakai's call for an ethics of turning away from desire to an analysis of the mechanisms by which desire is produced suggest the continuing importance of bringing experience and knowledge together, albeit in new ways. One of these ways might concern the subjectivity of the researcher, for example. Just as the relationship between a textual archive and a contemporary national formation can never be captured through the tropes of closure, organic relation, continuity, and possession, the relationship between the researcher and her object of study (culture X) can never be exhaustively described through the protocols of membership. In the engagement with the cultural text, one never stands in a relation of either/or exteriority/interiority.

A transformation of the magnitude proposed here will have to be accompanied by a radically different ontology from that upon which the modern human sciences have been constructed. It is in this sense that I understand Frédéric Neyrat's critique of "the ontological indemnity of capitalism" to reach one of its most poignant forms (Neyrat 2004: 147). Only further investigation will reveal the extent to which capitalism, as a form of ontological indemnity, has promoted the institutions of human speciation precisely because of the way they invoke a deficit of experience at the heart of national political subjects. Certainly, when Étienne Balibar talks about the "deficit of democracy" (cf. Balibar 2004) bedeviling the European Union, we can understand that democracy is neither an accumulated historical experience nor a gold-standard identity or property associated with a specific geocultural region or population, but is rather the ground upon which we, 'Europeans' or not, must continually renew our credit.

This cannot be accomplished by borrowing against the future, nor by leveraging the past, but must always return to the widest possible spread on our shared condition: the plastic indeterminacy of language(s) and people(s).

7 Convivial Institutions

It would be inappropriate in an essay devoted to institutions – such as national language, national history, area studies, and the state – to conclude by displacing the problem to ontology. Especially given the current situation, in which the only visible plan for institutional reform is restructuring along a corporate model, the importance of alternative proposals for deep institutional reform, rather than rearguard defensive actions of historically determined and compromised forms, cannot be overemphasized. One can discern two movements or tendencies in the current conjuncture that appear to be diametrically opposed, but which may, in fact, be the harbingers of transformational paths to come. The first is an institutional moment in which the burgeoning insecurities caused by the drastic reduction in funding for the humanities, including the outright elimination of many programs, are forcing intellectual laborers to pose questions about the constitution of the human sciences themselves. This may be a chance for those who are not yet addicted to the hollow pleasures of scapegoating and nostalgia to ask if the unprecedented debacle of the humanities is not, in some way, related to their own historicity? The second is an anti-institutional moment in which more and more people, forced by the precariousness of employment in the university, will look to build alternatives outside. Inevitably, part of the division between these two tendencies will work itself out through the different logics of institutions versus networks.

Within an institutional context, linguistic training could continue to play an irreplaceable role, now mobilized in support of the transition to a rebirth of the humanities, outside of the "Romantic Ideology," on the basis of the indeterminacy of people(s) and language(s). To give but one example pertinent to the institutions of speciation in the postimperial context, the incorporation of the learning of non-Western languages into programs of study that apparently have no connection to non-Western subjects could, by attacking one of the gross asymmetries in the institutional assemblage of bodies, tongues, and minds, provide institutional conditions for ending the dominant mode of speciation. To become accredited in Western philosophy, for example, it would be necessary to demonstrate professional linguistic competence (including active production skills) with regard to the body of related writing in at least one non-Western language. To be effective, the same logic would have to be applied in the reverse direction. Similarly, specialization in the concrete conditions of life in a particular geocultural area (Husserl's infamous "empirical anthropological types" for whom the "[Western] theoretical attitude" was foreclosed)[9] would have to be accompanied by the conceptual defamiliarization that only 'theory' or 'philosophy' could provide. Of course, such measures in and of themselves are not sufficient to change the institutional format. The point is to begin to attack deep-rooted asymmetries in the global assemblage that links tongues to bodies and minds as a first step, to produce entirely new assemblages and social relations that are not mystified by the mode of speciation.

The goal of such reforms would be, in a word, to create something like what Illich has termed "'convivial' institutions" (Illich 1971: 27). Illich's definition of conviviality in *Deschooling Society* in terms of aleatory, "spontaneous" encounter lacks precision and could be misleading, unless we take care to define it in terms, as I have suggested elsewhere, of the "non-relation" between experience and knowledge that exists prior to the establishment of their symmetrical opposition (cf. Solomon 2010). In *Tools for Conviviality* (1973), Illich considerably refines the definition of the concept, dialing it in on interdependent autonomy, rather than experience. Its affective disposition is described by austerity and playfulness. Its cognitive dimension is found in the distinction between machines and tools. This distinction is not a question of 'technological level' but of social relations. Machines favor centralization and domination; tools favor autonomy and equality. Significantly, Illich considers language, particularly the 'mother tongue,' to be a model for the essentially convivial tool, yet like the majority of socially engaged thinkers in the twentieth century, the framework in which he understands language and culture is formatted by the normativity of the nation-state. This leads Illich to view the "pernicious spread of one nation beyond its boundaries" (1973: 19) as a threat to conviviality, rather than the institution of the national frontier, or that of national language after its appropriation by the modern state. To be useful for guiding a transition out of the modes of speciation, it would be necessary to reconfigure Illich's idea of conviviality on the basis of an alternate ontology: Conviviality cannot be reduced to the relation between two or more unities' thought on the basis of individualism

---

9 "For Husserl's discussions about anthropological types, see *The Crisis of European Sciences and Transcendental Phenomenology*, pp. 11-18; and 'The Vienna Lecture', pp. 269-285. It is, however, crucial to acknowledge that Husserl's status as a Moravian Jew living and working within a Europe-wide climate of intensifying Fascism shaped the exposition of his ideas on race in sensitive ways. For an extensive treatment of this point, see my forthcoming *Dislocation of the West*" (cited in Sakai 2010: 463).

but rather results from, or accompanies, assemblages of bodies, tongues, and minds that are not aligned with specific difference. To pursue Illich's engagement with language, we would rather say that conviviality is to be found in translation and not in mother tongue – provided, of course, that we understand translation as a condition of linguistic exchange in general.

We want to fashion social subjects whose desire cannot be captured by the closure of cultural objects and cultural knowledge. It is high time to start making ourselves into subjects that do not fit well into curiosity cabinets, museum cases, and citation indexes run by real-time financial publishing conglomerates that form cultural capital and job security for the university-based critic. This does not mean an abandonment of knowledge, which in any case would be impossible for the instinct-deprived, neotenous species of *homo sapiens*. It means, rather, putting social relations before and after knowledge: 'before' in the sense that we understand the production of knowledge in which we are engaged as a social practice that cannot be contained in the epistemological models of representation and observation; 'after' in the sense that knowledge is never an end in itself. The challenge for the transnational study of culture as it moves forward is to remain resolutely focused on the problem of subjective formation. In simpler terms, this means problematizing the role of the intellectual and envisaging a new sociality for knowledge.

Giorgio Agamben, with whom we started, deserves credit for being one of the few philosophers to have followed, albeit for only a very brief moment, the implications of the indeterminacy of language(s) and people(s). However, in a final analysis, his work, as a form of investment in speciation through civilizational transfer, is symptomatic of *the globalization of class* in which intellectual labor is caught today (cf. Solomon "Invoking" 2013). Yet it is not enough to talk about the way in which structural relations of class have infiltrated systemic relations of international order and, then, conduct a critique of knowledge on that basis. That is why Agamben's comments about the "Romantic Ideology," recalling the historical repression of the essential indeterminacy of people(s) and language(s), remain important today. Although nowadays we can find some very interesting articulations of the anti-capitalist struggle to the anti-colonial struggle, these critical articulations come at the unacceptable price of a complete resubstantialization of the civilizational identities to which intellectuals subjectively suture themselves (much to the relief, one may suppose, of Eurocentric intellectuals like Giorgio Agamben who suture themselves to the position of the West). Although many theorists realize that capitalism used colonialism – an exhaustive project of both anthropological taxonomy and population management – as a means of total mobilization around the needs of capitalist accumulation, they are not ready to concede just how much the production of knowledge, expression, and identities, as well as surplus value, has also been indebted to or invested in that project. Many critics still hold on, in other words, to the fantasy of the "Romantic Ideology" *par excellence*, i.e., they still cling to the project of charting out origins and influences (and this is ultimately what the trope of 'entanglement' – as in 'entangled histories' – still cannot get away from), thereby mistakenly substituting determinate identities for language(s) and people(s). More than four decades ago, Foucault initiated a fundamental challenge to the "Romantic Ideology" of national humanism when, in his archaeological phase, he urged us to abandon the 'radiation model' of cultural study that charts out relations through the tropes of origin and influence altogether (cf. Foucault 2002). It is high time that we finally follow through.

The woeful truth is that, today, there are not yet any intellectuals, either postcolonial or postimperial, who can both practice the indeterminacy of people(s) and language(s) and think over the critique of capitalism at the same time. Perhaps the reasons for this impasse lie not just in the institutions of speciation inherited from the colonial/imperial modernity but also in the peculiar way in which knowledge has come to occupy a special position in the mode of production now known as 'cognitive capitalism' (cf. Moulier Boutang 2011). A direct result of this epochal transition is that academic labor is now constitutively part of the phenomenon that we have dubbed the globalization of class precisely at the historical moment when the historically determined assumptions of imperial/colonial modernity have become, for a brief moment, visible to critique. The reasons for this visibility lie in the metamorphosis being undergone by the state form, which is gradually moving from national formations to civilizational and global ones, as well as virtual forms. From nation-states to civilization-states to global-states, what remains the same is that 'stateness,' as a form of social organization suited to capitalist accumulation, is always inescapably an anthropological project of 'man knowing/creating/shaping/controlling man.'

Now, the contemporary globalization of class tears through the realm of knowledge production like a tsunami overwhelming a seaside nuclear powerplant. *Erudition*, directly subsumed, via the evaluation bureaucracy, into the economy, is the trap of subjective capture into which intellectuals irresistibly fall, simply following the flow. Those aspiring to enter or having recently entered the market for academic labor are particularly vulnerable, forced to oscillate between precarity and overproduction. Erudition is not only time-consuming in the traditional sense (i.e., it produces value under conditions of industrial capitalism by the measure of labor time), but it is also time-'consuming' (i.e., experience and life become fully commodified under conditions of cognitive capitalism). As a result, the division between experience and knowledge is further reinforced, while the categories themselves become reified.

A transnational study of culture resolutely devoted to subjective transformation rather than capitalistic accumulation will, thus, have to fight not only against the process of determination (through a refusal of the "Romantic Ideology") but also against the process of valorization (through a refusal of 'erudition') and the 'accumulation of difference and the logic of area' (through a reinvention of assemblages combining bodies, tongues, and minds). The subjective change envisaged here goes, finally, well beyond the limits of the stoutly meta-level at which this essay takes the liberty of operating. It means to reorganize the division of labor, the division of knowledge (within the humanistic disciplines, to begin with), and ourselves at the same time. The transnational study of culture, situated between an ending and a beginning, an inner and an outer practice, can make a positive contribution, guiding the changes ahead towards goals that will be well-received not by the images and figures of 'who-we-were' or 'are-supposed-to-be,' but by the gratitude and acceptance of 'those-to-come.'

References

Agamben, Giorgio. *Homo Sacer: Sovereign Power and Bare Life*. Trans. Daniel Heller-Roazen. Stanford: Stanford University Press, 1998 [1995].

Agamben, Giorgio. *Means without End: Notes on Politics*. Trans. Vincenzo Binetti and Cesare Casarino. Minneapolis: University of Minnesota Press, 2000 [1996].

Anghie, Antony. *Imperialism, Sovereignty and the Making of International Law*. Cambridge: Cambridge University Press, 2007.

Baldwin, James. *Notes of a Native Son*. Boston: Beacon Press, 1955.

Balibar, Étienne. "Sur la 'constitution' de l'Europe: Crise et virtualités." *Le passant ordinaire* 49 (juin 2004 – septembre 2004). http://www.passant-ordinaire.com/revue/49-635.asp (20 September 2013).

Bhabha, Homi K. *The Location of Culture*. New York/London: Routledge, 1994.

Cronin, Michael. *Translation and Globalization*. London/New York: Routledge, 2003.

Foucault, Michel. *The Order of Things: An Archaeology of the Human Sciences*. London/New York: Routledge, 2002 [1966].

Frassinelli, Pier Paolo, Ronit Frenkel, and David Watson. *Traversing Transnationalism: The Horizons of Literary and Cultural Studies*. Amsterdam/New York: Rodopi, 2011.

Holmes, Brian. "The Flexible Personality: For a New Cultural Critique." *Transversal* (2002). http://eipcp.net/transversal/1106/holmes/en (23 September 2013).

Illich, Ivan. *Deschooling Society*. http://www.davidtinapple.com/illich/1970_deschooling.html. New York: Harper & Row, 1971 (20 September 2013).

Illich, Ivan. *Tools for Conviviality.*
http://www.mom.arq.ufmg.br/mom/arq_interface/3a_aula/illich_tools_for_conviviality.
pdf. London/New York: Marion Boyars, 1973 (20 September 2013).

Laruelle, François. *Théorie des étrangers. Science des hommes, démocratie, non-psycho-analyse.* Paris: Kimé, 1998.

Latour, Bruno. *We Have Never Been Modern.* Trans. Catherine Porter. Cambridge, MA: Harvard University Press, 1993.

Malabou, Catherine. *What Should We Do with Our Brain?* Trans. Sebastian Rand. New York: Fordham University Press, 2008.

Mezzadra, Sandro. "Living in Transition: Toward a Heterolingual Theory of the Multitude." *Transversal* (2007). http://eipcp.net/transversal/1107/mezzadra/en (20 September 2013).

Moulier Boutang, Yann. *Cognitive Capitalism.* Cambridge/Malden, MA: Polity, 2011.

Neyrat, Frédéric. *Surexposés. Le monde, le capital, la terre.* Paris: Léo Scheer, 2004.

Neyrat, Frédéric. "Ce qui arrive aux images (aux passages des frontières)." *REVUE Asylon(s)* 7 (2009–2010), Que veut dire traduire. http://www.reseau-terra.eu/article919.html (23 September 2013).

Parisi, Luciana. "Biotech: Life by Contagion." *Theory, Culture & Society* 24.6 (2007): 29–52.

Parisi, Luciana, and Marek Kohn. "Dividing the Species: Race, Science, and Culture." *Mute* 2.2 (2006) http://www.metamute.org/editorial/articles/dividing-species-race-science-and-culture (16 September 2013).

Quijano, Anibal. "Coloniality of Power, Eurocentrism, and Latin America." *Nepantla: Views From the South* 1.3 (2000): 533–580.

Ross, Andrew. "Rise of the Global University." *Towards a Global Autonomous University.* Eds. Edufactory Collective. New York: Autonomedia, 2009. 18–31.

Sakai, Naoki. *Translation and Subjectivity: On "Japan" and Cultural Nationalism.* Minneapolis: University of Minnesota Press, 1997.

Sakai, Naoki. "How Do We Count a Language? Translation and Discontinuity." *Translation Studies* 2.1 (2009): 71–88.

Sakai, Naoki. "Theory and Asian Humanity: On the Question of *Humanitas* and *Anthropos*." *Postcolonial Studies* 13.4 (2010): 441–464.

Solomon, Jon. "Rethinking the Meaning of Regions: Translation and Catastrophe." *Transversal* (2008). Issue title: *Borders, Nations, Translations*.
http://eipcp.net/transversal/0608/solomon/en (20 September 2013).

Solomon, Jon. "The Experience of Culture: Eurocentric Limits and Openings in Foucault." *Transeuropéenes* 1.1 (2010) (Translations into French and Turkish).
http://www.transeuropeennes.eu/en/articles/108/The_Experience_of_Culture_Eurocentric_Limits_and_Openings_in_Foucault (20 September 2013). Chinese authorial version: 〈文化的體驗：傅柯的歐洲中心主義與文化製圖的生命政治〉，《文化研究》第十一期，臺北，2010年。.

Solomon, Jon. "Another European Crisis?! Myth, Translation, and the Apparatus of Area." *Transversal* (2013). Issue title: *A Communality that Cannot Speak: Europe in Translation.* (Translations into German, Spanish, and French).
http://eipcp.net/transversal/0613/solomon/en (20 September 2013).

Solomon, Jon. "Invoking the West: Giorgio Agamben's Philosophy and the Problems of Civilizational Transference." Presented at the International Conference, *Except Asia: Agamben's Work in Transcultural Perspective*, June 25–27, 2013. Taipei, 2013.

Thrift, Nigel. *Non-representational Theory: Space, Politics, Affect*. London/New York: Routledge, 2008.

Walker, Gavin. "The Accumulation of Difference and the Logic of Area." *Area and the Regime of Civilizational Difference*. Eds. Naoki Sakai and Gavin Walker. Special issue of *Positions*, 2014 (forthcoming).

Andreas Langenohl
Scenes of Encounter

A Translational Approach to Travelling Concepts in the Study of Culture

1 Introduction

This essay assigns itself a double task. It addresses the concept of 'translation' both as a (potentially) travelling concept and as a mode of travel (see also Bachmann-Medick's contribution in this volume). In the name of the first task, the essay will raise the question of possible convergences and crossroads of literary and sociological theory regarding the conceptual notion of translation, as both discourses have recently displayed an increasing amount of interest in this notion. This analysis will then inform the second question regarding the consequences of viewing travelling concepts themselves, of which 'translation' is one, from a translational perspective.

The notion of translation has gained prominence in the humanities and so-cial sciences in the last decade and can be counted among the major travelling concepts in both fields. Indeed, a "translational turn" has been heralded, sup-posedly inaugurating one of several "cultural turns" of its own (Bachmann-Medick 2009). Yet, at the same time, translation as a notion is far from univocal, let alone self-identical. What seems to constitute the translational turn is not so much a clearly distinguished epistemological shift of direction in (parts of) the humanities and social sciences but rather a mounting, yet sometimes vague, uneasiness with inherited analytical concepts, such as 'language,' 'culture,' and 'context.' This essay takes this ambivalence as its point of departure for recon-structing the appearance of 'translation' in recent discourses in literary and sociological theory and, from there, attempts to indicate possible conjunctures of the concept between these discourses. This discussion serves as a launching pad for suggesting a translational approach to concept-circulation in the study of culture.

In literary studies, and rather unsurprisingly, it is the field of comparative literature that especially refers to translation in order to take issue with some elements and notions of literary analysis (see, in particular, Apter 2001; Venuti

1995; Sakai 1991, 1997, 2009). At the same time, and more surprisingly, the notion reintroduces some questions into literary studies that seem to have gone overboard in much of poststructuralist literary theory – most prominently, the question of the relationship between what is translated and into what something is translated. For 'translation' as a concept carries the conundrum that the 'equivalence,' 'adequacy,' or 'fidelity' of a translation can never be vouched for, while the question of that very adequacy remains valid all the same (cf. Renn 2002; Schreiber 2006). In other words, the relationality between the *translatum* and the *translandum* cannot be disavowed from a theoretical point of view, because translation as a theoretical concept makes the interrogation of that relationality unavoidable. It poses a question that cannot be discarded, irrespective of whether it can be answered.

In sociology, translation has emerged both as a theoretical and as an analytical category at rather different points in the debate. On the one hand, 'translation' has been used by scholars in science studies to launch a critique against holistic notions in theoretical social analyses, like that of social structure, culture, or context. It was notably Bruno Latour (1986) and Michel Callon (1986) who argued as early as the 1980s that the substrate of the social does not involve overarching structures of meaning, social positions, or the distribution of social goods, usually referred to as 'collective consciousness,' 'values,' or 'social structure.' Instead, this substrate should be viewed as a series or sequences of interactions, among them 'translations,' between different agents that enforce notions of the social that only then become active as agents of their own. The 'social,' from this point of view, does not precede translation but is its effect. Other approaches, like that of Joachim Renn (2006), have tried to introduce 'translation' as a meta-theoretical term into existing theoretical confrontations and oppositions in sociology, like those between action theory and systems theory. Here, translation figures as a theoretical device that is used to advocate, as it were, a lifting of theorization above the level of the controversy between action-oriented and systemic approaches, as it views these approaches not as mutually contradicting theoretical alternatives but as modes of reflection on different ways of societal integration that can, in principle, be re-conjoined.

As this introductory overview indicates, 'translation' emerges as a key category at rather different sites in the humanities and social sciences. While this does not yet permit speaking of translation as a travelling concept, it invites the interrogation of possible conjunctures, common motives, and mutually translatable critiques that accompany the notion of translation. These critiques inevitably extend themselves into a redoubling of the notion of translation not only as a (potentially) travelling concept in the study of culture but also as a mode of travel. Put differently: is it possible to understand the conjunctures of transla-

tion as an important concept in the study of culture from a translational epistemological perspective, in their turn? And what are the implications of such
perspectivization for our understanding of the translation that takes (or ought to
take) place between different national and disciplinary contexts in the study of
culture?

This essay will outline different idioms of translation in the humanities and
social sciences in the first two sections and then move on to questioning, confronting, and interrelating them in the third section, using 'translation' not only
as the object of an epistemological investigation but also as a conceptual entry
point into the pursuit of said investigation. I will, thereby, concentrate on instances in which translation is involved in self-reflexive discourses that question their respective disciplines' epistemological strategies and interfere in what
they set out to describe and explain – for it is mainly in these discourses that
translation figures not only as a symptom but also as a reflective strategy. Accordingly, I will analyze and interrelate uses of the notion of translation in
comparative literature, especially its postcolonial strand, as well as in the
actant-network theory (ANT) of science and technology studies (section 3).
Postcolonial studies and ANT-approaches are united in what could be called
their established marginality: although far from forming the core part of their
respective disciplines' agendas (comparative literature, on the one hand, anthropology and sociology, on the other), they nevertheless have enjoyed some
prominence as loci of theory production, self-reflexivity, and epistemological
critique.

This analysis, finally, will be carried over into a reflection on translation as
a mode of travel in section 4. Translation has been characterized as a "metaphor
of metaphor," that is, as a performative *mis-en-scène* of the idea of transposing
meaning from one conceptual scene to another (Derrida 2002: 104; Sakai 2010:
1). As metaphor turned upon itself, 'translation' forces the study of culture into
reflexivity. Accordingly, to regard the travelling of concepts, including 'translation,' as a move from one scene to another is to provide clues as to how this
transposition may take place. This also has implications for our understanding
of the travelling of concepts throughout the humanities and social sciences,
since translation may be envisaged as a particular way of travelling. Therefore,
after having explored how translation might provide us with a novel perspective
on how to critically reconstruct notions like context, culture, society, etc. that
have been prominent in the traditional study of culture, this essay will end with
a translation-related suggestion that challenges ways of exploring the travel of
concepts (including translation) between disciplinary and national research
cultures, which operate with notions of contextuality, culturality, and, more
generally, the (mis-)match between different research backgrounds.

2 Scene I: Translation in Literary Studies

The uses of the category of 'translation' in contemporary literary studies is an interesting case of how a concept that was once relevant only within the confines of a rather technical discourse, namely that of translation studies, has moved to the theoretical centre-stage of the humanities. Thereby, it has undergone transformation in both its context of origin and mainstream debates within literary studies, providing an example of how translation works as a particular mode of cultural exchange and interaction.

Translation studies, as the original discourse of the travelling concept of translation, has, in recent years, tilted toward a less technical and more encompassing, broad, and general notion of translation, taking into account not only interlingual relations but also more general questions of intercultural convergence, translatability, and transferability (see the overview in Bachmann-Medick 2009: 3–5). Thus, not only questions regarding the social and cultural situatedness of the process of translation but also meta-approaches to the question of how criteria for a 'good' translation can actually be established have received increased attention (cf. Renn 2002; Böckler 2003; Cappai 2003; Lau et al. 2001; Plé 2003; Schreiber 2006; and Van Vaerenberg 2006). Recent questioning of the paradigm of equivalence – which proceeded from the presumption of direct translatability of lexemes from one language into another, by way of the paradigm of functional adequacy, which highlights the necessity of making an expression work within the target language's system – is a case in point (cf. Renn 2002). On the receiving end, 'translation' has been appropriated, even kidnapped, by mainstream literary studies. Under the impact of postcolonial, gender, and queer theory, it has contributed to the overall tendency in the last two decades to problematize conceptions of cultures as self-identical containers and, at the same time, helped connect these questions to epistemological issues in literary studies that concern the viability of literature and individual literary works as knowable entities, as voiced by Apter, Venuti, and Sakai and Hanawa.

Given this discussion in comparative literature, the question arises as to the peculiar epistemological and political quality that the concept of 'translation' introduces when compared to, for instance, hybridization (Bhabha 1994), creolization (Ashcroft et al. 1989), contact zones (Pratt 1992), cosmopolitanism (Brennan 1997), transculturality (Welsch 1994; Gvozdeva 2010), etc. Many of these concepts have been introduced into comparative literature and, more broadly, literary studies to challenge the existing power differentials between historically Western societies and the postcolonial non-West in the fields of culture and aesthetic production. In particular, they are directed against the essentialization of the West through the construction of an equally essentialized 'other' that underlies and legitimizes that power differential. 'Translation,' it would seem, needs to differ from these concepts in order to make a difference. Translation per se, as Emily Apter points out in "On Translation in a Global Market" (2001), does not guarantee a liberatory approach toward global inequalities but can just as well become a concept that serves the ends of dominant languages as target languages of translation and, thus, might even strengthen the domination of semi-peripheral and peripheral literatures, cultures, and people by the metropolises.

So, while, on the one hand, the discussion about translation has not yet found broad consensus as to what actually makes translation so special vis-à-vis other travelling concepts like those mentioned above; on the other hand, translation cannot be held innocent in the global division of cultural, mental, and aesthetic labor.[1] Yet, certain developments in recent discussion demonstrate that this *problématique* is undergoing reflection and that the notion of translation as a theoretical core concept in the study of culture is being further refined. In particular, scholars working in, and on, postcolonial sites have critically revisited the notion of translation and its implications in cultural processes of essentialization and global (post)colonial relations.

For instance, Naoki Sakai, a scholar of Japanese studies, has argued that translation involves an act of address. This act can assume different forms. Working on literary translations from Chinese into what was to become Japanese in the eighteenth century, Sakai depicts a historical moment that, in certain aspects, is highly indicative of the construction of cultural dividing lines in modernity. In *Voices of the Past* (1991) and *Translation and Subjectivity* (1997), Sakai argues that, precisely through articulating interlingual translation as an act in which meaning passes from one lingual context (Chinese) into another (Japanese), both contexts are symbolically constituted as (national) languages (see also Kim 2010). Here, translation figures as a clearly demarcated activity that involves professionalized knowledge about the other. This knowledge is epitomized in the figure of the translator. It presupposes the existence of different languages while, at the same time, this difference nevertheless emerges only as a result of the very act of translation. This type of translation has been worked out as 'homolingual address,' notably by Naoki Sakai and Jon Solomon in their introduction to *Translation, Biopolitics, Colonial Differences* (2006). It imaginarily presupposes, yet culturally produces, the notion that languages are

---

1 For translational processes in the realm of tertiary education and their relations to global division of intellectual labor, see the contributions in de Bary 2010.

distinct from each other yet homogeneous within themselves, which follows the 'container model' of society and, thus, inaugurates and reifies the national-modern episteme. This critical view on translation parallels other reservations about the term as, for instance, expressed by Apter in her essay "On Translation in a Global Market."

Yet, homolingual address has a counterpart, which does not figure as prominently and openly in the history of cultural relations but rather has to be retrieved from that history and set against the domination and abundance of instances of homolingual address in modernity. Sakai terms this counterpart 'heterolingual address.' It is a mode of translation that ought to be imagined as an instance of encounter in which mutuality is not achieved by way of a literal translation from one code into the other, but by gestures from various registers including, but not limited to, language used to provoke resonance in the other. The concept of heterolingual address calls a scene to mind: strangers using different forms of expression like speech, gestures, facial expressions, and touch to engage each other, prior to any categorization of the other person as an exemplar of this or that language, culture, or nation. As John Namjun Kim stresses:

> The point of departure for Naoki Sakai's work on translation is not translation itself, but the scene of address as the site of social practice. This unlikely methodological point of departure is explained by the epistemological observation that addressing precedes translation. (Kim 2010: 55)

This "scene" of translation advocates, accordingly, a separation between Sakai's conception of translation and the history of translation, if the latter is understood as a history of intercultural contact. The concept of heterolingual address, therefore, does not point to a transfer of meaning, like in the communication paradigm of interlingual translation, but to the creation of mutual responsiveness; its corresponding attitude is not the ordering penetration of what the other says but an attention to how the other articulates herself. In epistemological and political terms, heterolingual address remains a critical alternative to homolingual address and, thus, criticizes the historical hegemony of the latter in modernity (cf. Sakai and Solomon 2006). This already hints at the epistemological consequences and applicability of various uses of translation: far from relating only to the idea of a transfer of meaning from one discourse to another, 'translation' raises the question of the orders of knowledge it helps construct, with consequences for the study of culture to be returned to later.

Sakai terms heterolingual address a mode of "sociality," and does "not hesitate to call this approach a materialist resolution to incomprehensibility" (Sakai

2009: no page). This conception of sociality crystallizes much of the criticism that Sakai, in "The Dislocation of the West" (2001), directs against the construction of the self-consolidating other of Asia by the West-centrist humanities and social sciences. In particular, he criticizes the reifying effects of the national framing of cultures and their hierarchization along the lines of a continuum running between the West and the non-West, whereby, in modernity, the idea of the West has exerted the power of definition over what was supposed to be the non-West.[2] Against this colonial imagination – which is based to a great extent on the idea of homolingual address, the figure of the translator, and the doctrine of understanding the other – Sakai introduces a conception of sociality that is capable of making any self-identical, homogenizing representation of self and other questionable.

A comparable criticism of the nationalist and colonialist epistemologies of modernity in the humanities and beyond has been pursued by German studies scholar Anil Bhatti. Without giving the notion of translation as much explicit reference as Sakai, Bhatti nevertheless relies on a critique of interlingual translation as an instance of a nationalist order of knowledge that separates cultures along the lines of national languages, a tendency that Bhatti refers back to colonialism and its attempts to homogenize language practice within the colonies. The history of the Western understanding of translation is imbricated in a "process of the condensation of *colonial competence*" (Bhatti 1997: 5; my translation).[3] Bhatti argues in accordance with some major critics in postcolonial studies, among them Guha, Chatterjee, and Duara, in claiming that postcolonial nationalism continues colonialist epistemologies when it draws distinctions between religions, cultures, nations, and ethnic groups that hinge upon the assumption that these groups are homogeneous within themselves and radically different from one another. The practice of interlingual translation, from this point of view, and in correspondence with Sakai's argument, does not point to a

---

2 Japan serves as a particularly interesting and revealing point of observation, as it has figured in a double role within the colonial imagination: on the one hand, it was quasi-colonized by the West in the nineteenth century when U.S. naval forces pressed Japan to open its borders to international trade; on the other hand, Japan became a colonial regional power itself, claiming a status of domination in relation to its colonies that resembled that of Europe in relation to the European colonies (cf. Sakai 2001).

3 Referring to this complicity of the concept of translation and its hermeneutic underpinnings with imperialism, Martin Fuchs attempts to disentangle the hermeneutic enterprise of achieving an "understanding of *content* [...] to understand people," which, according to Fuchs, "was or is the goal both of imperialist translators and their anti- and postcolonial opponents" (Fuchs 2009: 25).

serious attempt to take the other's position, but rather to control the other through the image produced in translation and through the technique of hermeneutics (cf. Bhatti 2009: 118, 2010).

Against this register of mutual delimitation and attempts at 'understanding' that presuppose borders across which understanding can take place, Bhatti proposes looking for instances in political and cultural history of encounters based on the principle of 'similarity.' Similarity has to be understood not so much as a certain degree of (more or less superficial) resemblance between two different entities, but rather as the discovery that entities might not be as homogeneous and self-identical as supposed, which, only seemingly paradoxically, gives view to the possibility that they have things in common. In other words, similarity undermines the doctrine of essential differences, pointing to commonalities and shared spaces between lingual registers, gestures, or beliefs on the basis that those registers, gestures, and beliefs are not hermetically sealed from encounter. Similarity, thus, casts doubt on the idea of interlingual translation as transfer of meaning from one code into the other and which underlies the imaginary of "dialogicity" (orig. *Dialogizität*, Bhatti 2009: 122). It highlights the connections that languages or cultures have prior to any interlingual or intercultural (and, as we will see, interdisciplinary) translation.

The notion of similarity gains significance if understood in opposition to the culturalization of difference, to a strong notion of culture, and to a hermeneutical take that demands a definition of the conditions of understanding prior to any exchange (cf. Bhatti 2010). Much like Sakai's notion of heterolingual address, similarity ought to be seen as a concept that intervenes in a certain historical epistemology, its political implications, and its limits. Because the hermeticism and uniformity of national societies and cultures have become questionable in the postcolonial episteme, the question of how to deal with their actual and irreducible plurality and heterogeneity arises. Neither 'address' nor 'similarity,' according to my analysis, should be misconstrued as advocating a retreat from difference-theoretical positions and flight to some sort of melting-pot doctrine. Instead, both attempt to turn the principle of difference back upon entities that were considered, in the hermeneutic tradition, to be self-identical and homogeneous: cultures and languages. For Bhatti, the main alternative resulting from this radicalization of the principle of difference is this: either one insists on cultural differences and how they block intercultural understanding, or one turns away from a strong notion of understanding and, at the same time, from the doctrine of cultural wholeness to focus instead on hermeneutically less ambitious ways of "get[ing] along with the other" (Bhatti 2010: 264; my translation).

'Similarity' heralds a turn away from hermeneutics on several levels and re-places the strong notion of culture with a weak one that pinpoints not so much understanding between cultures but rather the conduct of encounter. Bhatti finds literary instances of attempts at getting along and discovering similarities prior to the emergence of full-fledged, culturalized discourse in, for instance, Goethe's *West-östlicher Divan* (cf. Bhatti 2009). The situational logic of similarity can be analogized with the concept of heterolingual sociality as articulated by Sakai. Both contradict a notion of translation as transfer of meaning between preexisting and self-identical codes and, instead, suggest a concept of transla-tion that avoids defining the conditionality of understanding prior to transla-tion.

3 Scene II: Translation in Science and Technology Studies

Like literary scholars Sakai and Bhatti, Bruno Latour, who has become one of the main proponents of science and technology studies, positions his notion of translation as a critique of established ways of thinking about social and cultur-al structures. That is, the basic gesture in which translation is introduced is comparable to those of Sakai and Bhatti. At the same time, Latour's endeavor is directed against a different, or rather more encompassing, discourse: the dis-course of Western science since Plato. According to Latour, this discourse has produced an utterly artificial confrontation between the realm of facts and the world of beliefs, which first took shape in Plato's ridicule of rhetoric as an art without substantial reference to the world ('mere words') and has since dynamized idolatric movements in Western thought that seek to expose false beliefs and discover hidden truth (cf. Latour 1999: 265–289). In short, what spoiled the occidental sciences (including the social sciences), according to Latour, was an artificial separation of knowledge practices into epistemology and ontology in which the two are constantly played out against each other. Latour terms this separation the "modernist settlement" (Latour 1999: 14).

Taking his past work ("The Powers of Associations" from 1986) and that of his colleagues in the social sciences (notably, Callon 1986) as points of depar-ture, Latour demonstrates that, to understand the emergence of scientific 'facts,' neither a realist nor a constructivist model is appropriate. Scientific facts are neither discovered nor socially constructed, as this would presuppose that they either existed all along or have no substrate other than their social constructed-ness. Against this dichotomy, Latour suggests a model circumscribed by interrelated concepts like 'articulation,' 'mediation,' 'transformation' – and 'transla-tion' (cf. Latour 1999: 89, 92, 100, 110). All of these notions point to the histori-cal moment(s) in which an entity emerges in connection to other entities, or, to use Latour's famous expression, as part of an "actant network." Such emer-gence typically takes place in scientific laboratories, in which substances are reconfigured in relation to other substances (and to the researchers and their instruments) to acquire new qualities. Thus, for Latour, scientific facts are nei-ther constructed nor real but both: they gain reality precisely in their new ar-rangements and networks with other entities as a result of the experiments they undergo. The thicker and denser the arrangements, the more constructed yet real the 'facts' become (cf. Latour 1999: 127–144). 'Reality,' thus, appears not as an ontological substrate that can be present or absent independent of its con-struction, but as a qualifier that directly depends on the work of construction allocated to the 'facts.' Latour calls this "articulation": far from referring to the expression of the meaning of a pre-given substrate, articulation interconnects facts and substances and, thus, yields reality (Latour 1999: 142).

Within this understanding of reality, translation assumes the meaning of a specific mode of articulation. Like articulation in general, translation serves as a notional device to overcome the dichotomization of facts and beliefs (or 'con-structions') by introducing another pair of notions: human and non-human beings. Translation takes place whenever different agencies, whether human or non-human, interrelate in their action procedures. To paraphrase one of Latour's most compelling, if somewhat macabre, examples, when a human being takes a gun and shoots at another human being, translation refers to both the shifting of the agential direction of the two actants (their 'goals,' 'functions,' 'dedications,' etc.) and their transformation into different entities. Joining two agential directions, a gun becomes a killing machine, and a shooter turns into a killer. For Latour, neither traditional sociological nor traditional materialist descriptions are appropriate for describing what happened. Only a translational description succeeds, because it is capable of depicting the moment in which action transforms both contributing vectors into different entities. This process of translation may occur between humans, between humans and non-humans as well as between non-humans (cf. Latour 1999: 176–193). In effect, this means that Latour eradicates the notions of intentionality and hermeneutics from his approach. Considering how current conceptualizations of translation may alter our understanding of travelling concepts in the study of culture, one begins to see that translation, when theorized along the lines reconstructed here, ought to be seen not as an epiphenomenon of the contact between two preexisting enti-ties but rather as a productive process that yields reality, irrespective of whether we localize this reality in science labs, in relations among humans and things, or in the circulation of concepts in the study of culture.

This becomes especially evident when one considers the fact that Latour's epistemological exposition includes a crucial critique of the notion of 'context.' For Latour, 'context' and 'content' have been used to inculcate the dichotomy between internalist and externalist explanations of science in the traditional history of science, which reproduces the pattern of realism vs. constructivism (cf. Latour 1999: 91–92, 109–110). The notion of 'translation' pinpoints this critique, since it makes clear that translation does not simply mediate between two different contexts that stay the same (to remain with the example above, between the intention to kill and the technical device that can fire a bullet). Instead, translation changes both contexts, exposing the fictitiousness of their wholeness and the stableness of their meaning. We can see a striking resemblance between the use of the notion of translation and the critique of hermeneutics in both sociology and literary studies.

As Latour uses an extremely extended notion of epistemology, treating science in its totality as the expression of the traditional Western 'settlement' based on the separation between epistemological and ontological questions 2,500 years ago, it is not surprising that he also articulates a critique of sociology as part of the modernist project that maintains this traditional settlement. 'Modernist' refers not to a specific historical period but to historical and epistemic moments in which the settlement is renewed, refurbished, and radicalized. According to Latour, the advent of the professional social sciences in the nineteenth century indicates such a moment of modernism. Taking issue especially with Émile Durkheim's foundation of sociology upon a functionalist notion of society, Latour reproaches Durkheim for having articulated the full-fledged emergence of the false dichotomy of realist vs. constructivist explanations (cf. Latour 1996, 2000). Durkheim, as Latour argues, construes the notion of 'society' as the core paradigm of all social constructivisms after him. As an alternative to Durkheimian sociology, Latour turns to the sociology of Gabriel Tarde (1969, 2009), who was an adversary of Durkheim at the turn of the twentieth century. In contrast to Durkheim, Tarde, somehow in line with Georg Simmel (1978), argues that society does not have any substrate outside of relationships between individuals. Tarde attempted to trace all relations between entities, whatever they are, back to the fundamental mechanism of 'emulation,' arguing that similarities as well as differences can be causally explained through this mechanism. What makes Tarde such an attractive alternative to Durkheim for Latour is his theory of society as sociality, as opposed to 'structure,' 'collective consciousness,' or 'context.' This allows for a form of conceptualization that remains open about whether emulation occurs only between humans, between humans and non-humans, or between non-humans. Tarde comes to stand for a radically alternative sociology that obviates the vague notion of society as a necessary mediator for any social analysis. Regarding Tarde's take on the relation between language as a system and language as practice, Latour explains that Tarde strictly avoids any reference to a preexisting *langue* (like in Saussure's *Course in General Linguistics*, 1960); Tarde interprets lingual rules as resulting from the rise of one particular language variety into a dominating position; yet, in this position, 'language' does not overarch individual speech acts but rather becomes the generator of differences itself (Tarde 2009: 73; Latour 2009: 48–49, 2005: 14–16). By way of extension, translation would imply not a transfer between two language systems, but the completely ordinary production of differences from prevalent lingual rules that lack systemic character.

The rather metaphorical notion of translation that Latour deploys can be anchored in a more literal meaning of translation without departing from the overall theoretical and epistemological framework of his argument. In particular, Tarde's conceptualization of language use as the seat of differentiality, to which Latour refers, can be aligned with the notions of translation articulated by both Sakai and Bhatti. The significance of difference within language, instead of figuring as a vehicle of the systematicity of *langue* in Saussure, becomes apparent only upon reflection of the uses of language by particular speakers in particular situations. Translation comes to stand for the differentiality of lingual and social practices that render 'language,' 'culture,' and 'context' heterogeneous, incoherent, and messy.

Having outlined recent discussions in the humanities and social sciences that involve the notion of translation, I will turn to possible conjunctures between these different discourses in the next section. As we have seen, all of these discourses take exception with notions of culture, language, or context as proxies for a holistic conception of the social and the cultural. Instead, they highlight the logic of the *encounter* as it subverts any such holistic conception. The notion of 'encounter' that I am using to circumscribe the logic of association that is common to all of the discussed uses of translation is borrowed from Erving Goffman's work of a similar name (1961). An encounter in Goffman's sense is a situation of co-presence in which certain norms for keeping the situation going are put to work by the involved actors, which also implies actors' strategic movements within such norms. It is crucial that they do not have to be traced back to a common culture, language or religion, not even to a mutual appreciation of the encounter itself, as their essence is not shared values, symbols, or beliefs. Instead, proper conduct in a situation of co-presence is a matter of *conventions* that need not be backed by a substantive semiosis in order to work. The notion of encounter in Goffman's sense, therefore, lends itself to describing a situation in which agency is shared by a multiplicity of actors and forgoes the intense questioning that defines the enterprise of hermeneutics.

Thus far, this account has concentrated on recent instances in which the notion of translation has been reconceptualized in literary studies and sociology. While this does not yet amount to a conceptual suggestion as to how the notion of translation may inform, and alter, our understanding of travelling concepts in the study of culture, a vista has been created in which we can begin to engage in this task. Before deliberately confronting this task in section 5, however, it is helpful first to interrogate the uses of translation more systematically with regard to their possible confluences and tensions.

4 Translating 'Translation' Between and Among the Humanities and Social Sciences

This section raises some questions in regard to the translatability of 'translation' across disciplines. The concept of translation, and the ways it is spelled out both in literary studies and sociology, announces a departure from the presumption of holistic and sealed cultures or cultural contexts and the aesthetic means through which this is achieved, which crucially relies on a foregrounding of encounters and associations among and between persons and things. To these already existing convergences, more potentialities can be added.

Firstly, as noted in the beginning, the critique of translation in its traditional sense, that is, as simultaneously a bridge and a boundary between two contexts or cultures, has been put forth in research areas beyond the mainstream of their respective disciplines. This points to a constellation of travelling concepts in need of further epistemological exploration. This constellation may be hypothetically described as a dual trajectory of concepts from peripheral sites of theory production to the core of the respective disciplines *and* to other disciplines at the same time. Marginality assumes a double meaning here: as a site not central, yet also adjacent to other disciplines' margins.

Secondly, the critique of context as holistic, all-encompassing, and different from other contexts, which is central to all the applications of 'translation' discussed here, points to a deepening critical awareness of epistemic dualisms in the humanities and social sciences. This applies to the distinction between text and context as well as between content and context (cf. Fuchs 2009). Criticism is articulated on two levels. On the one hand, the content/context distinction is critiqued because it extends an epistemological model that ends up in the self-sustaining impasse of realism (content) vs. constructivism (context). On the other hand, the text/context distinction is effectively rejected because it treats texts as mere exemplars of 'their' contexts and leaves the latter unchanged (and unchangeable). What, in my view, unites Sakai, Bhatti, and Latour's arguments is precisely the point that it is not context, understood as 'cultures,' 'languages,' or any other rigorously systematized set of meanings, that meet each other. Rather, through translation, texts, speech acts, and actions are *taken out* of their contexts in order to encounter each other. It is only from the angle of the encounter that contexts, cultures, etc., become articulated and reconstructed. This obviously has immediate consequences for arguments about the 'translatability between contexts' that, among other things, are currently circulating within the study of culture – to which this volume testifies.

Thirdly, and connecting to the point above, there is an uneasiness with all-encompassing concepts of sociality and culturality – for instance, 'society,' 'culture' or 'language' – which unite literary and social-scientific uses of translation. However, unlike earlier critiques, such as those of 'nation' or 'culture' within colonial discourse analysis and post-colonial literary studies, the tendency has advanced, as it were, half a step further. This applies in particular to science and technology studies (STS), which not only critiques the fictitiousness of holistic notions (which it associates with traditional, macro-sociological concepts like 'collective consciousness' or 'social structure') but also chooses to *ignore* them in the very act of rearticulating the notion of translation as association and encounter. Yet, while STS seems to have taken the lead in circumventing the laborious deconstruction of such macro-notions via the route of a fundamental critique of modernist epistemology, literary studies is catching up. If we take into account the recent interest in radically underlining the consequences behind the principles of aesthetic singularity, political plurality, and heterogeneity (cf. Hardt and Negri 2005; Casarino and Negri 2008), it seems that a move toward an epistemological condensation of the empirical critiques of "rational abstractions" is underway (Spivak 1993: 237).

Fourthly, the crisis of all-encompassing categories by no means results in a celebration of the local and denial of the global. On the contrary, a reconstellation of the micro/macro and the global/local divisions is currently underway. To cite an instance from STS, 'global microstructures' (cf. Knorr Cetina and Bruegger 2002), like those of the financial markets, gain their global momentum precisely because of a scaling-up of the situational logic of the countless encounters between traders and a globe-girdling network. But the disentangling of the short-circuit that associated situational logics with spatially circumscribed locales and macro-processes with globality does not stop at the margins of sociology. According to recent interventions in literary and film studies (notably by

Ezli 2009, 2010; Göktürk 2010), post-national trajectories of artworks disentangle the traditional affinity between a world perspective and the stipulation of macro-units like 'society.' These are recombined into an affinity between the local, situational logics of the encounter and a planetary scope of the nodes, hubs, and stretches of the networks within which these encounters take place. The notion of 'translation' and the situational logic of encounter do not so much subvert but rather *super*vert the macro-fictions of imagined communities. With regard to travelling concepts in the study of culture, this triggers consideration of the trans-local significance of situated encounters between concepts and how such encounters might be understood in a non-metaphorical way.

Apart from these potential convergences, however, open questions regarding the future of the travels of 'translation' remain within, among, and between the humanities and social sciences. Because this essay theorizes 'translation' as a model of how concepts travel in the study of culture, it will only focus on questions that are of immediate concern.[4] The most important question concerns the need for further theoretical specification of the 'encounter.' In literary studies, the scene of the encounter is still very much observed in terms of its opposition to both culturalism and the logics of identity and difference. 'Sociality' and 'similarity,' in invoking the figure of the encounter, appear as corrective devices that question the viability of hermeneutic understanding and the role

---

4 Further differences between the uses of translation discussed here concern points of entry of the concept of translation into respective discursive environments that co-determine these very points. For instance, comparative literature seems to imply that the notion of translation is a gesture that is continuous with a deconstructive and postcolonial idiom and, thus, exposes the cultural and aesthetic foundations of the West-centrism of academic and political discourse and its essentialization of the non-West. STS, in contrast, is less concerned with the (geo)political ramifications of macro-notions like those of 'society' or 'culture' and, instead, uses the notion of translation to reveal the methodological shortcomings of sociology as a science. The open question is thus: how does the (cultural) critique of the (political) representation that has driven postcolonial literary studies since its formation within comparative literature (cf. Langenohl 2007: 116–249) relate to the methodological critiques of science that sociological uses of translation pursue? Another, and related, question that arises in the borderlands of the epistemologies and politics of translation involves how one might decouple the legitimacy of the logic of the translational encounter from the deconstructivist critique of aesthetic-political constellations. As we have seen, there is a common tendency to immediately deny not only the saliency but also the relevance of traditional macro-categories. Is this an emancipation from, a putting to rest, or a downplaying of still-existent national and nation-state frames in aesthetic, cultural, and social constellations? If one takes into account the repeatedly articulated and ever-present cautions against an all-out deconstructivism, especially in postcolonial settings that might also destroy the agential resources for resistance (cf. Ahmad 1995), this question remains unaccounted for by most uses of translation thus far.

translation should play in this endeavor. But at the same time, they do not yet develop into full-fledged concepts on par with the theoretical and conceptual arsenal of literary studies. In STS, a concept like that of 'encounter' can, in principle, rely on a more affirmative heritage like micro-sociology (cf. Goffman 1961), ethnomethodology (cf. Garfinkel 1967), or Tarde's philosophy (see above). Yet, in Latour, it emerges mainly as a historicization that opposes a theoretically modernized, and ultimately over-generalized narrative. Consequently, different conceptual registers may be invoked to handle the theoretical vagueness of the encounter. While such vagueness often facilitates conceptual traffic across disciplinary boundaries, the question of how to further theorize the encounter cannot be avoided in the long run. In view of this desideratum, we will now turn to possible modes of circumscribing scenes of encounter in the study of culture, guided by the principle proposed here, namely, that a conceptualization of travelling concepts in the study of culture should be evoked along the lines of a notion of 'translation.'

5 Translating 'Translation': Toward an Understanding of Research Practice as a Scene of Encounter

Having outlined these (possible) conjunctures between uses of 'translation' in literary studies and sociology, I will now return to the task of conceptually elaborating translation as a (potentially) travelling concept on the level of an epistemology of the study of culture. If translation is conceptualized as an encounter, as suggested here, the following question needs to be posed: How does translation as encounter help to clarify the possibilities and manifestations of cross-cultural and cross-disciplinary research practices in the study of culture? Instead of putting these conceptual discussions to intellectual rest within the confines of safely guarded research cultures and contexts, we now need to apply the conceptual scene of translation to its travelling as a research practice. As I have demonstrated, current discussions invoke the notion of translation in order to critique those of 'context' and 'culture.' Accordingly, we need to question these notions in the analysis of cross-cultural, cross-national, and cross-contextual research encounters as well.

Translation is a conceptual scheme that is neither sealed nor univocal. And yet, it rests on a thick and growing layer of discussions in both the humanities and social sciences. It is the inheritor of multiple and pluralistic epistemological troubles and kinds of uneasiness. As an heir, it has no control over what it inherits, because heritage is handed over by history. From a purely conceptual point of view, as applied in the preceding sections, the question that arises, therefore, is how translatable 'translation' is, given the different troubles, concerns, and histories – in other words, the different 'cultures' – to which the concept must respond. For instance, is it not first necessary to go through all the stages in the theory of representation, which contemporary postcolonial theory and STS have both accomplished, in order to learn to appreciate a notion of translation that valorizes the encounter and discards 'language,' 'culture,' and 'context?' Are the concerns of different disciplines and discourses really translatable into each other – not only between disciplines but also between (trans)national research cultures? Can a postcolonial critique of modernity be made compatible with a post-socialist one, let alone a postmodern one? In other words, what degree of translatability between the contexts in which 'translation' figures must be presupposed in order to preempt any misunderstanding?

Questions like these are perfectly conceivable, given the current interest in cross-cultural, transnational, and interdisciplinary exchange in the study of culture. Yet, they fall back on the notion of translation as elaborated above. If we accept that 'translation' heralds an approximation, not as a confrontation of contexts or cultures but as an encounter in which agencies bring themselves into one another's reach precisely as they *are leaving* their contexts and cultures, we arrive at an utterly different picture of the travelling of translation as a concept. Since 'culture' and 'context' are radically critiqued through the conceptual notion of translation, they cannot return as explanatory or hermeneutic devices in understanding how 'translation' as a concept travels. At least, they cannot be the starting points of such a travelogue. Instead, they may begin to be seen as the *effects* of translation's travelling.

Context and culture can be regarded as effects of translation, understood as an act of address, insofar as they are used by the agents themselves to make sense of the encounter. Not every encounter, however, has to invoke culture or context to be understood. Most everyday interactions, sociological phenomenology argues, function through people signaling communicative reciprocity and normative referentiality vis-à-vis one another without intensely questioning the 'background' or symbolic system in which they themselves or others operate (Berger and Luckmann 1966; Garfinkel 1967). This phenomenological view has been supplemented by more structural accounts, which highlight that modern, functionally differentiated and pluralized societies rely on the principle of a kind of cultural 'don't ask, don't tell,' inasmuch as actors are expected to display agency within very different institutional settings – that is, in different social roles – without constantly explicating the cultural principles that govern their actions (Radtke 1991; Esser 2004). Social roles are composed of very mundane conventions, not of culture's 'deep play.'[5] In a famous essay, Alfred Schütz (1944) has argued that as soon as actors try to understand other actors' behavior as an expression of their 'culture,' that is, of a tightly integrated system of values and deep-seated beliefs, as often happens when they encounter situations unfamiliar to them, they are systematically misled: They confuse conventions, which need not at all be systematized and can be quite messy, with cultural systems.

Is research different from such mundane and everyday encounters? As researchers in universities or research institutes, most of us have been equipped with a habitus that tells us that science and research are different, because they require us to act according to rationalized standards – or, in other words, 'cultures' – of scientific conduct. Many of us also experience uneasiness with the idea that scientific conduct might itself be a mundane activity, governed by conventions, and that these conventions might not be very systematized. Therefore, when we encounter violations of conventions – for instance, when concepts travel not as we imagined they would – we tend to ascribe them to the influence of a different research 'culture' or 'context,' and we imagine this culture/context as being, in itself, just as systematic, coherent, and orderly as we imagine our own research performances to be.

However, keeping in mind the concept of translation as reconstructed in this essay, such ascription is a perfect example of Sakai's homolingual address. Researchers regularly reconstruct violations of norms and conventions as differences in 'culture' or 'context,' regardless of whether in cross-disciplinary, cross-lingual or cross-national encounters, without taking into account the conventionality, as opposed to culturality, of research on either side of the alleged divide. True, academic communication is different from other genres in that it relies on, and gains a reputation from, a comparatively high coherence pressure that urges it to constantly monitor, explicate, and question the epistemic conventions that underlie its modes of operation, such as the articulation of theories, concepts, and methods. However, the reference to different 'cultures' or 'contexts' of research circumvents and suspends this urge. By ascribing problems in interdisciplinary or inter-/transnational research to alleged untranslatabilities between cultures or contexts, the coherence of one's own con-

---

5 The use of the notion of 'deep play,' obviously referring to Clifford Geertz's seminal essay of the same name (1972), is based on a literal reading of his work. According to Geertz, deep play indicates social rituals that make culture legible for the subjects as well as for ethnographers in a hermeneutic sense. Consequently, deep play stands in contrast to everyday encounters, which may operate without hermeneutic readings.

ventional assumptions is not explicated, laid open, or questioned; instead, explication, elaboration, and the questioning of conventions is silenced as conventions are made the epiphenomena of 'culture' and 'context,' both endowed here with the phantasms of wholeness and coherence. From this point of view, 'untranslatabilities' in research exists only in the form of academic conventions that are denied reflection and scrutiny.

The presumption of academic 'cultures' and 'contexts,' while instrumental in everyday maneuvering within cross-disciplinary and cross-national academic settings, is therefore not a viable *epistemological* starting point for analyzing the possibility of a cross-study of culture. But it is an interpretive effect of a *vernacular* epistemology that characterizes the idioms of the humanities and social sciences. 'Context' and 'culture' are *in vivo* codes of research as a practice or encounter, not conceptual tools independent of encounter. From a translational perspective, as traced in this essay, 'cultures' and 'context' have no existence beyond their relation to encounter. The question, thus, is whether it is possible to come up with an alternative understanding of the travelling of concepts, or more precisely, with an understanding of the translational encounter in research as a possible site of heterolingual address or similarity. In a moment, I shall conclude by discussing this question with a focus on (and in the absence of more appropriate terms) cross-'disciplinary' and cross-'national' research practices in the humanities and social sciences.

The trouble with interdisciplinarity is that, as long as the disciplines remain its defining cornerstones, it will always be threatened with being abandoned as an illegitimate child. With 'disciplinary context,' 'disciplinary tradition,' etc., remaining the master frames from which to perspectivize an encounter with other disciplines, interdisciplinarity cannot move beyond being an extra outcome of research – a surplus, synergy, or supplement – without a right of its own. From a translational perspective, however, interdisciplinarity precedes and conditions disciplinarity. Michael Oakeshott (1978: 1–31) has argued that the constitutive moment of any discipline is the arrest of an epistemic movement and practice that is not yet confined to the definitions of research interests, theories, and methodologies. In other words, it is only through the encounter, intermingling, and crystallization of pre-disciplinary epistemic practices that disciplines are allowed to form in the first place. The history of science is full of examples that demonstrate the preexistence of epistemic practice prior to the crystallization and emergence of disciplines (cf. Rheinberger 1997; Lepenies 2006; Lindner 1990). The fact that modern science tends to proceed from the preexistence of the disciplines in order to approach interdisciplinarity effaces the constitutive work of an encounter, which our research conventions urge us to call interdisciplinary, in the articulation of the disciplines. A translational perspective on travelling concepts would focus on precisely this scene of the articulation of disciplines, namely the constitution of disciplinary contexts and cultures through the perspectivization characteristic of encounters in modern science.

The same holds true for national research cultures, which one might term more profoundly, if not very elegantly, nationally culturalized sets of research practices. For here we are confronted not so much with differences between research cultures, but with a culturalization of research practice that articulates differences. As long as we stick to the idea of preexisting national cultures in the study of culture, we miss the significance of the cross-'national' encounter in the constitution of research nationalities. An alternative route might, instead, proceed by taking stock of empirical encounters, that is, practices of cross-national research collaborations. For instance, one might conceive of the close observation of international conferences and the ways multi- or monolinguality becomes enacted (and sometimes institutionalized) in such settings.[6] We might even apply ethnography to the translation of written texts, an epistemological strategy that would reveal how texts become detached from their 'contexts' and 'cultures' as they face their own translation (cf. Zingerle 2003). Which sources are used by translators of academic texts to accomplish their tasks? How do they make use of dictionaries or reference texts other than the *translandum* and the *translatum* in order to check reference translations, to explore translational options, and to handle the unavoidable potentiality and excess of meaning? How do they interrelate the *translandum* and the *translatum* by dissociating them from their 'cultures' and 'contexts,' thus, perspectivizing both?

In short, what is heralded here is the idea of an epistemological laboratory of the study of culture. Such a laboratory would provide natural experimental settings (cf. Rheinberger 1997) of the encounter and approximation or dissociation of various agencies in the study of culture that could be made subject to observation and investigation. For instance, we have not yet made much epistemological use of the online revolution in the study of culture. Our infinite e-mail transactions; the endless plethora of commented and reworked text versions sleeping in mailboxes; posts in various academic forums; increasingly automatic cross-referencing social network applications; blogs and profiles; the use of online dictionaries; digitized corpora of literature and other references – all of these are archives of how the study of culture unfolds through associations and dissociations between researchers, technical apparatuses, profile algorithms, and the imagined communities we have become and in which we

---

6 See Ammon 2007 and the conference-website "Translating society."

are leaving traces. These archives, by the way, seem to be under more scrutiny by policing institutions than by ourselves. Finally, as academic teachers, we are already disposed towards an understanding of the usefulness, but also dangers, of such experimental settings, assigning exercises to our students that make the relations between different practices, sites, devices, and images in research palpable and reflective. Why should we not let our teaching teach us more about our research?

References

Ahmad, Aijaz. "The Politics of Literary Postcoloniality." *Race & Class* 36.3 (1995): 1–19.

Ammon, Ulrich. "Global Scientific Communication: Open Questions and Policy Suggestions." *Linguistic Inequality in Scientific Communication Today*. Eds. Augusto Carli and Ulrich Ammon. Amsterdam/Philadelphia: John Benjamins, 2007. 123–133.

Apter, Emily. "On Translation in a Global Market." *Translation in a Global Market. Public Culture* 13.1 (2001): 1–12.

Ashcroft, Bill, Gareth Griffiths, and Helen Tiffin. *The Empire Writes Back: Theory and Practice in Post-Colonial Literatures*. London/New York: Routledge, 1989.

Bachmann-Medick, Doris. "Introduction: The Translational Turn." *The Translational Turn*. Ed. Doris Bachmann-Medick. *Translation Studies* 2.1 (2009): 2–16.

Bachmann-Medick, Doris. *Cultural turns. Neuorientierungen in den Kulturwissenschaften*. 4th edition. Reinbek: Rowohlt, 2010 [2006].

de Bary, Brett, ed. *Universities in Translation: The Mental Labor of Globalization (Traces: A Multilingual Series of Cultural Theory and Translation)*. Hong Kong: Hong Kong University Press, 2010.

Berger, Peter L., and Thomas Luckmann. *The Social Construction of Reality: A Treatise in the Sociology of Knowledge*. Garden City: Doubleday, 1966.

Bhabha, Homi K. *The Location of Culture*. London/New York: Routledge, 1994.

Bhatti, Anil. "Zum Verhältnis von Sprache, Übersetzung und Kolonialismus am Beispiel Indiens." *Kulturelle Identität. Deutsch-indische Kulturkontakte in Literatur, Religion und Politik*. Eds. Horst Turk and Anil Bhatti. Berlin: Erich Schmidt, 1997. 3–19.

Bhatti, Anil. "Der Orient als Experimentierfeld. Goethes 'Divan' und der Aneignungsprozess kolonialen Wissens." *Goethe-Jahrbuch* 126. Göttingen: Wallstein, 2009. 115–128.

Bhatti, Anil. "Heterogenität, Homogenität, Ähnlichkeit." *Kulturwissenschaften in Europa. Eine grenzüberschreitende Disziplin?* Eds. Andrea Allerkamp and Gérard Raulet. Münster: Westfälisches Dampfboot, 2010. 250–266.

Böckler, Stefan. "Abbildung oder Rekonstruktion? Sprachphilosophische Grundfragen des Übersetzens und die Aufgaben des Übersetzers in der Beziehung zwischen Kulturen." *Sozialwissenschaftliches Übersetzen als interkulturelle Hermeneutik – Il tradurre nelle scienze sociali come ermeneutica interculturale*. Eds. Arnold Zingerle and Gabriele Cappai. Milan/Berlin: Franco Angeli and Duncker & Humblot, 2003. 51–78.

Brennan, Timothy. *At Home in the World: Cosmopolitanism Now*. Cambridge, MA/London: Harvard University Press, 1997.

Callon, Michel. "Some Elements of a Sociology of Translation: Domestication of the Scallops and the Fishermen of St Brieuc Bay." *Power, Action and Belief: A New Sociology of Knowledge?* Ed. John Law. London/Boston/Henley: Routledge & Kegan Paul, 1986. 196–233.

Cappai, Gabriele. "Einleitung: Übersetzen zwischen Kulturen als interdisziplinäre Aufgabe." *Sozialwissenschaftliches Übersetzen als interkulturelle Hermeneutik – Il tradurre nelle scienze sociali come ermeneutica interculturale.* Eds. Arnold Zingerle and Gabriele Cappai. Milan/Berlin: Franco Angeli and Duncker & Humblot, 2003. 11–29.

Cappai, Gabriele. "Grundlagentheoretische und methodologische Bemerkungen zum Interpretieren und Übersetzen als interkulturelle Operationen. Für einen möglichen Dialog zwischen analytischer Philosophie und Sozialwissenschaften." *Sozialwissenschaftliches Übersetzen als interkulturelle Hermeneutik – Il tradurre nelle scienze sociali come ermeneutica interculturale.* Eds. Arnold Zingerle and Gabriele Cappai. Milan/Berlin: Franco Angeli and Duncker & Humblot, 2003. 107–131.

Casarino, Cesare, and Antonio Negri. *In Praise of the Common: A Conversation on Philosophy and Politics.* Minneapolis: University of Minnesota Press, 2008.

Chatterjee, Partha. *The Nation and Its Fragments: Colonial and Postcolonial Histories.* Princeton: Princeton University Press, 1993.

Derrida, Jacques. "Des Tours de Babel." *Acts of Religion.* Ed. Gil Anidjar. New York/London: Routledge, 2002. 104–133.

Duara, Prasenjit. *Rescuing History from the Nation: Questioning Narratives in Modern China.* Chicago/London: University of Chicago Press, 1995.

Esser, Hartmut. "Welche Alternativen zur 'Assimilation' gibt es eigentlich?" *Migration – Integration – Bildung. Grundfragen und Problembereiche.* IMIS-Beiträge 23. Eds. Klaus J. Bade and Michael Bommes. Osnabrück: IMIS, 2004. 41–59.

Ezli, Özkan. "Von der interkulturellen zur kulturellen Kompetenz: Fatih Akıns globalisiertes Kino." *Wider den Kulturenzwang. Migration, Kulturalisierung und Weltliteratur.* Eds. Özkan Ezli, Dorothee Kimmich, and Annette Werberger. Bielefeld: transcript, 2009. 207–230.

Ezli, Özkan. "Von Lücken, Grenzen und Räumen: Übersetzungsverhältnisse in Alejandro Gonzáles Iñárritus 'Babel' und Fatih Akıns 'Auf der anderen Seite'." *Kultur als Ereignis. Fatih Akıns Film "Auf der anderen Seite" als transkulturelle Narration.* Ed. Özkan Ezli. Bielefeld: transcript, 2010. 71–88.

Fuchs, Martin. "Reaching Out; or, Nobody Exists in One Context Only: Society as Translation." *The Translational Turn.* Ed. Doris Bachmann-Medick. *Translation Studies* 2.1 (2009): 21–40.

Garfinkel, Harold. "Common Sense Knowledge of Social Structure: The Documentary Method of Interpretation in Lay and Professional Fact Finding." *Studies in Ethnomethodology.* Englewood Cliffs: Prentice-Hall, 1967 [1962]. 76–115.

Geertz, Clifford. "Deep Play: Notes on the Balinese Cockfight." *Daedalus* 101 (1972): 1–37.

Goffman, Erving. *Encounters: Two Studies in the Sociology of Interaction.* Minneapolis/New York: Bobbs-Merrill, 1961.

Göktürk, Deniz. "Mobilität und Stillstand im Weltkino digital." *Kultur als Ereignis.* Ed. Özkan Ezli. Bielefeld: transcript, 2010. 15–45.

Guha, Ranajit. "On Some Aspects of the Historiography of Colonial India." *Mapping Subaltern Studies and the Postcolonial.* Ed. Vinayak Chaturvedi. London/New York: Verso, 2000 [1982]. 1–7.

Gvozdeva, Katja. "Performative Prozesse der Kulturbegegnung und des Kulturkontakts: Hybrider und paradoxer Modus." *Kontaktzonen. Dynamiken und Performativität kultureller Begegnungen.* Ed. Christoph Wulf. *Paragrana: Internationale Zeitschrift für Historische Anthropologie* 19.2 (2010): 13–20.

Hardt, Michael, and Antonio Negri. *Multitude: War and Democracy in the Age of Empire.* New York: Penguin, 2005.

Kim, John Namjun. "Politics as Translation: Naoki Sakai and the Critique of Hermeneutics." *The Politics of Translation: Around the Work of Naoki Sakai.* Eds. John Namjun Kim and Richard Calichman. London/New York: Routledge, 2010. 52–71.

Knorr Cetina, Karin, and Urs Bruegger. "Global Microstructures: The Virtual Societies of Financial Markets." *American Journal of Sociology* 107.4 (2002): 905–950.

Langenohl, Andreas. *Tradition und Gesellschaftskritik. Eine Rekonstruktion der Modernisierungstheorie.* Frankfurt a.M./New York: Campus, 2007.

Latour, Bruno. "The Powers of Associations." *Power, Action and Belief: A New Sociology of Knowledge? Sociological Review Monograph* 32. Ed. John Law. London/Boston/Henley: Routledge & Kegan Paul, 1986. 264–280.

Latour, Bruno. "On Interobjectivity." *Mind, Culture, and Activity* 3.4 (1996): 228–245.

Latour, Bruno. *Pandora's Hope: Essays on the Reality of Science Studies.* Cambridge, MA/London: Harvard University Press, 1999.

Latour, Bruno. "When Things Strike Back: A Possible Contribution of 'Science Studies' to the Social Sciences." *British Journal of Sociology* 51.1 (2000): 107–123.

Latour, Bruno. *Reassembling the Social: An Introduction to Actor-Network-Theory.* Oxford: Oxford University Press, 2005.

Latour, Bruno. "Gabriel Tarde und das Ende des Sozialen." *Soziologie der Nachahmung und des Begehrens. Materialien zu Gabriel Tarde.* Eds. Christian Borch and Urs Stäheli. Frankfurt a.M.: Suhrkamp, 2009. 39–61.

Lau, Kin-chi, Po-keung Hui, and Shun-hing Chan. "The Politics of Translation and Accountability: A Hong Kong Story." *Specters of the West and Politics of Translation.* Eds. Naoki Sakai and Yukiko Hanawa. Ithaca: Cornell University, 2001. 241–267.

Lepenies, Wolf. *Die zwei Kulturen. Soziologie zwischen Literatur und Wissenschaft.* Frankfurt a.M.: Fischer, 2006 [1985].

Lindner, Rolf. *Die Entdeckung der Stadtkultur. Soziologie aus der Erfahrung der Reportage.* Frankfurt a.M.: Suhrkamp, 1990.

Oakeshott, Michael. *On Human Conduct.* Oxford: Clarendon Press, 1978.

Pickering, Andrew. *The Mangle of Practice: Time, Agency, and Science.* Chicago/London: Chicago University Press, 1995.

Plé, Bernhard. "Das Übersetzen als Moment kultureller Austauschprozesse: das Problem der Empathie." *Sozialwissenschaftliches Übersetzen als interkulturelle Hermeneutik – Il tradurre nelle scienze sociali come ermeneutica interculturale.* Eds. Arnold Zingerle and Gabriele Cappai. Milan/Berlin: Franco Angeli and Duncker & Humblot, 2003. 287–324.

Pratt, Mary Louise. *Imperial Eyes: Travel Writing and Transculturation.* London: Routledge, 1992.

Radtke, Frank-Olaf. "Lob der Gleich-Gültigkeit. Probleme der Konstruktion des Fremden im Diskurs des Multikulturalismus." *Das Eigene und das Fremde. Neuer Rassismus in der Alten Welt?* Ed. Ulrich Bielefeld. Hamburg: Junius, 1991. 79–96.

Renn, Joachim. "Die Übersetzung der modernen Gesellschaft. Das Problem der Einheit der Gesellschaft und die Pragmatik des Übersetzens." *Übersetzung als Medium des Kultur-*

verstehens und sozialer Integration. Eds. Joachim Renn, Jürgen Straub, and Shingo Shimada. Frankfurt a.M./New York: Campus, 2002. 183–214.

Renn, Joachim. *Übersetzungsverhältnisse. Perspektiven einer pragmatistischen Gesellschaftstheorie*. Weilerswist: Velbrück, 2006.

Rheinberger, Hans-Jörg. *Toward a History of Epistemic Things: Synthesizing Proteins in the Test Tube*. Stanford: Stanford University Press, 1997.

Sakai, Naoki. *Voices of the Past: The Status of Language in Eighteenth-Century Japanese Discourse*. Ithaca/London: Cornell University Press, 1991.

Sakai, Naoki. *Translation and Subjectivity: On "Japan" and Cultural Nationalism*. Minneapolis/London: University of Minnesota Press, 1997.

Sakai, Naoki. "The Dislocation of the West." *Specters of the West and Politics of Translation*. Eds. Naoki Sakai and Yukiko Hanawa (*Traces: A Multilingual Journal of Cultural Theory and Translation*). Ithaca: Cornell University, 2001. 71–91.

Sakai, Naoki. "Translation and the Schematism of Bordering." Paper for the Conference *Gesellschaft übersetzen: Eine Kommentatorenkonferenz*. University of Konstanz: October 2009. http://www.translating-society.de/conference/papers/2/ (28 October 2013).

Sakai, Naoki. "Translation as a Filter." *Transeuropéennes: Revue internationale de pensée critique* (2010). http://www.transeuropeennes.eu/en/articles/200/Translation_as_a-_filter (28 October 2013).

Sakai, Naoki, and Jon Solomon. "Introduction: Addressing the Multitude of Foreigners, Echoing Foucault." *Translation, Biopolitics, Colonial Differences*. Eds. Naoki Sakai and Jon Solomon. Hong Kong: Hong Kong University Press, 2006. 1–35.

Sakai, Naoki, and Yukiko Hanawa, eds. *Specters of the West and Politics of Translation* (*Traces: A Multilingual Journal of Cultural Theory and Translation*). Ithaca: Cornell University, 2001.

Saussure, Ferdinand de. *Course in General Linguistics*. London: Owen, 1960.

Schreiber, Michael. "Loyalität und Literatur – Zur Anwendung des Loyalitätsbegriffs auf die literarische Übersetzung." *Übersetzen – Translating – Traduire. Towards a "Social Turn"?* Ed. Michaela Wolf. Münster/Vienna: Lit, 2006. 79–87.

Schütz, Alfred. "The Stranger." *American Journal of Sociology* 49.6 (1944): 499–507.

Simmel, Georg. *Philosophy of Money*. Ed. David Frisby. London/New York: Routledge, 1978.

Spivak, Gayatri Chakravorty. "Reading the Satanic Verses." *Outside in the Teaching Machine*. New York/London: Routledge, 1993. 217–241.

Tarde, Gabriel. *On Communication and Social Influence: Selected Papers*. Ed. Terry N. Clark. Chicago: University of Chicago Press, 1969.

Tarde, Gabriel. *Monadologie und Soziologie*. Mit einem Vorwort von Bruno Latour. Frankfurt a.M.: Suhrkamp, 2009.

"Translating Society: A Commentator's Conference." October 29–31, 2009. University of Konstanz. http://www.translating-society.de (16 December 2013).

Van Vaerenbergh, Leona. "Die funktionale und kommunikative Dimension des Übersetzens: Funktionalistische und kognitive Translationstheorien im Vergleich." *Übersetzen – Translating – Traduire. Towards a "Social Turn"?* Ed. Michaela Wolf. Münster/Vienna: Lit, 2006. 99–108.

Venuti, Lawrence. *The Translator's Invisibility: A History of Translation*. New York/London: Routledge, 1995.

Welsch, Wolfgang. "Transkulturalität – Lebensformen nach der Auflösung der Kulturen." *Dialog der Kulturen. Die multikulturelle Gesellschaft und die Medien*. Eds. Kurt Luger and Rudi Renger. Vienna et al.: Österreichischer Kunst- und Kulturverlag, 1994. 147–169.

Zingerle, Arnold. "Was geschah zwischen Gaetano Moscas 'Elementi di scienza politica' (1923) und Franz Borkenaus Übersetzung 'Die herrschende Klasse' (1950)? Lehren aus einer Übersetzungsgeschichte." *Sozialwissenschaftliches Übersetzen als interkulturelle Hermeneutik – Il tradurre nelle scienze sociali come ermeneutica interculturale*. Eds. Arnold Zingerle and Gabriele Cappai. Milan/Berlin: Franco Angeli and Duncker & Humblot, 2003. 287–324.

Doris Bachmann-Medick
From Hybridity to Translation

Reflections on Travelling Concepts[*]

1 The (Transnational) Study of Culture as a "Study of Transportation?"

"Once again: in the crystallized world system, everything is subject to the compulsion of movement. Wherever one looks in the great comfort structure, one finds each and every inhabitant being urged to constant mobilization," writes the German philosopher Peter Sloterdijk in his book *In the World Interior of Capital*; yet – as he continues – "none of what changes and moves still has the quality of 'history'" (Sloterdijk 2013: 249). How can the study of culture contribute to a re-entry of history into this global circulation? For instance, how can awareness of contexts, local relations, and uneven developments, and, hence, the capacity for acting and intervening be maintained?

Globalized circumstances demand the development of new, transnational positions for the study of culture, its concepts and theories. The field is complex. On the one hand, concepts used in an intercultural study of culture set their sights on the power of global circulations. On the other hand, such concepts themselves cannot be taken out of these spheres of circulation. In particular, this applies to so-called 'travelling concepts,' which can all too easily be considered as global passageways of knowledge since, in their circulation, "they don't bring with them the field of production of which they are a product" (Bourdieu 1999: 221). But what does the metaphor of 'travelling concepts' actually mean, as it has been developed, above all, by Edward Said, Mieke Bal, and James Clifford (cf. Said 1983; Bal 2002; Clifford 1989, 1997)?

If, traditionally, key concepts and theories were predominantly 'at home' in western academia, they are being sent on a journey in the face of transnational challenges. They are being appropriated, reinterpreted, and altered in other, often non-European, places. Does this lead to a critical 'displacement' of west-

---
[*] My thanks go to Joanna White for the translation of this text.

ern European theory or, even, to its "provincializing," as Dipesh Chakrabarty puts it (cf. Chakrabarty 2000)? This is questionable, at least so long as the concept of 'travelling concepts' itself remains imprisoned in the tradition of a European history of travel, discovery, and expansion. This tradition has long been associated with concepts of mobility, flexibility, conquest, and expansionist ambition, which are not only eurocentric but also construed as middle-class and male dominated.[1]

This association even comes across in Goethe's talk of an "intellectual commerce" or "free spiritual trade" ("freier geistiger Handelsverkehr") in the early nineteenth century as a precondition for the development of an emerging World Literature. Certainly, with its supposition of an autonomously productive cosmopolitan individual, this concept might be considered as hardly suitable for times of global mass migrations. In such times as ours, the migration of concepts and theories also seems to run more along the lines of the commodity circulation of goods that is not "geistig" any more. To ask a provocative question, are concepts in the study of culture commensurate with consumer brands produced in the West (such as Coca-Cola or McDonalds)? After all, even these brands increase their rate of global circulation by making concessions to local circumstances – as can be seen in the appearance of a Ramadan-Burger and Barbie Dolls in saris in India. These marketing analogies cannot be overlooked, especially when one accepts – with Peter Sloterdijk – the "process of modernity as a project in transportation" (Sloterdijk 2013: 62). Accepting this could possibly lead to an understanding of the study of culture in general as a "study of transportation" ("Verkehrswissenschaft"), following globalization's increased demands for mobility. Anthropologist James Clifford's talk of new "ways of looking at culture (along with tradition and identity) in terms of travel relations" also resonates here (Clifford 1997: 25). Clifford, however, connects this to a critical approach: He maintains that concepts such as culture, tradition, and identity should not be fixed in national structures of transmission, but rather be developed in their contexts of intercultural contact.

At this point, going down the mobility route and following the paths of an intensified "nomadic criticism" (Braidotti 2011) would seem the obvious choice. But precisely here would be the place to stop and call the competence of inter/disciplinary as well as regional studies to mind. In this way, the rather free-floating key terms of cultural mobility (transit, travel, transfer) could be anchored more regionally and historically to avoid letting 'travelling concepts'

---

1 Cf. Wolff 1993: 224, 230; for a critique of the travel metaphor in favor of 'displacement' as a more adequate category to analyze mass migration, cf. Kaplan 1996: 3.

become seamlessly inserted into the "ungrounded movement" (Wolff 1993: 235) of the global sphere of circulation. And here a second dimension of 'travelling concepts' comes into play: Concepts and theories are *only* generated through travel. They are rounded out, take detours, overlap with other concepts, and even experience breaks. This does not happen in a vacuum, but in the field of relations between one's own and other regional academic traditions, with their different social conditions of origin.

The magic word 'mobility' is, thus, powerless unless the theories and concepts we work with become 'localized.' Area studies, with its certain mode of cultural and social 'groundedness,' seems particularly suited to this task of localization. What is meant here is its regional competence, which openly takes up the mode of systematic questioning practiced by a transnational or comparative study of culture, whilst at the same time being able to 'ground' this empirically. Is the study of culture, thus, not rather a 'study of translation' precisely because it dislocates transit, travel, and transfer from the well-worn tradition of western travel and, instead, strengthens categories of rupture such as translation and transformation; because it incorporates detours, displacements, breaks, obstacles; and because it shows how concepts only blaze their trails through these very distortions and hybrid overlapping by way of translations as transformations? Therefore, instead of transportation studies, I advocate a (transnational) study of culture as translation studies, which perhaps provides new impulses for the analysis of travelling concepts.

2 The Unbearable Lightness of the Concept 'Travelling Concepts'

In earlier times, concepts were treated as luggage to be stowed away. Today they have themselves become travelers. But what has happened to their carriers, intermediaries, and brokers? At the same time, talk of their cosmopolitan circulation seems to render them seemingly harmless. At what point does their active role in producing inequalities of power and asymmetries of knowledge become visible? Such questions are raised by the very concept of 'travelling concepts.' It is remarkable to what extent this concept itself has already become a kind of theory on the move, becoming more and more depersonalized over time, separated from people and occurrences of mediation.

Edward Said, in his famous essay "Traveling Theory" (1983), started from an understanding of theory explicitly connected to people. He sketched out how Georg Lukács' Marxist theories of reification and revolutionary class consciousness has been passed on by different people and through various places: starting in Hungary in 1919, travelling via Paris after World War II through Lukács' pupil Lucien Goldmann, and moving on to England with the help of Raymond Williams in Birmingham. In the process, however, the rebellious, critical content of the original theory was – as Said maintains – "during its peregrinations [...] reduced, codified, and institutionalized" (1983: 339). Above all, it became depoliticized, moderated, and "tamed" (Said 1983: 238). According to Said, this shows how essential it is to always link a theory with the specific social and historical circumstances of its space of production and reception (cf. 1983: 278). Theory alone cannot do this. One also needs critical consciousness in order to apply theory with an awareness of its political location and context as well as possible "resistances to theory," and one needs "to open it up toward historical reality, toward society, toward human needs and interests" (Said 1983: 242): "we distinguish theory from critical consciousness by saying that the latter is a sort of spatial sense. A sort of measuring faculty for locating or situating theory" (Said 1983: 241, see also the revision of his own originally too linear perception of travelling theories, Said 1994).

Locating theories and the investigation of their respective spatial, historical relations, therefore, seem to be essential.[2] It seems surprising in this context how light-heartedly the journey of the concept of 'travelling theory' or 'travelling concepts' itself has proceeded through the hands of Homi Bhabha, Mieke Bal, James Clifford and others, on a journey appearing to be virtually placeless and barrier free. How has this been possible? As Clifford noted in a distancing and somewhat cynical form of critique vis-à-vis Said, theory does not have to travel in an "immigrant boat" anymore; it is transmitted, rather, in a non-linear mode of production, circulation, and reception: It "takes the plane, sometimes with round-trip tickets" (Clifford 1989). Against this figurative explanation, I would like to argue that the concept has become ubiquitous because the metaphor of 'travelling theory' has fallen into the clutches of a worn-out concept of 'hybridity.' The concept of hybridity, as it has entered the mainstream of theory discussions worldwide, celebrates perhaps all too quickly both the blending and borderlessness of global relations, and the eclectic exchangeability of theoretical positions.[3] Perhaps we should investigate the routes travelled by the

---

2 As a convincing example for a location of theory in the specific case of Australian cultural studies, cf. Christa Knellwolf King's contribution to this volume.
3 For a critical reconsideration of the concept and the patterns of hybridity, the contemporary "hybridity talk" and the "anti-hybridity backlash," cf. Pieterse 2001.

category of hybridity itself with a more critical eye – and hereby reach a point at which the importance of the category of 'translation' becomes apparent.

3 Routes of 'Hybridity'

As is well-known, hybridity has many faces: On the one hand, it is a specific concept (a synonym for complex systems and for a negotiation – not a fixing – of differences in a 'third space'). On the other hand, hybridity is also a mode of a concept's movement itself, and, moreover, stands for a transnational form of blending communication in a globalized world. Today's understanding of hybridity, however, represents just one particular stage in a surprisingly long journey – from nineteenth-century biology right up to post-colonial and postmodern cultural theory, with the following stages:

The 'origin' of this concept (if it makes sense at all to speak of 'origins' in matters of hybridity) lies in the racist discourse of nineteenth century biology. Here, hybridity asserted miscegenation and became a term of racial discrimination (cf. Young 1995). However, already in the field of biology, as it evolved at the time, a turnaround to a positive revaluation of impurity was taking place – due to the theory of evolution and the discovery of Mendel's laws. Hybrid breeds and gene combinations were recognized as sources of innovation. Thus, it stood to reason for literary studies and the humanities to also answer the question of how novelty is generated by pointing to the mixing of, and even the tensions between, differences.

On its journey through linguistic fields, hybridity was also taken up as a positive term, above all by Mikhail Bakhtin in his essay "Discourse in the Novel" from the mid-1930s (1981: 259–422). Here, important foundations were laid for the development of the concept in postmodernism and postcolonialism later on. "What is a hybridization? It is a mixture of two social languages within the limits of a single utterance, an encounter [...] between two different linguistic consciousnesses, separated from one another by an epoch, by social differentiation or by some other factor" (Bakhtin 1981: 358). What is meant here is not a harmonious *mélange*. The reference is rather to a dialogic confrontation or "collision between differing points of views on the world," which "consciously fight it out on the territory of the utterance" (Bakhtin 1981: 360). Bakhtin's battlefield is the novel in its polyphony. The unified, canonical language of a national culture, the hegemonic standard language with all the power of its traditions can be shattered – precisely through hybridization, that is to say, through exposure to "social heteroglossia [...] where the dialogue of voices arises directly out of a social dialogue of 'languages'" (Bakhtin 1981: 284–285). The baroque novel, for example, uses irony, parody, and satire to relativize the dominating standard language as well as heroic poetic genres. These are provided with a "polemic counterpoint" through the incursion of everyday genres such as the letter, the diary, the ego-document and conversation and, above all, a variety of social languages into the world of the novel. Through this kind of "tension-filled interaction" (Bakhtin 1981: 279), which produces collisions instead of mere mixings, the novel deliberately refers back to the capacity of social groups to articulate themselves and their differences. Linguistic hybridization, thus, shifts the power of articulation to a certain extent, aiming to empower marginalized groups and subjects to articulate their own forms of cultural self-expression.

Leading on from Bakhtin's questioning of the authority of dominant discourses, hybridity has been pushed by Edward Said and Homi Bhabha into a new field of enquiry, by being developed as the key concept for a postcolonial theory of culture (cf. Beecroft 2001: 217). They have questioned the discourse of a one-sided authority of colonialism, seeing the colonial constellation itself as hybridized – as an ambivalent, two-way interaction between the colonizer and the colonized. More can be read about the journey of the hybridity concept itself in Robert Young's study on *Postcolonialism* (Young 2001). In the following, however, I will emphasize and criticize a dominant, reductionist aspect: the epistemologization and, with it, the de-politicization and de-historization of this concept.

It is true that the postcolonial career of the hybridity concept may well have begun with historical-political impulses arising from the 'original scene' of hybridized colonial relations with their unequal power structures. But, increasingly, hybridity's horizon has been narrowed down to the level of mere representations, leading to shifts in the dominant regime of signs. Even culture in general has, in this way, come to be seen as fundamentally hybrid, internally contradictory and multi-layered, whereby the center and peripheries overlap and mix in dynamic tension.

This nowadays well-known insight has methodological consequences, not least for a trans/national study of culture. It suggests the need to de-essentialize key terms such as race, nation, modernity, identity, etc. and to critically pry them open as generalizations. A polyphonic identity is no longer at issue, as was still the case with Bakhtin. Rather, there is a complete departure from the notion of 'identity' itself. The focus has shifted to multiple codings and the scope for change in occupying an 'in-between' position: Only an "interstitial passage between fixed identifications" – according to Homi Bhabha – "opens up the possibility of a cultural hybridity that entertains difference without an assumed or imposed hierarchy" (Bhabha 1994: 4). And yet this kind of productive 'in-between' space is still not conceptualized enough in terms of spatiality; instead, it is conceived as an epistemological dimension. Historical subjects come too little into focus as actors. They are figured, instead, as "junctions or crossing points in languages, orders, discourses and systems" (Bronfen and Marius 1997: 4).

Restricted to the level of signs and representations, the hybridity concept currently seems to be losing itself ever more in a de-spatialized and de-historicized sphere of theory. Although Homi Bhabha developed his understanding of hybridity in the context of migration, he has neglected the concrete conditions of migration, which are accompanied by a large degree of suffering. In contrast, he overestimates the creativity and power of innovation that he ascribes to the hybrid overlapping of different affiliations. The destabilization of fixed categories, which is Bhabha's critical aim, is thus robbed of its historical grounding. As Edward Said in his critique of 'orientalism,' Bhabha also uses the concept of hybridity to counter dichotomies (the self and the other, colonizer and colonized, Europe and Orient). At this junction on its journey into the transnational study of culture, the concept of hybridity has definitely met the path of western deconstructive theory: A travelling back to the West has taken place – in spite of the postcolonial signposts put up by Said and Bhabha.

Why has the concept of hybridity at all been so successful in the West? To be sure, it fits more easily into world-capitalist mobility flows because of its placelessness. It is not only the Ford car company's ad-slogan, "Feel the difference" – one of many other difference-celebrating advertisements – that shows how hybridity has found its way into the world-capitalist marketing strategies of a transglobal consumer culture. Here the 'different' has become a kind of 'selling concept' within a market of the conformist mainstream.[4] What remains of subversion and critique – one has to ask – in this permanent, neoliberal assertion of flexibility? Has everything really become hybrid? Has the concept of hybridity, too, become so boundless that even theory formation itself has been hybridized – as, for example, one can see in the overlapping between different cultural turns (cf. Bachmann-Medick 2014)?

What needs to be done to lead hybridity's journey through different contexts out of its flattened, epistemological dead-end? Travelling theories – I would suggest – need to be explicitly followed up along their journey through processes of cultural translation: "Traveling theories, in other words, have to go through translation" (Mignolo 2000: 210). It is no coincidence that this quote

---

4 For a massive critique of 'hybridity' as a dominant phenomenon of cultural industry in the context of capitalist commodification cf. Ha 2005.

comes from a scholar of Latin American studies, Walter Mignolo, who draws our attention to the Latin American transformation of 'hybridity.' To me, this seems to offer a particularly strong impetus for further historical-political development of the concept.

The hybridity concept's Latin American journey has taken place on extremely winding and manifold paths. One of these paths has been opened up by the reception of Bakhtin in Brazil in the 1970s. This interesting incursion, to date, has largely been ignored in favor of the US-American reception of Bakhtin with its celebration of 'polyphony.' Above all, in Brazil, the so-called "anthropophagy movement," which can be traced back to the 1920s, has called not merely for hybrid mixings, but also explicitly for an irreverent, cannibalistic assimilation of European traditions and hegemonies from a local perspective of resistance (cf. Oswald de Andrade's "Cannibalist Manifesto" of 1928). Translation is understood here as appropriative and all-consuming. In this tradition, Bakhtin's notion of the "carnivalesque" has adopted a new costume. This occurs precisely through a decentering of accustomed notions of Europe and Latin America, center and periphery, and original and translation. It has taken place prominently in the sphere of Latin American concrete poetry and in practices of willful plagiarism and parody. But, beyond this, it has been developed as a more general 'cannibalistic' cultural style that can also be found in contemporary fields of social critique and sociologically relevant organizational appropriations in Brazil (cf. Islam 2012). In this context, Brazilian organizational studies – as the article "Can the Subaltern Eat?" illustrates – have considered an "anthropophagous model of cultural portability" explicitly as a self-conscious and creative practice of the implementation of managerial techniques from the U.S. and Europe (Islam 2012: 172).

Another path towards establishing a socially effective elaboration of the 'hybrid' leads to the Argentinian cultural theorist Néstor García Canclini living in Mexico. He writes not of hybridity in general, but rather of the dynamics of hybridization, based on the conflict-ridden processes of transformation of a whole nation or network of nations, peoples, and social groups in their everyday relationships:

> One also encounters economic and symbolic reconversion strategies in the popular sectors: rural migrants who adapt their knowledges in order to work and consume in the city, or who connect their traditional craftwork with modern uses in order to interest urban buyers; workers who reformulate their culture on the job in the face of new technologies of production; indigenous movements that renovate their demands in transnational politics or in an ecological discourse and learn to communicate these demands via radio, television, and the Internet. For reasons such as these, I maintain that the object of study is not hybridity but the processes of hybridization. (Canclini 1995: xxvii)

In contrast to Bhabha, concrete social and economic problem-fields, skills, and practices are studied here, above all in the context of urbanization. Canclini's own work is based on rural migrants who, in the cities, have to adapt their traditional knowledge and handicraft know-how to modern, urban technologies of production and the mass media.

The key point here is that these occurrences of hybridity in the context of urbanization are not conceived of as mixings but rather as translations, since they involve strategies in which exclusions also occur. The question of "what is left out of the fusion" (Canclini 1995: xxvii) arises when one is confronted with the resistant, contradictory, or conflictual.[5] These challenges emerge when traditional patterns of behavior assert themselves in areas of advanced technology and postmodern social processes under conditions of globalization. When there is talk of Hispano-Americanization in relation to the ownership of banks, airlines and telecommunications, then the concept of hybridity has clearly left the field of mere cultural and textual representation.

Hybridity moves on to become a main category of empirical sociological and historical analysis – merging at this point with the more precise category of translation. Spelled out as hybridization, it becomes a "comparative concept" in a wider context of "comparative cultural studies" (Clifford 1997: 18), which seems to be an important approach for any transnational study of culture. Precisely in the sense of a "translation term" (Clifford 1997: 11, esp. 39),[6] the concept could be used to critically question the notion of a pure, authentic identity: "These diverse, ongoing processes of hybridization lead to a relativizing of the notion of identity" (Canclini 1995: xxviii). Under the sign of 'translation,' this cultural-theoretical kind of questioning shows how hybridization and self-hybridization are actively carried out, in particular in the fields of social integration and migration (cf. Renn 2006; Fuchs 2009). But also, to mark the space of a transnational circulation of theory itself, processes of translation can become

---

5 For Canclini, hybridization means explicitly a process of uncovering conflicts instead of describing mere fusions. It "rather can be helpful in accounting for particular forms of conflict generated in recent cross-cultural contact and in the context of the decline of national modernization projects in Latin America" (Canclini 1995: xxiv).

6 "I consider it attractive to treat hybridization as a translation term along with syncretism, fusion, and other words employed to designate particular kinds of mixing. Perhaps the decisive issue is not how to come to an agreement about which of those concepts is most inclusive and fertile but how to continue constructing theoretical principles and methodological procedures that can help us make the world more translatable, which is to say more cohabitable in the midst of differences, and to accept at the same time what each of us gains and loses through hybridization" (Canclini 1995: xliii).

eye-openers for the different receptions and transformations of the model of hybridity in various knowledge traditions and intellectual cultures.[7]

4 Translation and the Reclamation of Historical Contexts

But which understanding of translation is actually at work here? Certainly, this understanding has also travelled far: from its uses in the philological-linguistic sphere through the perspective of cultural translation as a dimension of every cultural encounter to the field of social conflicts and processes of negotiation. Jürgen Habermas, for example, recently called on religious communities in post-secular societies to "translate" their religious language into a publicly accessible secular language (cf. Habermas 2006). The sociologist Joachim Renn bases an entire conception of sociology on "relations of translation" – especially concerning a new approach to processes of integration (cf. Renn 2006). Migration, too, has recently been reinterpreted in terms of translational action and the necessity for active self-translation in situations of multiple cultural belongings.[8] In more obviously textual terms, the Translation Studies scholar Susan Bassnett talks about "Translating Terror" (Bassnett 2005) and Sherry Simon deals with *Cities in Translation* (Simon 2012). Countless other examples – such as Robert Stam and Ella Shohat's *Race in Translation* (2012) – demonstrate the huge range of areas of inquiry within the study of culture, which currently make use of the category of translation.

Many of these specific uses assume that there is more to the translation category than just the use of 'translation' as a mere metaphor – as, for example, in the general talk of migration as translation, or culture as translation. Such inflationary metaphorical uses need to be broken down into the investigation of interaction scenarios in their concrete steps of translational activities, transmissions, negotiations, and mediations. In this sense, travelling concepts can also be grounded historically, by following their trails in specific empirical case studies (see, for example, Matthias Middell's contribution in this volume). They can be connected not only to the mediating practices of subjects but also to the

---

7 On the specific "transfer" and transformation of the model of hybridity within German theoretical discourse, cf. Standke 2008.
8 Cf. the debate on "Translation and Migration" in the Forum of the journal *Translation Studies* 5.3 (2012), 6.1 (2013), 6.3 (2013).

whole chain of translations via institutions, instruments, and technical conditions that have long been ignored in their active mediating function: Travelling concepts are, thus, constituted in a translational "collective" – in terms of Bruno Latour's actor-network theory (also discussed in Andreas Langenohl's contribution in this volume).[9] Only by elaborating such multidimensional findings into a dissecting approach can 'translation' serve as a new analytical category and a category of action itself – two important steps towards the emerging interdisciplinary "translational turn" in the humanities and social sciences (Bachmann-Medick 2009; 2014).

In such elaborated and concretized new understandings of 'translation,' a change from a deeply flawed concept of hybridity to translation can be located. On the one hand, this change is affirmed by increasingly complex global lifeworlds themselves. On the other hand, it marks an important conceptual shift in the field of the study of culture: It may turn out to be more productive to look at travelling concepts not through the model of hybridization but through the model of translation. Why? An understanding of travelling concepts along the model of hybridity has the disadvantage that it often lacks precise contextualizations und historicizations and leaves universalizing assumptions unreflected. Thus, for example, western feminism has regarded women in the countries outside Europe and the U.S. as a homogenous, monolithic, oppressed group. This happened with a western lens still part of the colonial discourse "Under Western Eyes," as Chandra Talpade Mohanty has critically phrased it in her famous and influential essay of 1988 (Mohanty 2003: 17–42, 255–257) and in her revisited version of 2003 (Mohanty 2003: 221–251, 270–273).[10] The focus of her critique reaches beyond a questionable extrapolation of universalist lines, based on the assumption of shared, hybridized concepts under the guise of "solidarity" with these groups. It exposes a still dominating research practice that operates in the mode of "the global hegemony of Western scholarship –

---

9 In the volume Czarniawska and Sevón (2005), numerous examples for a detailed analysis of singular steps and phases in translation processes can be found. Though elaborated in the field of management studies, this specific method of a detailed translational analysis can be applied to other phenomena in the study of culture.

10 Mohanty's revision of her classic article entitled "'Under Western Eyes' Revisited: Feminist Solidarity through Anticapitalist Struggles" can really be considered a translational research practice of its own. Working towards a "comparative feminist studies model" (Mohanty 2003: 238), Mohanty translates the insights of her former article into the changed political and economic global framework at the beginning of the new millennium: "Perhaps it is no longer simply an issue of Western eyes, but rather how the West is inside and continually reconfigures globally, racially, and in terms of gender" (Mohanty 2003: 236).

that is, the production, publication, distribution, and consumption of information and ideas" (Mohanty 2003: 21).

This mode has been countered by explicitly differentiating concepts that call for a "politics of location" (Rich 1986: 210, 215), "situated knowledges" (Haraway 1988), and "situated theories" (Hoving 2001: 198). On the corresponding levels of political activism, new light has been shed on different forms and self-representations of feminism in specific world regions (cf. Basu 2010). Such insights into the workings of localized concepts and local practices could be deepened further through the investigation of localizing processes of translation. Hereby, a focus on local or regional reinterpretations of universalistic umbrella terms – for instance, human rights – could be seen as a productive strategy. It has already been pointed out that universal corridors of translation can enable marginalized groups or societies to make strategic and, at the same time, practically useful claims for their rights: environmental, general human as well as civil political rights (cf. Tsing 1997; Bachmann-Medick 2013).

This ambivalence between universalism, on the one hand, and "situated theories" and their application, on the other, surely has to do with historical rupture and "displacement" caused by colonialism: "what happens when theories travel through the colonial difference?" (Mignolo 2000: 173). In this case – as Walter Mignolo has maintained – 'travelling theories' can easily be turned into catalysts for new forms of intellectual colonialism. Mignolo's critical counter-question is: "Where are theories produced? Where do they come from?" [...] What is the ratio between geohistorical location and knowledge production?" (Mignolo 2000: 173). Where and in what context does the theory in question arise and what role does it play in its place of origin, and at its destination? Translation becomes a crucial practice for connecting (universalizing) concepts back to historical life-worlds and "local histories." This means that people enter the stage as cultural brokers and insert themselves into theories' travels. By their actions, connections, renunciations, fears, and self-assertions they open up spaces for intervention, not least for accentuating gender-oriented dimensions in theories' travels.

With reference to this dimension of agents, actions, and interactions, the concept of 'travelling concepts' gains even wider practical and historical relevance by including "travelling objects/facts" (Howlett and Morgan 2011; Czarniawska and Sevón 2005) and especially by turning towards different "travelling traditions" (Pannewick 2010), such as storytelling, and focusing on "travelling debates" (Stam and Shohat 2005), such as debates on multiculturalism, postcolonialism, race (Stam and Shohat 2012), and diversity (Lammert and Sarkowsky 2010). This brings another question to the fore: How are travelling concepts passed on in concrete terms? Here we should look more carefully at the differences between cultural semantics, knowledge traditions, and knowledge gaps. But we should also concentrate on the smaller units of social interactions, on misunderstandings, or even battles over interpretation. Ultimately, travelling concepts are actively in motion: They are appropriated, gain ground, or are turned away; they are made to stay or get thrown out. Sweeping statements about (automatic) circulation, distribution, diffusion, and mixing in an information-networked world do not help us here. They have to give way to precise contextualizing analyses and new insights into the ruptures or resistances involved in local appropriations.

Only in this way will it become at all possible to dislodge western theories, so to speak, with the help of these theories themselves. Research should aim for intersections that could serve as new locations for the production of theory in transnational constellations and co-operations. 'Travelling concepts,' which have strong links to the practical sphere, do indeed constitute such intersections. I am thinking of the concept of 'empowerment' here, which has increasingly been moving away from its beginnings as a critical grass-roots concept of environmental movements and farmers' protests in India, towards becoming a mainstream term utilized by official UN-development programs. But this happened with the consequence that what was originally self-empowerment has then come to stand for a paternalistic bestowal of rights. 'Sustainability' has also travelled in a similar way. It is no longer merely a normative principle of critical environmental policy. It has found its way into the mission statements of multinational companies, the business models of their Corporate Social Responsibility (CSR) programs, and their annual "sustainability reports" as – for example – with the German detergent company Henkel. If in the social sciences the current suggestion is for "translating sustainability into the principles of ecological justice" (Leist 2007), one should critically ask: What does this translation really amount to?

In this context of intersections and connectivities, it seems especially urgent to follow the translational transformations by which the travelling of the concept of human rights is characterized today. Human rights are western in origin, as they imply individualization and secularization. Beyond this, one should imagine human rights as a multi-vocal, diverse, and unsettled field of contending ideas. They can only be considered as basic rights in a transnational world when they are localized and regionalized outside Europe and developed out of transnational constellations of translation (cf. Merry 2006; for a wider reflection on human rights as a problem of translation, cf. Bachmann-Medick 2013). For example: The conflicts surrounding the building of the Narmada dam in India have shown how questions of human rights can be connected to concrete, local disputes about eco-social justice. This dam destroyed the means of existence of thousands of small-scale farmers and, in the process, it gave rise to a powerful protest movement in which human rights came to be reformulated as environmental rights (cf. Linkenbach 2014).

Concepts can, therefore, be translated into real life contexts through both their localization and historicization. The actual appropriation of 'travelling concepts' takes place on a social and political level (creating debates or even conflicts), not just on the level of discourse in the academic community. It seems to be essential, therefore, for a transnational study of culture to open to worldwide demands for acknowledging different traditions of knowledge and research and their pragmatic impact. In this process, one not only encounters other theories but also, perhaps, wholly other conceptions of what theory even means. This becomes visible only when spaces of theory are not separated off as spaces of reflection but are 'translated' into social fields of appropriation. It is in this respect that we come, finally, to a third meaning of 'travelling concepts': The key task in transnational times is not to send concepts on a journey but, instead, to develop them at productive intersections 'between' disciplines and cultural formations in the first place. The various conceptual 'cultural turns,' for example, can be considered as embodiments of translational procedures. From this point of view, they can be associated with culturally different ideas of "epistemic spaces" and are, therefore, particularly suited to a transnational study of culture, assuming, however, that they can be re-localized within disciplines and regions.

Within this perspective, one could finally try to find an alternative to the hybridized understanding of 'travelling concepts' that has dominated the discussion so far. An approach that takes us further in this direction is that of the multilingual book series in the field of cultural theory, *Traces,* which gives attention to the global production of theory in all its disparate sites and places of production at once – that is, to "global traces in the theoretical knowledge produced in specific locations and [...] constituted in, and transformed by, practical social relations at diverse sites" (Sakai and Solomon 2006: v; see also de Bary 2010). Following this trail might lead to a new, geopolitically reflected, comparative and multilingual cultural theory constituted 'in translation,' as well as to new insights into the co-existences, constellations, and networks of theories. This approach is directed against the colonial, or neo-colonial, one-way streets of travelling theories (which too often travel from the U.S. to Europe or other parts of the world).[11]

---

11 "Since its inception, *Traces* has explicitly sought to provide readers with the elements for a strategic intervention into the neo-colonial distribution of theory and data [...] By proposing to

To sum up: Instead of 'travelling concepts,' it might perhaps be better to speak of 'concepts in translation' in order to call for more historical grounding and contextualization. This would allow for a more detailed exploration of exactly which social practices and social relations lie behind the specific concepts at issue, which intermediaries are active, and what obstacles and local resistances arise. Will 'cross-categorical translations' become inevitable (because the transnational field exploits and lives off the power of its monopolies on terms and categories)? Partaking in this power are, above all, the research terms and concepts elaborated and used in the western humanities: religion, god, society, state, work, etc. Yet, to what extent are these terms and categories really universally valid? Should not these terms of analysis themselves be explored with more critical regard to their inter-cultural translatability – thus, working toward a "global lexicon" of travelling/translational concepts (cf. first significant approaches in Gluck and Tsing 2009)? To what extent is a "categorical mobility" (Greenblatt et al. 2010: 11) on the level of structures, definitions, and codes really feasible – or, more precisely, can they arrive at what Dipesh Chakrabarty has fruitfully called "cross-categorical translation" (not only cross-cultural translation), as already mentioned in the introduction to this volume (Chakrabarty 2000: 83–86)? And why are 'hybridity/hybridization' and, above all, 'translation,' so important for our line of questioning in this regard? The fact seems crucial that each of these two categories not only represents a specific concept in the study of culture but also a significant mode by which concepts travel (and not only concepts but also people, religious groups, and different forms of cultural articulation). The question, thus, remains: Do we perceive travelling concepts in their convergences and 'immigrations' as hybrid or translated? Do concepts only travel because they are 'translated' by people and intermediaries? Could translation in the sense of trans-location not also mean becoming, at least temporarily, 'settled' in concrete historical and regional surroundings? Follow-up questions like these could pave the way for a "growing two-way traffic" (Sloterdijk 2013: 142), as opposed to just moving along the worn-out western tracks of a transnational transportation network of concepts.

---

provide [...] the same content at the same time to readers in several different language markets, the performative synchronicity created by *Traces* directly intervenes in the field of 'linear progress' and 'developmental stages' invariably favored by the powerful historical narratives of colonial modernity" (Sakai and Solomon 2006: 1).

References

Andrade, Oswald de. "Cannibalist Manifesto." [1928]. Trans. Leslie Bary. *Latin American Literary Review* 19.38 (1991): 38–47.

Anfeng, Sheng. "Traveling Theory, or, Transforming Theory: Metamorphosis of Postcolonialism in China." *Neohelicon* XXXIV.2 (2007): 115–136.

Bachmann-Medick, Doris. "Introduction: The Translational Turn." *Translation Studies* 2.1 (2009) (special issue *The Translational Turn*): 2–16.

Bachmann-Medick, Doris. "The 'Translational Turn' in Literary and Cultural Studies: The Example of Human Rights." *New Theories, Models and Methods in Literary and Cultural Studies.* Eds. Greta Olson and Ansgar Nünning. Trier: WVT, 2013. 213–233 (extended German version: "Menschenrechte als Übersetzungsproblem." *Geschichte und Gesellschaft* 38.2 (2012): 331–359).

Bachmann-Medick, Doris. *Cultural Turns. Neuorientierungen in den Kulturwissenschaften.* 5th edition. Reinbek: Rowohlt, 2014 [2006] (English translation: *Cultural Turns: New Orientations in the Study of Culture.* Berlin/Boston: De Gruyter, 2016).

Bakhtin, Mikhail M. *The Dialogic Imagination: Four Essays.* Ed. Michael Holquist. Austin: University of Texas Press, 1981.

Bal, Mieke. "Introduction: Travelling Concepts and Cultural Analysis." *Travelling Concepts: Text, Subjectivity, Hybridity.* Eds. Joyce Goggin and Sonja Neef. Amsterdam: ASCA, 2001. 7–25.

Bal, Mieke. *Travelling Concepts in the Humanities: A Rough Guide.* Toronto: University of Toronto Press, 2002.

Bary, Brett de. *Universities in Translation: The Mental Labor of Globalization* (Traces 5). Hong Kong: Hong Kong University Press, 2010.

Bassnett, Susan. "Translating Terror." *Third World Quarterly* 26.3 (2005): 393–403.

Basu, Amrita, ed. *Women's Movements in the Global Era: The Power of Local Feminisms.* Boulder/New York: Westview Press, 2010.

Beecroft, Simon. "Mikhail Bakhtin and Postcolonial Hybridity." *Travelling Concepts: Text, Subjectivity, Hybridity.* Eds. Joyce Goggin and Sonja Neef. Amsterdam: ASCA, 2001. 212–223.

Bhabha, Homi K. *The Location of Culture.* London/New York: Routledge, 1994.

Binder, Beate, Ina Kerner, Eveline Kilian, Gabriele Jähnert, and Hildegard Maria Nickel, eds. *Travelling Gender Studies.* Münster: Westfälisches Dampfboot, 2011.

Bourdieu, Pierre. "The Social Conditions of the International Circulation of Ideas." *Bourdieu: A Critical Reader.* Ed. Richard Shusterman. Oxford/Malden, MA: Blackwell, 1999. 220–228.

Braidotti, Rosi. *Nomadic Subjects: Embodiment and Sexual Difference in Contemporary Feminist Theory.* 2nd edition. New York: Columbia University Press, 2011 [1994].

Bronfen, Elisabeth, and Benjamin Marius. "Hybride Kulturen. Einleitung zur anglo-amerikanischen Multikulturalismusdebatte." *Hybride Kulturen. Beiträge zur anglo-amerikanischen Multikulturalismusdebatte.* Eds. Elisabeth Bronfen and Benjamin Marius. Tübingen: Stauffenburg, 1997. 1–30.

Canclini, Néstor García. *Hybrid Cultures: Strategies for Entering and Leaving Modernity.* Minneapolis: University of Minnesota Press, 1995.

Chakrabarty, Dipesh. *Provincializing Europe: Postcolonial Thought and Historical Difference.* Princeton/Oxford: Princeton University Press, 2000.

Clifford, James. "Notes on Travel and Theory." *Inscriptions* 5 (1989) ("Traveling Theories – Traveling Theorists").
http://www2.ucsc.edu/culturalstudies/PUBS/Inscriptions/vol_5/clifford.html (12 August 2013).

Clifford, James. "Traveling Cultures." *Routes: Travel and Translation in the Late Twentieth Century.* Cambridge, MA/London: Harvard University Press, 1997. 17–46.

Czarniawska, Barbara, and Guje Sevón, eds. *Global Ideas: How Ideas, Objects and Practices Travel in the Global Economy.* Malmö: Liber & Copenhagen Business School Press, 2005.

Fuchs, Martin. "Reaching Out; or, Nobody Exists in One Context Only: Society as Translation." *Translation Studies* 2.1 (2009): 21–40.

Gluck, Carol, and Anna Lowenhaupt Tsing, eds. *Words in Motion: Toward a Global Lexicon.* Durham, NC/London: Duke University Press, 2009.

Greenblatt, Stephen, Ines G. Županov, Reinhart Meyer-Kalkus, Heike Paul, Pál Nyíri, and Friederike Pannewick. *Cultural Mobility: A Manifesto.* Cambridge: Cambridge University Press, 2010.

Ha, Kien Ngui. *Hype um Hybridität. Kultureller Differenzkonsum und postmoderne Verwertungstechniken im Spätkapitalismus.* Bielefeld: transcript, 2005.

Habermas, Jürgen. "Religion in the Public Sphere." *European Journal of Philosophy* 14.1 (2006): 1–25.

Haraway, Donna. "Situated Knowledges: The Science Question in Feminism and the Privilege of Partial Perspective." *Feminist Studies* 14.3 (1988): 575–599.

Hoving, Isabel. "Hybridity: A Slippery Trail." *Travelling Concepts: Text, Subjectivity, Hybridity.* Eds. Joyce Goggin and Sonja Neef. Amsterdam: ASCA Press, 2001. 185–201.

Howlett, Peter, and Mary S. Morgan, eds. *How Well Do Facts Travel? The Dissemination of Reliable Knowledge.* Cambridge: Cambridge University Press, 2011.

Hüchtker, Dietlind, and Alfrun Kliems, eds. *Überbringen – Überformen – Überblenden. Theorietransfer im 20. Jahrhundert.* Cologne/Weimar/Vienna: Böhlau, 2011.

Islam, Gazi. "Can the Subaltern Eat? Anthropophagic Culture as a Brazilian Lens on Post-Colonial Theory." *Organization* 19.2 (2012): 159–180.

Kaplan, Caren. *Questions of Travel: Postmodern Discourses of Displacement.* Durham, NC/London: Duke University Press, 1996.

Lammert, Christian, and Katja Sarkowsky, eds. *Travelling Concepts: Negotiating Diversity in Canada and Europe.* Wiesbaden: Springer, 2010.

Leist, Anton. "Ökologische Gerechtigkeit als bessere Nachhaltigkeit." *Das Parlament* 24 (11.6. 2007).

Linkenbach, Antje. "Übersetzungsprozesse. Soziale Bewegungen für Umweltgerechtigkeit in Indien und das Idiom der Menschenrechte." *Menschenrechte und Protest. Zur lokalen Politisierung einer globalen Idee.* Ed. Andreas Pettenkofer. Bielefeld: transcript, 2014.

Merry, Sally Engle. *Human Rights and Gender Violence: Translating International Law into Local Justice.* Chicago/London: University of Chicago Press, 2006.

Mignolo, Walter D. "Are Subaltern Studies Postmodern or Postcolonial? The Politics and Sensibilities of Geohistorical Locations." *Local Histories/Global Designs: Coloniality, Subaltern Knowledges, and Border Thinking.* Princeton: Princeton University Press, 2000. 172–215.

Mohanty, Chandra Talpade. *Feminism without Borders: Decolonizing Theory, Practicing Solidarity.* Durham, NC/London: Duke University Press, 2003.

Neumann, Birgit, and Frederik Tygstrup, eds. *Travelling Concepts* (special issue of *European Journal of English Studies*) 13.1 (2009).

Neumann, Birgit, and Ansgar Nünning, eds. *Travelling Concepts for the Study of Culture*. Berlin/Boston: de Gruyter, 2012.

Pannewick, Friederike. "Performativity and Mobility: Middle Eastern Traditions on the Move." *Cultural Mobility: A Manifesto*. Stephen Greenblatt et al. Cambridge: Cambridge University Press, 2010. 215–249.

Perry, Nick. "Travelling Theory/Nomadic Theorizing." *Organization* 2.1 (1995): 35–54.

Pieterse, Jan Nederveen. "Hybridity, So What? The Anti-Hybridity Backlash and the Riddles of Recognition." *Theory, Culture & Society* 18.2/3 (2001): 219–245.

Pollock, Griselda, ed. *Conceptual Odysseys: Passages to Cultural Analysis*. London/New York: Tauris, 2007.

Renn, Joachim. *Übersetzungsverhältnisse. Perspektiven einer pragmatistischen Gesellschaftstheorie*. Weilerswist: Velbrück, 2006.

Rich, Adrienne. "Notes toward a Politics of Location (1984)." *Blood, Bread, and Poetry: Selected Prose 1979–1985*. New York: Norton, 1986. 210–231.

Said, Edward W. "Traveling Theory (1982)." *The World, the Text, and the Critic*. Cambridge, MA: Harvard University Press, 1983. 226–247.

Said, Edward W. "Traveling Theory Reconsidered (1994)." *Reflections on Exile and Other Essays*. Cambridge, MA: Harvard University Press, 2000. 436–452.

Sakai, Naoki, and Jon Solomon, eds. *Translation, Biopolitics, Colonial Difference*. (*Traces* 4). Hong Kong: Hong Kong University Press, 2006.

Simon, Sherry. *Cities in Translation: Intersections of Language and Memory*. Abingdon/New York: Routledge, 2012.

Sloterdijk, Peter. *In the World Interior of Capital: Towards a Philosophical Theory of Globalization*. Cambridge/Malden, MA: Polity, 2013.

Stam, Robert, and Ella Shohat. "Traveling Multiculturalism: A Trinational Debate in Translation." *Postcolonial Studies and Beyond*. Eds. Ania Loomba, Suvir Kaul, Matti Bunzl, Antoinette Burton, and Jed Esty. Durham, NC/London: Duke University Press, 2005. 293–316.

Stam, Robert, and Ella Shohat. *Race in Translation: Culture Wars Around the Postcolonial Atlantic*. New York/London: New York University Press, 2012.

Standke, Jan. "Hybride Theorien? Transkultureller Theorietransfer in den deutschsprachigen Kulturwissenschaften." *'Meine Sprache grenzt mich ab....' Transkulturalität und kulturelle Übersetzung im Kontext von Migration*. Eds. Gisella M. Vorderobermeier and Michaela Wolf. Münster: Lit Verlag, 2008. 251–272.

Susam-Sarajeva, Şebnem. *Theories on the Move: Translation's Role in the Travel of Literary Theories*. Amsterdam/New York: Rodopi, 2006.

Tsing, Anna Lowenhaupt. "Transitions as Translations." *Transitions, Environments, Translations: Feminisms in International Politics*. Eds. Joan W. Scott, Cora Kaplan, and Debra Keates. New York/London: Routledge, 1997. 253–272.

Werbner, Pnina, and Tariq Modood, eds. *Debating Cultural Hybridity: Multi-Cultural Identities and the Politics of Anti-Racism*. London/New Jersey: Palgrave, 1996.

Wolff, Janet: "On the Road Again: Metaphors of Travel in Cultural Criticism." *Cultural Studies* 7.2 (1993): 224–239.

Young, Robert J.C. *Colonial Desire: Hybridity in Theory, Culture and Race*. London: Routledge, 1995.

Young, Robert J.C. *Postcolonialism: An Historical Introduction*. Oxford/Malden, MA: Blackwell, 2001.

Matthias Middell
Is there a Timetable when Concepts Travel?

On Synchronicity in the Emergence of New Concepts Dealing with Border-Crossing Phenomena

1 Travelling Concepts – A Metaphor among Others

The idea that concepts may travel (cf. Bal 2002; Czarniawska and Joerges 1996) is part of a larger spectrum of perceptions focusing on the circulation of goods, capital, people, ideas, viruses, and many other things. This very specific terminology of travelling concepts has its origins in postcolonial cultural studies of the 1980s (cf. Said 1983; Knapp 2005; for an overview on current trends in the field, see Herren et al. 2012), but its development is undoubtedly a result of break-ups in countries beyond the Anglo-Saxon world. It seems as if scholars with very different backgrounds discovered the same set of problems – of course, at different places, in different languages, and with different theoretical-methodological luggage.

The metaphor of 'travelling concepts' invites reflection on synchronicity in the search for formulations that may describe things that have come into focus for more and more researchers: transnational border-crossings of ideas, people, capital, and goods. These were of course not observed for the first time within this context. It is, however, possible to chart when and how a community of scholars began to question new dimensions of these movements within societies.

An area of inquiry that opened at almost precisely the same moment as that of travelling concepts, with similar lines of argument, is that of cultural transfers. Two French specialists in German Studies, Michel Espagne and Michael Werner, suggested overcoming the obvious limitations of investigation that focuses on influences of one culture on another by turning to research on why, how, and when the appropriation of foreign cultural elements occurs (cf. Espagne and Werner 1985, 1987). The study of cultural transfers drew its inspiration from the study of translation, but it goes far beyond the limits of a history of ideas and texts: it ranges from the social practice of appropriation and the social histories of intermediates and translators to the study of media involved in those histories. Investigations from the perspective of cultural transfers also extend into processes of politics, especially when it comes to the explanation of successful and unsuccessful attempts to transfer desirable foreign elements into one's own culture. This approach, which was (and still is) a decisive challenge to the dominant, diffusionist paradigm in many social sciences, was first tested in the French-German context (cf. Espagne and Werner 1988) and has been implemented in other fields over the years.

One may think, here, of Arjun Appadurai's attempt to insist on the permanent reframing of socio-cultural action in what he called "modernity at large" (cf. Appadurai 1988, 1996).[1] Sociologists insisted on placing the local in seemingly universal processes of globalization: Roland Robertson promoted the term 'glocalization' (cf. Robertson 1992), while others focused on the new level of connectivity of societies as a challenge to classical sociological theory (cf. Mol and Law 1994, 2002). Shmuel Eisenstadt further expanded the idea, which led to a theory of multiple modernities (cf. Eisenstadt 2000, 2002) that disputes two notions: Western modernity being the benchmark for all development in the world, and the West's unilateral influence on the rest of the world. The concept of multiple modernities is not only an invitation to frame classical accounts of historical development anew, but also to investigate the interaction between societies and cultures. From an anthropologist's point of view, this was the call for multi-sited ethnography (cf. Marcus 1995).

What should be clear at this point is that the idea of travelling concepts has no single origin but echoes a variety of conceptual proposals meant to encompass fundamental transformations that have occurred across the globe since the 1980s. Near the end of the Cold War, transnational movements (especially the protesting of dangerous armament on both sides) nourished the feeling that crossing even the most protected borders was possible (cf. Evangelista 1999; Della Porta et al. 2009). In addition, an enormous increase in new communication technologies became available in the civilian sphere (cf. Abbate 1999). Observing these new realities led authors from different disciplines to rather similar formulations of a new research agenda. It became quite obvious that new frames were needed to understand a world that was seen as entering a phase of transition and reorganization.

---

1 A somewhat similar approach is taken by Zygmunt Bauman (2000), who emphasizes the fluidity of current social processes in comparison to those of the past.

Some authors concerned with travelling concepts concentrate on categories like 'narrative,' which has been at the heart of a discourse that took its inspiration from literary studies (see, for example, the contribution to a conference in Helsinki by Doloughan 2006), but the main idea of concepts that travel has long since left its original context behind and has been translated into a wider range of social sciences, including history. This broader interest is, again, not wholly new (see, e.g., Tarde 2003), though it has received much more attention in recent times in which the hype about globalization has led to scholarly interest not only in the phenomena of resulting encounters but also in the issue of explaining periods and spaces of more intense entanglements in world history.

The most popular version of this trend sings the praises of globalization as the – often somehow mysterious – source of increasing flow across national borders, insisting on the (circular) idea that globalization flows and is itself characterized by such flows. Accordingly, cultures are described as intermingling and hybrid (cf. Brathwaite et al. 2002); they encounter other cultures and people who move between cultures create transnational spaces (cf. Pries 1999; Faist and Özveren 2004) that are populated by diasporas (cf. Dufoix 2011; Rürup 2009). This may result in creolization (cf. Cohen 2007; Burton 1995). In general, increased migration leads to the idea that these flows of people generate transnationalism (cf. Glick Schiller et al. 1992). It has been argued, furthermore, that an age of network society (cf. Castells 1996) has emerged from not only people moving beyond borders but also technological advances in modes of communication, which minimizes or even denies geographical distance. The more cultures and societies come into contact, the more translation and brokers are obviously needed (cf. Rottenburg 2008). Moreover, these translations or cultural transfers (cf. Espagne 1999), as ample evidence shows, also occur within influential local contexts (cf. Spittler 2003). However, these local circumstances are, of course, not neutral but rather influenced by power asymmetries and the long-lasting practice of interpreting synchronously acting societies as diachronically arranged along a timeline of modernity (cf. Mosse and Lewis 2006; Büschel and Speich 2009). What appear as universal values have to be interpreted – as authors like Shalini Randeria argue – as the result of negotiations between actors with different types and scopes of agency to assert their particular world views and interests (cf. Randeria 2003).

What I have summarized in a rather broadly sketched reminder is evidently inspired by an alarmist perception of a fast-changing world in which new border-crossing phenomena grab the centre of attention. What can be called a discourse of newness is widespread, especially in the social sciences, and is echoed by policy-makers who like to present themselves as actors without alternatives, forced by overwhelming trends to do what they do because of floods of migrants, uncontrollable capital flows, worldwide divisions of labor that escape all forms of local and national policies, and new forms of communication within the global village that make the world flat.

It should come as no surprise that the metaphor of travelling concepts is used increasingly in very different contexts to signal that the character of the problem reaches far beyond the canonical borders of any one discipline, and that the author who employs it is willing to go beyond these limitations. The emergence of a discourse that relies on the omnipresence of travelling concepts can therefore be interpreted as expressing discontent with the disciplinary character of our knowledge production: namely, that it was seated in institutions organized into fields and disciplines established during the first major wave of global connections between the 1860s and the First World War.[2] What we should not forget is that the frame of the nation-state, together with modernized forms of imperial power exercised by the most powerful nation-states (cf. Burbank and Cooper 2010), guaranteed control over a world order by adapting the internal regulation and identification processes of societies to increasingly important global markets, international organizations (cf. Herren 2009), and cultural learning processes across national borders. Academic disciplines, mainly in the humanities and social sciences, were part of this process of societal reorganization and contributed to its self-understanding by focusing on society as a sort of closed box that developed primarily because internal constellations changed. At the same time, the observation of 'others' was transferred to disciplines like ethnography and anthropology as well as to a bundle of regional or area studies dealing with different world regions (cf. Szanton 2002; Appadurai 2000). This guaranteed the availability of necessary information and skills (we should not forget that growing colonial administrations and, later on, apparatuses of developmental aid relied on professionals trained in the languages of the colonies and who had a basic understanding of what happened in a world controlled and exploited by imperialist powers – cf. Büschel and Speich 2009) but left the explanatory power of this information in a cage of exoticism – one that is called into question today.

---

2 During this time, the nation-state and nationalized society were very much seen as efficient frames for developing new tools of control over global flows – flows that became obvious in the period between 1840s and 1870s, as Michael Geyer and Charles Bright (1995) argue in an article that inspires writing on global history to this day.

2 New Observations and the Search for Metaphors that May Express Newness

The prevailing view of knowledge production has changed dramatically over the past thirty years, during which postcolonial criticism undermined the established knowledge order and reacted to the changing weight of what has at times been called the 'Third World.' Transnationalism also became an issue, as the corporate world developed, since the 1970s, more and more transborder configurations concerning production and distribution. The global moment of 1989 gave this development a further push (cf. Lawson et al. 2010). Global commodity chains gained attention, and new political alliances made the formerly clear divide between the Global North and the Global South not entirely obsolete but less stable; they raised doubts about the effectiveness of a world view based on such a clear divide. New challenges ranged from supranational coordination of political order (as within the European Union and similar forms of new regionalism – cf. Breslin et al. 2002; Grant and Söderbaum 2003; Söderbaum and Shaw 2005; Robinson et al. 2009) to ideas of humanitarian intervention – which resulted in the establishment of institutions of transitional justice – and to methods of transnational conflict prevention (cf. Behrends and Rottenburg 2011) and solutions. These issues repeatedly raised concerns about how to better understand the workings of a world that had moved neither towards absolute global governance nor back to an old regime of international cooperation exercised by states whose sovereignty was protected (or frozen) by the Cold War configuration. Today, with an increasing amount of people engaged in these kinds of border-crossing activities, the impact of such activities needs to be measured and explained more than ever.

As a consequence, it has become more and more difficult to treat society as a container within which interesting things happen (due to social composition and the relationship between socio-economic and politico-cultural dimensions) and external connections are only of marginal or secondary interest. On the contrary, the issue of how to manage connectivity has become a central issue, while this new interest in the entangled character of society clashes with the old disciplinary configurations of knowledge production. Dissatisfaction with what has been called methodological nationalism (cf. Wimmer and Glick Schiller 2002) and a container-like understanding of society has come more and more to the fore.

And yet, disciplines persist. They remain powerful principles of organization in higher education and research. All the talk about interdisciplinarity cannot hide the fact that disciplines provide the power to control immense parts of knowledge production. What speaks most for the persistence of disciplinary training and the 'gatekeeper function' of institutions like journals, congresses, and professional associations – deliberatively disciplinary – is the need for methodological control over innovative knowledge. Over the past century, disciplines have developed increasingly sophisticated practices and discourses that integrate new findings into canonized methodologies. One of the difficulties with such canonization is that it forces authors of new ideas to use metaphorical language, because the existing disciplinary language is too embedded and canonized to allow for the expression of tentative thinking. Before new paradigms emerge, we often observe a phase of rather vague expressions of discontent with the existing narratives and interpretations of current changes. This vagueness inspires metaphorical expression. Metaphors allow for the escape, at least partially, from the control of an established set of methods. Notwithstanding, this is exactly what also makes new ideas suspect to mainstream science. We can risk the hypothesis that transitional times are, on the one hand, particularly favorable for the use of new metaphors. On the other hand, metaphoric language sometimes makes it easy to criticize new ideas for lacking precise argumentation.

3 Parallel Innovation in Different Contexts

All these methodological propositions evolved more into parallel disciplinary worlds across the humanities and social sciences than into one integrated discussion. The situation is further complicated by the fact that, despite all new transnational forms of communication, some ideas travelled better than others across the persisting borders between national academic communities. It is, therefore, interesting to observe how these ideas travelled and why some were perceived with more interest in some contexts than in others. In what follows, I will try to read into some of the timetables with a special emphasis on the world of historians.

While some French cultural historians developed the concept of cultural transfers in the late 1980s to address the problem of interactions between different societies, the dominant strand of historiography in France was much more concerned with redefining the relationship between the *Annales* school's tradition of social history and the analysis of cultural representations.[3] It was not

---

3 See two editorials of the *Annales* from 1988 and 1989: "Histoire et sciences sociales. Un tournant critique." *Annales E.S.C.* 43.2 (1988): 291–293; "Tentons l'expérience." *Annales E.S.C.*

until a decade later that the *Annales* reconsidered the problem of global history.[4]

At more or less the same time, U.S. historiography mobilized its considerable resources in the study of different world regions in an attempt to address issues of historical globalization. *The World History Association*, with its *Journal of World History* (founded in 1989), became a focal point of these efforts, with an underlying paradigm of 'cultural encounters' (cf. Bentley 1993). As the book description states, the aim was to examine "major cross-cultural influences that transformed Asia and Europe" over long historical periods and to demonstrate that, on the one hand, cultural encounters have a long history and, on the other hand, that they are not unidirectional and by no means support the idea of a dominating West and a 'rest' that is only the target of Western innovations and values (cf. Bentley 1993). This approach proved to be influential, inspiring a broad movement of scholarly work and newly emerging study programs both at high school and university levels. Within only a few years, world history as the history of long-lasting encounters that produce cultures and mutually influence one another became extremely prominent (while disputed by conservatives in the U.S.). In turn, the idea of focusing on cultural encounters proved to be a fruitful tool for a fundamental revision of history that undermined the classical narrative of 'Western Civilization' courses.[5] The notion of cultural encounters was broad enough to allow for empirical work on all kinds of patterns of conversion, conflict, and compromise that emerged from cross-cultural encounters. The study of cultural encounters became a success story in North American historiography, which may explain the region's interest in world and global history. The argument that became so convincing was that Americans would need, during times of globalization, a form of orientation when confronted with an increasing number of cultural encounters. The concept was vague enough to leave room for various interpretations of what might occur as a consequence of such encounters. It proved capable of encompassing both diffusionist interpre-

---

44.6 (1989): 1317–1323; Roger Chartier. "Le monde comme representation." *Annales E.S.C.* 44.6 (1989): 1505–1520; Christophe Charle, ed. "Histoire sociale, histoire globale?" Actes du colloque des 27–28 janvier 1989. Paris 1993.

4 We should not forget that the *Annales*, under the leadership of Fernand Braudel, developed innovative world history approaches but, since the 1970s, the prominent French school of historical writing increasingly removed itself from its geographically widespread ambition to focus more on the history of mentalities and sociopolitical orders in Europe, or even more narrowly, in France.

5 Perhaps the most prominent textbook, one that inspired many others as well as the majority of courses taught at U.S. colleges, is Bentley and Ziegler 2000.

tations (those generously accepting of the claim that other past empires and societies might have been influential) and interpretations that critically examined the assumed divide between a powerful West and a rather passive rest-of-the-world. It is, perhaps, not an overstatement to conclude that, under the political and epistemological conditions of U.S. historiography, the precondition for the success of cultural encounters as a concept was a lack of intense theoretical and methodological debate regarding its further definition.[6]

This new paradigm emerged more or less at the same time that the above-mentioned concepts of cultural transfer were formulated in France. Notwithstanding, neither respectively travelled across the Atlantic. While the cultural transfer approach – despite its observable presence in publications and conferences – remained at the institutional margins of French historiography, the investigation of cultural encounters became the dominant feature within a fast-growing world-history movement in the U.S., and this movement started influencing other historiographies (Manning 2003). At this particular moment, there was unmistakably no need for North American historians, who, in the past, had been greatly inspired by the *Annales* school and Foucault's reinterpretation of history, to look into recent French developments. Subaltern studies and post-colonialism became more prominent – and what were previously very-often-used routes across the Atlantic for travelling concepts between France and the U.S. became less frequented after the reconceptualization of an entangled world in the 1990s.

At the same time, cultural transfer gained prominence in German debates. In this context, the point of departure is quite different. Since the 1970s, societal history (*Gesellschaftsgeschichte*) had expanded its rather classical, comparative approach. German unification and the search for a new role in a reconfigured Europe challenged existing interpretations, and it became rather unclear, at the beginning of the 1990s, if these challenges would lead to increased (re-)nationalization, a European history organized along the lines of East-West comparisons, or new thoughts about Germany and Europe's position in the world inspired by discourses on globalization (Jarausch and Geyer 2003; Middell 2002). This moment of uncertainty about future master narratives led to an interest in methodological questions about how and what to compare.[7] Research on cultural transfer was seen as a fundamental challenge to the centrali-

---

6 For an insightful description of North American historiography, see Novick 1988.

7 It is interesting to compare the German edition of papers presented at a conference in 1993: Haupt and Kocka 1996, and the much later English version, which reflects the results of sharp methodological confrontation by including some of the positions developed between 1993 and 2009: Haupt and Kocka 2009.

ty of comparison for any historical explanation.[8] The opponents of comparative historiography, as it was practiced especially in Germany (in search for an explanation to the German *Sonderweg*), argued that, despite the fact that comparison claims to work transnationally, it risks confirming an image of societies as self-contained, closed entities and, even worse, constructing these entities in a way that undermines their distinctiveness. Comparison systematically underestimates interaction between entities and their working perceptions of each other. Not by necessity but as an observable danger, comparative historiography often went hand in hand with diffusionist concepts.

But, of course, historians focusing on cultural transfers had to recognize that all perceptions, appropriations, and incorporations of foreign cultural elements are based upon comparative activity by the historical actors. Without looking beyond the borders of one's own society or culture, there would not be any kind of cultural transfer.

The outcome of the debate was at least twofold. Firstly, it made clear that comparative history cannot be naively understood as the golden way to historical explanation but has its limitations, as do all other methods. As Jürgen Osterhammel once put it: Comparison tends to decontextualize its objects for the sake of analytical strength and clarity, while research on cultural transfers recontextualizes the phenomena under investigation but risks losing analytical rigor (cf. Osterhammel 2003). Secondly, it became evident that comparative history could no longer neglect the importance of connected histories, as Marc Bloch had already argued in his groundbreaking article presented at the International Congress of Historical Sciences in Oslo in 1928 – a work often selectively quoted to legitimize comparison between two or more cases without including Bloch's insistence of the fact that cases influence one another as well as the terminology used in describing them, creating a situation of mutual interdependency (cf. Bloch 1928). At certain points, the conclusions drawn from the debate between comparative historians and researchers investigating cultural transfers went in the direction of a more encompassing understanding of comparison and a more flexible application of the comparative method (cf. Kaelble 1999; Paulmann 1998),[9] while, in other cases, priority was given to studies sole-

---

8 It is not by accident that the paper submitted by Michel Espagne on the self-limitations of classical comparative historiography to the conference mentioned above (Espagne 1994) was not included in the proceedings but appeared in a French journal that, at the time, was considered a challenge to the dominance of the *Annales*.
9 Jürgen Kocka describes the tradition of a Bielefeld-born and now Berlin-based historical school of social history as the core of German comparative history writing (Kocka 2006).

ly on cultural transfers.[10] These differences, if slight, still confirm the idea that concepts travel, even though they travel at different points and are perceived with differing levels of sensitivity to phenomena of entanglement.

A cooperation between researchers in Paris and Leipzig added two dimensions to the original investigation of national cultural spheres and their influences on one another. The first of these dimensions is a regional one. The perception of 'France' and 'French' was nearly homogeneous across Germany, especially in the eighteenth and nineteenth centuries, while a strong regionalization of German history can also be observed after the German unification in 1871 and especially after the divide in 1945/1949. The question of regional differences in exchange with France led to the conclusion that some regions – including Britain, Belgium, and the Netherlands, as well as countries from the south and northeast of the European continent – have been particularly attentive to French (and other) cultural inspirations. This gave birth to the idea that some regions can be characterized as "European regions," in the sense that they tried to promote identification with elements appropriated from other European societies rather than become subordinate to a monolithic national culture (cf. Espagne 1995, 2000; Hollwedel et al. 2004).

The second dimension was a concern with the constructivist approach towards space in modern writing on world history (cf. Middell 2006). It became evident that cultural transfers do not occur between container-like societies, whether national or regional, nor do they express increasing connectedness between these societies alone. On the contrary, cultural transfers produce new spaces populated by active intermediaries who select, translate, transport, and integrate seemingly foreign cultural elements. Prominent examples of these intermediaries are translators, booksellers, art brokers, architects, and so on (cf. Espagne and Greiling 1996). They move between places located within different states, and they build networks across borders – weaving transnational spaces where a permanent evaluation of what might be worth translating occurs. Researchers observing intermediaries in transnational and transcultural spaces experience their border-crossing character first hand, simply because they visit

---

10 Responding to the book series "Deutsch-Französische Kulturbibliothek" (29 volumes since 1993; edited by Michel Espagne, Etienne François, Werner Greiling, and Matthias Middell), I argued why research on cultural transfer might have been more attractive to historians based in East Germany than for an unchallenged mainstream of comparative historians from the former West. My argument addressed the specific situation at the end of the 1990s and has, of course, lost parts of its value over the following decade, as particular features of East German historiography have lost increasing ground to the subsequent transformation and integration of German historiography (see Middell 2000).

archives in many different locations, which highlights that various institutions and countries claim their written legacy (cf. Espagne et al. 2000).

Another example that demonstrates successful travelling is the attention that has been given to the conceptualization of cultural transfers in Canada. The bilingual situation made it easier for an approach that was mainly available in French, while, at the same time, the Canadian context added a transatlantic dimension that had been missing (cf. Turgeon et al. 1996). The same holds true for the enrichment of the concept via the Russian tradition that sustains a history of *world literature* (cf. Dmitrieva and Espagne 1996), as well as with scholars from Italy and Scandinavia who studied exchanges across the North-South divide in European history (cf. Espagne 2005, 2006). All of these interactions contributed to further exploration of multipolar transfers (cf. Middell 2011). Another important step in the development of the investigation of cultural transfers, which became increasingly popular across different communities of historians, was the integration of postcolonial studies. Diffusionism, which was prevalent in the historiography of empires for so long, became more and more questioned and replaced by concepts of entangled or connected histories that insisted on the agency of historical actors far from the former metropolis of widespread imperial configurations (examples of this trend taking hold in France and Germany can be found in Subrahmanyam 1997; Conrad and Randeria 2002). The similarity of these approaches of cultural transfer and connected history is prominent, but neither is a simple effect of the expansion of transfer studies or postcolonial studies into new fields of interest. On the contrary, the two developed rather independently of each other and its representatives only slowly became aware of possibilities for cross-fertilization.

The various additions to and modifications of the original concept of cultural transfer research, above and beyond the multidirectional travels of the 1990s, led to a split between the two French scholars who had originally formulated the approach. While Michel Espagne insisted on the capacity of the original idea to integrate all new dimensions, Michael Werner became critical towards the notion of cultural transfer and started favoring concepts like *histoire croisée* (cf. Werner and Zimmermann 2006). Here, a new chapter on itineraries of travelling concepts begins, since we now have the curious (and more complex) situation of two competing concepts going more or less in the same direction yet calling for attention and productive response by mobilizing alliances of cooperation and support. Instead of following the rather Gordian ways of such entanglements, which cannot be unscrambled without taking the complex histories of academic institutions and power relations into consideration, I would like to conclude by emphasizing one last station our travelling concept has reached in the early 2000s.

The emerging debate (or better: debates) on transnational histories helped mobilize, on the one hand, the integration of previously fragmented levels and spaces of discussion, and, on the other hand, the attention of historians who were not yet familiar with categories like cultural transfer. Related debates began in the U.S. and Germany more or less at the same time. Historians in various areas were concerned with how to relate their subjects to the increasing prominence of global and entangled histories (cf. Siegrist 2007) – as in the case of German studies in the U.S.[11] or Eastern European history in Germany (cf. Creuzberger et al. 2000) – while, at the same time, many expressed the wish to overcome a traditional divide between research on non-Western societies and the history of the West.[12]

The debate on transnational history, often described as an approach open to different methods in the investigation of social and cultural interaction as well as inter- and transcultural phenomena,[13] nevertheless gave the search for a more explicit foundation and distinct methodology a push. It is now widely accepted that cultural interaction does not start with the expansion of certain features, as diffusionists assumed, but with the recognition of a deficit that inspires the search for patterns already established in other cultures and that fit better with the needs of the society than those practiced in the past. This leads to the activities of intermediaries, identifying such external patterns and translating them into new contexts. At the same time, translation requires media and places of production. Intermediaries, media, and places are specifically qualified for transfer due to their individual capacities to 'read' and translate foreign cultural elements as well as the presence of cultural institutions representing a tradition of openness to the foreign.[14] A last analytical step involves reviewing the way societies deal with elements borrowed and appropriated from foreign contexts. In some cases, these elements are openly advertised as exotic; in other cases, foreign origins are carefully hidden and overwritten by legends about long-lasting internal traditions.

---

11 Cf. Boettcher et al. 2006.

12 See the contributions to the e-platform *geschichte.transnational* (Espagne and Middell 2004–2013) and the inspiring example of Conrad and Osterhammel 2004.

13 On the various approaches towards transcultural history today, see Herren et al. 2012.

14 This quality of certain places remaining prominent centers of transfer activities has recently inspired a debate on "portals of globalization," relating, thus, again to the investigation of cultural transfers to broader narratives of global history (see Geyer 2010). Among the many examples that have been discussed in that respect, see Bandau et al. 2010; Driver and Gilbert 1999; Masashi 2008; Newman 2007.

4 Conclusion

In summary, the cultural transfer approach is a travelling concept par excellence. It was enriched by contact with various academic communities, it has integrated new empirical evidence and new theoretical inspiration, and it has transformed into an ever-more precise methodology.

Our example demonstrates, on the one hand, that, at times of substantial change in the perception of society and politics, an increasing number of more or less similar proposals for interpreting new phenomena emerges. These proposals are characterized by the use of a metaphoric language that indicates a willingness to be emancipated from the fixed categories of established theories and disciplinary frameworks as well as a search for originality within a broader spectrum of attempts to cope with the new. Such approaches emerge in different places at approximately the same time, and what makes them part of a broader movement is their reaction to similar sets of problems. On the other hand, we have to be aware that these suggestions travel and influence one another.

Initially faced with the idea of an easy border crossing, we can conclude that if, when, and how fast concepts travel depends on various factors ranging from previous connections between academic communities to shared languages. In contrast to what adherents of diffusionism believe, the travel of concepts is mainly determined by the context of perception. Decisions are made based on an idea's allure and its usefulness upon being incorporated into its new context. Ironically, this is also true for concepts that are meant to put travelling concepts into focus. The research on cultural transfers undertaken over the last two decades and described here has been successful in some but by no means all academic communities that deal with problems of interactions between different societies and cultures. Insofar as this has been a revealing exercise, it is worth applying the theory developed to analyze cultural transfers to that theory itself. What researchers in the field of cultural transfer studies insist on is the role of motivation for such an appropriation or incorporation – and it is obvious that, in some contexts, the motivation to incorporate cultural transfer studies has been more intense than in others.

References

Abbate, Janet. *Inventing the Internet*. Cambridge, MA: MIT Press, 1999.

Appadurai, Arjun. *Modernity at Large: Cultural Dimensions of Globalization*. Minneapolis: University of Minnesota Press, 1996.

Appadurai, Arjun. *Globalization and Area Studies: The Future of a False Opposition. The Wertheim Lecture 2000*. Amsterdam: Centre for Asian Studies, 2000.

Appadurai, Arjun, ed. *The Social Life of Things: Commodities in Cultural Perspective*. Cambridge/New York: Cambridge University Press, 1988.

Bal, Mieke. *Travelling Concepts in the Humanities: A Rough Guide*. Toronto: University of Toronto Press, 2002.

Bandau, Anja, Marcel Dorigny, and Rebekka von Mallinckrodt, eds. *Les mondes coloniaux à Paris au XVIIIe siècle. Circulation et enchevêtrement des savoirs*. Paris: Karthala, 2010.

Bauman, Zygmunt. *Liquid Modernity*. Cambridge: Polity Press, 2000.

Behrends, Andrea, and Richard Rottenburg, eds. *Translating Technologies of Social Ordering: Travelling Models in African Conflict Management*. Leiden: Brill, 2011.

Benjamin, Walter. "Die Aufgabe des Übersetzers." *Illuminationen*. Frankfurt a.M.: Suhrkamp, 1977. 50–62.

Bentley, Jerry H. *Old World Encounters: Cross-Cultural Contacts and Exchanges in Pre-Modern Times*. Oxford: Oxford University Press, 1993.

Bentley, Jerry H., and Herbert Ziegler. *Traditions & Encounters: A Brief Global History*. Toronto: McGill, 2000.

Bloch, Marc. "Pour une histoire comparée des sociétés européennes." *Revue de Synthèse Historique* 46 (1928): 15–50.

Boettcher, Susan, Eve Duffy, Christopher Fischer, Will Gray, David Imhoof, and Paul Steege, eds. "Transnationalism." www.hnet.org/~german/discuss/Trans/forum_trans_index.htm. 2006 (10 November 2013).

Brathwaite, Kamau, Verene Shepherd, and Glen L. Richards, eds. *Questioning Creole: Creolisation Discourses in Caribbean Culture*. Oxford: James Currey Publishers, 2002.

Breslin, Shaun, Christopher W. Hughes, and Nicola Phillips, eds. *New Regionalisms in the Global Political Economy: Theories and Cases*. London: Routledge, 2002.

Burbank, Jane, and Frederick Cooper. *Empires in World History: Power and the Politics of Difference*. New Jersey: Princeton University Press, 2010.

Burton, Richard D. E. "The Idea of Difference in Contemporary French West Indian Thought: Négritude, Antillanité, Créolité." *French and West Indian: Martinique, Guadeloupe and French Guiana Today*. Eds. Richard D. E. Burton and Fred Reno. London: Macmillan, 1995. 137–166.

Büschel, Hubertus, and Daniel Speich, eds. *Entwicklungswelten. Globalgeschichte der Entwicklungszusammenarbeit*. Frankfurt a.M./New York: Campus, 2009.

Castells, Manuel. *The Information Age: Economy, Society, and Culture, Volume 1: The Rise of the Network Society*. Oxford/Malden, MA: Blackwell, 1996.

Cohen, Robin. "Creolization and Cultural Globalization: The Soft Sounds of Fugitive Power." *Globalizations* 4.3 (2007): 369–383.

Conrad, Sebastian, and Jürgen Osterhammel, eds. *Das Kaiserreich transnational. Deutschland in der Welt 1871–1914*. Göttingen: Vandenhoeck & Ruprecht, 2004.

Conrad, Sebastian, and Shalini Randeria, eds. *Jenseits des Eurozentrismus. Postkoloniale Perspektiven in den Geschichts- und Kulturwissenschaften*. Frankfurt a.M./New York: Campus, 2002.

Creuzberger, Stefan, Ingo Mannteufel, Alexander Steininger, and Jutta Unser, eds. "Wohin steuert die Osteuropaforschung? Eine Diskussion." Cologne: Verlag Wissenschaft & Politik, 2000.

Czarniawska, Barbara, and Bernward Joerges. "Travels of Ideas." *Translating Organizational Change*. Eds. Barbara Czarniawska and Guje Sevón. Berlin/New York: de Gruyter, 1996. 13–48.

Della Porta, Donatella, Hanspeter Kriesi, and Dieter Rucht, eds. *Social Movements in a Globalizing World*. Basingstoke: Palgrave Macmillan, 2009.

Dmitrieva, Katia, and Michel Espagne, eds. *Transferts culturels triangulaires France-Allemagne-Russie*. Paris: Editions de la Maison des Sciences de l'Homme, 1996.

Doloughan, Fiona J. "Narratives of Travel and the Travelling Concept of Narrative: Genre Blending and the Art of Transformation." http://www.helsinki.fi/collegium/e-series/volumes/volume_1/001_10_doloughan.pdf. 2006 (9 November 2013).

Driver, Felix, and David Gilbert, eds. *Imperial Cities: Landscape, Display and Identity*. Manchester/New York: Manchester University Press, 1999.

Dufoix, Stéphane. *La dispersion. Une histoire des usages du mot diaspora*. Paris: Editions Amsterdam, 2011.

Eisenstadt, Shmuel N. "Multiple Modernities." *Daedalus* 129.1 (2000): 1–29.

Eisenstadt, Shmuel N. *Multiple Modernities*. New Brunswick, NJ: Transaction Publishers, 2002.

Engel, Ulf, Frank Hadler, and Matthias Middell, eds. *1989 in a Global Perspective*. Leipzig: Leipziger Universitätsverlag, 2012.

Espagne, Michel. "Sur les limites du comparatisme en histoire culturelle." *Genèses* 17 (1994): 112–121.

Espagne, Michel. *Transferts culturels et region. L'exemple de la Saxe*. Lyon: Université Lumière, 1995.

Espagne, Michel. *Les transferts culturels franco-allemands*. Paris: PUF, 1999.

Espagne, Michel. *Le creuset allemand. Histoire interculturelle de la Saxe XVIIIe–XIXe siècles*. Paris: Presses Universitaires de France, 2000.

Espagne, Michel, and Michael Werner. "Deutsch-französischer Kulturtransfer im 18. und 19. Jahrhundert. Zu einem neuen interdisziplinären Forschungsprogramm des CNRS." *Francia* 13 (1985): 502–510.

Espagne, Michel, and Michael Werner. "La construction d'une référence culturelle allemande en France. Genèse et histoire (1750–1914)." *Annales. E.S.C.* 42.4 (1987): 969–992.

Espagne, Michel, ed. *Russie, France, Allemagne, Italie. Transferts quadrangulaires du néoclassicisme aux avant-gardes: Textes rassemblées*. Tusson: Du Lérot, 2005.

Espagne, Michel, ed. *Le prisme du Nord. Pays du Nord, France, Allemagne (1750–1920)*. Textes réunis. Tusson: Du Lérot, 2006.

Espagne, Michel, and Matthias Middell, eds. "Forum." *geschichte.transnational*. http://geschichte-transnational.clio-online.net/forum/type=diskussionen. 2004–2013 (10 November 2013).

Espagne, Michel, and Michael Werner, eds. *Transferts. Les relations interculturelles dans l'espace franco-allemand (XVIIIe–XIXe siècle)*. Paris: Éditions Recherche sur les Civilisations, 1988.

Espagne, Michel, Katharina Middell, and Matthias Middell, eds. *Archiv und Gedächtnis. Studien zur interkulturellen Überlieferung*. Leipzig: Leipziger Universitätsverlag, 2000.

Espagne, Michel, and Werner Greiling, eds. *Frankreichfreunde. Mittler des französisch-deutschen Kulturtransfers (1750–1850)*. Leipzig: Leipziger Universitätsverlag, 1996.

Evangelista, Matthew. *Unarmed Forces: The Transnational Movement to End the Cold War*. Ithaca: Cornell University Press, 1999.

Faist, Thomas, and Eyüp Özveren, eds. *Transnational Social Spaces: Agents, Networks and Institutions*. Aldershot: Ashgate, 2004.

Geyer, Michael. "Portals of Globalization." *The Plurality of Europe: Identities and Spaces*. Eds. Winfried Eberhard and Christian Lübke. Leipzig: Leipziger Universitätsverlag, 2010. 509–520.

Geyer, Michael, and Charles Bright. "World History in a Global Age." *American Historical Review* 100.4 (1995): 1034–1060.

Glick Schiller, Nina, Linda Basch, and Cristina Blanc-Szanton. "Transnationalism: A New Analytic Framework for Understanding Migration." *Towards a Transnational Perspective on Migration: Race, Class, Ethnicity, and Nationalism Reconsidered*. Eds. Nina Glick Schiller, Linda Basch, and Cristina Blanc-Szanton. New York: New York Academy of Science, 1992. 1–24.

Grant, J. Andrew, and Fredrik Söderbaum, eds. *The New Regionalism in Africa*. Aldershot: Ashgate, 2003.

Haupt, Heinz-Gerhard, and Jürgen Kocka, eds. *Geschichte und Vergleich. Ansätze und Ergebnisse international vergleichender Geschichtsschreibung*. Frankfurt a.M./New York: Campus, 1996.

Haupt, Heinz-Gerhard, and Jürgen Kocka, eds. *Comparison and Transnational History: Central European Approaches and New Perspectives*. New York/Oxford: Berghahn Books, 2009.

Herren, Madeleine. *Internationale Organisationen seit 1865. Eine Globalgeschichte der internationalen Ordnung*. Darmstadt: Wissenschaftliche Buchgesellschaft, 2009.

Herren, Madeleine, Martin Rüesch, and Christiane Sibille, eds. *Transcultural History: Theories, Methods, Sources*. Berlin/New York: Springer, 2012.

Hollwedel, Alke, Jörg Ludwig, and Katharina Middell, eds. *Passage Frankreich-Sachsen. Kulturgeschichte einer Beziehung 1700 bis 2000*. Halle: Mitteldeutscher Verlag, 2004.

Jarausch, Konrad H., and Michael Geyer. *Shattered Past: Reconstructing German Histories*. Princeton/Oxford: Princeton University Press, 2003.

Kaelble, Hartmut. *Der historische Vergleich. Eine Einführung zum 19. und 20. Jahrhundert*. Frankfurt a.M./New York: Campus, 1999.

Knapp, Gudrun-Axeli. "Traveling Theories. Anmerkungen zur neueren Diskussion über 'Race, Class, and Gender.'" *Österreichische Zeitschrift für Geschichtswissenschaften* 16.1 (2005): 88–110.

Kocka, Jürgen. "Wandlungen der Sozial- und Gesellschaftsgeschichte am Beispiel Berlins 1949 bis 2005." *Wege der Gesellschaftsgeschichte*. Eds. Jürgen Osterhammel, Dieter Langewiesche, and Paul Nolte. Göttingen: Vandenhoeck & Ruprecht, 2006. 11–31.

Lawson, George, Chris Armbruster, and Michael Cox, eds. *The Global 1989: Continuity and Change in World Politics*. Cambridge: Cambridge University Press, 2010.

Manning, Patrick. *Navigating World History: Historians Create a Global Past*. New York: Palgrave Macmillan, 2003.

Marcus, George E. "Ethnography in/of the World System: The Emergence of Multi-Sited Ethnography." *Annual Review of Anthropology* 24 (1995): 95–117.

Masashi, Haneda, ed. *Asian Port Cities 1600-1800: Local and Foreign Cultural Interactions.* Singapore: NUS Publishing, 2008.

Middell, Matthias. "Kulturtransfer und Historische Komparatistik. Thesen zu ihrem Verhältnis." *Comparativ. Leipziger Beiträge zur Universalgeschichte und vergleichenden Gesellschaftsforschung* 10.1 (2000): 7–41.

Middell, Matthias. "Europäische Geschichte oder global history – master narratives oder Fragmentierung? Fragen an die Leittexte der Zukunft." *Die historische Meistererzählung. Deutungslinien der deutschen Nationalgeschichte nach 1945.* Eds. Konrad H. Jarausch and Martin Sabrow. Göttingen: Vandenhoeck & Ruprecht, 2002. 214–252.

Middell, Matthias. "Die konstruktivistische Wende, der spatial turn und das Interesse für die Globalisierung in der gegenwärtigen Geschichtswissenschaft." *Geographische Zeitschrift* 93.1 (2006): 33–44.

Middell, Matthias. "Deutsch-russisch-französische Kulturbeziehungen im 18. und 19. Jahrhundert – ein Feld triangulärer Kulturtransfers." *Naturwissenschaften als Kommunikationsraum zwischen Deutschland und Russland im 19. Jahrhundert.* Eds. Ortrun Riha and Marta Fischer. Aachen: Shaker Verlag, 2011. 49–74.

Mol, Annemarie, and John Law. "Regions, Networks, and Fluids: Anaemia and Social Topology." *Social Studies of Science* 24.4 (1994): 641–671.

Mol, Annemarie, and John Law, eds. *Complexities: Social Studies of Knowledge Practices.* Durham: Duke University Press, 2002.

Mosse, David, and David Lewis, eds. *Development Brokers and Translators: The Ethnography of Aid and Agencies.* Bloomfield: Kumarian Press, 2006.

Newman, Karen. *Cultural Capitals: Early Modern London and Paris.* Princeton: Princeton University Press, 2007.

Novick, Peter. *That Noble Dream: The "Objectivity Question" and the American Historical Profession.* Cambridge/New York: Cambridge University Press, 1988.

Osterhammel, Jürgen. "Transferanalyse und Vergleich im Fernverhältnis." *Vergleich und Transfer. Komparatistik in den Sozial-, Geschichts- und Kulturwissenschaften.* Eds. Hartmut Kaelble and Jürgen Schriewer. Frankfurt a.M./New York: Campus, 2003. 439–468.

Paulmann, Johannes. "Internationaler Vergleich und interkultureller Transfer. Zwei Forschungsansätze zur europäischen Geschichte des 18. bis 20. Jahrhunderts." *Historische Zeitschrift* 267 (1998): 649–685.

Pries, Ludger, ed. *Migration and Transnational Social Spaces.* Aldershot: Ashgate, 1999.

Randeria, Shalini. "Domesticating Neo-Liberal Discipline: Transnationalisation of Law, Fractured States and Legal Plurality in the South." *Entangled Histories and Negotiated Universals.* Ed. Wolf Lepenies. Frankfurt a.M./New York: Campus, 2003. 146–182.

Robertson, Roland. *Glocalization: Social Theory and Global Culture.* London: Sage, 1992.

Robinson, Nick, Ben Rosamond, and Alex Warleigh-Lack, eds. *New Regionalism and the European Union: Dialogues, Comparisons and New Research Directions.* London: Routledge, 2009.

Rottenburg, Richard. "Übersetzung und ihre Dementierung." *Bruno Latours Kollektive. Kontroversen zur Entgrenzung des Sozialen.* Eds. Georg Kneer, Markus Schroer, and Erhard Schüttpelz. Frankfurt a.M.: Suhrkamp, 2008. 401–424.

Rürup, Miriam, ed. *Praktiken der Differenz. Diasporakulturen in der Zeitgeschichte.* Göttingen: Vandenhoeck & Ruprecht, 2009.

Said, Edward W. "Traveling Theory." *The World, the Text, and the Critic.* Cambridge, MA: Harvard University Press, 1983. 226–247 (dt. "Theorien auf Wanderschaft." *Die Welt, der Text und der Kritiker.* Frankfurt a.M.: Fischer, 1997. 263–292).

Siegrist, Hannes. "Transnationale Geschichte als Herausforderung der wissenschaftlichen Historiographie." *Dimensionen der Kultur- und Gesellschaftsgeschichte.* Ed. Matthias Middell. Leipzig: Leipziger Universitätsverlag, 2007. 40–48.

Söderbaum, Fredrik, and Timothy M. Shaw, eds. *Theories of New Regionalism: A Palgrave Reader.* Basingstoke: Macmillan, 2005.

Spittler, Gerd. "Globale Waren – Lokale Aneignungen." *Ethnologie der Globalisierung. Perspektiven kultureller Verflechtung.* Eds. Brigitta Hauser-Schäublin and Ulrich Braukämper. Berlin: Dietrich Reimer, 2003. 15–30.

Subrahmanyam, Sanjay. "Connected Histories: Notes toward a Reconfiguration of Early Modern Eurasia." *Modern Asia Studies* 31 (1997): 735–762.

Szanton, David L., ed. *The Politics of Knowledge: Area Studies and the Disciplines.* Berkeley/London: Berkeley University Press, 2002.

Tarde, Gabriel. *Die Gesetze der Nachahmung.* Frankfurt a.M.: Suhrkamp, 2003.

Turgeon, Laurier, Denys Delâge, and Réal Ouellet, eds. *Transferts culturels et métissages. Amériques/Europe XVIe–XXe siècle.* Laval: Presses Universitaires de Québec, 1996.

Werner, Michael, and Bénédicte Zimmermann. "Beyond Comparison: Histoire Croisée and the Challenge of Reflexivity." *History and Theory* 45.1 (2006): 30–50.

Wimmer, Andreas, and Nina Glick Schiller. "Methodological Nationalism and Beyond: Nation-State Building, Migration and the Social Sciences." *Global Networks* 2.4 (2002): 301–334.

Christina Lutter
What Do We Translate when We Translate?

Context, Process, and Practice as Categories of Cultural Analysis[*]

Even after decades of research and theoretical examination, both 'culture' and 'translation' – not to mention their (inter-)relations – remain intriguing, albeit controversial and fuzzy, categories of description and analysis. These categories are entangled within and between different contexts of practice, theoretical approaches, and academic disciplines, as an ever growing body of research literature shows.[1] The concept and title of this volume *The Trans/National Study of Culture* rightly suggest that one reason for this confusion is that the term 'cultural translation' still needs thorough examination and differentiation, especially as it has been appropriated by and become a keyword in rather different academic and national traditions, such as *cultural studies, sciences humaines,* and *Kulturwissenschaften.* What is more, it seems that using the term 'translation' demands a cautious differentiation from related terms used to describe cultural encounters, contacts and changes – for example, 'exchange,' 'transfer,' 'transition,' or 'transformation' – and it also calls for a review of the relations between different modes of translation, especially between linguistic and cultural ones.

The notions I have mentioned so far, and their partially overlapping meanings, all have one thing in common: they postulate and execute a turn away from the idea of a unified 'Culture with a capital C'[2] to contextual, process-

[*] I am grateful to Max Diesenberger, Stefan Erdei, Susan Ingram, Markus Reisenleitner, and Birgit Wagner for discussion and comments, as well as for help with the translation.
1 See the Routledge journal *Translation Studies*, founded in 2008; Bal 2002; St-Pierre and Kar 2007. For an extensive bibliography, also see the chapter "Translational Turn" in Bachmann-Medick 2006: 238–283.
2 In analogy with Stuart Hall's famous rejection of a "Theory" for its own sake, articulated twenty-five years ago: "I am not interested in Theory, I am interested in going on theorizing" (quoted in Grossberg 1996 [1986]: 150; cf. also the other contributions in Morley and Chen 1996, and in Hall 2000).

related, and practice-oriented conceptions of how the cultural production of meanings, as well as cultural encounters, exchange processes and conflicts, in past or present times, might have worked. In a subtle essay on the reception of Homi Bhabha's work, Birgit Wagner (2009, cf. also 2012) has recently explored the term 'cultural translation' that, at least in the German-speaking world, has been flourishing ever since the publication of Bhabha's seminal work *The Location of Culture* (1994). As Wagner shows, when a term enjoys a "career" of fashionability, as Bhabha's 'cultural translation' has, there is always a downside – its inflationary use, for example, which more often than not involves a blurring of terms. In this article I, therefore, first want to outline some of the problems that are caused by such an inflationary use of concepts like translation and culture. In its second part, I will accentuate the advantages of a more rigorous combination of the study of history and cultural analysis by using an example from early medieval history to show the contextual specificity of cultural translations, which are often associated with today's recent phenomena of globalization.[3]

The first challenge I want to address concerns the relations between language and culture. I am a historian, and neither a linguist nor a translator, even if I may pride myself in roughly meeting the criteria that Umberto Eco, specialist in semiotics and, at the same time, essayist and translator himself, has defined as the minimal requirements to be able to theoretically inquire into the issue of translation: "translation scholars should have had at least one of the following experiences during their life: translating, checking and editing translations, or being translated and working in close co-operation with their translators" (Eco 2004: 1). Eco himself has dealt with issues related to inter-lingual, inter-semiotic, and cultural translations for more than half a century – the work of a lifetime. And in each of his works he has dealt with these problems by staying close to the object, striving for precision, and always giving a wide range of context-specific examples. Looking at his work certainly makes me feel very cautious when it comes to big claims – especially as Eco always demonstrates the author's and translator's respect for the object of translation and for his readers (cf. also Bal 2002).

Linguists speak about translations from one 'natural' language into the other, while 'cultural translation' widens the concept to characterize the transfer of ideas and values, of patterns of thought and behavior between different cultural contexts (cf. Wagner 2009: 1; Wagner et al. 2012). The link between these approaches is that both describe changes, to which both language and the 'ob-

---

3 For a subtle and comprehensive interdisciplinary approach, see, e.g., Kreff et al. 2011.

jects' of cultural translation are subjected as complex processes of *de-* and *re-*contextualization. According to Walter Benjamin, language is always already translated (cf. Benjamin 2002: 76; cf. Wagner 2009: 3). It continually changes in the process of translation between linguistic and cultural contexts, without any identifiable 'starting point.' Drawing on Benjamin, Homi Bhabha develops a similar argument for cultural translation: culture is always already translation. Still, there are important differences: in "translation proper," to draw on one of Eco's main arguments in his recent work on "translation as negotiation," "faithfulness to the original text" plays an important role, even if the expression – in Eco's own words – might seem somewhat "outdated" in light of contemporary literary and translation theories that "stress the principle according to which, in the translating process, the impact a translation has upon its own cultural milieu is more important than an impossible equivalence with the original" (Eco 2004: 4–5). Nonetheless, there are, in fact, certain commonsensical rules defining the "limits of interpretation" (cf. the title of Eco 1994) as well as what may distinguish a 'good' translation from a 'bad' one, in keeping with the translator's aim of rendering the text's intentions as well as its context. However, this stands in contrast to cultural translation in Bhabha's sense, which is basically in line with literary theory, and which foregrounds the shifts and changes of meaning in the process of recontextualization and reception – that is, the performative and transformative aspects of translating (cf. Bhabha 1994; Burke 2000, 2007).

These are doubtlessly some of the most compelling aspects of this concept, when one looks into the reasons and processes of cultural change. Still, at the same time, a closer look at the notions of 'translation' and 'transformation' is needed. 'Translation' and also 'transfer' derive from the same Latin stem, *ferre*, which means to carry something from one place to another; 'transformation,' on the other hand, derives from *formare*, which means 'to form.' In the practice of encounters and exchanges, contacts and conflicts (eventually resulting in cultural changes), single constituents cannot remain unchanged. Actors, texts, and objects are changed within processes of translation; they are not only trans-*lated* but eventually trans-*formed*. At this point, we can obviously no longer deal with questions of 'faithfulness' to an 'original,' to which an interlingual translation in Eco's terms would be committed. Rather, at this point we reach the limits of the metaphorical equivalence between the idea and practice of interlingual and cultural translations. These are the distinctions we should discuss further, and we would suffer a distinct loss to take up the question formulated in the title of this volume, if we were to level these differences too quickly.

I am thus worried by hasty analogies that, especially within debates about cultural translation, may result in 'short circuits.' Firstly, it seems that 'language' and 'culture' are often short-circuited to resemble one another. This cannot merely be demonstrated by a multitude of non-academic cases, for example the meta-discourse on the European Union, but also in academic debates on this issue. Birgit Wagner (2009) quotes a very telling example from the mission statement of the important and commendable online journal *Eurozine*, a network of more than 75 European cultural journals. Under the heading "Translation of cultures," the journal claimed in 2008 that "by translating articles *from different European cultures*, *Eurozine* enables a rich and freewheeling dialogue, which is the foundation of a European public space worthy of its name" (cf. Wagner 2009: 2). This somehow floating equation of languages with "cultures" is by no means 'innocent,' but highly problematic, as, on the one hand, 'culture' is reduced to language, and, on the other hand, supposed 'differences' between cultures are, thus, reified by means of differences between languages. Fortunately, the people responsible for this text seem to have noticed the problem, or been prompted to do so, for the passage – though retaining the header "The philosophy: translation of cultures" – now reads: "Translation is the key to creating a European public space that respects diversity. By translating texts into one of the widely-spoken European languages, *Eurozine* creates the possibility for texts to be understood and valued outside of their original context" (Buljevic et al. 2013).

Secondly, the focus inherent in the keyword of 'globalization,' on spatial rather than other aspects of cultural difference, including 'transnational' translations, often effects a certain (perhaps unintended) 'short circuit' between culture and space. While Homi Bhabha, in his book *The Location of Culture*, distinguishes between 'transnational' and 'translational,' this stands in contrast to the reception of his texts, where the very terms of 'space' and 'culture' are, implicitly or explicitly, equated, as in the case of 'language' and 'culture': *transnational, transcultural,* and *translational* become interchangeable. As in the case of the implicit identification of language with culture, 'translation,' thus, is reduced to just a few aspects of its spectrum of meanings (cf. Bachmann-Medick 2010: 260–262).

Another issue addressed in the title of this volume and in need of clarification is the relation between different research cultures. Inter- and transdisciplinarity are specific forms of transcultural communication and translation. Even more fundamentally, each form of scholarly reception, and the incorporation of new elements into existing traditions involved, is an instance of such a process. For example, by drawing on Walter Benjamin, postcolonial theorist Bhabha integrates one of the founding fathers of German *Kulturwissenschaften* into his body of thought (cf. Bhabha 1994: 163–164; Wagner 2009: 4). Another example is the theoretical turn in British cultural studies connected with Stuart Hall, which would not have been possible without the reception of then-contemporary French poststructuralism (cf. Hall 2000; Morley and Chen 1996). By now it has become quite commonplace to insist that cultural studies and *Kulturwissenschaften* only exist in the plural, and that the ancient dichotomies like cultural studies vs. *Kulturwissenschaften*, history vs. theory, cultural studies vs. history, and even cultural studies vs. political economy hardly facilitate down-to-earth research and, what is more, are mere constructions themselves. As early as 1995, Lawrence Grossberg playfully subtitled an essay dealing with the relations between cultural studies and political economy with "Is Anybody Else Bored with this Debate?" (Grossberg 1995). Birgit Wagner entitled her paper at the *3rd Crossroads in Cultural Studies Conference* in Birmingham (2000), a discussion of literary and personal relations between Antonio Gramsci, Walter Benjamin and Antonio Machado, as "Thinking and Writing in Networks" (Wagner 2001). And Meaghan Morris, in her *Too Soon Too Late: History in Popular Culture* (1998), points out the need for locating cultural studies' issues in a proper historical context. She pinpoints some of the problems related to a "culture of theory" that applies to many traditions within cultural studies (as well as within the field of *Kulturwissenschaften*, one might add) as well as meta-theories that represent big entities and 'monolithic' subjects – the West, Modernity, Fordism – and phrases such as "ever since Plato/Descartes/the Enlightenment" (you name it). All of these do not leave much room for contextually oriented work, particularly as a "culture of theory" is more often than not characterized by debates about theoretical or bibliographic frames of reference rather than about specific objects of analysis (Morris 1998: 2).

Against this background, it seems especially helpful to draw from a multifaceted concept of culture, such as that which developed within and out of the very tensions between different traditions of cultural research and analysis of historical material and from the development of the viewpoint of the *longue durée* in historical changes (cf. Lutter and Reisenleitner 2002; Lässig 2012). Within this context, the following assumptions seem especially important: cultural contacts and conflicts, translations and transformations always happen in specific locations (spaces and places); they are always situated in specific historical contexts; and they are always enacted by specific persons. Just as Meaghan Morris points out the importance of a historical perspective for research on popular culture, historians of globalization such as Jürgen Osterhammel illustrate the need to historically contextualize processes of 'globalization' in the long nineteenth century, as do cultural historians like Peter

Burke in his studies on early modern cultural contacts and conflicts, negotiations, and translations; (cf. Osterhammel 2009; Burke 2000, 2007).

I would now like to discuss an example deliberately taken from medieval history to accentuate what might be evident – namely, that cultural translations, with all their respective specificities, are in no way restricted to a certain historical era. In the context of the comprehensive research conducted on Late Antiquity and the European Early Middle Ages during the last decades, the grand narratives of what was formerly called the Great Migration and the corresponding grand historical entities of 'peoples' or 'cultures' have been comprehensively deconstructed. Instead, medievalists talk about the "Transformation of the Roman World," and this is all about long processes of imagining and constructing communities.[4] Still, when Benedict Anderson wrote his groundbreaking book on *Imagined Communities* (1983) and touched on the early medieval period, he only quoted works on medieval history published more than forty years prior.[5] This is a very practical example of the lack of 'translation' between disciplines (or if you like, research cultures) – but in no way a conceptual or necessary one.

The Great Migration was not a single, coherent migration but a multitude of 'migrations' that were in no sense directed toward any predefined or common goal. They constituted vastly diverse major and minor conquests, long-term population shifts and complex processes of integration spanning several centuries, just as 'frontiers' constituted border areas and contact zones spanning hundreds of kilometers. Especially from AD 400 to 900, border areas repeatedly underwent fundamental change (cf. Pohl et al. 2000; McKitterick 2001; Pohl 2005).

Life in these border areas in the final decades of the fifth century is described by a unique document for the time, the so-called *Vita St. Severini*. It is an early hagiographic account of the Saint Severinus, who was probably a former Roman official in the border region of Noricum at the Danube in what is today's Upper and Lower Austria, but, in fact, very little is known about his personal background. This region sets the scene for the events reported, which took place during the 480s, when the remaining Roman population of the region decided to leave its dwellings and what was left of Roman infrastructure and move south to Italy, which still constituted the center of the Roman world (cf. Lotter 1976;

---

4 For major comparative research projects undertaken since the early 1990s, see the book series *Transformation of the Roman World* (Leiden/Boston: Brill); for projects since 1997, see also Pohl and Reimitz 1998; Pohl et al. 2000; Corradini et al. 2003.
5 I am grateful to Walter Pohl for this observation.

Wolfram 1995). Eugippius, the author of the text and a member of the Saint's community, wrote the story down decades later, after the group had left the Danube region and settled in Naples in 511, about twenty-five years after the migration and the protagonist's death (cf. Noll 1981). It is not clear whether Eugippius had ever even personally met the protagonist of his account.

The *Vita*, as a piece of hagiography from the very beginnings of Christianity in West and Central Europe, is an extremely precious source that gives at least some insights into the living conditions and everyday life of these decades of accelerated transformation, during which the Roman infrastructure lost significance and early structures of Christian communities took over the organization of what was needed at the time. So, the "Saint" Severinus – and, in fact, there was nothing like a procedure of canonization at the time – simply did what was necessary: negotiate with the non-Roman neighbors, defend his community against sometimes hostile raids, and fend off floods, storms and plagues of locusts. To be sure, as demanded by the genre, he did all of this on behalf and by order of God and by means of miracles, as one would expect from a decent saint. Therefore, the account gives a lot of information both on contemporary needs, beliefs, and ways of life, but also, and most importantly within this context, on contacts and conflicts between different groups not only simultaneously present but, at least for a certain time, actually co-existing in the region.

I would finally like to link some of the theoretical debates about concepts of 'culture,' and its translation and transformation, in the field of cultural and postcolonial studies to similar discussions in medieval studies that pursue comparable questions about the specificity of source materials and the possibilities and limits of their analysis (cf. Spiegel 1990). In doing so, I will draw on the *Vita St. Severini*, a seminal text for medievalists, to consider the advantages and disadvantages of the terms in question.

One of the basic assumptions uniting contemporary cultural theory and medieval studies is the concept of individual and social identities as constructed (e.g., in Hall and du Gay 1996; Hall 1997). Their cultural constituents are seen as multiple and mostly ambivalent, if not contradictory forms of shared signs and narrations in the past and present (on early medieval history, see Pohl and Reimitz 1998; Corradini et al. 2003). 'Culture' is not an articulation of stable identities of ethnic or religious communities but conceived as the manifold and changing categories and formations of knowledge by which communities define themselves and are defined by others (cf. Anderson 1983; Geary 2002; Pohl 2005). Cultural identities, thus, are never confined or fixed but fragmented and constantly translated.

Identities constitute relations between individuals and social groups. They are constructed within cultural processes of identifying with and differentiating between others. They work by means of classification and representation – a framework within which people make sense of their experiences by marking their belongings and non-belongings symbolically. Symbolic signs, in turn, have real social effects and play an important role within power relations, as their function is to tell who is part of and who is excluded from a group. Identities, thus, are produced by and through culture (cf. Hall 2004).

Where, then, do we find such processes of cultural formation and translation in the *Vita St. Severini*? Does it tell a story of conflicting cultures – of a Roman culture vs. 'barbarians,' as it was predominantly read for a long time, i.e. as one of the most impressive textual sources from the end of the Roman Empire and the decline of Roman culture at its northern frontier, brought about by a clash with the barbarian peoples? Is it a narrative about a sharp contrast between Roman and barbarian populations?[6] In fact, at first glance, the *Vita* provides a wide range of examples that might substantiate these kinds of readings: barbarian raids against remaining towns in Roman Noricum at the end of the fifth century; military and social conflicts in little villages and province towns that seem to prove that a coexistence between 'Romans' and 'barbarians' in a community was not considered possible. The most prominent and powerful example for this type of interpretation is the narration of the Saint's announcement of the Roman exodus from Noricum and the actual event, which took place a few years after his death. This example was so powerful because it drew a comparison to the biblical Egyptian captivity of God's people. Clearly, influential cultural narratives embedded in the Christian imaginary were used for different reasons (and not least to gloss over 'internal' conflicts within the community), and they had their effects both on contemporaries and historians (Pohl 2001: 16; Wood "Monastic Frontiers" 2001: 45).

On the other hand, though, the *Vita St. Severini* represents a wide range of 'alternative' stories contradicting a grand narrative of clearly defined conflicting 'cultures' of Romans and non-Romans (Pohl and Diesenberger 2001): first, there is a variety of differentiated representations of the concept of 'barbarians,' which is, in the first place, a linguistic one, used from a Roman perspective to designate people talking in a foreign language – i.e. not in Latin. In the *Vita*, 'barbarians' are assessed quite differently, both in terms of their denominations and narrative descriptions (Pohl 2001). We find barbarian robbers and monks of barbarian origin within Severin's community, just as hostile barbarian groups, whose assaults were expected daily; and barbarian kings, with whom the Saint

---

6 For an overview and detailed discussions of the older research on the topic, see the contributions in Pohl and Diesenberger 2001.

negotiates and who he advises in accordance with the Christian principle of charity.

The category of the 'true spiritual life' embodied in and represented by the holy man Severin clearly cuts across the identity categories of 'Romans' and 'barbarians.' What really counts is not who you are, but what you do. Corresponding to the biblical exhortation to follow Christ without regard to age, gender, origin, or social rank, the *Vita* focuses on 'social sins' for which people are punished regardless of their ethnic or cultural categorization. In Eugippius' account, barbarian raids – just like earthquakes, floods, and famine – serve the 'function' of reckoning the misbehavior and the sins of people and, at the same time, illustrate the Saint's holy deeds. Thus, emerging Christianity clearly seems to have been a powerful means of cultural translation and integration between seemingly different groups (cf. Diesenberger 2001: 87–89; Wood "Monastic Frontiers" 2001: 47), and we should not forget that, in the subtext of his narrative, Eugippius constantly negotiates the theological discourse of his time. Moreover, conflicting cultural practices become manifest at other levels of social life, for example, in negotiations about the 'right' way of living – monastic or secular, within or outside communities such as towns or monasteries. Similarly, the interests of individuals and social groups within different communities confront each other and are mediated by Severinus, not to mention ambivalent political interests, partialities, and mostly temporal alliances of different groups, both 'Roman' and 'barbarian,' that constitute another strand of the narrative.

The Roman Empire had already been a highly differentiated and also 'internally' mobile and fragmented society for centuries. Thus, the complex web of interests, conflicts, translations – literal and cultural – and negotiations represented in the *Vita St. Severini* is interwoven with different cultural patterns and role models articulated by often contradictory practices. After all, if 'culture' is everywhere in the *Vita St. Severini*, it is articulated differently and according to various contexts, just not as a grand subject of singular opposed identities (cf. Wood "Monastic Frontiers" 2001: 46). One might rather read the text as a contemporary narrative that represents a range of role models transporting, translating, and eventually transforming cultural patterns that had powerful social effects. These patterns, though, do not exist independently of cultural practices; historical facts are inseparably intertwined with how they are discursively shaped. They only 'make sense' and become meaningful in relation to discursive models and cultural patterns – whether corresponding to or diverging from them. Cultural models, as part of complex discursive configurations that provide individuals with options to appropriate existing discourses in different ways, are rearticulated and changed by the cultural practices of people using them.

We are obviously dealing with processes of cultural transformation. This is evident in the multiplicity of contextual appropriations and translations between the author Eugippius' world – Naples at the beginning of the sixth century – and the world of his protagonist Severinus. In the south of Italy, where refugees from all over the Roman Empire came together, Eugippius addresses another highly heterogeneous, multi-ethnic community struggling for new patterns of belonging and identity (see, e.g., Cooper 2001). The *Vita St. Severini* is such a telling source, exactly because it fails to construct one single grand narrative of homogeneity; the text succeeds not by glossing over the heterogeneity of views, values, interests, and practices of its protagonists or of the author's contemporaries but rather by making the tensions and ambiguities of both historical communities visible. The *Vita St. Severini* exhibits textual strategies that prevent the blurring of cultural categories (whether framed in terms of spirituality, community, or ethnicity) and that cut across such categories in multiple ways. It is a good example of how different categories of self-perception and construction of the 'Other' overlap in very complex and often contradictory ways.

Therefore, I would like to advocate a less nominal and monumental use of the term 'culture,' precisely because culture, whether past or present, cannot simply be equated with language, class, or conceptions of 'nation' – nor can it be equated with a 'post-national' concept of space. For even if 'culture' is not construed nationally or within an ethno-linguistic framework, the question still remains whether, perhaps, the construction of a nominal concept of 'Culture with a capital C' itself leads to the idea of cultural entities that can be sharply distinguished from one another. Is it not precisely these constructions that potentially render all the transitions, ambivalences, contradictions, multiplicity of interests, conflicts, negotiations and translations invisible, which are always part of the game? Differentiations between the 'same' and the 'other' are often found within what is called 'one's own culture.' Telling alternative stories about the forms and processes of social communication and cultural translation in specific contexts enables us to take cultural texts as flexible models between representations and practices more seriously and to show the usefulness of a concept of 'culture' that goes beyond its construction as a 'grand subject.'

Thus, I want to advocate a concept of culture that is able to describe contexts, processes, and practices and, at the same time, use them as analytical categories. Taking up one of the volume's basic questions of how the notion of 'translation' benefits our understanding of 'culture,' I consider the metaphor of cultural translation as negotiation to be most fruitful and, to draw on Umberto

Eco again (2004), I do so with all due respect for the specific object of translation and for the often laborious, even tedious research involved in the endeavor. Of course, I do not argue for abandoning comprehensive, global relations and interactions to understand what is going on in our complex world. But I do plead for an approach that acknowledges that not all types of 'translations' proceed along the same axis. Literal, semiotic, and cultural translations are always specific to their historical contexts and mostly operate in ambivalent ways. These contexts have to be explored and analyzed comparatively. Such analyses can lead to a better understanding of culture without a capital C – if we accept the limits of a "translational study of culture" and do not stretch the metaphor of translation beyond the limits of our source material, and if we meet the variety and heterogeneity of cultural change with terminological variety and precision (Burke 2000: 36). I, therefore, do not think that *one* practice or *one* set of "transnational" *translational studies* can or should be defined (as that would seem just as strange as claiming one historiography or ethnography). I would rather support equipping a toolbox with which a variety of *studies of culture* can be undertaken that live up to the exigencies of their objects of study, contexts, and the people involved.

References

Anderson, Benedict R. *Imagined Communities: Reflections on the Origin and Spread of Nationalism*. London: Verso, 1983.

Bachmann-Medick, Doris. *Cultural Turns. Neuorientierungen in den Kulturwissenschaften*. 4th edition. Reinbek: Rowohlt, 2010 [2006].

Bal, Mieke. *Travelling Concepts in the Humanities: A Rough Guide*. Toronto/Buffalo/London: University of Toronto Press, 2002.

Benjamin, Walter. *Medienästhetische Schriften*. Frankfurt a.M: Suhrkamp, 2002.

Bhabha, Homi K. *The Location of Culture*. London: Routledge, 1994.

Buden, Boris, and Stefan Nowotny. "Cultural Translation: An Introduction to the Problem." *Translation Studies* 2.2 (2009): 196–208.

Buljevic, Miljenka, Göran Dahlberg, Marc-Oliver Padis, and Elke Rauth. *Eurozine*. http://www.eurozine.com/about_Eurozine.html (16 October 2013).

Burke, Peter. *Kultureller Austausch*. Frankfurt a.M: Suhrkamp, 2000.

Burke, Peter. "Cultures of Translation in Early Modern Europe." *Cultural Translation in Early Modern Europe*. Eds. Peter Burke and R. Po-chia Hsia. Cambridge: Cambridge University Press, 2007. 7–38.

Butler, Judith. *Das Unbehagen der Geschlechter*. Frankfurt a.M.: Suhrkamp, 2008.

Cooper, Kate. "The Widow as Impressario: Gender, Legendary Afterlives, and Documentary Evidence in Eugippius' *Vita Severini*." *Eugippius und Severin. Der Autor, der Text und der*

Heilige. Eds. Walter Pohl and Max Diesenberger. Vienna: Verlag der österreichischen Akademie der Wissenschaften, 2001. 53–75.

Corradini, Richard, Max Diesenberger, and Helmut Reimitz, eds. *The Construction of Communities in the Early Middle Ages: Texts, Resources and Artefacts*. Leiden/Boston: Brill, 2003.

Diesenberger, Maximilian. "Topographie und Gemeinschaft in der *Vita Severini*." *Eugippius und Severin. Der Autor, der Text und der Heilige*. Eds. Walter Pohl and Max Diesenberger. Vienna: Verlag der österreichischen Akademie der Wissenschaften, 2001. 77–97.

Eco, Umberto. *The Limits of Interpretation*. Bloomington: Indiana University Press, 1994.

Eco, Umberto. *Mouse or Rat? Translation as Negotiation*. London: Phoenix, 2004.

Geary, Patrick J. *The Myth of Nations: The Medieval Origins of Europe*. Princeton: Princeton University Press, 2002.

Grossberg, Lawrence. "Cultural Studies vs. Political Economy: Is Anybody Else Bored with this Debate." *Critical Studies in Mass Communication* 12 (1995): 72–81.

Grossberg, Lawrence. "On Postmodernism and Articulation: An Interview with Stuart Hall." *Stuart Hall: Critical Dialogues in Cultural Studies*. Eds. David Morley and Kuan-Hsing Chen. London: Routledge, 1996 [1986]. 131–150.

Hall, Stuart. "New Ethnicities." *'Race', Culture and Difference*. Eds. James Donald and Ali Rattansi. London: Sage, 1997. 252–259.

Hall, Stuart. *Ein politisches Theorieprojekt. Ausgewählte Schriften 3*. Hamburg: Argument, 2000.

Hall, Stuart. *Ideologie, Identität, Repräsentation. Ausgewählte Schriften 4*. Hamburg: Argument, 2004.

Hall, Stuart, and Paul du Gay, eds. *Questions of Cultural Identity*. London/Thousand Oaks/New Delhi: Sage, 1996.

Kreff, Fernand, Eva-Maria Knoll, and Andre Gingrich, eds. *Lexikon der Globalisierung*. Bielefeld: transcript, 2011.

Lässig, Simone. "Übersetzungen in der Geschichte – Geschichte als Übersetzung? Überlegungen zu einem analytischen Konzept und Forschungsgegenstand für die Geschichtswissenschaft." *Geschichte und Gesellschaft* 38.2 (2012): 189–216.

Lotter, Friedrich. *Severinus von Noricum. Legende und historische Wirklichkeit. Untersuchungen zur Phase des Übergangs von spätantiken zu frühmittelalterlichen Denk- und Lebensformen*. Stuttgart: Hiersemann, 1976.

Lutter, Christina, and Markus Reisenleitner. "Introducing History (in)to Cultural Studies: Some Remarks on the German-Speaking Context." *Cultural Studies* 16.5 (2002): 611–630.

McKitterick, Rosamond, ed. *The Early Middle Ages: Europe 400–1000*. Oxford: Oxford University Press, 2001.

Morley, David, and Kuan-Hsing Chen, eds. *Stuart Hall: Critical Dialogues in Cultural Studies*. London: Routledge, 1996.

Morris, Meaghan. *Too Soon Too Late: History in Popular Culture*. Bloomington: Indiana University Press, 1998.

Noll, Rudolf, ed. *Eugippius. Das Leben des Heiligen Severin*. Lateinisch und Deutsch. 2nd edition. Passau: Passavia Universitätsverlag, 1981.

Osterhammel, Jürgen. *Die Verwandlung der Welt. Eine Geschichte des 19. Jahrhunderts*. Munich: Beck, 2009.

Pohl, Walter. "Einleitung: Commemoratorium – Vergegenwärtigungen des heiligen Severin." *Eugippius und Severin. Der Autor, der Text und der Heilige*. Eds. Walter Pohl and Max

Diesenberger. Vienna: Verlag der österreichischen Akademie der Wissenschaften, 2001. 9–23.

Pohl, Walter. *Die Völkerwanderung. Eroberung und Integration.* Stuttgart: Kohlhammer, 2002.

Pohl, Walter. "Aux origines d'une Europe ethnique: Identités en transformation entre antiquité et moyen âge." *Annales: Histoire, Sciences sociales* 60.1 (2005): 183–208.

Pohl, Walter, and Helmut Reimitz, eds. *Strategies of Distinction: The Construction of Ethnic Communities, 300–800.* Leiden/Boston: Brill, 1998.

Pohl, Walter, Helmut Reimitz, and Ian Wood, eds. *The Transformation of Frontiers – From Late Antiquity to the Carolingians.* Leiden/Boston: Brill, 2000.

Pohl, Walter, and Max Diesenberger, eds. *Eugippius und Severin. Der Autor, der Text und der Heilige.* Vienna: Verlag der österreichischen Akademie der Wissenschaften, 2001.

Spiegel, Gabrielle M. "History, Historicism, and the Social Logic of the Text in the Middle Ages." *Speculum* 65.1 (1990): 59–86.

St-Pierre, Paul, and Prafulla C. Kar, eds. *In Translation – Reflections, Refractions, Transformations.* Amsterdam/Philadelphia: John Benjamins, 2007.

Wagner, Birgit. "Denken (und Schreiben) in Netzwerken: Antonio Gramsci, Walter Benjamin und Antonio Machado." *Die Werkzeugkiste der Cultural Studies. Perspektiven, Anschlüsse und Interventionen.* Eds. Udo Göttlich, Lothar Mikos, and Rainer Winter. Bielefeld: transcript, 2001. 223–243.

Wagner, Birgit. "Kulturelle Übersetzung. Erkundungen über ein wanderndes Konzept." *Kakanien Revisited* (2009). http://www.kakanien.ac.at/beitr/postcol/BWagner2.pdf. (16 October 2013).

Wagner, Birgit. "Kulturelle Übersetzung. Erkundungen über ein wanderndes Konzept." *Dritte Räume. Homi K. Bhabhas Kulturtheorie. Kritik. Anwendung. Reflexion.* Eds. Anna Babka, Julia Malle, and Matthias Schmidt. Vienna: turia + kant, 2012. 29–42.

Wagner, Birgit, Christina Lutter, and Helmut Lethen, eds. *Übersetzungen. Zeitschrift für Kulturwissenschaften* 2 (2012). Bielefeld: transcript.

Wolfram, Herwig. *Grenzen und Räume. Geschichte Österreichs vor seiner Entstehung.* Vienna: Ueberreuter, 1995.

Wood, Ian. *The Missionary Life: Saints and the Evangelisation of Europe 400–1050.* New York: Longman, 2001.

Wood, Ian. "The Monastic Frontiers of the *Vita Severini*." *Eugippius und Severin. Der Autor, der Text und der Heilige.* Eds. Walter Pohl and Max Diesenberger. Vienna: Verlag der österreichischen Akademie der Wissenschaften, 2001. 41–51.

II. Knowledge Systems and Discursive Fields

Boris Buden
Translation and the East

There is No Such Thing as an 'Eastern European Study of Culture'

Asked to provide an account of what is called 'Eastern European study of culture,' one is not only confronted with an impossible task but also arbitrarily cast
into a role with which it is hard to identify both intellectually and morally. In
addition to this, any possible answer, including the refusal to answer – the
option chosen here – will necessarily have political meaning.

Imagine first that we have chosen the opportunistic option instead, which is
usually preferred and almost automatically performed in the academic production of knowledge. In this case, the task of providing a report on an Eastern
European study of culture is taken seriously. The procedure is, then, a routine.
One selects a case study considered to be exemplary of the way culture is theorized in Eastern Europe – the curriculum at a local university, the publications
surrounding it, its impact on a broader public, etc. –, puts it in the context of an
alleged 'country-specific' culture of knowledge and compares it, finally, with
the international study of culture, or better, the study of culture on its way to
inter- or trans-nationalization.

Let us put the fact that one cannot arbitrarily generalize such a case, neither
on the level of a particular culture of knowledge, nor on the level of Eastern
Europe itself, aside. Simply speaking, we cannot choose a case, a country or
region-specific culture of knowledge and say that it is representative of the
Eastern European study of culture. Who can speak in the name of Eastern Europe?

Another question regards what this East of Europe actually means beyond
simply the name of a certain geopolitical space? The idea of an Eastern European study of culture implies that the East is a cognitive Other, or, more precisely,
a cluster of different, that is, particular or 'country-specific' cultures of knowledge. In other words, it figures the East as the place where culture is theorized
differently. But differently than what, differently than who? Germany's or any
other country's specific study of culture? A Western study of culture, that is,
another culturally specific study of culture? In both cases, the gaze at Eastern
Europe implied in the question about its study of culture cannot be identified

with the international study of culture – and if it can, only as another culturally specific international study of culture, which would be a contradiction.

1 "I Don't Want to Be Your Native Informant"

Now we cannot but ask: what actually makes Eastern Europe appear as a general cultural concept, this especially in relation to the place from where it is perceived in terms of cultural and cognitive otherness?

This is, for sure, not a question of a generality that is immanent to the cultural concept of Eastern Europe itself – for instance, the most general features of Eastern European cultural identity. This wouldn't suffice. The generality at stake here must include both the cultural concept of Eastern Europe and the gaze in which it appears as a general cultural concept. In other words, we are searching for what in Eastern Europe is culturally more than Eastern Europe.

The only concept that is able to provide sufficient cultural generality to the notion of Eastern Europe and, moreover, to establish its relation to the international study of culture today is the concept of modernism. It is only within this concept that Eastern Europe transcends its cultural particularity.

But before we explain this, let us go back to the problem of a subject who is supposed to provide an account of the 'Eastern European study of culture.' This, namely, concerns a specific role one must assume in fulfilling the task: the role of the so-called native informant. This figure, as is well-known, originated in anthropological fieldwork. The task of the native informant is to supply 'indigenous knowledge' on colonial subjects, thereby facilitating exchange between the metropolis or country of origin.

The figure of the native informant stars in Gayatri Spivak's *Critique of Postcolonial Reason*. Spivak argues that the planetary humanism that emerges with the Enlightenment and found its theoretical foundation in the European ethical philosophical tradition of Kant, Hegel and Marx, has foreclosed the 'native informant' as the condition of its possibility. For Spivak, the role of the native informant is to possess a necessary complicity in humanist knowledge-production. The native informant is a character that substitutes an imaginary or absent figure. In our case, this would be the Eastern European study of culture. Spivak defines the native informant as "a name for that mark of expulsion from the name of Man – a mark crossing out the impossibility of the ethical relation" (Spivak 1999: 6). In other words, there is no innocent theory production, which is the reason why we must become aware of its complicity with imperialist or neo-imperialist projects, or, to quote Spivak, "acknowledge a responsibility toward the trace of the other, not to mention toward other struggles" (Spivak 1999: 198).

This awareness, which takes the form of a "transcendental critique of post-colonial reason" in terms of becoming aware of its conditions of possibility – that is, of its limits, both ethical and cognitive – is, for Spivak, the precondition for moving from postcolonial discourse studies to what Spivak proposes as a kind of transnational cultural studies or transnational cultural literacy as discipline, which is precisely what is at stake here. Or, to apply it directly to our situation: on the way to an inter- or transnational study of culture, the figure of native informant is a necessary bump in the road, which we cannot avoid if we really want to reach this goal.

However, there is a curious moment in Spivak's theory of the foreclosed native informant. She argues that, with the end of the Cold War in 1989, things changed: a certain postcolonial subject – a metropolitan migrant, a citizen of the decolonized nation-state or, as she calls him, a "benevolent cultural nativist" – started to appropriate the native informant's position. However, Spivak does not spell out the factors that led to this. She does not tell us exactly why the year 1989 marks this transformation in the traditional figure of native informant. But we can try to figure it out ourselves.

2 The Task Fulfilled: It Is Underdeveloped, Belated, Provincial, Peripheral...

So, what actually happened in 1989? An explanation that expresses today's hegemonic view on the events that brought East European Communism to collapse was succinctly provided by Jürgen Habermas in 1990. He summed up the meaning of what happened back then, in Eastern Europe, under one single phrase: "the catching up revolution" (*die nachholende Revolution*), or, as he also wrote, a rewinding (*rückspulende*) revolution; the purpose of the revolution, according to Habermas, was to clear the way for catching up with missed development (Habermas 1990: 180). But what had been missed in the Communist East?

In one of the pamphlets that, during the nineties, was still euphorically celebrating the fall of Communist Totalitarianism, we find the following sentence: "The Bolshewik Revolution was a titanic effort to stop the invasion of Western culture" (Pellicani 1998: 15). It defines the October Revolution and historic communism as, essentially, a cultural event and, concretely, an act of resistance to a particular – Western – cultural development; and it also implicitly determines what the process of the so-called post-communist transition should essentially be about: contrary to the Bolsheviks, the post-communist democrats of the East should not only allow but also facilitate the invasion of Western culture, which, for the author, is identical to democracy. Habermas' concept of "the catching up revolution" implies the same. With the removal of Communists in 1989/1990, the expansion of modernity ("Ausgreifen der Moderne") towards the East could be resumed, as Habermas writes (Habermas 1990: 185). The East can finally catch up with the West in terms of modern cultural development, which is just another phrase for democracy. However, this also defines the post-communist East as a space of belated modernity, essentially, a cultural time-space.

The belatedness of the East designates a cultural difference in time, which also implies the difference between cultural universality and cultural particularity. As Slovenian Philosopher Rastko Močnik (2009) argues, the belatedness of the East makes it particular, specific and localized in relation to the West. The West, on the other side, is not only always already in its proper place but also always on time. In other words, the West is timeless, canonic and general; it is a norm, a measure against which the peripheral, the provincial, is to be measured. This has a huge impact on our relationship to the past. According to Močnik, the East-West difference is an ideological phenomenon. Its ideological function is to rob both sides of their history: the West appears as emancipated from its own history, moreover from any history, which is why it can be imposed as general and canonic. The notion of the East, on the contrary, is associated with amnesia, for its telos is to get rid of history, to become an a-historical non-space like the West. Its own history is what makes the East peripheral and provincial. In short, the East has a history that would be better forgotten. Moreover, the West-East divide, according to Močnik, robs both sides of their common history and prevents them from having a common history in the future. The East is doomed to struggle for recognition, and the form of this struggle is called identity.

This applies to knowledge, too. Knowledge of the East has no past but rather an identity: the Eastern European study of culture! The East is determined by its cultural particularity, which arises only in relation to knowledge that is supposed to be universal: the study of culture on its way to inter- or trans-nationalization.

This is what we have been asked to supply in the role of the native informant: information about the particular identity of the Eastern European study of culture. One doesn't have to know much about this identity to provide information: the study of culture in Eastern Europe is underdeveloped, belated, provincial, peripheral, desperately dependent on local knowledge traditions and cultures. At the same time, it is both in the process of catching up with the development of the international study of culture that is taking place almost exclusively in the West, and it constantly struggles for recognition from what is supposed to be this international study of culture. The task is fulfilled, the question about the Eastern European study of culture properly answered, without us having to do the usual homework of a native informant.

In other words, an inter- or transnational cultural theory cannot innocently use the cultural concept of the East without reactivating its ideological effects. This is why the East is a challenge for any trans/national study of culture. Without being critically examined, in terms of a contemporary critique of ideology, the use of the cultural concept of the East leads necessarily to what Spivak calls complicity with imperialist or neo-imperialist projects. This is why a genuinely transnational cultural theory must go beyond the East-West difference. It must work with concepts whose generality critically sublates this ideological difference, that is, this relation between an allegedly pre-given, original universality and its particular translations.

3 Translating Modernism

It is not by chance that we are now opening up the problem of translation. According to Peter Osborne, in order to become truly transnational, cultural theory must work with cultural concepts that are sufficiently general to embrace its full geopolitical range, that is, to come to terms with its global character (cf. Osborne 2000: 53). This is, namely, what we expect of a transnational cultural theory – to be globally applicable. As Osborne argues, it is precisely the concept of translation that is able to provide a model of theoretical generality. In our concrete case, it offers the possibility to understand a cultural form – 'modernism,' for instance – beyond the ideological East-West difference, that is, beyond the difference between modernism as an originally Western cultural form and its particular translations in non-Western contexts – a Chinese or an African or an East European modernism. Of course, we are not talking about the traditional concept of translation based on the primacy of an original context and obsessed with the idea of understanding translations as secondary productions. We rather think of translation as providing a model for forging certain types of cultural generality or universality. For Osborne, translatability is inherent in the concept of modernism and, therefore, responsible for its translations into non-Western contexts, as well as for its universalization in the form of a general cultural concept (cf. Osborne 2000: 56). From this perspective, modernism cannot claim an original Western context, for it is exposed to historicity – both the original and its translation undergo changes in time, to use Walter Benjamin's words from his essay "The Task of the Translator." Translation, in this case, is not a metaphor for a relation between different, in themselves always already existing languages, cultural entities or identities, but, to quote Osborne: "the metonymic register of the interpretive dimension of the process of social intercourse and exchange in general" (Osborne 2000: 57). In short, translation is a social relation.

What does it then concretely mean for modernism as a cultural form when it enters the process of translation? First of all, it does not mean that it necessarily enters the binary relation between an original – say the Western modernism in its authenticity and uniqueness – and, on the other hand, a plurality of its translations that will always lack this or that quality of the original and can be conceived of as, for instance, its "belated," "underdeveloped," "missed," "failed," "in need of catching up with" copies. At stake is, rather, modernism as a Western cultural form that has been subsequently generalized at a global level. Precisely through this generalization, which is nothing but an activation of the translatability that is immanent in the concept, modernism has finally detached itself from the Western context and has become, to quote Osborne again, a "cultural affirmation of a particular temporal logic of negation (the new)" (Osborne 2000: 59).

What makes Western modernism translatable into all other cultural contexts is its introduction of a cultural difference in time, concretely, the difference between 'old' and 'new' that is imminent to the concept. This abstract difference is what has been translated in local contexts all over the world and, in its abstractness, can never be valued as "belated," "less authentic" or "underdeveloped." At the same time, it discloses modernism as an inherently future-oriented form of cultural experience that is, at the same time, an experience of history as temporal form. There is a temporal formalism in the concept of modernism – it structures our time-consciousness – this is what makes it translatable, capable of universalization and generalization, and, finally, suitable for a transnational study of culture.

However, such a concept of translation as universalization necessarily confronts us with its social and political meaning, or, to repeat Osborne's words, with the processes of social intercourse and exchange, which are never free of conflict and struggle, be it a struggle for hegemony or a struggle for recognition. As Gayatri Spivak warns us, cultural theory on its way to internationalization must acknowledge a responsibility for other struggles (cf. Spivak 1999: 198).

4 Resistance: Necessary Even If Doomed to Fail

Let us, at this point, move to the empirical side, that is, to what has been ex-pected of a native informant asked to provide the case studies of cultural knowledge production in Eastern Europe. We are not interested in any knowl-edge that is produced in cultural studies departments of Eastern European Uni-versities but rather in knowledge that is forged and rooted in the struggle against Western hegemony that constantly reproduces the notion of the East as its cultural and cognitive other.

There are generally two different strategies of this struggle: The first one is a sort of struggle for recognition in the form of cultural translation. It is best pre-sented in Maria Todorova's famous book *Imagining the Balkans*. In short, Todorova shows how 'the Balkans' has become a European swear word, that is, a cultural concept of exclusion and suppression. She discloses the complicity of imperial politics in forging this concept and misusing it in introducing a frontier between a civilized and a barbarian part of Europe. "As in the case of the Orient, the Balkans have served as a repository of negative characteristics against which a positive and self-congratulatory image of the 'European' and 'the West' has been constructed," she writes (Todorova 1997: 188). Her book concludes with a sort of plea: "If Europe has produced not only racism but also antiracism, not only misogyny but also feminism, not only anti-Semitism, but also its repu-diation, than what can be termed Balkanism has not yet been coupled with its complementing and ennobling antiparticle" (Todorova 1997: 189). In fact it is a plea for cultural translation in the sense Judith Butler (1996) uses it – as a model for cultural universality. Butler's formula is: universality can be articulated only in response to its own excluded outside. Consider the following example: wom-en had been earlier excluded from the idea of the universally human and, in consequence, from public political life in Europe. After having put this concept of universality under pressure – precisely from the position of their exclusion – women succeeded in being accepted, which finally changed the idea of what is universally human; now the idea includes women, too. Something similar has happened to other formerly excluded minorities like Jews, Roma, people of color, etc. What Todorova's *Imagining the Balkans* finally argues is that the Bal-kans, too, should undergo this process of inclusion of an excluded outside that constructs the concept of cultural universality, a process Judith Butler calls 'cultural translation.'

The second strategy of the East European struggle against Western hegemony can be called 'over-identification' – the concept allegedly coined by Slavoj Žižek. Back in 1983, the first public appearances of the Slovenian music and cross-media group *Laibach* – in uniforms resembling *Hitlerjugend* – shocked the public in Slovenia and the former Yugoslavia, immediately initiating a heated discussion about the question of whether they are truly fascists or not. Some argued that what we see is what we get while others stated that their outfit and gestures are merely ironic and, therefore, harmless imitations of totalitarian rituals. In contrast, the group of Slovenian Lacanians associated with Slavoj Žižek understood *Laibach's* artistic practice as a form of successful subversion of totalitarianism: it frustrates the system and the ruling ideology precisely to the extent that it is not its ironic imitation but rather represents an over-identification with it (cf. Žižek 2013). Through over-identification, *Laibach* brings the obscene, superego underside of the system to light. The music group depicts fascism in all its totalitarian rhetoric and ritual as part of a strategy that confronts us with fascism. They expose the hidden flipside of fascism's true nature, which must remain invisible and unspoken in order for it to hold sway over the people.

Later, it was asked many times, what came first, the theory, that is, Žižek and Slovenian Lacanians, who invented the concept of over-identification, or the cultural practice, that is, *Laibach*, who articulated it culturally? Eda Čufer, an artist, curator and, at that time, active member of the whole artistic and cultural movement to which *Laibach* loudly belonged, once perfectly answered this question: "[A]t that time this way of thinking was already in the air; it was the language of alternative society. You didn't need to read the books, the original Lacan or Žižek; you could get it from the journal Mladina, or from Radio Student – it was everywhere in the media, in private talks, etc." (Čufer 2000). This dynamic should be recalled today, when we all too quickly mistake the academy for the exclusive space of the study of culture, especially when it comes to cultural and intellectual life, as well as to the production of theory, in the former socialist East.

The same concept of over-identification has lately been applied by another Slovenian artistic collective precisely in the context of the Eastern European struggle against Western cultural hegemony – Irwin's *East-Art Map*. The curiosity of this artistic project lies in the fact that it tries to reconstruct fifty years of art history in Eastern Europe without any reference to the Western – almost exclusively understood as universal – history of art. However, another curiosity of the *East-Art Map* project is that it was exhibited in 2003 at the exhibition entitled *Blood and Honey: Future's in the Balkans*, curated by the legendary Harald Szeemann and one of three large and quite ambitious art exhibitions dealing with the Balkans that were all organized within just one year in Austria and Germany.

To sum up: not only has an artistic subversion of the Western cultural hegemony quickly succeeded in entering the Western art-system, that is, in gain-
ing recognition – as a Western cultural commodity under the label of 'Balkan-
art' – precisely from the power it dared to challenge. Todorova's plea for European recognition of the Balkans was soon fulfilled, at least in the European art
scene.

5 A Struggle and Nothing More

Although failed, both strategies of resistance have clearly laid bare the antagonistic character of today's 'inter- or transnational' knowledge production, deeply trapped in the contradictions of its cultural articulations. An East that is supposed to differentiate the so-called Eastern European study of culture from its
Western (international, universal) counterpart is not simply just a cultural location. It is the name of a struggle, either in the guise of an excluded outside that
seeks inclusion into the West or as a paroxysm of itself that, in the act of an
excessive self-easternization, repeats the claim to hegemony of the West and, at
the same time, excludes it completely. And it will remain the name of that
struggle even if it designates nothing but its own defeat.

Is there, thus, any Eastern European study of culture beyond this struggle?
One that patiently learns from the Western study of culture and creatively applies this knowledge to its own cultural context – in short, one that can claim to
be a faithful translation of its Western original? If there is such a study of culture, it would be admitting that the so-called inter- or transnationalization of
cultural theory is nothing but a translational expansion of a Western original.
And because this notion of an original implies spatiality, we can simply visual-
ize this translation as a centripetally controlled enlargement of the Western
circle. Is that really what a truly transnational study of culture should look like?

No, there is no such thing as an Eastern European study of culture. There is
only a struggle going on, a struggle in which what is at stake is more than this
or that cultural theory and even more than the divisions and hierarchies among
geo-cultural regions. It is vehemently fought – in the name of emancipation,
what else – with all available cultural forms, cognitive concepts, and aesthetic
practices, but it is a struggle that has lost its social ground. This, too, is what a
study of culture on the move to its trans-nationalization should be reminded of:
not only can it not avoid getting involved in this struggle; it must recover its
social dimension long ago disavowed, not least by the studies of culture itself. It

is only in bringing together knowledge and social cause that it will be able to hold its ground in this struggle.

References

Butler, Judith. "Universality in Culture." *For Love of Country? Debating the Limits of Patriotism.* Martha C. Nussbaum with respondents, ed. Joshua Cohen. Boston: Beacon Press, 1996. 45–52.

Čufer, Eda. "NSK 2000? Irwin and Eda Čufer interviewed by Joanne Richardson." Ljubljana, 2000. http://subsol.c3.hu/subsol_2/contributors/nsktext.html (8 October 2013).

EAM, East-Art-Map Project. http://www.eastartmap.org/ (8 October 2013).

Habermas, Jürgen. "Nachholende Revolution und linker Revisionsbedarf. Was heißt Sozialismus heute?" *Die nachholende Revolution. Kleine politische Schriften VII.* Frankfurt a.M.: Suhrkamp, 1990. 179–203.

Močnik, Rastko. "Will the East's Past Be the West's Future?" *Les frontières invisibles.* Ed. Caroline David. Oostkamp: Stichting Kunstboek, 2009.

Osborne, Peter. *Philosophy in Cultural Theory.* London/New York: Routledge, 2000.

Pellicani, Luciano. "Modernity and Totalitarianism." *Telos* 112 (Summer 1998): 3–23.

Spivak, Gayatri Chakravorty. *A Critique of Postcolonial Reason: Toward a History of the Vanishing Present.* Cambridge, MA/London: Harvard University Press, 1999.

Todorova, Maria. *Imagining the Balkans.* Oxford/New York: Oxford University Press, 2009 [1997].

Žižek, Slavoj. "Why are Laibach and NSK not Fascists?" http://www.reanimator.8m.com/NSK/zizek.html (8 October 2013).

Christa Knellwolf King
Australian Cultural Studies

Intellectual Traditions and Critical Perspectives[*]

Simon During describes cultural studies as "a discipline continuously shifting its interests and methods both because it is in constant and engaged interaction with its larger historical context and because it cannot be complacent about its authority" (During 1999: 17). During's criteria apply strongly to Australian cultural studies, which is not only intimately linked to the cultural formations it critiques, but is also ambivalently positioned between defending Australian cultural practices against the belittling attitudes of its former colonial motherland and exposing the racism and jingoism of homegrown traditions.

The methodological and thematic heterogeneity of Australian cultural studies has sometimes been criticized as a sign that it lacks a distinctive character. Graeme Turner asserts that "[t]here are no myths of origin for Australian cultural studies. [...] By contrast with cultural studies in Britain, there are no key institutions around which Australian cultural studies can be said to have formed. Cultural studies is multiply fragmented in Australia" (Turner "Nation, Culture, Text" 1993: 4–5). However critical British cultural studies may have been, its location in the metropolis suggests complicity with metropolitan theory which, according to Tania Lewis, "has overwhelmingly tended to see itself as unmarked by specificity and therefore able to 'travel' globally" (Lewis 2003: 200). For non-western varieties of cultural studies, by contrast, it has become ever more important to respond with sensitivity to the postcolonial conditions which contributed to the formation of cultural studies groups. This is because cultural analysis that comes from the margins is more cautious about claims to universality and, instead, "openly acknowledges the relative autonomy of cultures in different geopolitical locations" (Chen 1998: 4).

While a certain sense of institutional and methodological indeterminacy undercut the attempt to articulate a shared agenda, the openness of Australian

[*] I want to thank Greg Dening for explaining the empowering ways in which the past is entangled in the present and Peter King for his inspiring comments on a draft version of this essay. I would also like to acknowledge support for my research on this topic by the Austrian Science Fund (FWF), project M 1290–G20.

cultural studies as a critical practice has also ensured its resilience at a time when cultural studies was established as a mainstream development in most humanities disciplines worldwide, so that it can remain an "eclectic and cautiously multidisciplinary field" (Turner in Storey 1996: 325), which challenges established beliefs about aesthetic standards and cultural values.

Cultural studies originated as a political analysis aimed at empowering marginalized members of society, and it continues to treat culture as a political arena that reflects the expectations and projections of a society that identifies with particular cultural formations. A major aim continues to be that of enabling interventions. The study of boundaries and conceptions of cultural difference, as they constitute ideas of national identity, is undoubtedly a seminal target of the individual national varieties of cultural studies. While critiques of globalization have always been an important feature of cultural studies, interest in local practices, particularly of marginal groups, has added impetus to the development of a nationally grounded community of scholars with a shared commitment to exploring the economic and political conditions behind the production of culture (cf. Docker 1974).

In the Australian context, cultural studies evolved into a critical practice and academic discipline at the same time that Australian studies established itself as a discipline that sought to overcome the legacy of colonial disparagement. Eduardo Marks de Marques (2005) describes the search of Australian studies for theory as an occasion for the, by no means uncontested, confluence of the two disciplines. However hostile the controversies about the usefulness of theory may have been, Australian cultural studies and Australian studies have experienced a similarly urgent need to expose the sexist and racist foundations of white Australian self-definitions.

Australia's history as a British colony meant that British standards influenced the procedures of settlement as much as the principles of government, which explains why British standards and values were a major point of reference into the late twentieth century. This is also reflected by the fact that the British monarch continues to be the sovereign of Australia to the present day. Analysis of Australian cultural formations needs to draw attention to the fact that Australian society, at least initially, imported its imaginative works from Britain, which is to say that in the nineteenth century, the bulk of printed material – canonical literature, sentimental fiction, gothic novels, and non-fiction – was imported from Britain (cf. Webby 2000). While homegrown journalism, literature, drama, and art began to thrive in the course of the twentieth century, British beliefs and standards retained a powerful influence. British guardianship over the standards of high culture was preserved through the recruitment policies of Australian universities, which continued to hire the majority of their staff in Britain, even holding job interviews for senior positions in London into the 1990s.

As a result of the close entanglement with the intellectual and institutional traditions of Britain, it was almost a matter of course that the principles of cultural studies resonated in Australia. But the Birmingham School's critical experiments in cultural analysis were more than an intellectual fashion that was taken over lock, stock, and barrel. It was welcomed as a rigorous political theory that enabled the analysis of the "hierarchical distinctions between the public and the private, the major and the minor, the 'great' and the 'everyday', as these regulated the field of culture (and the discipline of English) in Britain" (Frow and Morris 1993: xxiii). For the intellectual community of a country that was urgently exploring what it might mean to be Australian, theoretical interrogations of meaning had to go hand in hand with outspoken demands for change in aesthetic and political representation (cf. Docker 1974). The animated climate of the 1970s and 80s enabled a context for "the remarkable explicitness of public debate in Australia about power, propriety and representation (who has, and who should have, the power to represent whom; how; and under which conditions)" (Frow and Morris 1993: xiii).

The grounding of British cultural studies in the analysis and empowerment of working class culture is generally accepted (cf. During 1999: 3; Weedon 2001: 161). Working in agreement with workers' associations and the trade unions, leftist intellectuals sought to oppose the elitist and white supremacist mentality of British culture, which was seen to back up the xenophobia disseminated by Cold War propaganda. In this fraught political context, ideas of un-Australian behavior were used to defeat political opposition. The award-winning novelist Frank Moorhouse gives a grueling account of the crude practices of surveillance with which leftist Australian intellectuals were intimidated during the Cold War (cf. Moorhouse 2006; Ward 1958). Rather than silencing oppositional voices, these practices stoked the anger of Australian intellectuals, causing political debates to reach a previously unknown level of intensity. It is self-evident that there were disagreements between the overlapping camps of writers, journalists, and academics. But the controversies evolving from diverging views about cultural standards and their implied messages about Australian identity generated a locally specific interrogation of identity.

Cultural practices are closely enmeshed with the preoccupations of culture analysis. When talking about Australian efforts to challenge the supremacist beliefs engrained in the cultural bastions of the establishment, it is important to recall that the community spirit of Australian working-class culture permitted a great deal of solidarity with the intellectual elite. The image of Australia as "the lucky country" (Horne 1964), in which the harsh conditions of the bush were supposed to even out social differences (cf. Ward 1958), was undoubtedly part of Australian myth making but, as John Hurst points out, an egalitarian myth was called into existence by a society that at least feels strongly about equal opportunities (cf. Hurst in Goldberg and Smith 1988: 58). Egalitarian values also prevailed in academic institutions that chose to have less rigid hierarchies. This structural detail opened up a space for imaginative critical responses that challenged the boundaries between theory, cultural production, and political activism. John Frow and Meaghan Morris state that:

> Australian work in cultural studies has generally been less concerned to debate the pros and cons of 'essentialism' as a philosophical stance than to examine the *political* conflicts at stake, in concrete contexts and for particular groups of people, between differing stories of community or nation, and to articulate the *historical* struggles occurring in the gaps between competing narrative programs (of 'prosperity', for example), and the complex social experiences that these aspire to organise. (Frow and Morris 1993: xii)

The uncompromising scrutiny of political, social, and historical factors was particularly welcomed by marginalized cultural institutions, while the mainstream universities – called 'sandstone universities' because they imitated Oxford and Cambridge even in the architectural design of their buildings – continued to focus their teaching on high or canonical culture. In defiance of their more conservative outlook, it was the polytechnics, city, and arts colleges that embraced a radical interrogation of the economic and political conditions for the production of culture. It was also the more marginal tertiary institutions that began to shift the interest of critical analysis onto popular art forms, cinema, and TV (cf. Frow 2005).

The heterogeneity of Australia, a society of migrants, has characterized the nation's self-perception from the time of Federation (when five former British colonies merged into one political unit in 1901) to the twenty-first century, a time marked by polemics around multiculturalisms (cf. Turner 2007).

1 Contested Histories

For British cultural studies, the survival of colonialist hierarchies beyond the demise of the British Empire was a vital area of interest. The resulting investigation of the political and historical discourses unraveled hidden divergences within Britain, and it also provided a space for the articulation of critical oppositions to the conditions that prevailed in the former colonies. For Australian cultural studies practitioners, researching colonialist legacies meant speaking out against the continuing exploitation of the country's indigenous population.

Owing to the country's origin as a settler colony, Australia is marked by a jarring contradiction: the main representatives of a colonized country were – and continue(d) to be – the colonizers of its indigenous people. Cultural studies, hence, offered itself as a tool for the identification of abusive mechanisms, such as 'White Australia Policy' (a policy used to safeguard the status quo of white rule that prevailed between 1901 and 1973). Analysis of the myths with which those in power protected their claims revealed that these myths had also infiltrated established historiography so that it could be used as an instrument for the consolidation of white dominion.

Research into Australia's origins as a settler colony, from the period of its foundation in 1788 to the twentieth century, showed that Aboriginal people had never welcomed the arrival of the white man. It also became clear that the supposedly accepting attitude of Aboriginal people towards the presence of white settlers had been used as an insidious tool to rationalize discriminatory treatments. Detailed research by historians, such as Henry Reynolds (1981) and Stuart Macintyre (Macintyre and Clark 2003), provided evidence for friendly interactions during the first phase of cultural contact, but it became clear that serious conflicts erupted as soon as the white settlers arrived in large numbers and fenced in farm land without consulting the traditional owners of the country, threatening their hunting and fishing grounds (cf. McKenna 2002). Evidence that Aboriginal people fought back refuted the argument that Australia had been *terra nullius*, that is, land that had not been owned by any organized cultural community and could, therefore, legitimately be claimed for Britain.

The demystification of narratives of national identity, which had been grounded in colonialist myths about the supposedly benign dominance of white people over the indigenous population, threatened to overturn all notions of what it meant to be Australian. Initiatives such as the Australian *Freedom Ride* of 1965 (cf. Curthoys 2002), in which students joined activists in order to raise consciousness about the injustices of the past, marked a moment when the country's intellectuals were able to make a difference. The *Freedom Ride* contributed to the positive outcome of the referendum in 1967, ensuring that Aboriginal people officially received full citizenship rights.

Open debates, in public and in the academic arena, about the legacy of colonial abuses provided valuable support for the struggle for Native Title. A turning point in the battle of indigenous people for their traditional land was reached in 1992, when Eddie Koiki Mabo, a member of a Torres Strait Island community, put a successful case to the Australian High Court to prove the legality of indigenous claims to ancestral land. This court case officially overturned the argument that Britain had been justified in claiming Australian soil on the grounds that it had been unpopulated, or rather, that its population had failed to cultivate the soil, which meant that it remained *terra nullius* in legal terms.

The Mabo case was a landmark on the road to the recognition of Aboriginal claims to ancestral land (cf. Attwood 1996; Behrendt 2002). However, for the majority of white Australians, this decision gave rise to dramatic fears that it might bring about a situation in which all white ownership of land might be annulled. What came to be known as the 'Australian History Wars' began as a controversy between Manning Clark's demand for an uncompromising admission of guilt and Geoffrey Blainey's insistence that the revised view of Australian history belittled the hard labor by which the white farmers had claimed and cultivated their land. Stuart Macintyre and Anna Clark explain:

> The risks of a Black Armband view of Australian history that Geoffrey Blainey identified included intolerance of old Australia, loss of sovereignty, the tying up of productive resources, disunity, pessimism and guilt. Both analyses of the options for Australia invested remarkable significance in the proper interpretation of its past. (Macintyre and Clark 2003: 14–15)

Blainey's metaphor of a "Black Armband" view of the past lent itself as a polemical catch phrase with which the long-standing conservative Prime Minister John Howard (1996 to 2007) attacked the human rights activists in order to reassure all those who felt threatened by the consequences of Mabo.

As a result of the mudslinging controversies over the implications of Mabo, the vast majority of those who practiced cultural studies in Australia understood themselves in opposition to an increasingly conservative political climate (cf. Attwood 1996; West-Pavlov and Wawrzinek 2010). While the endeavor to redress the wrongs of the past continued, the methodological rigor of cultural analyses became a target of attack. Keith Windshuttle, in particular, objected that the maltreatment of Aboriginal people had been far less severe than was claimed. In an endeavor to rehabilitate the Australian nation, he launched an aggressive attack on the validity of research that argued that Aboriginal communities had been exterminated by the means of armed force, malnutrition, illness, and the removal of children (cf. Windshuttle 2002). His indictment of fellow historians, provocatively entitled *The Killing of History* (1994), targeted the content and methodologies of the historical analyses by "literary critics and social theorists" (mentioned explicitly in the book's subtitle).

Although Windshuttle's arguments were defeated by research that produced painful evidence of the brutal suppression of Aboriginal defenses of their territory (cf. Attwood 2003), the 'history wars' seriously damaged public perceptions about the entitlements to compensation of Aboriginal people (cf. Darian-Smith 2002; Manne 2004). Their damaging impact on endeavors to return land to indigenous hands may explain why Prime Minister Kevin Rudd was able to sidestep the land issue in his public apology to Aboriginal people on 13 February 2008, instead concentrating on the removal of children as the only cause of past grievances (cf. Rudd 2008). The history wars undermined the public credibility of cultural studies practitioners, and they also served as a reminder that much important critical work remained to be done.

2 Postcolonial Australia and Critical Whiteness

While some insist that Australia will only become a postcolonial nation when it has become a republic, others maintain that the passing of the *Native Title Act* (1992–1993) was the distinctive moment of transition. In the academic arena, categories of race and ethnicity have acquired new meanings, although there is a sense that the still mainly white intellectual elite spends too much energy on definitions of cultural difference, while disregarding the problems of those concerned.

Aileen Moreton-Robinson develops the argument that whiteness features as an unmarked category in the standard responses to representations in the west. She claims that "[w]hiteness remains the invisible omnipresent norm. As long as whiteness remains invisible in analyses 'race' is the prison reserved for the 'Other'" (Moreton-Robinson 2000: xix). Her work reveals the existence of implied hierarchies that structure cultural representations as well as critical discourses. When she talks about "representations of whiteness as dominance" (Moreton-Robinson 2000: 33), she draws attention to the damages caused by well-meaning notions of solidarity that involve patronizing subjection of non-white people. By insisting that whiteness needs to be interpreted in the context of privilege she reminds us that white working-class people – men and women – profit from racially defined forms of exploitation. Even though her writing is more interested in intervention than critical analysis, it demonstrates a refreshing return to the core concerns of cultural studies. By asking who benefits from racist practices, she exposes the economic and political conditions behind oppression.

While arguing that "[i]ndigenous women are the bearers of subjugated knowledges" (2000: xxiii), Moreton-Robinson also calls for a systematic repudiation of the moral and intellectual hegemony of white domination. Her study of the impact of ideas of rationality, civilization, and progress pursues a similar goal to that of Dipesh Chakrabarty's discussion of the idea of Europe as a 'hyperreal' abstraction that dominates non-western narratives of modernization and modernity. He says: "'The modern' will then continue to be understood, as Meaghan Morris has so aptly put it in discussing her own Australian context, 'as a *known history*, something which has *already happened elsewhere*, and which is to be reproduced, mechanically or otherwise, with a local content" (Chakrabarty 2000: 39; Morris 1990: 10).

It is worth remembering at this point that Chakrabarty, as well as Morris, are intellectual migrants who, as part of their official appointments, regularly traverse geopolitical boundaries: India, Australia, and the United States (Chakrabarty) and Asia and Australia (Morris). The regular experience of long-distance air travel reinforces Chakrabarty's vantage point for seeing Europe as a hyperreal space. Using Morris as a case study, Tania Lewis argues that

> the intersections between transnational and local knowledges that have been central for the formation of Australian cultural studies have often been marked by an active process of exchange in which local Australian intellectual traditions have been strengthened and foregrounded rather than effaced. (Lewis 2003: 199)

Morris' case shows that the groundedness of a comparative perspective in the personal backgrounds of 'traveling critics' sharpened these critics' abilities to see the culturally specific themes and practices of interpretation that are favored in particular locations.

Chakrabarty radically interrogates the theoretical categories of western thought (see also his contribution to this volume). Referring to Carole Pateman's book *The Sexual Contract*, he describes the intrinsic complicity between critical categories and practical forms of oppression: "the very conception of the modern individual belongs to patriarchal categories of thought" (Chakrabarty 2000: 42; Pateman 1988: 184). It is in a similar vein of examining the influences of hegemonic thought that Ghassan Hage emphasizes that

> an entity such as "White multiculturalism" is a *subjective* formation. By saying that it is a White fantasy, I am interested in making claims about how some White Australians experience multiculturalism rather than grand statements about what multiculturalism is or is not. (Hage 1998: 18)

Graeme Turner has pointed out that the target of Hage's subsequent book, titled *Against Paranoid Nationalism* (2003), reflects a symptomatic change in the public perception, from a simplistically homogeneous but nevertheless inclusive understanding of Australian society to a paranoid rejection, particularly of Muslim influences. The idea of a multicultural Australia had dominated the public discourse of the 1980s and 1990s because it "had enabled a fundamental break with the early Anglocentric accounts of Australian culture and society" (Turner 2007: 10). But after 9/11, the longstanding difficulties of many Australians in experiencing a sense of belonging unleashed dormant fears of refugees, asylum seekers, and "those Australians of Middle Eastern extraction, whether Christian or Muslim (media representations routinely disregard that distinction)" (Turner 2007: 11).

3 Gender

Traditional notions of Australian identity operate with oppositional gender stereotypes that date back to the early days of settlement, when male muscle power and female endurance were described as seminal features. Images of the bushman, the drover, and their female partners describe the indomitable spirit of the men and women who were carving out a living in the hostile environment of the outback (compare Henry Lawson's influential short story "The Drover's Wife," 1892). These images dominated the Australian imagination into the later twentieth-century, even though Australia had from an early time been one of the most urbanized societies worldwide (cf. Kiernan 1997). The image of the muscular – and white – male body, therefore, continues to be targeted by Australian analyses of gender difference. It is seen to have been a formative influence on the conception of early twentieth-century, middle-class identities (cf. Crotty 1998) and to have informed contemporary uses of the Australian beach by the advertising industry.

Australia embraced a progressive policy when it gave (almost) equal suffrage to women in 1902, although it notably excluded Aboriginal women. As is documented by the personal reminiscences of Janine Haines (1992), the first female leader of an Australian political party, the right to vote enabled white women to gain a place in a harshly masculine world (cf. Scutt 1992), but critics are still struggling against the enduring presence of unhelpful gender stereotypes.

The themes pervading the seminal cultural works of Australia also set the scene for their critical assessment. On an immediate level, critics point out that the Australian stereotype of the masculine hero who triumphs over bush, outback, city, and women is not limited to blockbusters like *Crocodile Dundee* (1986). By noting that even *Priscilla, Queen of the Desert* (1994), a gay, or transgender, parody of established views, is structured around the idea that an authentic experience of gendered Australian identity requires mastery over the red center, cultural studies illustrates the groundedness of parodic treatments in traditional images. This can be pinpointed in the episode in which the film's three drag artists from Sydney climb King's Canyon dressed up for a performance in a night club – the only compromise is their choice of mildly suitable footwear – in order to inscribe their ambiguously gendered identities into the Australian landscape. For a critic of culture, such feature films document that the red center continues to be used as a point of reference for the conception of gendered identity, even in a work that seeks to subvert traditional ideas about masculinity and femininity. Graeme Turner comments on Australian self-representation by saying:

> The curious thing about Australian nationalism is not only its varied political potential; it is also the narrow range of images and iconography through which it has signified itself: imagery which locates an essential and distinctive national character in the landscape, in the social structures of the bush, and in a masculinist/social pioneering ethic. (Turner in Storey 1996: 328)

When drawing comparisons between the critical traditions of different nations and cultures, it is worth remembering that European gender stereotypes are modeled on a particular relationship to nature. The idea of nature as a benign and nurturing mother, reinforced by the literature of European Romanticism, has been a major factor in the definition of European gender roles. Perhaps it is another consequence of the predominantly British roots of Australian intellectual traditions that notions of femininity generate expectations about a particular relationship to nature. Owing to the forbidding conditions of Australia's outback, the nurturing mother becomes an unfeasible ideal. An Australian sense of femininity which is modeled on the country's nature undergoes an insidious translation of values, generating the view of Australian women as hard, indifferent, and even cruel mothers. The sensational circumstances of the trial of Lindy Chamberlain, convicted of murdering her baby Azaria during a camping trip to Uluru in 1980, sparked fierce debate in cultural studies about the role of the media in the construction of a verdict that was recognized as tendentious and, therefore, repealed in 1986. The historical event triggered discussions about the hostile views of Australian femininity and maternity (cf. Howe 2005; Sanders 1993). The Chamberlain case illustrates that the concrete factors of Australia as a geographical space and political formation may have granted women more freedom than they had in the colonial motherland, but it has also shown that Australian feminism is still struggling to get rid of deeply hostile ideas of femininity (cf. Schaffer 1988).

A striking example of the Australian influence on the international feminist scene is Germaine Greer. The daring with which she named the sexual parts of the (female) body in interviews and public speeches that followed the publication of *The Female Eunuch* (1971) were associated with her Australian accent, although she spent most of her career outside her country of origin. The energy with which Greer challenged the deeply engrained misogyny of the seventies made it clear that challenges to the patriarchal status quo had to be open and outspoken, defeating all prohibitions of female self-expression. The need to gain public presence emphasized the significance of performance – of bodies and ideas. Feminists like Germaine Greer, who came from a non-western background, exposed the strong parallels between imperialist, patriarchal, and economic (or class) oppression.

Tania Lewis quotes Andrew Milner's observation that the 'New Australian Feminism' is a term that was coined by the British-based feminist theorist Michèle Barrett, arguing that "the peculiar mixture of 'feminist rhetoric, Lacanian psychoanalysis and Barthesian semiotics' that distinguished post-structuralist feminist work in Australia in the late 1980s, made (and continues to make) a significant impact on the international intellectual community" (Lewis 2003: 196). Australian feminists have played an important role in valorizing the role of the body in gender theory. Rita Felski and Zoe Sofia even talk about an "Australian 'school' of corporeal feminism" (Felski and Sofia 1996: 386). Critics like Elspeth Probyn (1993) and Rita Felski undoubtedly develop European and American traditions, but their analyses may appeal so strongly because they are motivated by the need to set themselves off against the sexist stereotypes of Australian culture. Although they work on similar topics as their international colleagues, these scholars' Australian background has encouraged the recognition that misogynist stereotypes are not only ubiquitous but also latent in the academic descriptions of embodied experience, thus offering a welcome precedent for the case studies of their international colleagues.

4 The Spaces of Australia

Australian landscape is a key topic of analysis precisely because it continues to inspire ambivalent feelings – to such an extent that there are, for example, virulent campaigns to uproot the European tree species, aiming to replace the willows and oak trees, which had been imported as part of an ecological process of colonization, with the native gum trees, wattle, bottle brush, etc. Beyond this, cultural studies has long emphasized that 'the Australian imagination' is marked by intricate entanglements between space and ideas of displacement. A deeply engrained unease about the experience of the bush, for example, gave rise to stories about lost children whose prominence in public consciousness greatly exceeds the statistical occurrence of such fatality (cf. Torney 2005).

Australia's settler society sought to claim the spaces of Australia's vast, open landscape by a politics of naming, which means that the Aboriginal names for topographic features were systematically overwritten and erased (cf. Carter 1988). In spite of endeavors to revert to the original names, prominent landmarks, such as Uluru, continue to be known as Ayer's Rock. While the legal appropriation by the white settlers has been completed, discussion of the thematic emphases of Australian literature shows that white – but also multicultural – Australians are still finding it difficult to claim the land emotionally (cf. Gelder and Jacobs 2001; Knellwolf King 2009). The struggle for belonging has, indeed, been described as a typically Australian experience (cf. Read 2000).

Cultural studies emerged in an urban environment and, hence, has typically addressed the concerns of an urbanized society, giving rise, for example, to Drusilla Modjeska's study of gendered experiences of the city (1989). A similarly relevant trajectory of Australian cultural studies deals with the fantasies and images about the back of beyond which, as is illustrated by Roslynn Haynes' study of the continuing relevance of the desert in Australian culture and art (cf. Haynes 1998), was generated by the inhabitants of Australian cities.

Concerning the significance of space and place, Graeme Turner asserts, "even theory has to have some historical location, specific contexts within which it works to particular ends" (Turner 1996: 334). On one level, he makes this claim with a view to exposing the still insufficiently challenged influence of British and other international traditions. On another level, however, he draws attention to the significance of location – as a real or imaginary space enveloped by fictions and histories – for the articulation of theory. The idea that every discourse is sited and, hence, reflects the tenets prioritized by those who participate in its interpretative community goes hand in hand with the recognition that the practice of cultural studies is always a matter of border crossing. Edward Said offered the eloquent reminder that "the specific situation or locality of a particular intellectual task seems uneasily distant from, and only rhetorically assisted by, the legendary wholeness, coherence, and integrity of the general field to which one professionally belongs" (Said 1991: 228). Said goes on to express the concern "that once an idea gains currency because it is clearly effective and powerful, there is every likelihood that during its peregrinations it will be reduced, codified and institutionalized" (Said 1991: 239).

Said's fear of theoretical self-defeat is primarily addressed to critics unable to grasp the interrelations between theories and the particular circumstances analyzed by them (cf. Said 1991: 239). It was in response to such concerns that the Australian historian Greg Dening developed a critical practice that experimented with the modalities of critical discourse. Allowing himself to be inspired by poststructuralist explorations of the blurred boundaries between fiction and theory, Dening set out to find new ways of reconciling scholarly rigor with critical self-reflection. I met him in the final years of his life (he died in 2008) and will never forget the energy with which he described criticism as a creative act. He encouraged the participants of his memorable workshops to 'perform' their arguments, which means that he invited them to come up with a physically grounded version of their critical ideas by, for example, presenting them as a song, a poem, or to experiment with any other creative form that drew attention to the physical presence of the critic in the critical argument.

While expanding on the interspaces between criticism and fiction, Dening employs Australian experiences of transition and arrival to outline a critical discourse that is particularly relevant to the cultural crossings that happened in Australian history:

> Experience is something reflected upon, something pulled out of the flow of things. We humans are very ingenious in creating a hedged-around space and time to have our experiences. It is an in-between space and in-between time [...]. We sometimes call this hedged-around space ritual, sometimes theatre. I'd like to call it, here, limen, threshold, or in a metaphor that has occupied my attention through many years, a beach. (Dening 2002: 8)

Dening's metaphorical use of the "beach" is an eloquent reference to the most important space of encounter in Australia's contested history of discovery and settlement. While drawing attention to the power differentials of cross-cultural encounters, he also reminds us that the beach, as a metaphor for the space of encounter, is a space of negotiation that requires its participants to shed their privileges and meet on quasi-equal terms. Dening's conscious use of the metaphor of the beach draws attention to the relevance of metaphors and images in critical discourse. While using it as a framework for his discussion of particular encounters between westerners and indigenous people in the Pacific region, he also encourages his readers to coin other metaphors suitable for other encounters. It is difficult to say to what extent Dening's creative treatment of critical concepts may have influenced other critics. In any event, the conception of the "contact zone" as a space (cf. Pratt 1992) similarly points to the need to imagine a cross-cultural encounter as a physical event that forces its participants to step outside their comfort zones and to explore new ways of dramatizing themselves, their emotions, and their needs.

5 New Directions

The twenty-first century began as a moment of crisis for cultural studies, when academics worldwide had to come to terms with the conservative backlash that happened in the wake of 9/11. When the Howard government joined forces with Tony Blair and George Bush in order to invade Iraq in 2003, the Australian humanities were confronted by a disturbing sense of helplessness. The polemics around the War on Terror and the associated conflicts about the premises of representation went hand in hand with cuts in funding, which further undermined the public perception of the value of the human and social sciences. But Australian critics responded by returning to the question of whether academics could make a difference at a time when global media and consumer industries did everything to exploit the marketing value of popular culture and marginal voices (cf. McRobbie and Morris 1997).

The upsurge of xenophobia in the first decade of the twenty-first century was also a time when Australian scholars recognized the overarching need for new studies of peaceful solutions for the co-existence between ethnic groups in order to challenge sentiments of paranoia which were stirred by the mass media. This endeavor was helped by Australian interests in studying cultural exchanges within and across national boundaries. It prompted a flow of ideas between Asia and Australia, which was accompanied, or indeed accelerated, by the physical move, for example, of Meagan Morris to a chair at Lingnan University in Hong Kong in 2000 (cf. Lewis 2003) and, subsequently, to a dual appointment between Lingnan and the University of Sydney. However, dual appointments and the move of senior academics between international institutions is an increasingly familiar phenomenon in contemporary academia. Rather than watering down critical responses to local specificities, such exchanges enable comparative approaches and heighten the awareness of local concerns. At a time of almost global anxiety about security issues, the comparative perspective on hostility towards immigrants enables a new debate on the meanings of culture and ethnicity.

Intellectual exchanges happen fast, making it difficult to say where new critical concepts emerge and in which directions they flow. The metaphor of a travelling theory, which transforms and is transformed similar to how a traveler is affected by the experiences of the journey, draws on the habits of travelling that were customary in the twentieth century. It may, therefore, seem appropriate to adjust the metaphor to the current academic situation, in which travelling is a part of daily life. The emergence of new approaches to theories of identity may, indeed, be a response to the routine physical and electronic encounters between international academics. New ways of being an academic may also have given rise to a call for theories that move beyond the binary oppositionality implied by twentieth-century theories of difference. For example, eloquent expressions of a new understanding of the co-existence of colonizers and colonized as a mutual entanglement that affected both sides of the colonial relationship are emerging in response to the conditions in South Africa in the second decade since the demise of apartheid (cf. Nuttall 2009).

Australian critics are similarly pushing for theoretical accounts of difference that offer a more fluid understanding of the interactions between members of different ethnic groups. Ann Game and Andrew Metcalfe (2011) give voice to the Australian call for theories of identity that imagine a self that is genuinely capable of belonging to a multicultural community. Concentrating on the Australian context, Game and Metcalfe claim that the focus on difference should be replaced by relationality. They assert that the possibility for a productive understanding of the living interrelations between different cultural communities presupposes that the boundaries beyond self and other should be considered as fluid, arguing that identities are shaped flexibly in response to the relations that are realized by the practices of daily life.

Comparative studies of South-African and Australian conditions, conducted, for example, by Kate Darian-Smith, Liz Gunner, and Sarah Nuttall (1996), point towards new conceptions of identity that are emerging in the context of comparative analyses of Australian and South-African ways of coping with historically generated power differentials. Such studies are important instruments for discovering new ways of overcoming deeply engrained hurts. Comparative cultural studies harbors unique critical energy, provided that it is motivated by the desire to make an intervention that benefits those who are affected by it.

I want to conclude with the observation that the application of critical concepts to concrete circumstances always involves an act of translation in which the institutional and national background of a critic's training influences his and her approach to a particular set of circumstances. Critical idioms and methods travel easily – at least as easily as the critics who embrace them – but it is imperative to resist the conclusion that interpretive methods are universally valid. The translation of critical concepts produces important results if they are employed pragmatically as a rapprochement to the particular circumstances and vocabularies to be studied, but it is crucial to refrain from making universalizing pronouncements.

References

Ang, Ien, and Jon Stratton. "Asianing Australia: Notes toward a Critical Transnationalism in Cultural Studies." *Cultural Studies* 10.1 (1996): 16–36.

Ashcroft, Bill, Gareth Griffiths, and Helen Tiffin. *The Empire Writes Back*. London: Routledge, 1989.

Attwood, Bain, ed. *In the Age of Mabo: History, Aborigines and Australia*. Sydney: Allen and Unwin, 1996.

Attwood, Bain, and Stephen Forster, eds. *Frontier Conflict: The Australian Experience*. Canberra: National Museum of Australia, 2003.

Behrendt, Larissa. *Mabo: Ten Years On*. Canberra: Australian National University, 2002.

Bulbeck, Chilla. *Living Feminism: The Impact of the Women's Movement on Three Generations of Australian Women*. Cambridge: Cambridge University Press, 1997.

Calhoun, Craig. "Belonging in the Cosmopolitan Imaginary." *Ethnicities* 3.4 (2003): 531–568.

Carter, Paul. *The Road to Botany Bay: An Exploration of Landscape and History*. New York: Knopf, 1988.

Chakrabarty, Dipesh. *Provincializing Europe: Postcolonial Thought and Historical Difference*. Princeton: Princeton University Press, 2000.

Chen, Kuan-Hsing. *Trajectories: Inter-Asia Cultural Studies*. London: Routledge, 1998.

Crotty, Martin. *Making the Australian Male: Middle-Class Masculinities*. Brisbane: University of Queensland Press, 1998.

Curthoys, Ann. *Freedom Ride: A Freedom Rider Remembers*. Sydney: Allen and Unwin, 2002.

Darian-Smith, Kate, ed. *Challenging Histories: Reflections on Australian History*. Special Issue of *Australian Historical Studies* 118 (2002).

Darian-Smith, Kate, Liz Gunner, and Sarah Nuttall, eds. *Text, Theory, Space: Land, Literature, and History in South Africa and Australia*. London: Routledge, 1996.

Dening, Greg. "Performing on the Beaches of the Mind." *History and Theory* 41 (2002): 1–24.

Docker, John. *Australian Cultural Elites: Intellectual Traditions in Sydney and Melbourne*. Sydney: Angus and Robertson, 1974.

Docker, John. *Postmodernism and Popular Culture: A Cultural History*. Cambridge: Cambridge University Press, 1994.

During, Simon, ed. *The Cultural Studies Reader*. 2nd Edition. London: Routledge, 1999.

Felski, Rita, and Zoe Sofia. "Introduction to 'Australian Feminism'." *Cultural Studies* 10 (1996): 383–392.

Frow, John. "Australian Cultural Studies: Theory, Story, History." *Australian Humanities Review* 37 (2005). http://www.australianhumanitiesreview.org/archive/Issue-December-2005/frow.html. (14 October 2013).

Frow, John, and Meaghan Morris, eds. *Australian Cultural Studies: A Reader*. Sydney: Allen and Unwin, 1993.

Game, Ann, and Andrew Metcalfe. "Belonging: From Identity Logic to Relational Logic." *Continuum: Journal of Media & Cultural Studies* 25.3 (2011): 347–357.

Gatens, Moira, and Barbara Caine, eds. *Australian Feminism: A Companion*. Melbourne: Oxford University Press, 1998.

Gelder, Ken, and Jane M. Jacobs. *Uncanny Australia: Sacredness and Identity in Postcolonial Australia*. Carlton: Melbourne University Press, 2001.

Goldberg, S. L., and F. B. Smith, eds. *Australian Cultural History*. Cambridge: Cambridge University Press, 1988.

Greer, Germaine. *The Female Eunuch*. New York: Harper Perennial Modern Classics, 2008 [1970, 1971, 1991].

Grossmann, Michèle, gen. ed. *Blacklines. Contemporary Critical Writing by Indigenous Australians*. Carlton: Melbourne University Press, 2005.

Hage, Ghassan. *White Nation: Fantasies of White Supremacy in a Multicultural Society*. Annandale: Pluto Press, 1998.

Hage, Ghassan. *Against Paranoid Nationalism: Searching for Hope in a Shrinking Society*. Sydney: Pluto Press, 2003.

Haines, Janine. *Suffrage to Sufferance: A Hundred Years of Women in Politics*. Sydney: Allen and Unwin, 1992.

Haynes, Roslynn D. *Seeking the Centre: The Australian Desert in Literature, Art and Film*. Cambridge: Cambridge University Press, 1998.

Horne, Donald. *The Lucky Country: Australia in the Sixties*. Ringwood: Penguin, 1964.

Howe, Adrian. *Lindy Chamberlain Revisited: a 25th Anniversary Retrospective*. Sydney: LhR Press, 2005.

Kiernan, Brian. "Sydney of the Bush: Some Literary Images." *Studies in Australian Literature*. Sydney: Shoestring Press, 1997. 129–156.

Knellwolf King, Christa. "Settler Colonialism and the Formation of Australian National Identity: Praed's 'Bunyip' and Pedley's 'Dot and the Kangaroo'." *Imagined Australia: Reflections Around the Reciprocal Construction of Identity between Australia and Europe*. Ed. Renata Summo-O'Connell. Zürich: Peter Lang, 2009. 107–121.

Lake, Marilyn. *Getting Equal: The History of Australian Feminism*. Sydney: Allen and Unwin, 1999.

Lewis, Tania. "Intellectual Exchange and Located Transnationalism: Meaghan Morris and the Formation of Australian Cultural Studies." *Continuum: Journal of Media & Cultural Studies* 17.2 (2003): 187–206.

Mabo, the High Court Decision on Native Title: Discussion Paper. Canberra: Australian Government Publication Service, 1993.

Macintyre, Stuart, and Anna Clark. *The History Wars*. Carlton: Melbourne University Press, 2003.

Manne, Robert, ed. *The Howard Years*. Melbourne: Black Inc, 2004.

Marks de Marques, Eduardo. "Understanding Australia: Notes on the Australian Studies vs Australian Cultural Studies Debate." *Journal of Australian Studies* 28.84 (2005): 117–124.

McKenna, Mark. *Looking for Blackfellas' Point: An Australian History of Place*. Sydney: University of New South Wales Press, 2002.

McRobbie, Angela, and Meaghan Morris, eds. *Back to Reality? Social Experience and Cultural Studies*. Manchester: Manchester University Press, 1997.

Milner, Andrew. "Cultural Studies and Cultural Hegemony." *Arena Journal* 9 (1997): 133–155.

Modjeska, Drusilla. *Exiles at Home: Australian Women Writers 1925–1945*. London: Sirius, 1981.

Modjeska, Drusilla. *Inner Cities: Australian Women's Memory of Place*. Ringwood: Penguin, 1989.

Moorhouse, Frank. "The Writer in a Time of Terror." *Griffith Review : A Quarterly of New Writing and Ideas* 14 (2006). http://griffithreview.com/edition-14-the-trouble-with-paradise/the-writer-in-a-time-of-terror (16 October 2013).

Moreton-Robinson, Aileen A. *Talkin' Up to the White Woman: Indigenous Women and Feminism*. St Lucia: University of Queensland Press, 2000.

Moreton-Robinson, Aileen A. "Whiteness, Epistemology and Indigenous Representation." *Whitening Race: Essays in Social and Cultural Criticism*. Ed. Aileen A. Moreton-Robinson. Canberra: Aboriginal Studies Press, 2004. 75–88.

Morris, Meaghan. *The Pirate's Fiancée: Feminism, Reading, Postmodernism*. London: Verso, 1988.

Morris, Meaghan. "Metamorphoses at Sydney Tower." *New Formations* 11 (1990): 5–18.

Morris, Meaghan. *Identity Anecdotes: Translation and Media Culture*. London: Sage, 2006.

Muecke, Stephen. *Textual Spaces: Aboriginality and Cultural Studies*. Australian Research Institute: Curtin University of Technology, 2005.

Nile, Richard, ed. *Australian Masculinities*. Brisbane: University of Queensland Press, 1998.

Nuttall, Sarah. *Entanglement: Literary and Cultural Reflections on Post-Apartheid*. Johannesburg: Wits University Press, 2009.

Pateman, Carole. *The Sexual Contract*. Stanford: Stanford University Press, 1988.

Pratt, Mary Louise. *Imperial Eyes: Travel Writing and Transculturation*. London: Routledge, 1992.

Probyn, Elspeth. *Sexing the Self: Gendered Positions in Cultural Studies*. London: Routledge, 1993.

Read, Peter. *The Stolen Generations: The Removal of Aboriginal Children in New South Wales 1883 to 1969*. New South Wales Ministry of Aboriginal Affairs, 1981. http://indigenousartmagazine.com/upload/3282/StolenGenerations.pdf (5 September 2013).

Read, Peter. *Belonging: Australians, Place and Aboriginal Ownership*. Cambridge: Cambridge University Press, 2000.

Reynolds, Henry. *The Other Side of the Frontier*. Ringwood: Penguin, 1981.

Reynolds, Henry, ed. *Dispossession: Black Australians and White Invaders*. Sydney: Allen and Unwin, 1989.

Rudd, Kevin. "National Apology to the Forgotten Australians and Former Child Migrants." Archived 16 November 2009. Speech in House of Representatives, Parliament House, Canberra. 13 February 2008. http://pandora.nla.gov.au/tep/81551 (28 October 2013).

Said, Edward. "Traveling Theory." *The World, the Text and the Critic*. New York: Vintage, 1991. 226–247.

Sanders, Noel. "Azaria Chamberlain and Popular Music." *Cultural Studies: A Reader*. Eds. John Frow and Meaghan Morris. Sydney: Allen and Unwin, 1993. 86–104.

Schaffer, Kay. *Women and the Bush: Forces of Desire in the Australian Cultural Tradition*. Cambridge: Cambridge University Press, 1988.

Schwarz, Anja. *Beached: A Postcolonial Reading of the Australian Shore*. Berlin: Free University, Diss., 2008.

Scutt, Jocelynne A., ed. *Breaking Through: Women, Work and Careers*. North Melbourne: Artemis, 1992.

Smith, Bernard. *Australian Painting, 1788–2000*. Melbourne: Oxford University Press, 1971.

Storey, John, ed. *What is Cultural Studies? A Reader*. London: Arnold, 1996.

Summo-O'Connell, Renata, ed. *Imagined Australia: Reflections Around the Reciprocal Construction of Identity between Australia and Europe*. Zürich: Peter Lang, 2009.

Torney, Kim. *Babes in the Bush: The Making of an Australian Image*. Fremantle: Curtin University Books, 2005.

Turner, Graeme. *National Fictions: Literature, Film and the Construction of Australian Narrative*. Sydney: Allen and Unwin, 1993.

Turner, Graeme. "'It Works for Me': British Cultural Studies, Australian Cultural Studies, Australian Film." *What is Cultural Studies? A Reader*. Ed. John Storey. London: Arnold, 1996. 322–335.

Turner, Graeme. "Shrinking the Borders: Globalization, Culture, and Belonging." *Cultural Politics* 3.1 (2007): 5–19.

Turner, Graeme, ed. *Nation, Culture, Text: Australian Cultural and Media Studies*. London: Routledge, 1993.

Ward, Russel. *The Australian Legend*. Melbourne: Oxford University Press, 1958.

Webby, Elizabeth. "Colonial Writers and Readers." *The Cambridge Companion to Australian Literature*. Cambridge: Cambridge University Press, 2000. 50–73.

Weedon, Chris. "Cultural Studies." *The Cambridge History of Literary Criticism*, vol. 9: *Twentieth-Century Historical, Philosophical and Psychological Perspectives*. Eds. Christa Knellwolf and Christopher Norris. Cambridge: Cambridge University Press, 2001. 155–164.

West-Pavlov, Russell, and Jennifer Wawrzinek, eds. *Frontier Skirmishes: Literary and Cultural Debates in Australia after 1992*. Heidelberg: Winter, 2010.

White, Richard. *Inventing Australia: Images and Identity 1688–1980*. Sydney: Allen and Unwin, 1981.

Whitlock, Gillian, and David Carter, eds. *Images of Australia: An Introductory Reader in Australian Studies*. St Lucia: University of Queensland Press, 1992.

Whitlock, Gillian, and Gail Reekie, eds. *Uncertain Beginnings: Debates in Australian Studies*. St Lucia: University of Queensland Press, 1993.

Windshuttle, Keith. *The Killing of History: How Literary Critics and Social Theorists are Murdering our Past*. Paddington: Macleay Press, 1994.

Windshuttle, Keith. *The Fabrication of Aboriginal History*, vol. 1: *Van Diemen's Land 1803–1847*. Paddington: Macleay Press, 2002.

Rainer Winter
Cultural Studies
Critical Methodologies and the Transnational Challenge[*]

1 Introduction

Almost four decades ago, cultural studies developed in Birmingham as a transdisciplinary enterprise, which successfully initiated a dialogue and collaboration between the humanities and the social sciences. From early on, enabled by publications and travelling or emigrated scholars, its theoretical perspectives, critical approaches, and research agendas were taken up in many parts of the world. Today there are different formations of cultural studies in Europe, Australia, North America, Latin America, Africa, Asia, and the Middle East.

If ideas travel, they occasionally change, and so it was with the Birmingham approach that had to be adapted for different national and cultural backgrounds. The Inter-Asia formation even remade cultural studies for the multilingual, geographically distinctive, and transnational region in which it was to be used (cf. Turner 2012: 139–141). These varying alterations lead to intense debates and arguments about the original project and its reassessments in different contexts. For example, it was often lamented that, after the institutionalization of cultural studies in the U.S., its critical spirit almost completely dissipated at many universities (cf. Cruz 2012: 257). This critical diagnosis has been corroborated by institutionally established practices in the context of the corporate university worldwide; they often lose the connection with the initial spirit of the project and its political, ethical, and pedagogical mission. Graeme Turner, in his new book *What's Become of Cultural Studies?* (2012), even comes to the conclusion that the future of cultural studies is uncertain. "[T]he one that I connect most with 'the project' of cultural studies is its claim to employ a mode of academic practice that is fundamentally committed to the social and political usefulness of the knowledge it produces" (Turner 2012: 158). Cultural studies is a critical project that attempts to produce a "public good" (Turner 2012: 184). Its

---

[*] This text has been translated into English by Andrew Terrington.

knowledge shall not be sold. It shall be used to advance "the social and cultural wellbeing of a society, and not just its economic development" (Turner 2012: 184).

I agree with Graeme Turner. It is time to come back to our project. Cultural studies should be more than research on contemporary culture. It should be strictly connected to the analysis and critique of power relations within and through culture (cf. Winter 2001; Gilbert 2008). Cultural studies is mainly interested in cultural and social change that creates radical democracy. This might serve as a timely reminder of the emerging *Kulturwissenschaften* in German-speaking countries, which, while it does not deny the existence of forms of subordination, social inequality, or discrimination, is not focused on the political; there is no determining desire to overcome the existing society. A 'translation' of cultural studies can only be possible if research in *Kulturwissenschaften* is directed by an 'emancipatory knowledge interest' (cf. Habermas 1968). This is the prerequisite link to cultural studies: "Cultural Studies contributes to illuminating how force and resistance operate in the world, through the relationship of culture to scarcity, inequality and the active material forces of coding, representation and theming. It is why Cultural Studies must ultimately be ranked as a contribution to that best of all human practices: *emancipation*" (Rojek 2007: 161).

For this reason, my contribution to this volume will set out the critical methodological fundamentals of cultural studies that have not been explicitly discussed for a long time. Under transnational circumstances, we need a common ground that preserves the political project. But it is not enough to remember its original aspirations. We have not only to reconstruct its critical methodologies but also renew them as well (cf. Smith 2011; Winter 2011).

2 The Transdisciplinary Perspective of Cultural Studies

The transdisciplinary approach of cultural studies that usually connects different disciplinary perspectives from the humanities and social sciences applies to the analysis of lived experiences, social practices, and cultural representations, which are considered in their network-like or intertextual links, from the viewpoints of power, difference, and human agency. From early on, cultural studies has been shaped by an interest in equality, democracy, and emancipation (cf. Williams 1961). It does not entail the analysis of an isolated practice or event but is rather driven by the attempt to radically contextualize cultural processes (cf.

Grossberg 2010). Every practice is connected to other practices. An assemblage of practices is part of a conjuncture, an intersection of discourses, practices, technologies of power, and everyday life (cf. Grossberg 2010: 25). Conjunctures and contexts are changing; cultural studies in its intended form reacts to these changes. It is a committed and engaged intellectual-political practice that attempts to describe the complexity, contradictions, and relational character of cultural processes. It wants to produce (politically) useful knowledge to understand the problems and questions of a conjuncture. It hopes to help people struggle against and transform power structures in order to realize radical democratic relations.

Its approach regards culture not as a subsystem or a field but rather as something that penetrates and structures every aspect of social life and subjectivity. From this perspective, therefore, culture does not belong to a single individual nor does it distinguish individuals; rather, it is the medium by which shared meanings, rituals, social communities, and identities are produced. The researcher is located "inside culture" and has to consider the complex, contradictory, and many-layered context of reality in the global era of the twenty-first century (cf. Couldry 2000). The knowledge produced by cultural studies ought to increase the reflexivity of those acting in everyday life – a life formed by power relationships and structured by a discursive order of representation – and reveal to them the possibility of changing restrictive and repressive living conditions.

Theories can help explore and illuminate contexts, but they are not enough. Understanding a conjuncture is only possible with a transdisciplinary approach. This orientation can lead to complex theoretical work, based on different approaches, that carefully describes and analyses discourses and practices (cf. Grossberg 2005). It can also include qualitative-empirical research. Since its beginnings in Birmingham, cultural studies has used and developed qualitative methods (cf. Willis 1977, 1978). The central characteristic of research in the context of cultural studies is the theoretical and empirical examination of the relationship between experiences, practices, and cultural texts in a specific context. It is the researcher's task to construct or reconstruct this context.

The tripartite focus of cultural studies on experiences, practices, and texts carries various methodological orientations, and their mutual connections have dominated the approach since its beginnings. Its singularity and creativity touches on mutual endorsement and enrichment but also on causes of friction, which, despite resulting from different theoretical and methodological options, are used productively (cf. Saukko 2003; Johnson et al. 2004). For example, the qualitative empirical research of media reception and appropriation has a phenomenological-hermeneutical focus on the one hand, because it deals with cultural experiences in order to understand the 'lived realities' of experiences and practices in different social contexts; the analysis of social and political contexts in which media texts are perceived and appropriated has to have a 'realistic' character, for example, in the description of the situational settings in which media reception is carried out or in the grasping of the increasingly global network of media flows. On the other hand, the analysis of media texts is often based on structural or poststructural approaches. The logic of a film or a TV series can be deduced by revealing the cultural values (which are hidden in the binary logic of texts), by examining discursive frameworks (which structure media realities), or by disclosing intertextual relationships (which exist between media texts and emphasize the mediated character of our knowledge and experience of reality).

Cultural studies is characterized by the focusing of analysis on tensions, contradictions, and conflicts that arise in the process of production and analysis of data and by generating, at times, surprising insights into the connection between different perspectives. The 'bricolage' of the research process, the triangulation of various methods and theories depending on the question being researched, demonstrates that this research tradition has divided from a positivistic agenda. The aim of this research is to produce hypotheses or theories about what 'really' takes place in the world and find out, through methodically produced and controlled analysis, if this is 'real.' Cultural studies also shows that research questions, methods, and interests are characterized by social, political, and historical contexts. In research, reality cannot be analyzed 'objectively' but rather research is part of the reality that it (co-)produces and socially (co-)constructs. Because the researcher's methodologies and writing styles do not reflect reality, it is reasonable that different methods will produce and present different perspectives on reality as well. Once we understand this, the particularity of perspectives becomes clear, and different constructions of reality can be taken into account. Knowledge is always socially and politically localized, and the researcher is also required to critically question the discourses and positions that characterize her own thinking. As always, the aim is to understand the complexity of contextual relations.

Considered epistemologically, cultural studies champions an anti-objectivistic view of knowledge like pragmatism or social constructionism. It is always directed at particular contexts, which are shaped locally and historically (cf. Grossberg 2010). Its knowledge objects do not exist independently from research but are rather (co-)created by it and considered as contingent, theoretical object constructions. The confession of "partiality" is defined by Donna Haraway (2004), who describes both the limits of research through temporal, physical, and social factors; the motivation caused by ideologies, interests, and desires; and also the positioning within power structures. These concessions distinguish this approach, which strives not for 'objectivity' in the classic sense but rather for dialogue, reflexivity, and self-understanding. Thus, since the beginnings of cultural studies in adult education in Great Britain, for instance, students were inspired to reflect on their own living conditions, social backgrounds, and personal development to bring these reflections to their research in order to explain their own social positions and relationships to that research object (cf. Winter 2004).

The confession of the approach's positionality, of the situating and localizing of knowledge, does not mean, however, that cultural studies proceeds in a reductionist way, nor that it gives up on demands for rigorous research and systematic knowledge. On the contrary, in accordance with the research questions being pursued, both theoretical approaches and methods of various disciplines are combined to construct research objects in multifaceted and sophisticated ways. "[T]he task for cultural studies, from the beginning, was precisely to develop methods to do things that have never been done before" (Turner 2012: 53). In the ideal case, cultural practices and representations are analyzed from multiple perspectives in the dialogue of different approaches and methods (cf. Kellner 2009). This both reveals and bypasses the necessary limit of single methodological or disciplinary approaches. Cultural studies demands that there is joint reflection on the design of research and the presentation of research results, and that other methods – or even a combination of them – are possible. Transgressions are also desired in order to attain different perspectives (cf. Johnson et al. 2004: 42). The radical contextuality of the approach demands careful (re-)construction of context by the use of suitable methods to understand it.

In the process of research, the realization of reflexivity is essential. In this way, for example, it can be made clear how the researcher's spatial and temporal localization plays a part in the research. Even dialogue with others intensifies desired reflexivity. Thus, cultural studies' newer approaches have performed a "performance turn" (cf. Denzin 2003): they recognize that culture is 'performed' in contradictions and conflicts through research and writing. 'Reflexive performance' and (auto-)ethnography has become the focus of the latest qualitative research.

3 Power, Culture, and Resistance

From its beginnings in the context of the New Left in Great Britain, cultural studies has examined the power structures of society and the possibilities of their transformation. *Resistance* has become a basic concept in cultural studies, which is defined according to Antonio Gramsci's analysis of hegemony (cf. Gramsci 1971), his reflections on popular culture, and, above all, Michel Foucault's analytics of modern power (cf. Foucault 1979, 1997). Despite massive criticism, resistance still occupies a very important role in the analysis of lived experiences and practices. That it is still of such significance demonstrates that cultural studies has continued to consider cultural and media processes in the context of social and cultural inequality as well as structures of power. Also, its perspective is always that of the underclass, subjugated or marginalized, a viewpoint that registers and analyses suffering in society and grief in the world but, at the same time, would also like to reveal the possibility of utopia and social transformation (cf. Kellner 1995).

Thus, it is no surprise that resistance became the central category of this critically interventionist theory and research practice in the 1980s and 90s. It was precisely in the everyday use of cultural and media texts, in their reception and (productive) appropriation that the characteristics and traces of rebellious practices and creative *Eigensinn* ("stubborn obstinacy") were found (cf. Winter 2001). Media texts were read differently than intended and used for the articulation of their own perspective by the readers. Therefore, questions of how far-reaching this resistance against power could be, and what significance it should be given in the context of the present, came to the fore. Did resistance (only) have a symbolic nature or did it also have a 'real' effect? Methodologically, of course, it proved difficult to grasp the creative and resistive elements of everyday experience, because these were already always informed and structured by discourses of the ruling elites. Often, analysis of the polyphonic character of media texts could give insight into potential and subversive readings that opposed those echoing dominant ideologies.

In early research that focused on resistance, which does not clearly show a uniform tradition ensuing from a program, a central aspect of cultural studies had already become clear: its (radical) *contextualism* (cf. Grossberg 2009, 2010). Resistant practices could only be understood when the context in which they occurred – one which they jointly set up – was (re-)constructed. Thus, Paul Willis shows in his (now classic) ethnographic study *Learning to Labour* (1977), how the "lads," working class boys, created a living and a rebellious counter-culture, which disapproved of the middle-class norms of school and subversive-ly circumvented them. Their creative practices rejected the boredom and aliena-tion of educational socialization but did not lead to a transformation of 'real' power structures because, of course, the badly educated "lads" had no recourse but to accept manual jobs after their education. Their protest, which they sub-jectively experienced as freedom, was thus actively involved in the reproduction of social inequality. Willis came to this conclusion by doing ethnographic field-work (participant observation) at a local school and analyzing interviews and discussions with the "lads." He studied their points of view and how they resist-ed. As a second step, he developed a sociological theory of the social reproduc-tion of inequality and applied it to his own ethnographic findings.

In her now equally famous study *Reading the Romance* (1984), which is ar-ranged multi-dimensionally via a combination of methods, and which links his-torical reflection to narrative analysis of novels and empirical research of the reader's perspective, Janice Radway concludes that the reception of romance novels, at first independent of their content, could have an essentially positive significance for women. She felt that regular and enthusiastic reading, losing oneself in reading, helped women in particular to distance themselves from social obligations and everyday relationships; women created spaces for them-selves amongst the domestic noise of the everyday, an everyday in which they were expected to be available exclusively for the family, their source of self-realization. Furthermore, Radway demonstrates through textual analysis how, in romance novels, female sensitivities could be upgraded and played off against those of the patriarchal order. The apparently harmless practice of read-ing relatively standardized romances proved to be unruly and led to the for-mation of a vibrant, resistant subculture. Admittedly, Radway concluded that real patriarchal structures, which penetrated family and social relationships, were not transformed. Resistance could even help strengthen them.

The analysis of resistance within cultural studies is concerned with the practices of subordinate groups and everyday experiences, which are, at first sight, trivial and insignificant. Their unique characters are examined, particu-larly for how they resist real structures of power. Even if, from the perspective of cultural studies, ideologies and hegemonic culture convey the subjects' rela-tionship with the world, they know these structures most closely by means of the practical knowledge that is the necessary prerequisite for their resistance. As a rule, this resistance remains in the imagination and is in vain, until explic-itly investigated. Thus, methodologically, everyday experiences and practices are taken seriously; qualitative interviews and group discussions are conducted and analyzed closely.

Admittedly, the researcher contextualizes the verbal data and, therefore, actually determines its meaning by applying the analytics of power in the work of Foucault, Gramsci's theory of hegemony, or other approaches that deal with the relationship between culture and power. Critiques of this approach often make the point that the researcher's theoretically-based view stands in the way of his/her self-reflexivity. Therefore, he/she cannot recognize, for example, how the 'real' power structures, which he analyzes, only gain a notional shape due to his own theoretical presuppositions (cf. Marcus and Fischer 1986: 81–83). Both Willis and Radway were criticized for allowing their theoretical presuppositions to lead to the development of blind spots, though, admittedly, this could be said of all empirical research and, more generally, all kinds of research.

In more recent ethnographic discussions, slightly exaggerated critiques claim that researchers learn more about their own theoretical perspectives than about the people being examined. Above all, this criticism has been aimed at John Fiske (1989), considered the most important representative of the resistance paradigm. For many, his analysis exploring the possibilities of agency in the 'lifeworld' (*Lebenswelt*) had overly optimistic conclusions. In his analysis of the popular in the present (Fiske 1989), he drew closely on Foucault's (1997) distinction between power and resistance. 'Resistance' can arise in specific historic situations in the relationship between discursive structures, cultural practices, and subjective experiences. Following Michel de Certeau (1984), Fiske conceived of postmodern everyday life as a continuous battle between the strategies of the 'strong' and the guerrilla tactics of the 'weak.' By using resources, which makes the system available in, for example, media texts and other consumer objects, everyday agents try to define their living conditions and express their interests on their own. Therefore, Fiske was not only interested in the process of appropriation, which contributed to social reproduction, but also in secret and hidden consumption, which, according to de Certeau (1984), is a fabrication and even an active producer of meanings and enjoyment. These meanings are used by consumers to make their own issues more clear and can (perhaps) contribute to gradual cultural and social transformation (cf. Winter 2001).

In his analysis, Fiske (1993, cf. also 1994 "Audiencing") critically deconstructs popular texts, from the video performances of Madonna and *Die Hard* (1992) to *Married...With Children* (1987–1997), revealing their potential for plural meanings, which were differently realized by the viewers as was appropriate for their particular social and historical situation. He revealed the inconsistencies, incompleteness, and contradictory structure or polyphony of media texts by structuralist (i.e. structural analysis of narrative codes) and post-structuralist methods (i.e. the analysis of style). He worked out how closely popular texts were related to the particular reality of the postmodern conjuncture and how they articulated social difference by articulating different ideologies. As my own studies have shown (cf. Winter 2010, 1999), reception and appropriation of texts examined by participant observation and the analyzing of interviews became social practices, which were contextually anchored and in which the texts were not predefined as objects with determined meanings but rather were only produced on the basis of social experiences. In combining different methods, Fiske (cf. 1994 "Audiencing") successfully revealed the situational uniqueness and significance of cultural practices, which took place in particular places at particular times. Especially his late work is a good example of radical contextualism and the attempt to determine the conjuncture of the U.S. in the 1990s (cf. Fiske 1993, 1994 *Media Matters*).

As with Radway and Willis, criticism directed at Fiske questioned what significance could lie beyond the immediate contexts of these symbolic battles. An obvious criticism was that resistive media consumption, as Fiske (1992) revealed in his famous and strongly disputed study of Madonna, remains ineffective because it does not change the patriarchal power structure. Arguing in this way, however, ignores the fact that Fiske did not claim that it caused such change in the first place. For him, his study was more about taking the significance of being a Madonna fan seriously, the subjective perspective of the fans, and – particularly in his later work – about working out the uniqueness of cultural experiences and practices in specific contexts, without at all claiming generalizations or immediate transformations of power structures. Admittedly, Fiske himself could not escape the criticism that, as a researcher, he pretended to understand the significance of the practices of the examined better than the examined themselves understood these practices.

Later works in cultural studies have tried to escape this dilemma by considering phenomena from different viewpoints so that, in this way, the methodological tools might become more sensitive to the experience of the other (cf. Saukko 2003: 55–73). For example, biographical interviews and narrations are used to understand the cultural situation of research partners (cf. Winter 2010). Popular cultural phenomena are analyzed from as many points of view as possible (cf. Morris 1998) in order to reveal the different forms of symbolic struggle with dominant meaning structures and the discrepancies and conflicts resulting from those struggles. Many doubt that these unruly or resistant practices have wider-reaching, systemic consequences. Thus, it is necessary to examine whatever specific effects a particular form of local resistance can have and how this influences other experiences, events, and practices in different areas of social life – to demonstrate the breadth of impact (cf. Winter 2001). Furthermore, experiences, practices, and discourses can be analyzed in multiple, local contexts with the result that different forms of subordination and resistance are revealed (cf. Saukko 2003: 40–42). These extensions of the scope of research show that, within cultural studies, the analysis of subversive media consumption, in particular, plays a role even when the optimistic hopes initially linked to it are no longer central.

In current discussions of cultural studies, a variety of topics are considered, from media spectacles (cf. Kellner 2012) and cultural industries (cf. Hesmondhalgh 2007) to sports (cf. Giardina and Newman 2011) and indigenous voices (cf. Denzin et al. 2008). As a rule, questions develop in local contexts, particular 'objects' are chosen for analysis that produces knowledge about particular situations from particular perspectives. Nevertheless, the central aim is to construct different contexts and understand particular conjunctures and their problems and conflicts (cf. Grossberg 2010). Due to historical and geographical contingencies, which influence cultural practices and contexts across the world, there is a variety of cultural studies traditions formed nationally or regionally. However, culture is not on the same level as language, nor is it treated as the 'essence' of a nation or a region. Rather, it is understood as an open, frequently embattled, polyphonic and relational process (cf. Frow and Morris 2003: 498).

4 Analysis of Texts and Cultural Formations: Important Approaches and Developments

Cultural studies strives to analyze cultural processes from as many perspectives as possible in order to reveal frames and discourses that structure them, research strategies, and also our understanding of everyday life. "Mapping the field" (Johnson et al. 2004: 31) is an important step in all cultural studies research; the researcher has to familiarize him- or herself with the particular theoretical frameworks or approaches relevant to his research topic. His orientation is transdisciplinary. He appropriates theories and methods from different disciplines to construct the particular context and its problems. Over the course of this process, the researcher must determine his own commitments, interests, and concepts, which are shaped historically, politically, and socially.

A central methodological characteristic of research in cultural studies is that it examines cultural texts not as discrete entities but as objects of research in contextual settings. The focus is on how texts and discourses are articulated within social, historical, or political contexts. From the beginning, cultural studies has rejected the traditionally Marxist view that culture can be understood primarily in the framework of a dominant ideology. Above all, Stuart Hall's famous "Encoding/Decoding"-model emphasizes that, in the production and reception of news programs, there is a struggle for meaning of the events presented (cf. Hall 1980). Media texts become sites of debate between different social groups that wish to assert their own interpretations and views of the world.

Hall's work is one example of how semiotic and structural analysis of qualitative data came to play an important role, and context became a key aspect of research. Signs were defined as polysemous, with a range of different foci; the link between signifier and signified was primarily, from the perspective of cultural studies, politically motivated. Media texts, as shown, for example, in a well-known study of James Bond (cf. Bennett and Woollacott 1987), are analyzed in their intertextual settings in order to overcome the often formalistic character of semiotic and narrative analysis, which is aimed at primary texts. Instead, the authors analyze "the social organization of the relations between texts within specific conditions of reading" (Bennett and Woollacott 1987: 45). The social contexts of reading frame the meanings of texts. By considering textual and social contexts, the analysis of popular texts gains depth and complexity, because their social meaning is analyzable in the context of complex social and cultural powers. For example, in *Cinema Wars* (2010) Douglas Kellner examines how popular Hollywood movies articulate the right-wing discourses of the Bush-Cheney era, its militarism and racism. He also shows that there are movies criticizing this system. In addition, Henry Giroux (2002) deconstructs the politics of representation in Hollywood movies by critically analyzing the discourses and images of race, gender, class, and sexuality. These studies on visual media illustrate that close reading techniques can be transferred from the field of literary criticism to TV series and shows, because, in contrast to research on the effects of media, the analysis of the cultural meaning of media texts can be considered centrally. From the start, however, these were not regarded as isolated, discrete entities but rather in their inter- and contextual relations. The *radical contextualism* of cultural studies (cf. Grossberg 2009) assumes that the meaning of texts and practices can only be determined in relation to more complex social and cultural power relationships.

Therefore, the focus becomes the semiotic "surroundings" of research objects and the relationships between media and other spatial and temporal contexts of social life (Frow and Morris 2003: 501). This is because, for example, media texts on the coverage of scandals are placed in the context of the contemporary U.S. media culture of spectacles (cf. Kellner 2012). Cultural texts are linked in a type of network to cultural and social practices, which they have initiated or modified.

One essential insight issuing from research in cultural studies is that interpretations always vary and that there are always several possible uses for each text. As John Frow and Meaghan Morris write: "[S]tructures are always structures-in-use and that uses cannot be contained in advance" (Frow and Morris 2003: 506). Therefore, there is no 'right' or 'true' reading of media texts from the perspective of cultural studies. Media texts are not monologic; they are not completed entities but rather a complex constellation of signs and meanings, the result being that they are interpreted and understood differently, even contradictorily, in each social context. Their social (further) existence is an open and incomplete process. Against this background, the readings by researchers must also be qualified and they must be considered in their contextual bonds.

Bringing this observation to bear on a work already mentioned, in *Reading the Romance* (1984) Janice Radway contrasted the interpretations of readers trained in literary criticism with those of fans of the genre. Her aim was to research as comprehensively as possible the experiences and practices of women who deal with this popular genre. Therefore, she combined analysis of literary texts with the analysis of quantitative and qualitative data (generated by surveys, group discussions, interviews). In addition she introduced psychoanalytical and feminist-theoretical positions to the discussion. The deliberate dialogue between theories and methods helped her to overcome the limits of a purely textual analysis and, tellingly, to show how texts can be construed and experienced differently in interpretive communities.

This is a marked departure from previous methods in that, as far as the analysis of media texts has been concerned, the first interpretive strategies to dominate cultural studies were structuralist. Above all Roland Barthes' *Mythologies* (1972) and the narratological analyses by Vladimir Propp, Umberto Eco, and Gérard Genette supplied the methodical basis for the analysis of popular texts. Thus the structural analysis of social ideologies and contexts are, in turn, placed in context. Genre analysis as a contextualizing research strategy is directed at intertextuality because it examines how films, for example, repeat, vary, or introduce new elements to the conventions of a genre (cf. Johnson et al. 2004: 163–167). In addition, the cultural and political dimensions of a genre are examined by relating textual forms and reception practices to each other in context. The popularity of film genres is created together with the viewers, who delight in the predictable order of events and in the surprising variations that are incorporated into it (cf. Winter 2010). Popularity is bound to a time and a place, as well as being situated in social and cultural contexts to which media texts refer and which they supply with stories. In everyday contexts, these stories can lead to personal narrations, and so, in the course of broad research developments from structuralist to radical contextualism, a newly important question of research is: by what means does a genre remain interesting as it successfully keeps, changes, or regains an audience?

One aim of cultural studies is to consider how texts are designed, for example, for the context of production and the economic relationships linked to it. This is done in the midst of broader cultural contexts and social power relationships. Therefore, the tensions between text and context take centre stage, and media texts become moments of greater cultural formations. Thus, in post-structuralist approaches, the polysemous potential, contradictions, and the possibility of diverse readings are worked out in social contexts. For this reason, Yvonne Tasker (1993) shows how action films do not simply reproduce dominant ideas of masculinity, but they also play with these categories, and can even encourage a critical reading. In the framework of cultural studies, texts are therefore contextualized and conventional divisions between text, experience, and practice are discussed and often abolished.

Examinations on the processes of political hegemony approaches focus, for example, on 'close reading' of political speeches in order to reveal the connections between the popular and the dominant. Thus, the analysis of small cultural units (as in the speeches of Bush and Blair on the 'war against terror') can give insights into complex strategic power relationships (cf. Johnson et al. 2004: 170–186): A close reading of their speeches shows that both politicians use strong moral distinctions between good and evil; they equate their Islamic enemies to aliens and demons by rhetorical means. Media texts are read here in their contribution to the stabilization of power and the justification of military strategy.

However, this is only one of many approaches. A feature of cultural studies is its revelation of the *'partiality'* of its approaches, which allows for a dialogue with others about their construction of objects and readings. As Donna Haraway writes: "Objectivity turns out to be about particular and specific embodiment, and definitely not about the false vision promising transcendence of all limits and responsibility. The moral is simple: Only partial perspective promises objective view" (Haraway 2004: 87). Therefore, detailed analysis can show singular situational moments in the cultural production, circulation, and reception of a popular genre in which complex cultural and social debates are hidden, but which contain the possibility of both (transgressive) pleasure and the construction of meaning. For example, Fiske (1994 "Audiencing") showed how the reception of *Married...With Children* enabled teenage viewers who attended a Catholic university to reflect on the relations with their absent parents. But this was only one particular part of the cultural circulation of meanings and pleasures around the production and reception of this postmodern sitcom.

The characteristics of postmodern media texts were also defined early on, borrowing from the archive of available media texts and understood primarily in the context of these circular references – and not in reference to a "primary reality" unaffected by the media (cf. Denzin 1991). Thus, a controversial film like *Natural Born Killers* (1994) deals self-reflexively and critically with media images as well as with our knowledge of serial killers, as garnered by media consumption. However, not everyone has formed a postmodern sensibility and can understand the film as a parody of media violence. Cultural studies emphasizes, therefore, that every reading is contextually bound and has political character. The knowledge of texts and practices whose spatial and temporal characteristics have to be defined is always knowledge of a particular context. As research into popular culture shows, texts, and practices exist in particular locations at particular times for particular people (cf. Jenkins 2002 et al.). Thus, the significance of a media text can never be determined definitively. In the field of popular culture, meanings multiply whenever consumers and researchers understand the texts in the context of their own social life and cultural identity. In the framework of cultural studies, personal experiences of dealing with media texts are often the starting point for critical analysis (cf. Johnson et al. 2004), thereby continuing the methodology of defining, in a self-reflexive way, the social basis of our interpretations and the limits of these interpretations.

In cultural studies research orientated toward post-structuralism, genealogical and deconstructive analyses are also carried out (cf. Saukko 2003: Ch. 6–7). Following Foucault (1979, 1997), genealogy can reveal how our perceptions, ideas, and descriptions of problems or scientific truths develop out of historic contexts and specific social and political processes. The images we make of ourselves, our society, and our history are never complete or independent. They remain partial, linked to the social practices from which they have arisen. A cultural genealogist attempts to understand the media practices in the culture we share with others and which have also made us what we are today.

Deconstruction makes possible a critical analysis of the logic behind media texts (cf. Bowman 2008). For example, dichotomous oppositions are revealed and discussed; behind these hide values, ideological presuppositions, and cultural hierarchies. Furthermore, deconstructive readings reveal the essential uncertainty and multivalency of the meaning of media texts, which are constituted by an unlimited play of differences and receptive to diverse readings in different contexts. Therefore, deconstructive cultural studies also has an interventional character, one that seeks to "expose the underlying 'structural' preconceptions that organize texts and to reveal the conditions of freedom that they suppress" (Denzin 1994: 196).

5 The Importance of Self-Reflexivity

In the analysis of reception and appropriation processes, the *ethnographic perspective* is at the fore of cultural studies. However, at the same time and as a rule, this is not meant to be an extensive ethnographic piece of fieldwork, as is appropriate for sociology or anthropology, but rather (short-time) participant observation of cultural practices in modern and postmodern life. This makes possible an approach to the inevitable circulation of meanings, and, therefore, access to cultural circulation (cf. Johnson et al. 2004). Often the ethnographic perspective is even linked to autobiographical elements.

For example, Ien Ang (1985), in her study *Watching Dallas* (1978–1991), has linked the analysis of female viewers' reactions to her own assessment of the series. Personal affinity to an object of research, even to the point of being a fan, as well as self-reflection, are all important resources in the research process of cultural studies. "My existence as a fan, my experiences, along with whatever other responses are available for describing the field of popular practices and their articulation to social and political positions are the raw material, the starting point of critical research" (Grossberg 1988: 68). Drawing on affinity in such a way can be fruitful while also being an active source of contention.

As has already been mentioned, the criticism of the overly theoretical nature of research, and particularly into resistance, both of which accentuate the researchers' theoretical view over the lived reality being researched, led within cultural studies to the discussion and development of new research strategies being more suitable for the examination of lived experience and reality. Greater significance has been since given to dialogue between the perspective of the researcher and that of the other, the object of study (cf. Lincoln and Denzin 2003). The researcher's world should not be described from an outsider's perspective, but rather in terms of the interaction or meeting between different worlds, in which the perspective of the other should, as far as possible, be understood 'authentically' along with his active contribution. Therefore, the researcher must first examine what might be preventing him/her from understanding the world of the other, who, for example, watches horror films or listens to gangsta rap. To be aware of one's own restricted frames of understanding demands sensitivity towards strange and radically different worlds of experience. For this reason researchers in cultural studies highlight the ethical duty to do justice, as far as possible, to the worlds of others. Dialogues between researchers and subjects should be possible, and must be conducted. Such dialogues would help reduce prejudices and overcome the limits of personal understanding and, therefore, be a more just approach for the texture of the lived experience from the point of view of the participants.

Staged against this backdrop, *self-reflexivity* is an important feature of this new form of ethnography. The researcher should reflect intensively on his/her own situation, social and political obligations, as well as any theoretical pre-suppositions, in order to find easier access to the subject's world. That said, self-reflexivity does not imply that a "true" knowledge of the world is possible (cf. Haraway 2004); instead, it shows the limits of our own world view, and reveals that different interpretations of our own world and that of others are always possible. In the form of critical autoethnography, self-reflexivity prompts a researcher to examine which events and social discourses have defined his/her experiences (cf. Bochner and Ellis 2002) and to carry this process of reflection to completion via new forms of writing (cf. Richardson 2000). In a personal, literal, and experimental way, these writings show aspects of the researcher's experience, particularly those that are not rational and that concern the (media) worlds of others.

In the global media world of the twenty-first century, ethnographic practices within the framework of cultural studies prove to be a moral discourse (cf. Denzin 2010), one that makes (problematic) life and media experiences available and can give insight into (new) forms of social and cultural inequality. A further step would involve questioning existing power relationships even in the everyday: "Research that is more fully participatory will aim to use the research process itself to empower those who are being researched" (Johnson et al. 2004: 215). Moreover, it is imperative to capture the polyvocality within the field of ethnographic research. Lived experiences should be rendered by a number of diverse voices in such a way as to preclude a single voice standing for the "truth" of an experience, and instead grasping the peculiarity of individual experiences (Saukko 2003: 64–65). Even the presentation of research results comes down to an interaction between the researcher's voice and those of the others. Autobiographers are a case in point: their experiences tend to lead them to experiment with their presentation, which can even become a "performance" of happenings and practices (cf. Denzin 2003, 2010). In qualitative media research, furthermore, such methodological reorientation is given great significance. On the one hand, dialogic relationships call on the researcher to challenge his/her own media 'profile,' preferences, and aversions. On the other hand, informants who, for example, report on forms of problematic media consumption are taken seriously as subjects who have developed their own particular viewpoint. They are then called to bring this to bear in their presentation. Given the widespread reverence for objectivity in science, it is a notable turn of events when the researcher leaves the role of independent observer to become more like a supporting teammate. Like the member of any team, one's own sub-jectivity becomes marked by media practices in modern societies, especially by popular culture. The researcher should, thus, be clear about this throughout the research process. "Popular culture matters [...] precisely because its meanings, effects, consequences, and ideologies can't be nailed down. As consumers and as critics, we struggle with this proliferation of meanings as we make sense of our own social lives and cultural identities" (Jenkins et al. 2002: 11).

Even in the new forms of ethnography, the critical analysis of social forms of injustice and inequality is central (cf. Denzin 2009; Niederer and Winter 2010). These should be revealed, analyzed from different perspectives, and in-spected for both the possibility for change and the increase of agency amongst those researched. Above all, it is the aim of 'Critical Pedagogy' within the field of cultural studies to contribute knowledge to this struggle and to improve the lives of those affected by social injustice and discrimination (cf. Kincheloe et al. 2011).

6 Outlook

Fleshing out the critical methodological fundamentals of cultural studies that are closely connected to the original political spirit of its project, as I have done here, should prove useful for the transnational study of culture. Modernity and capitalism are now established in different forms worldwide, and what we need now is a critical approach to analyze the complex relationship between culture and the other domains of global society. Certainly, critical methodologies have to be adapted to different contexts as well, but their core should not be changed. Cultural studies should still remain true to its origins and seek to link criticism of power to opportunities for intervention and democratic change. Stuart Hall defines its aim as "to enable people to understand what [was] going on, and especially to provide ways of thinking, strategies for survival, and re-sources for resistance" (Hall 1990: 22). If cultural studies wants to be more than the analysis of contemporary culture, it has to preserve its emphasis on the political. The political may be unlikely, contingent, and rare, but it still exists today, and should be held up for inspection.

Cultural studies is not dispensed with the task to develop new theoretical and empirical tools, in the event they are necessary in order to grasp and under-stand the contemporary shape of the political. To my understanding, this orien-tation is what distinguishes cultural studies from the field of *Kulturwissen-schaften* in the German sense of the term. Considering the growing forms of economic crisis and social inequality worldwide, both traditions should begin debating the role of critical academic research and practice in a changing world. The 'transnational' has opened up a potential space of exchange and discussion, and this should be used productively. The contemporary university may be in ruins (cf. Readings 1996), but it should redefine its role in an emerging global society. Here, the discourse of 'excellence' (especially in Germany) seems not to be the solution, but rather part of the problem. The critical project of cultural studies can be an outstanding example of the attempt to explore disciplinary frontiers and to connect academic knowledge with a political understanding of culture and society. We can still learn from it.

Kulturwissenschaften could 'translate' the political into German speaking contexts in order to delve into the interconnections between cultural objects, cultural practices, and forms of power and domination. In this way, it would deepen its understanding of resistance, agency, and (political) subjectivization. *Kulturwissenschaften* could revisit the questions and concerns of the Frankfurt School and other critical traditions – which would, in turn, link back to the project of cultural studies (cf. Kellner 1997) – in order to enrich its theoretical and methodological perspectives. That said, cultural studies could learn from the rich and complex traditions of *Kulturwissenschaften* as well, particularly those that analyze cultural forms and practices innovatively and profoundly, in order to better understand the relationships between culture and power.

References

Ang, Ien. *Watching Dallas: Soap Opera and the Melodramatic Imagination*. London: Methuen, 1985.

Barthes, Roland. *Mythologies*. London: Cape, 1972.

Bennett, Tony, and Janet Woollacott. *Bond and Beyond: The Political Career of a Popular Hero*. London: Macmillan Press, 1987.

Bochner, Arthur P., and Carolyn Ellis, eds. *Ethnographically Speaking: Autoethnography, Literature, and Aesthetics*. Walnut Creek, CA: Altamira Press, 2002.

Bowman, Paul. *Deconstructing Popular Culture*. New York: Palgrave, 2008.

Certeau, Michel de. *The Practice of Everyday Life*. Berkeley/Los Angeles/London: University of California Press, 1984.

Couldry, Nick. *Inside Culture: Re-imagining the Method in Cultural Studies*. London/Thousand Oaks, CA/New Delhi: Sage, 2000.

Cruz, John D. "Cultural Studies and Social Movements: A Crucial Nexus in the American Case." *European Journal of Cultural Studies* 15.3 (June 2012): 254–301.

Denzin, Norman K. *Images of Postmodern Society: Social Theory and Contemporary Cinema*. London/Newbury Park/New Delhi: Sage, 1991.

Denzin, Norman K. "Postmodernism and Deconstructionism." *Postmodernism and Social Inquiry*. Eds. David Dickens and Andrea Fontana. London: UCL Press, 1994. 182–202.

Denzin, Norman K. *Performance Ethnography*. London/Thousand Oaks, CA/New Delhi: Sage, 2003.

Denzin, Norman K. *Qualitative Inquiry Under Fire: Toward a New Paradigm Dialogue*. Walnut Creek, CA: Left Coast Press, 2009.

Denzin, Norman K. *The Qualitative Manifesto: A Call to Arms*. Walnut Creek, CA: Left Coast Press, 2010.

Denzin, Norman K., Yvonna S. Lincoln, and Linda Tuhiwai Smith, eds. *Handbook of Critical and Indigenous Methodologies*. London/Thousand Oaks, CA/New Delhi: Sage, 2008.

Fiske, John. *Understanding Popular Culture*. London/Sidney/Wellington: Unwin Hyman, 1989.

Fiske, John. "British Cultural Studies and Television." *Channels of Discourse, Reassembled*. Ed. Robert C. Allen. Durham, NC/London: Duke University Press, 1992. 284–326.

Fiske, John. *Power Plays – Power Works*. London/New York: Verso, 1993.

Fiske, John. "Audiencing: Cultural Practice and Cultural Studies." *Handbook of Qualitative Research, First Edition*. Eds. Norman K. Denzin and Yvonna S. Lincoln. London/Newbury Park/New Delhi: Sage, 1994. 189–198.

Fiske, John. *Media Matters: Everyday Culture and Political Change*. Minneapolis/London: University of Minnesota Press, 1994.

Foucault, Michel. *History of Sexuality: An Introduction*, vol. 1. London: Allen Lane, 1979 [1978].

Foucault, Michel. *Discipline and Punish: The Birth of the Prison*. London: Allen Lane, 1997 [1977].

Frow, John, and Meaghan Morris. "Cultural Studies." *The Landscape of Qualitative Research: Theories and Issues*. Eds. Norman K. Denzin and Yvonna S. Lincoln. London/Thousand Oaks, CA/New Delhi: Sage, 2003. 489–539.

Geertz, Clifford. *The Interpretation of Cultures*. London: Hutchinson, 1973.

Giardina, Michael D., and Joshua L. Newman. "Cultural Studies: Performative Imperatives and Bodily Articulations." *The Sage Handbook of Qualitative Research*. 4th edition. Eds. Norman K. Denzin and Yvonna S. Lincoln. London/Thousand Oaks, CA/New Delhi: Sage, 2011. 179–194.

Gilbert, Jeremy. *Anticapitalism and Culture: Radical Theory and Popular Politics*. Oxford/New York: Berg, 2008.

Giroux, Henry A. *Breaking in to the Movies: Film and the Culture of Politics*. Malden, MA/Oxford: Blackwell, 2002.

Gramsci, Antonio. *Selections from the Prison Notebooks*. Eds. and trans. Q. Hoare and G. Smith Nowell. London: Lawrence & Wishart, 1971.

Grossberg, Lawrence. *It's a Sin: Essays on Postmodernism, Politics and Culture*. Sydney: Power Publications, 1988.

Grossberg, Lawrence. *Caught in the Crossfire: Kids, Politics and America's Future*. Boulder/London: Paradigm Publishers, 2005.

Grossberg, Lawrence. "Cultural Studies: What's in a Name." *Media/Cultural Studies: Critical Approaches*. Eds. Rhonda Hammer and Douglas Kellner. New York: Peter Lang, 2009. 25–48.

Grossberg, Lawrence. *Cultural Studies in the Future Tense*. Durham, NC/London: Duke University Press, 2010.

Habermas, Jürgen. *Erkenntnis und Interesse*. Frankfurt a.M.: Suhrkamp, 1968.

Hall, Stuart. "Encoding/Decoding." *Culture, Media, Language.* Eds. Stuart Hall, Dorothy Hobson, Andrew Lowe, and Paul Willis. London: Hutchinson, 1980. 128–138.

Hall, Stuart. "The Emergence of Cultural Studies and the Crisis of Humanities." *October* 53 (1990): 11–23.

Haraway, Donna. "Situated Knowledges: The Science Question in Feminism and the Privilege of Partial Perspective." *The Feminist Standpoint Theory Reader: Intellectual and Political Controversies.* Ed. Sandra Harding. New York/London: Routledge, 2004. 81–102.

Hesmondhalgh, David. *Cultural Industries: An Introduction.* 2nd edition. London/Thousand Oaks, CA/New Delhi/Singapore: Sage, 2007.

Jenkins, Henry, Tara McPherson, and Jane Shattuc, eds. *Hop on Pop: The Politics and Pleasure of Popular Culture.* Durham, NC/London: Duke University Press, 2002.

Johnson, Richard, Deborah Chambers, Parvati Raghuram, and Estella Tincknell. *The Practice of Cultural Studies.* London/Thousand Oaks, CA/New Delhi: Sage, 2004.

Kellner, Douglas. *Media Culture.* London/New York: Routledge, 1995.

Kellner, Douglas. "Social Theory and Cultural Studies." *Sociology after Postmodernism.* Ed. David Owen. London/Thousand Oaks, CA/New Delhi: Sage, 1997. 138–157.

Kellner, Douglas. "Toward a Critical/Media Cultural Studies." *Media/Cultural Studies: Critical Approaches.* Eds. Rhonda Hammer and Douglas Kellner. New York: Peter Lang, 2009. 5–24.

Kellner, Douglas. *Cinema Wars: Hollywood Film and Politics in the Bush-Cheney Era.* Oxford: Wiley-Blackwell, 2010.

Kellner, Douglas. *Media Spectacle and Insurrection 2011: From the Arab Uprisings to Occupy Everywhere.* New York/London: Bloomsbury, 2012.

Kincheloe, Joe, Peter McLaren, and Shirley R. Steinberg. "Critical Pedagogy and Qualitative Research: Moving to the Bricolage." *The Sage Handbook of Qualitative Research.* 4th edition. Eds. Norman K. Denzin and Yvonna S. Lincoln. London/Thousand Oaks, CA/New Delhi/Singapore: Sage, 2011. 163–178.

Lincoln, Yvonna S., and Norman K. Denzin, eds. *Turning Points in Qualitative Research.* Walnut Creek, CA: Altamira Press, 2003.

Marcus, George E., and Michael M. Fischer. *Anthropology as Cultural Critique: An Experimental Moment in the Human Sciences.* Chicago: University of Chicago Press, 1986.

Morris, Meaghan. *Too Soon Too Late: History in Popular Culture.* Bloomington: Indiana University Press, 1998.

Niederer, Elisabeth, and Rainer Winter. "Poverty and Social Exclusion: The Everyday Life of the Poor as the Research Field of a Critical Ethnography." *Qualitative Inquiry and Human Rights.* Eds. Norman K. Denzin and Michael D. Giardina. Walnut Creek, CA: Left Coast Press, 2010. 205–217.

Radway, Janice A. *Reading the Romance: Women, Patriarchy, and Popular Literature.* London/New York: Verso, 1984.

Readings, Bill. *The University in Ruins.* Cambridge, MA/London: Harvard University Press, 1996.

Richardson, Laurel. "Writing: A Method of Inquiry." *Handbook of Qualitative Research.* 2nd edition. Eds. Norman K. Denzin and Yvonna S. Lincoln. London/Thousand Oaks, CA/New Delhi: Sage, 2000. 923–948.

Rojek, Chris. *Cultural Studies.* Cambridge: Polity Press, 2007.

Saukko, Paula. *Doing Research in Cultural Studies: An Introduction to Classical and New Methodological Approaches.* London/Thousand Oaks, CA/New Delhi: Sage, 2003.

Smith, Paul, ed. *The Renewal of Cultural Studies*. Philadelphia: Temple University Press, 2011.

Tasker, Yvonne. *Spectacular Bodies: Gender, Genre and the Action Cinema*. London/New York: Routledge, 1993.

Turner, Graeme. *What's Become of Cultural Studies?* London/Thousand Oaks, CA/New Delhi/Singapore: Sage, 2012.

Williams, Raymond. *The Long Revolution*. New York: Columbia University Press, 1961.

Willis, Paul. *Learning to Labour: How Working-Class Kids Get Working-Class Jobs*. Westmead: Saxon House, 1977.

Willis, Paul. *Profane Culture*. London: Routledge and Kegan Paul, 1978.

Winter, Rainer. "The Search for Lost Fear: The Social World of the Horror Fan in Terms of Symbolic Interactionism and Cultural Studies." *Cultural Studies: A Research Volume*, No. 4. Ed. Norman K. Denzin. Stanford: JAI Press Inc., 1999. 277–298.

Winter, Rainer. *Die Kunst des Eigensinns. Cultural Studies als Kritik der Macht*. Weilerswist: Velbrück, 2001.

Winter, Rainer. "Critical Pedagogy." *Encyclopedia of Social Theory*, Vol. 1. Ed. George Ritzer. London/Thousand Oaks, CA/New Delhi: Sage, 2004. 163–167.

Winter, Rainer. *Der produktive Zuschauer. Medienaneignung als kultureller und ästhetischer Prozess*. 2nd edition. Cologne: Herbert von Halem, 2010.

Winter, Rainer. "Cultural Studies – Jetzt und in der Zukunft." *Die Zukunft der Cultural Studies. Theorie, Kultur und Gesellschaft im 21. Jahrhundert*. Ed. Rainer Winter. Bielefeld: transcript, 2011. 7–14.

Thomas Weber
Translating 'Media' and 'Communication'
National Assignment and Transnational Misunderstanding[*]

1 Introduction

If one posits translation as a guiding concept in research, differentiating between various epistemological interests becomes virtually inevitable, not only
as a matter of 'translation' as such but also as a meta-reflection on the practice
of translating. This practice can be viewed from various perspectives within a
broadly defined concept of cultural studies, with each perspective focusing on a
different set of phenomena: (1) the group of problems related to linguistic translation, which corresponds to our everyday understanding of translation as rendering an adequate expression of a text in a given target language through a
hermeneutic process of contextually understanding the text in its source language; (2) the manner in which various disciplines subsumed under cultural
studies are manifested in different nation-specific academic cultures; (3) the
relationships between social and cultural power expressed in the act of translation that can, for example, be described in terms of cultural dependence or hegemony as analyzed by cultural studies in recent decades; and (4) the translation from one milieu to another, in which the gesture of translation and the
aspect of transmission are more significant than linguistic problems.

These four sets of concerns prove to be difficult to isolate from one another.
That said, certain similarities can be revealed as superficial; even if all processes of translation navigate sites of misunderstanding and difference, these must,
in turn, be pried apart and shown to be distinctive. Linguistic translation and
translating between disciplines are primarily matters of translation in the nar-
rower sense; here, the guiding assumption is that selecting suitable terminology
will improve mutual understanding and that this is, indeed, desirable. In cultural studies, however, questions of hegemony and situational barriers arise
and translation is primarily a matter of 'transmission' in which relationships of

---

[*] Translated by Maureen Roycraft Sommer.

power become visible. An examination of transmission also encompasses corresponding 'transformations,' which are determined not only by cultural 'contexts' but also by modes of behavior and specific constellations of interests and, thus, in equal measure, by the media and media culture.

The claim that questions of translation are radicalized in the field of media and communication may, at first, seem surprising, given the common assumption that, due to the fact that media and communication are perceived as structurally indispensable elements of every translation process, there are fewer translation problems in this particular context. The goal and ideal of translation is, ostensibly, to become a medium itself and facilitate communication. In fact, media and communication form an intellectual horizon and make a utopian promise (on this subject, see also Buden and Nowotny 2008), the realization of which usually ends in national attributions.

Armand Mattelart critically deconstructs 'communication' as having emerged as a utopian promise, a kind of "ideology of world understanding" in which fears and hopes were combined, even in its early beginnings in the eighteenth century (Mattelart 2007).[1] In fact, communication is, to this day, employed as a promise, especially the form of communication conveyed through mass media and/or technical media, which generally experienced its baptism by fire in military conflicts. Its concrete manifestations initially tended to reflect claims to power on the part of elites rather than truly cross-border or border-opening forms of communication. These claims to power are now found in national, social, cultural, and environment-related appropriations and attributions and, thus, also in the academic world. Here, Eric Hobsbawm (1990) comes to mind; his definition of nation-states in the nineteenth century includes not only an organized territory but also media and a cultural elite who knew how to make the best use of it. In this context, communication is not only a matter of propagating an idea of the national but, even more importantly, of displacing its physical and material conditions, or – as the Swiss 'mediologist' Vincent Kaufmann (2004) more precisely expresses – of organizing the process of forgetting. Under the banner of globalization, there are not so much national ideas as there are autopoetic tendencies related to the idea of global communication promoted by globalized elites. Globalized elites seem, on the one hand, to organize themselves transnationally and, on the other hand, to demonstrate

---

1 Armand Mattelart has been one of the most prominent globalization theorists since the 1970s, but his work has never been widely translated into German and, if at all, only recently, when he began serving as a scientific advisor to UNESCO on world communication development (e.g. for the UNESCO Convention on Cultural Diversity of 2005).

tendencies of 'localization,' i.e. persistence. These tendencies sometimes converge in the same environments, or individuals, and result in an idiosyncratic mixture of legitimation discourses and claims to power, each appealing to different criteria.

I do not want 'translation' to be misunderstood as a concept of exclusively successful communication but grasped, instead, as a process of cultural and social appropriation and attribution (in certain cases by the media); hence, it is also a category or an indicator of unsuccessful, i.e. faulty or 'misleading,' transnational and media communication. Thus, translation must not be taken merely as a technique that objectively conveys meaning from one linguistic context to another. Birgit Mersmann has already drawn attention to the fact "that one of the problems that led to the debates concerning translation and culture in the age of globalisation lies in the fact that insufficient differentiation is made between translation as communication and translation as transmission" (Mersmann 2008: 152–153). In this context, limited concepts of translation arise out of confusing the technical/physical transfer of information with the transfer of social knowledge, which is influenced by claims to power or the often-cited *differences cachés*. Translation should, therefore, be understood in the expanded sense outlined by Doris Bachmann-Medick (2009), which goes beyond the traditional concept of translation by including the idea of transmitting and transforming cultural practices.

Questions related to how translation comes about, why it is neglected in certain cases, how a cultural paradigm shift fails to take place, and how a 'turn' appears in the culture of academic discourse will be discussed via examples from three different arenas: (1) television's potential for organizing cross-border communication as an illustration of borders that are not exclusively determined by political systems or language; (2) translations that are required to provide the basis and medium for intellectual communication between two countries; (3) an account of the divergent self-conceptions of the disciplines of media and communication studies in Germany and France (in which the U.S. also plays a certain role).[2] If translation is always also understood as the transformation of social and cultural fields, then what is essential for its success or failure is not an individual idea, concept, institution or person, but the collaboration be-

---

2 In this context, the more fundamental question arises as to whether there could be alternative, well-grounded systems of organizing knowledge in ways other than according to the disciplines. Encyclopedias could be one example: the rise in recent years of Wikipedia via the Internet shows their continued importance, even if they lack an orientating function to determine the relative weight of facts.

tween various protagonists as outlined in actor-network theory (cf. Latour 1999) or mediology (cf. Mersmann and Weber 2008).

2 Television, ARTE, and the Collaboration between Human and Non-Human Actors

"A picture is worth a thousand words" is a common saying, but do pictures also speak the same language in different national contexts? "Every country has its own concept of communication," claims the former director of audience research at ARTE, Michael Schroeder (1993: 21). With this statement, he identifies a problem: although conceived as a 'window to the world,' television generates a specific national view, which cannot be perceived beyond the borders of a country for reasons that are more than just technical. Television does not travel. It stops at national borders, even in cases where this is not assumed to be true. In this context, one must let go of the idea of immediate understanding often attributed to images and gestures. Even a medium as familiar as television, which has triumphed globally within just a few decades and is, therefore, often used as a paradigm of global culture in cultural studies, can hardly escape national attribution. National forms of communicative attribution are not only determined by cultural and political elites, but also by everyday habits and idiosyncrasies, not least of all by their organization, pattern of use (e.g. the programming scheme), and the design and arrangement of material.

Ostentatious national attributions are found not only in conjunction with events such as international football matches, but also in forms of relatively obvious national usurpation. One example of the latter would be cooking shows: the German flag was seen fluttering in front of the official presidential residence, Schloss Bellevue, during the show *Zu Gast bei Christiane Herzog* ("A Visit with Christiane Herzog" – Germany's "first lady" at that time); and, in *La cuisine des mousquetaires*, the decoration of an open hearth with an old musket and the presentation of recipes such as wild boar stew in blood sauce revived not only nationally oriented cuisine but also the *ancien régime* in culinary terms (cf. Woltersdorff 2001). In fact, differences in national viewing habits are so great that most television programs cannot even be exported to neighboring countries. With an export rate of only 6%, television channels lack important opportunities to generate income by selling programs. However, even greater problems arise for the advertising industry, since most commercials must be nation-specific and even allude to national clichés.[3] Even where there is political will to organize international and cross-border cooperation, it is by no means a guarantee that communication will be successful; the very existence of a channel like ARTE is all the more surprising, because the ideas on the German and French sides were, particularly in the beginning, so divergent. ARTE, as an instrument of French foreign policy, on the one hand, and as an economical opportunity for re-using German television productions, on the other, required more than just harmonization. This was, not least of all, due to the fact that France's president François Mitterrand was confronted by an unwieldy number of German minister-presidents (i.e. premiers). They were responsible, within the framework of Germany's federal structure, for regulating the media. However, they were by no means all of the same opinion, and, even more importantly, from the standpoint of the French, they were operating on a different level of official protocol. A national treaty between two sovereign states could not be organized in this manner, since an ideal could not be simply conveyed or translated in this context. A national treaty establishing ARTE could only be signed in the wake of a special law passed by the French parliament; the channel has been operating on this basis ever since.

In addition to institutional problems, aesthetic conventions also demonstrate remarkable persistence in the face of institutional dynamism and become evident when certain formats are rejected by viewers.[4] This was the experience

---

3 Hidden cultural differences emerge, such as the well-studied intra- and intergroup image perceptions sometimes expressed in advertising clips in which, for example, German cars are attributed the characteristic of dependability, whereas French cars display creativity. Beyond this, different concepts of explicit and implicit communication, as described by Edward and Mildred Hall (1992), are expressed in the manner in which messages are conveyed. Since, here, to a great extent, social and cultural forms of the construction of identity must also be addressed, these cannot be transmitted through simple linguistic translations and, thus, necessitate nationally differentiated advertising clips. In the 1990s, enjoyment of *Jacobs Krönung* coffee was explicitly presented, in a rather convoluted manner, to German audiences as the most perfect form of a Sunday-afternoon family gathering. The French, who exhibit a greater preference for sensual seduction, saw, in short advertising clips for the *Carte Noir* brand of coffee, a man and woman swirling around each other, like coffee being stirred in a cup; a cut from the dancers to the cup sufficed to illustrate the association.

4 Cf. Machill (1997), Keusen (1997), and Landbeck (1991). Media systems arise at the intersection of technology, economy, politics, and cultural tradition. They not only convey the content of media but also, simultaneously, the systems of values and standards for judging reality that influence social and cultural manners of thought. In this respect, there is a relationship between questions of comparative literature and intercultural and media studies. Hence, an integrating – in part also "mediological" – approach is proposed here, one that combines aspects of media, cultural, and, in part, communication studies.

in the early days of ARTE, when the channel was in search of a concept for their news format (cf. Gräßle 1995). This was no easy task, because national differentiation begins with the news. While images are produced and marketed globally, they are organized and commented upon nationally.[5] To this day, there are no really 'global' news broadcasts, and even CNN differentiates its programs, as Europeans can apparently be confronted with different images than U.S. audiences. There are also differences regarding where things fit into program schedules, the lengths of programs, and styles of depiction. In addition to issues of selection, placement, and the weighting of topics noted in previous studies on communication, special consideration should be given to visual design, one aspect of which has been chosen here for the purpose of illustration: the position of the speaker or presenter.

One of the most notable differences between German and French practices, at first glance, is the distance established between the audience and the speaker in Germany. The latter is always shown in an upper-body shot in an obvious attempt at objective and impartial portrayal. In France, on the other hand, the anchor – usually a famous journalist such as Patrick Poivre d'Arvor – is shown in a close-up, making it possible to recognize even the slightest emotional reaction on his face, which, at times, almost completely fills the frame. Through his direct mediation, he becomes a broker who assumes the task of explaining the world to his community. If there were no friendly wink, or no commentary (regardless of how cryptic), one can suspect that the French audience might be disappointed or even feel neglected.

These differences led to translation problems for ARTE during the 1990s: how could a new program be established that would be equally accepted in both countries? The French insisted on a broadcasting slot at 20:30, with news stories presented as longer reports, while the Germans were in favor of the 20:00 slot, with short, concise reports featuring off-camera commentary. The final result was ARTE Info, broadcast at 19:45, which presents not only current news but also background information given by a news anchor who moves freely around the studio, thereby actually varying his position. The result: a news program that is ignored in equal measure by both French and German audiences.

---

5 *Euronews* may be an exception to the rule: the same images are broadcast from Lyon, generally without commentary, and the few sections with commentary are translated into various languages, but – in all honesty – who watches *Euronews*?

3 *Au Jardin des Malentendus* – In the Garden of Misunderstandings

When Jacques Leenhardt and Robert Picht published their book *Au Jardin des Malentendus* – which can be loosely translated as "In the Garden of Misunderstandings" – in 1990, they presented an overview of the rich history of mistrust, misunderstanding, and divergent expectations between French and German cultural elites in the centuries-old Franco-German relationship, which has wavered between animosity and neighborliness and has, now, become one of friendship. Regardless of whether we are led to the world of academia by Charlemagne, Hegel, or critical theory, discourses are repeatedly adopted from other discourses, weighted with national attributes, and transformed to the point that they become unrecognizable. This applies, in principle, to the present day, in which the success or failure of intellectual and scientific concepts is dependent, not least of all and quite essentially, upon the situation of translation itself. And this is, in a word, disastrous.

Thus, one should not be misled by the number of existing translations, or even by the hype regarding certain authors, into believing that the percentage of translations from each language into the other has not been sinking for years, despite numerous programs that provide public funds to support translation, or that a marked shift to translations of English-language texts has not taken place. While French is still the second most frequently translated language internationally, and while France exports roughly five times as many titles to Germany as it imports from Germany, the share of translations from the German, in relation to all translations, has fallen from 25% in the 1960s to 4.9% in 2007 (Papouschek 2009: 33). Stated in concrete numbers, an average of 23.4 titles of fiction were translated into French between 2001 and 2008 per year (Papouschek 2009: 40). In the field of cultural studies, the situation with regard to translations is only slightly better. I will refrain from listing the authors who have not been translated here; suffice it to say that, in the last five years, works by better-known authors, such as Peter Sloterdijk, Ulrich Beck, and Siegfried Kracauer, have, at least, been translated.

Therefore, it is not surprising that, for a long time, there were no translations of highly relevant works in the field of media and communication studies or works on systems theory, such as those by Niklas Luhmann. In France, just as little was known about constructivism as about the technology-centered media theory of scholars like Friedrich Kittler, or about Siegfried Zielinski's media archaeology. Even the texts – mainly by English-speaking authors – that have been translated into German and have found a strong resonance in Germany are only rarely found in France, and then only as recent translations. This dearth includes not only numerous works on gender theory, particularly Judith Butler's, but also the broad field of cultural studies, with texts by Stuart Hall and many other authors having been almost entirely absent until quite recently.

However, there are also many gaps in translation into German in this respect; younger, but nevertheless important and well-connected authors, are unknown here. These include the communication scholar Dominique Wolton, the media philosopher Pierre Lévy, and the (media) sociologist Bernard Lahire; within the growing field of mediology (Régis Debray, Louise Merzeau, and many others), very few works have been translated.[6] The low number of translations is, however, not just the result of a lack of market demand or insufficient financial support. Often, new approaches in research are received with very little enthusiasm or even actively ignored. Even translations which we now take for granted – those of better-known authors such as Derrida, Lacan, Nancy, Lyotard, and Rancière – were only published in Germany after considerable delays and, often, only by way of American academic circles.

The dedication of certain individuals has always been (and still is) responsible for lifting the 'ban' in this area. One such individual is Peter Engelmann, who founded the publishing house *Passagen Verlag* in the late 1980s. Somewhat ironically, he initiated the German reception of postmodernism by leaving Germany and establishing his business in Vienna. Engelmann notes, in this context:

> It is hard to imagine from today's perspective the difficulties the Passagen project faced in the mid-eighties. [...] Although in the United States, the works of Michel Foucault, Jacques Derrida or Jean-François Lyotard had been an important part of philosophical discourse for quite some time, Western German intellectuals, who until then had been uncontested, felt their monopoly jeopardized, and mobilized all their political and cultural influence, revving up important publishers and the media against the new French philosophy. (Engelmann 2013)

Even if Engelmann tends to be somewhat polemical in his criticism of the so-called 'Suhrkamp culture,' he does address an important problem. What is ultimately translated is not merely subject to logical economic decisions regarding potential sales; the field of academic literature is always deeply dependent upon state subsidies (here, very few exceptions may prove to be the rule). The translations that are funded are, however, those for which influential support-

---

6 The authors and works cited as examples are those for which the author of this paper, as acting director of the publishing company AVINUS Verlag, has been attempting to improve the availability of translations.

ers are willing to make a case, either as editors, publishers, or translators. The latter, in particular, are the unsung and underpaid pariahs of the publishing industry, as Stephanie Grillo calls them (1999: 102), who undertake the painstaking work of translating, i.e. translation in terms of language, as well as of conveying ideas between corresponding cultural or academic contexts.

4 Media and Communication Studies

The problem of 'translation' in media and communication studies begins with the terms used to designate these disciplines, which elude clear definition in much the same way as social studies and, perhaps even more so, the field of cultural studies as a whole. During the 1970s, the communication researcher Klaus Merten (1977) identified as many as 160 different definitions of the term 'communication,' and the media scholar Hartmut Winkler (2004) counted as many as 63 different meanings of the term 'media'; they could all be logically aligned to specific differentiations within the discipline, thereby making way for a German *Sonderweg*. In Germany, media and communication studies developed in strict separation from each other and – a matter of no small importance – were organized into two separate, and sometimes mutually antagonistic, professional organizations: the *Gesellschaft für Medienwissenschaft (GfM)* and the *Deutsche Gesellschaft für Publizistik und Kommunikationswissenschaft (DGPuK)*. The discipline of communication studies was established in Germany during the 1950s, inspired by empirical social research of American origin, while, at the same time, integrating the German legacy of newspaper studies in the form of *Publizistik* (a discipline positioned somewhere between journalism and media studies). Since then, it has mainly been characterized by quantitative empirical methods and has focused on journalistic forms of presentation, media economy, empirical reception research, and corporate communications.

The somewhat smaller discipline of media studies emerged in the 1970s, out of one of the crises of German studies, and has since focused, above all, on fictional forms of presentation in different media, popular culture, and the technicity of cultural media, particularly from a hermeneutic perspective. Within technology-centered media theories, or theories of mediality, inspired by McLuhan and, in no small measure, Friedrich Kittler, German media studies has since earned a reputation of leading the field, while, at the same time, it has established its own German *Sonderweg*. In other countries, such as Switzerland and, especially, the United States, media and communication studies are combined in a single discipline, as communication or media studies – although there is sometimes a special local focus, such as television or film studies. They form a common field of analysis of aesthetic design, technical and economic production processes, sociological or ideological implications, and reception practices.

What, on the other hand, is the situation in France? Here, one also finds a separation between two academic disciplines concerned with media and communication; this separation is reminiscent of the situation in Germany. On the one hand, the various courses in film and television studies, long dominated by structuralism and post-structuralism, were viewed as aspects of the field of *sciences humaines* (provided they offered no artistic training) and primarily concentrated on interpretation, aesthetics, and history of artistically successful productions without developing a concept of the materiality, or even just the mediality, of the media. On the other hand, the *sciences de l'information et de la communication,*[7] which became the 71st section of the *French Scientific Council* in 1975, called *Infocoms* for short, but also referred to as SIC, covers a far broader spectrum. It includes information sciences – which leads a shadow existence in Germany and tends to be confused with informatics and library sciences – as well as a communication science derived from sociology, yet it sees itself as less indebted to empirical research methods of American origin than to approaches focusing on the critique of ideology as encountered in critical theory, particularly in the work of Jürgen Habermas and his theses on the structure of public space, which were translated into French quite quickly.[8]

The German concept of 'science' cannot easily be translated into English, as the word is reserved for the natural sciences. And, in France, a qualification is always required in order to establish precise differentiation between the natural sciences and other sciences. On the other hand, the English term 'studies' leads to misunderstandings in Germany and is ambiguous in French, because *études* can designate both courses of study and individual studies. It becomes even more difficult when translating the terms 'media' and 'communication,' which exist in Germany, the United States, and France but mean different things in each setting due to different disciplinary evolutions within divergent national discourses. It is clear that the problem cannot be solved solely through the technical translation of terms.

---

7 It should be mentioned that there is also a *sciences des médias*, which covers training in and research on journalism.

8 For additional details, see the book by Averbeck-Lietz (2010), in which the history of the discipline of communication studies in France was surveyed for the first time.

During the first larger-scale meeting between German and French media and communication researchers in Potsdam in 2001, which was organized by Philippe Viallon and included nearly forty invited speakers from both countries, non-linguistic comprehension problems persisted despite fast and efficient professional interpreting.

> Concerning the organisation of the discipline, the situation in France is clearly characterised by 'sciences de l'information et de la communication,' which were established in the 1970s [...]. The centralistic French structure ensures that all students receive similar training in the various sub-segments and that all future academics are trained according to a common norm. (Viallon 2002: 11–12)

In view of the situation in Germany, Viallon goes on to say:

> The situation in Germany is completely different, nearly incomprehensible, even for a German. This is due to individual Länder being responsible for education and research, as well as the great autonomy of universities, the even greater independence of professors, and the liberal organisation of most courses of study. In addition, terms such as media sciences, communication sciences and *Publizistik*, to name just a few of those most frequently used, have given rise to such divergent courses of study at different universities that it sometimes seems dubious whether they mean the same thing for those responsible. (Viallon 2002: 12)

Indeed, terms like 'communication,' 'medium,' 'media,' 'mediality,' 'medialization,' or 'mediatization' cannot be easily translated without explicitly defining what, precisely, is meant in each case and to which of the – nationally adapted – disciplines one is referring. Claims of transnational or even global validity in associating the terms 'media' and 'communication' often break down in relation to claims regarding definitions and sovereignty, which are limited to local contexts, individual professorships, or organizations, and sometimes lead to absurd and, for external observers, virtually inexplicable aberrations in the field of translation.

In the meantime, some attempts have been made, in both Germany and France, to overcome this fragmentation. In Germany, younger colleagues have, for the most part, begun to think beyond the divisions of professional societies. In France, the discipline referred to as 'mediology' evolved out of *Infocoms* during the 1990s, although it never focused solely on mass media, but, instead, on the materiality and mediality of processes of cultural communication in general. In this sense, mediology also built a bridge to the *sciences humaines*, filling the gap left by the absence of cultural studies, which were long unknown in France. The success of this approach, however, could not be translated into an institutionalization of mediology. Hence, to this day, there is neither a professorship nor a course of study in mediology, although its focus on technical/ material, economic, social, institutional, and aesthetic aspects of media communications processes displays great potential for integration – and is likely to be viewed as particularly interesting outside of France. After the first translations of Régis Debray's concept of 'cultural transmission' in the United States, the term 'mediologie' (or, as an alternative, 'mediology') was adopted. Meanwhile, in Germany, only a few, albeit very high-ranking, scholars took an interest in mediology: Frank Hartmann, Lorenz Engell, and Hans Belting.

Yet, even when media and communication researchers in different countries speak of an internationalization of their discipline, they by no means always mean the same thing, but are, instead, subject to national filters. Content is not the only thing perceived in a highly selective manner; the external forms of transmission also play a decisive role in this context, including the frequency of translation, the prevalence of the original language, the discursive form of the discipline (and with it also the horizon that provides orientation, e.g., empirical or hermeneutic ideals), and, not least of all, different forms of ignorance regarding innovations or approaches that come from outside of a discipline. In the academic world, these by no means always lead to serious attempts to come to terms with new ideas, but, instead, often lead to forms of structural exclusion, for example, bodies within an organization that only take note of 'papers' and the terminology related to them when they are forced to do so by a majority decision or by public discussions that can no longer be ignored.

Translations can hardly dispel this logic. They tend, rather, to adhere to it, thereby providing reinforcement; the courage is seldom found to retain the foreign as something that offers resistance or demonstrates independence in an attempt to transform a field. With translation alone, and even with highly circumspect 'translation' characterized as the transmission of cultural and/or scientific practices, one soon encounters limits. Yet, despite all warnings against excessive idealism, the latter is perhaps the only way to push against these limits.

References

Averbeck-Lietz, Stefanie. *Kommunikationstheorien in Frankreich. Der epistemologische Diskurs der Sciences de l'information et de la communication (SIC) 1975 – 2005*. Berlin: Avinus, 2010.
Bachmann-Medick, Doris, ed. *The Translational Turn*. Special Issue *Translation Studies* 2.1 (2009).

Buden, Boris, and Stefan Nowotny, eds. *Übersetzung. Das Versprechen eines Begriffs*. Vienna: Turia + Kant, 2008.

Debray, Régis. *Jenseits der Bilder. Eine Geschichte der Bildbetrachtung im Abendland*. Berlin: Avinus, 1999.

Debray, Régis. "Le médiologue et les medias." *médium* 8 (2006): 3–15.

Engelmann, Peter. "Passagen Verlag: About Us/History." http://www.passagen.at/cms/index.php?id=16&L=1 (26 October 2013).

Gräßle, Inge. *Der europäische Fernseh-Kulturkanal ARTE. Deutsch-französische Medienpolitik zwischen europäischem Anspruch und nationaler Wirklichkeit* (Deutsch-französische Studien zur Industriegesellschaft, 18). Frankfurt a.m./New York: Campus, 1995.

Grillo, Stephanie. *Frankreich literarisch. Übersetzungen französischsprachiger Literatur ins Deutsche von 1983–1994* (Düsseldorfer Materialien zur Literaturübersetzung, Transfer 14). Tübingen: Narr, 1999.

Hall, Edward T., and Mildred R. Hall. *Understanding Cultural Differences*. Yarmouth: Intercultural Press, 1992.

Hamm, Ingrid, ed. *Fernsehen auf dem Prüfstand. Aufgaben des dualen Rundfunksystems. Internationale Studien im Rahmen der Kommunikationsordnung 2000*. Gütersloh: Verlag Bertelsmann-Stiftung, 1998.

Hartmann, Frank. *Mediologie. Ansätze einer Medientheorie der Kulturwissenschaften*. Vienna: WUV, 2003.

Hobsbawm, Eric J. *Nations and Nationalism since 1780: Programme, Myth, Reality*. Cambridge/New York: Cambridge University Press, 1990.

Kaufmann, Vincent. "Medien und Nationalismus – Einleitung." *Medien und nationale Kulturen* (Facetten der Medienkultur, 4). Ed. Vincent Kaufmann. Bern: Haupt, 2004. 7–22.

Keusen, Kai P. *Studien zur Medienpolitik in Europa. Die Deregulierung der Fernsehsysteme in Großbritannien und Frankreich bis Mitte der 90er Jahre*. Alfeld: Coppi, 1997.

Koch, Ursula, Detlef F. Schröter, and Pierre Albert, eds. *Deutsch-französische Medienbilder; images médiatiques franco-allemandes*. Munich: R. Fischer, 1993.

Krämer, Sybille. *Medium, Bote, Übertragung. Kleine Metaphysik der Medialität*. Frankfurt a.M.: Suhrkamp, 2008.

Lahire, Bernard. *La Condition littéraire. La double vie des écrivains*. Paris: La Découverte, 2006.

Landbeck, Hanne. *Medienkultur im nationalen Vergleich. Inszenierungsstrategien von Fernsehnachrichten am Beispiel der Bundesrepublik Deutschland und Frankreich* (Medien in Forschung + Unterricht, 33). Tübingen: Niemeyer, 1991.

Latour, Bruno. *Pandora's Hope: Essays on the Reality of Science Studies*. Cambridge, MA: Harvard University Press, 1999.

Leenhardt, Jacques, and Robert Picht. *Au jardin des malentendus. Le commerce franco-allemand des idées*. Arles: Actes Sud, 1990.

Lévy, Pierre. *Die kollektive Intelligenz. Für eine Anthropologie des Cyberspace*. Mannheim: Bollmann, 1997. (Trans. of *L'intelligence collective. Pour une anthropologie du cyberspace*. Paris: La Découverte, 1994).

Lüsebrink, Hans-Jürgen, Klaus Peter Walter, Ute Fendler, Georgette Stefani-Meyer, and Christoph Vatter. *Französische Kultur- und Medienwissenschaft. Eine Einführung*. Tübingen: Narr, 2004.

Machill, Marcel. *Frankreich Quotenreich. Nationale Medienpolitik und europäische Kommunikationspolitik im Kontext nationaler Identität*. Berlin: Vistas, 1997.

Mattelart, Armand. *Kommunikation ohne Grenzen? Geschichte der Ideen und Strategien globaler Vernetzung.* Foreword by Mechtild Rahner and Thomas Weber. Berlin: Avinus, 2007 [1999].

Mersmann, Birgit. "(Fern-)Verkehr der Bilder. Mediologie als methodischer Brückenschlag zwischen Bild- und Übersetzungswissenschaft." *Mediologie als Methode.* Eds. Birgit Mersmann and Thomas Weber. Berlin: Avinus, 2008. 149–167.

Mersmann, Birgit, and Thomas Weber, eds. *Mediologie als Methode.* Berlin: Avinus, 2008.

Merten, Klaus. *Kommunikation.* Opladen: Westdeutscher Verlag, 1977.

Merzeau, Louise. "Ceci ne tuera cela." *Les Cahiers de médiologie,* 2.6 (1998): 27–39.

Merzeau, Louise, and Thomas Weber. *Mémoire et Médias.* Paris: Avinus, 2001.

Papouschek, Iris. "Routine oder reger Austausch? Eine Analyse deutscher Gegenwartsliteratur in Lizenzausgaben auf dem französischen Buchmarkt von 2000 bis 2007." Erlangen: Universität Erlangen-Nürnberg, 2009. http://www.alles-buch.uni-erlangen.de/Papouschek.pdf (23 January 2013).

Schroeder, Michael. "Frankreich-Deutschland. Zwei unterschiedliche Auffassungen von Kommunikation." *Deutsch-französische Medienbilder; images médiatiques franco-allemandes.* Eds. Ursula Koch, Detlef F. Schröter, and Pierre Albert. Munich: R. Fischer, 1993. 21–42.

Synergies – Pays germanophones, n° 2 (2009): *L'interculturel à la croisée des disciplines: theories et recherché interculturelles, état des lieux.*

Todorov, Tzvetan. *Nous et les autres. La réflexion française sur la diversité humaine.* Paris: Édition du Seuil, 1989.

Uhde, Kathrin. *KARAMBOLAGE oder die deutsch-französischen Eigenarten mit fremden Augen sehen.* Berlin: Avinus, 2006.

Viallon, Philippe. "Bilden eine Wissenschaft und zwei Kulturen zwei Wissenschaften? Eine vergleichende Ansicht der Kommunikationswissenschaft in Frankreich und Deutschland." *Kommunikation – Medien – Gesellschaft.* Eds. Philippe Viallon and Ute Weiland. Berlin: Avinus, 2002. 9–17.

Viallon, Philippe, and Ute Weiland, eds. *Kommunikation – Medien – Gesellschaft. Eine Bestandsaufnahme deutscher und französischer Wissenschaftler.* Berlin: Avinus, 2002.

Weber, Thomas. "Perspektiven interkultureller Forschung in der deutschen Medienwissenschaft." *Identität und Diversität. Eine interdisziplinäre Bilanz der Interkulturalitätsforschung in Deutschland und Frankreich/Identité et diversité. Etat des lieux interdisciplinaire de la recherche sur l'interculturalité en France et en Allemagne.* Eds. Carolin Fischer, Helene Harth, Philippe and Virginie Viallon. Berlin: Avinus, 2005. 119–131.

Weber, Thomas, and Stefan Woltersdorff, eds. *Wegweiser durch die französische Medienlandschaft.* Marburg: Schüren, 2001.

Werner, Michael. "Dissymmetrien und symmetrische Modellbildungen in der Forschung zum Kulturtransfer." *Kulturtransfer im Epochenumbruch. Deutschland – Frankreich, 1770–1815,* vol. 1. Eds. Hans-Jürgen Lüsebrink and Rolf Reichardt. Leipzig: Leipziger Universitätsverlag, 1997. 87–102.

Winkler, Hartmut. "Mediendefinition." *medienwissenschaft* 1 (2004): 9–27.

Woltersdorff, Stefan. "Kochsendungen als Spiegel nationaler Eigenheiten." *Wegweiser durch die französische Medienlandschaft.* Eds. Thomas Weber and Stefan Woltersdorff. Marburg: Schüren, 2001. 104–105.

Wolton, Dominique. *Kommunizieren heißt Zusammenleben.* Berlin: Avinus, 2010.

Birgit Mersmann

D/Rifts between Visual Culture and Image Culture

Relocations of the Transnational Study of the Visual

Was it just a coincidence when, in independent publications of the year 1994, two visual turns, the iconic turn in Germany and the pictorial turn in the U.S., were concurrently announced?[1] Did this historical synchronicity mark the beginning of a new era of transatlantic, even transnational, studies of the visual? Or was it the re-emergence and revaluation of the image that has given way to the transnationalization of the study of culture, which is a more global research perspective?

Twenty years after the proclamation of the iconic/pictorial turn, the impact on academia, its research agendas, and institutional frameworks has become perceptible. As an integrative part of a broader cultural turn, the iconic/pictorial turn has not only affected (and infected) the humanities and social sciences but also the natural and technical sciences. For the first time in history, a transnational and transdisciplinary study of the visual appears on the horizon, arousing great expectations but also confronting us with unforeseen challenges and obstacles. However, as transnational as the cultural study of the visual might look,[2] and as identical (or basically interchangeable) as the iconic and pictorial turn seem to be in their general orientation of expressing the cultural and societal (need to) turn towards images, they stand for different historical and academic traditions, methodological approaches, disciplinary discourses and institutional practices in the treatment of the visual. In the German-speaking aca-

---

1 In his article "Die Wiederkehr der Bilder," the German art historian and philosopher Gottfried Boehm coined the formula of the iconic turn. It was identified as an epochal "entrance of the image as an autonomous, substantial instance into the very core of hermeneutics and philosophizing" (Bredekamp 2004: 16). At the same time, W.J.T. Mitchell, a trained literary historian who had just entered the art-historical department at the University of Chicago, observed a pictorial turn within the humanities and started to confront this new phenomenon with the conceptual design of a picture theory.

2 The wording 'study of the visual' is used here as the most neutral and general term to express the cultural study of images, vision, and visuality, since the English term 'visual' covers both the visual as picture/image and the visual as sensory modality.

demic community, the iconic turn has led to the formation of a relatively independent area of research defined by the term *Bildwissenschaft* (image studies), whereas in Anglophone academia the pictorial turn has resulted in the formation and institutional establishment of visual culture or visual studies.

In the aftermath of the iconic/pictorial turn as a historical point of inflexion, one can observe a drift between visual studies and *Bildwissenschaft*, the study of visual culture(s) and the study of the image as cultural phenomenon, that has, meanwhile, caused a paradoxical 'split' or 'rift' constellation. On one side, visual studies, or visual culture, which originally took shape as "preeminently an American movement" (Elkins 2003: 2), has since developed more and more into a transnational movement, conquering research agendas and academic institutions in various, albeit selected, regions of the world. By contrast, *Bildwissenschaft* has developed as a primarily national, or more precisely transnational, German movement that has stayed mostly within the boundaries of German-speaking academia in Germany, Austria, and Switzerland – apart from some German-French and German-Italian border crossings. Another crucial difference in addition to respective national and transnational orientations lies in forms of academic institutionalization. Whereas the German-based *Bildwissenschaft* has almost not been academically institutionalized at all in the form of specific study programs and/or related professorships and has remained restricted to research programs and schools,[3] the visual studies/visual culture initiative has led to the design and implementation of new study programs at all levels (BA, MA, and PhD) and even departments on the North American continent and beyond.[4]

------

3 Only one university department of *Bildwissenschaften* offering MA programs was established at the Donau Universität Krems in Austria, and only one Virtual Institute for Bildwissenschaft (VIB) was founded, providing an online research platform for creating a General Iconology (*Allgemeine Bildwissenschaft*) as a new autonomous discipline. Only one institute for art history in Germany has renamed itself by adding the component of image studies: the Humboldt Universität zu Berlin's art-historical institute is now called Institut für Kunst- und Bildgeschichte. This non-institutionalization stands in stark contrast to the variety of introductory literature on how to approach and study images that has been published (see Schulz 2005; Bruhn 2009; Probst and Klenner 2009; Frank and Lange 2010; Burda 2010; Hornuff 2012).
4 Since 2000, the trans-North-American outreach of the visual study movement has become manifest: new academic programs (and departments) in visual studies have been implemented in the UK, Australia, New Zealand, South Africa, Scandinavia, Hong Kong, Taiwan, and Pakistan. These wanderings of the visual studies movement on the world map make very clear that the spread is dependent on existing tracks of geopolitical dissemination and influence of Anglophone (world) culture, together with English as the lingua franca.

The split situation between Anglophone studies of visual culture and the German-based *Bildwissenschaft/en* is so pronounced that it calls for a profound analysis. The examination performed here will be primarily conducted from the perspective of *Bildwissenschaft*. Why is it that the transnational study of visual culture has gained almost no ground in the German-speaking visual-research landscape and academic institutions?[5] How is it that the concept (and study programs) of visual culture successfully travels to specific cultural regions and academic places but hits a functional limit when crossing the border of German academia?[6] In what respect is *Bildwissenschaft* a German *Sonderweg* incompatible with Anglo-American approaches to visual culture? Is this untranslatability due to different concepts of both the idea of culture and cultural studies/*Kulturwissenschaften* as (inter)disciplines? Why has *Bildwissenschaft* principally remained restricted to the scientific community of German-speaking countries and not spread internationally, apart from some exchanges with their neighboring countries France and Italy?

1 Iconic versus Pictorial Turn: Transatlantic Divergences and Confluences

The "Two Letters" exchanged between Gottfried Boehm and W.J.T. Mitchell in 2006 in order to intellectually position the emergence of the study of images can serve as a point of access not only to discern shared views on the visual turn in general but also to gain insight into the different orientations and implications

---

5 The only institutionalized form of visual studies in Germany is the Institute for Studies in Visual Culture (ISVC) in Cologne. It was founded as a research platform in 2000 by Tom Holert and Mark Terkessidis with the goal – as stated on the German website – to 'document developments of contemporary visual culture' and 'promote a critical understanding of visual processes in national globalized media societies.'

6 French academia has, so far, been confronted with the same limitation: a lack of academic recognition and, as a result, a lack of institutionalization of visual culture studies. At the London conference "Visual Cultural Studies in Europe" (2010), which, for the first time, explored the European terrain of visual culture studies, Lorrain Audric described the state of visual culture studies in France as "quite a desolated landscape;" what she laments most is the paradox that, despite the unquestionable influence of French critical theory on the formation of Anglophone visual culture studies, the presence of visual culture studies in France "remained marginal and their legacy stayed outside of the institutional framework" (Audric 2010). Starting in 2010, the first institutional changes can be observed in French academia: at the University of Lille, the first professorship for visual culture (*Culture visuelle*) was established.

of the pictorial and iconic turn, as related to the study domains of visual culture and *Bildwissenschaft*. As personal as the correspondence between Boehm and Mitchell had been, it has nonetheless reached representative status, reflected by the fact that the "Two Letters" have been included in publications that seek to survey the emerging field of visual studies.[7] The comparative analysis of the iconic versus the pictorial turn will focus on the following common points of discussion: interpretation of the turn towards the visual and its relation to the linguistic turn; methodological and disciplinary approaches to the study of images; definition of the iconic and the pictorial; critical dimensions of the study of images; and the role of image studies as a (trans)discipline.

1.1 The Turn towards the Iconic/Pictorial

Boehm and Mitchell agree that the iconic/pictorial turn expresses both a contemporary paradigm shift in the sciences and a recurrent trope. For Boehm, the iconic turn signifies a profound cultural turn in that "the image question touches upon the foundations of culture and poses quite novel demands"; it implies a "different mode of thinking, one that has shown itself capable of clarifying and availing itself of the long-neglected cognitive possibilities that lie in non-verbal representations" (Curtis 2010: 9). Taking the iconic turn seriously as a new paradigm of scientific thinking would mean establishing a new theory and science of images that transgresses the boundaries between the humanities and the natural sciences. For Mitchell, the significance of the pictorial turn lies in the argument that it has not only initiated a "powerful account of visual representation that is dictating the terms of cultural theory," but that it has also become a paradigm, "a kind of model or figure of other things (including figuration itself), and as an unsolved problem, perhaps even the object of its own 'science'" (Mitchell 1994 quoted in Curtis 2010: 20).

While the iconic/pictorial turn is often considered to be a novel paradigm shift within the sciences, both Boehm and Mitchell interpret it as a recurrent trope in the sense of a return of images and questions related to images. In his essay "Die Wiederkehr der Bilder," in which Boehm (1994) defines the iconic turn for the first time, he actually speaks of an iconic *re-turn*. How are we to understand this return of images? Is it related to historical paradigm shifts according to which images/image discourses have been there before, but disap-

---

7 The English version of the "Two Letters" is included in Curtis 2010; the German version is found in Belting 2007.

peared from view, and finally reappeared? Does it allude to the fact that images return in constantly new forms and via constantly new carrier-media? In Boehm's interpretation, the return of images primarily refers to the unique phenomenon of images being able to change their form and content yet still remain images. This leads directly to the fundamental question Boehm poses: "What and when is an image?"

Mitchell, on the contrary, describes the popular pictorial turn as a recurrent trope. This definition is referred to as "a kind of 'iconic panic' usually accompanied by hand-wringing and iconoclastic gestures" (Curtis 2010: 20). In general, it is argued that a pictorial turn does not necessarily depend on new technology but may also be the result of a social movement mobilized by fear of a new image, be it a self-image or worldview. In line with this psychological explication, he admits that there has been more than one pictorial turn in history – thus, emphasizing the socio-cultural meaning of the pictorial turn as a recurring figure.

The central, seemingly bizarre question Mitchell asks in search of a way to describe the pictorial turn in both cultures – intellectual high culture and popular, mass-media culture – is: "What do pictures want?" (Mitchell 2004). In comparison to Boehm's ontological question "What is an image?" (Boehm 1994), this one seems, at first sight, to be the inverse in terms of its de-ontologizing and post-structuralist tendency. Upon closer consideration, however, this impression can be corrected, due to the fact that images are attributed a life, an existence, a will (to power), and a desire of their own. By enquiring into the deep-rooted fear of images as the uncanny, ungraspable Other, Mitchell's pictorial-theoretical approach reveals its psychoanalytical foundation.

1.2 Visual Turn(s) versus Linguistic Turn

Regarding the relationship between the iconic/pictorial turn and the linguistic turn, Mitchell and Boehm agree that the iconic/pictorial turn is not just a 'new' turn succeeding and replacing the linguistic turn: it also directly springs from the latter and is, thus, interwoven with it. Whereas Mitchell points to U.S. semiotics and Derrida's grammatology,[8] Boehm refers to German philosophy of lan-

---

8 Besides semiotics and grammatology, he also names phenomenology, Wittgensteinian philosophy of language, the Frankfurt School, with its analysis of modern mass culture, and Foucault's history and theory of power, which opened a gap between the articulatable and the visible as harbingers of the pictorial turn.

guage and language critique as a departure point for the pictorial/iconic turn. For Mitchell, Charles Peirce's semiotic studies and Nelson Goodman's *Languages of Art* are agents of the pictorial turn in Anglo-American countries, as both "explore the conventions and codes that underlie non-linguistic symbol systems and (more important) do not begin with the assumption that language is paradigmatic for meaning" (Mitchell 1994: 12). Also, Derrida's *Of Grammatology* is said to have widely contributed to the revision of the phonocentric view of language and directed focus on the visibility and materiality of writing.[9]

Boehm's reading of the iconic turn confirms this assumption, although his arguments are different. In his view, the linguistic turn consequently leads to the iconic turn, because investigating how much thought and knowledge depend on language necessarily leads to its transgression. As a result, the image grows out of and beyond language. Significantly, Boehm does not give up the concept of 'logos'; rather, he tries to redefine it in the beyond of language as an iconic logos. The logos is increased beyond its limited verbality by the power of the iconic and, thus, transformed. Boehm, therefore, distinguishes between linguistic and iconic logos. The latter is eventually transferred to the 'logic of images' and bound to his leading research question: How do images produce meaning? How do they generate sense? (cf. Boehm 2010). Boehm's 'iconic criticism' (*Bildkritik*) directly emerges from language criticism (*Sprachkritik*),[10] as it is found in phenomenological, ontological, and language philosophy. Three philosophers are named as enactors of a criticism of language that gave way to the rise of the iconic logos: Husserl, Heidegger, and Wittgenstein, as they were among the first to locate the generation of meaning in acts of viewing, processes of existence, and practices of language play. In addition to German (and, in part, French) philosophy, with its specifications in phenomenology, hermeneutics, and ontology, modern art, with its iconoclastic tendencies to undermine forms of visual representation and display image presence as a strategy of self-reflection, is seen as a trigger of an iconic turn. Language-critical philosophy

---

9 When Mitchell directly relates grammatology to iconology in his book *What Do Pictures Want?* (2004) by identifying their analogous motivations, he supports the view of the pictorial turn having a family resemblance, to use Wittgenstein's phrase, with the linguistic turn.

10 "The turn towards the image is a consequence of the turn towards language; it adheres to the insight that [...] reflection on the conditions for knowledge is an indispensable premise of any science that does not wish to subject itself to reproach a lack of intellectual rigour, e.g. to that of a naïve objectivism" (Boehm quoted in Curtis 2010: 10).

and modern art, as sources and enactors of the iconic turn, are consolidated in order to install the image as a new paradigm of thinking.[11]

1.3 Iconic versus Pictorial

The introduction and definition of the iconic, including the theorems of the 'iconic logos' and 'iconic difference,' follows disciplinary lines and conceptual roots of the iconic turn. Boehm stresses that his conceptualization of the iconic has nothing to do with Peirce's semiotic definition (Peirce 1955: 104–105). He even strictly dissociates his theorem of the iconic from any form of semiotic approach, be it U.S.-American or French, not wanting to commit images to a universal sign system.[12] A reason why the concept of the iconic seems appropriate to Boehm is that it implies a stronger generalization behind the complexity of image phenomena, the range between 'picture' and 'image,' and also underlines the claim of images being objects *and* processes of meaning creation *and* knowledge generation at the same time.[13]

As a remedy for all previous – according to Boehm, failed – attempts at finding a satisfying answer to what makes an image and what makes images recurrent, Boehm proposes the theorem of 'iconic difference.' The inspiration for the definition of iconic difference is Heidegger's ontological difference.[14] Just as Heidegger demands, in a critique of metaphysics, that being 'as itself' must

---

11 The academic opening of the image debate in Germany – with Boehm's anthology *Was ist ein Bild?* (2004) that included contributions by Maurice Merleau-Ponty, Hans-Georg Gadamer, Hans Jonas, Bernhard Waldenfels, Michael Polanyi, and Max Imdahl, among others – made clear that the study of the image and the iconic (turn) took philosophy and modern art theory as constitutive disciplinary approaches, thereby promoting a new philosophy of the image on the basis of modern art studies.

12 Boehm's main motivation for implementing an iconic turn was the challenge of "protecting images from linguistic heteronomy" (Boehm quoted in Curtis 2010: 15). In his view, the semiotic approach represents an expansionist form of linguistic imperialism.

13 This discourse function is precisely what distinguishes the iconic turn: "[...] although capable of representing meaning, [the image] lacked the ability to function as a medium of discourse on meaning, i.e. to function as a meta-entity. What is completely new is an emergence of image-generating processes that have led to cognitive processes at the heart of the hard sciences being driven by the iconic, and the fact that the image now plays a role in the day-to-day business of science, which even a generation ago would have been utterly unthinkable" (Curtis 2010: 12).

14 Boehm points to this in a footnote explaining the iconic difference in "Die Wiederkehr der Bilder" and in his essay on "Das Bild und die hermeneutische Reflexion," where he notes that the turn from the linguistic toward the iconic 'logos' is prefigured in Heidegger.

be deployed in its difference to beings, Boehm tries to ascertain the image 'as itself,' in its autonomy, and to fathom the iconic logos, which is determined by difference, because it shows something as something.

Mitchell's choice of the adjective 'pictorial' might not be as intentional as Boehm's systematization of the iconic into two related concepts, 'iconic logos' and 'iconic difference.' However, it indicates from which disciplinary approaches and theories the adjective derives, leading to a picture theory and inquiry into the implications and prospects of the pictorial turn. The title of Mitchell's book, *Picture Theory: Essays on Verbal and Visual Representation* (1994), which also includes the first publication of his essay "Pictorial Turn," reveals that comparative studies in visual art and literature – the so-called 'sister arts' – became the points of departure for reflections about the differences between verbal and visual expression and the elaboration of a picture theory by which the peculiarities of visual forms and functions of representation could be captured. This approach makes clear that research on the specificity of pictorial qualities was, from its outset, driven by questions of (inter)mediality.[15] This stands in stark contrast to Boehm's iconic approach dedicated to investigating processes of image emergence and recurrence independent of mediality and other contexts. Belting has noticed, with regard to this point, that the English term 'pictorial,' related to the category 'picture,' refers to artifacts and, thus, is rebound to visual media and technologies as enactors/agents of picture production and proliferation (Belting 2007: 20). This relational focus is confirmed by Mitchell's interest in the history and theory of the technical picture and visual technologies in both the natural sciences and the arts, as well as his fascination for media studies as a way to access visual culture(s). Mitchell's interpretation of the pictorial turn follows these lines but stresses that the picture-as-artifact is unthinkable and cannot be processed without the image as its counterpart of visual actualization in the beholder. It is the objectification of this relationship that characterizes the pictorial turn. As the picture/image relation is crucial for visual perception, it is seeing, viewing, and observing that gain prominence in the argument for the pictorial turn and the study field of visual culture.

---

15 Mitchell also defines the pictorial turn as word/picture relation (Mitchell in Sachs-Hombach 2005: 322).

1.4 *Bildwissenschaft* versus Image Science

The conclusion to be drawn from the iconic/pictorial turn in the humanities, social sciences, and physical sciences is obvious for Boehm and Mitchell: it is time to build a new, truly transdisciplinary science of the image. Despite the parallels in Boehm's and Mitchell's evaluations of the emerging field of image studies and the scientific anchorage of the visual turn, their respective concepts also vary. Whereas Boehm envisages a 'science of the image' (*Bildwissenschaft*) as a cognitive science and epistemology of the image, Mitchell projects an image science that would also include the 'hard' or 'experimental' sciences – signaled by the meaning of the English word 'science.' The turn towards the life sciences that motivated Mitchell's theoretical question "What do pictures want?", posed in his book of the same title, has also led him to bring the sciences of images into the arena of visual studies; these include the physical, chemical, biological or, simply put, life sciences of images. These two positions elucidate an enduring cleavage with regard to the spectrum of sciences and disciplinary approaches involved in the design of a new science of images. The rift is to be found between *Bildwissenschaft*, still dominated by a humanities approach, in particular philosophy and art history, and image science as a true transdiscipline crossing all existing sciences and related disciplines.

1.5 Visual Culture versus Iconic Criticism: The Factor of Critique

The critical approach involved in the study of the visual is the crossroad where the divergences between Mitchell's assessment of the pictorial turn and Boehm's understanding of the iconic turn become most evident, ultimately leading to different orientations and conceptualizations, as represented by visual culture studies versus *Bildwissenschaft*, critical iconology versus iconic criticism. As already mentioned in the discussion of the relation between the iconic and linguistic turns, Boehm's iconic criticism (*Bildkritik*) is modeled through an analogy with language critique (*Sprachkritik*) in its philosophical orientation of cognitive criticism and epistemology. It self-reflectively inquires the conditions and potentials of images as generators of knowledge and creators of meaning, thereby envisioning an image theory as a critical theory of cognition. Critique is understood in its original meaning, as the art and practice of discrimination. The theorem of iconic difference reflects this 'critical' faculty of differentiation as a precondition for any cognitive process or act by which the image is constituted as an autonomous thought-image. Social aspects are basically excluded from *Bildkritik* by this self-reflective, mind-encapsulating conceptualization of the image. This approach stands in firm opposition to Mitchell's concept of a critical picture theory or critical iconology, as he has often named his approach an ideology-critical (re)turn to Panofsky. For him, the extension of the pictorial turn to the field of social and political issues is essential. By correlating iconology and ideology,[16] Mitchell aims to reveal how much the notion of ideology is based on and infiltrated with icon(ism)s. It is these socio-political and pictorial entanglements that have led Mitchell to establish not only a critical iconology but also a critique of visual culture.

By following the different meanings and interpretations of critique in Boehm's theory of iconic criticism and Mitchell's model of critical iconology, the transatlantic conceptual rift between visual culture and image philosophy is disclosed. Visual culture is shaped by a predominantly political and social agenda derived from the legacy of Marxism-rooted British cultural studies. It is mostly concerned with popular culture and shows a strong interest in actively engaging political discourse by dismantling ideology and power relations. This politicized orientation distinguishes the study of visual culture from the more philosophical and system-oriented image studies affiliated with the German *Kulturwissenschaften* (study of culture) and its legacy of cultural philosophy, cultural anthropology, and criticism of culture. Mitchell's critical picture theory can be qualified as image sociology, deeply anchored in social psychology with additional elements of visual anthropology. Because of this orientation, it can be productively connected to political and communication sciences, as well as to cultural and media studies. In contrast to this definition, Boehm's iconic criticism can be categorized as image phenomenology. With iconic difference as its key concept, it builds upon *Gestalt* and perception theory. Because of its ontological motivation to determine the autonomous power of the image without making extra-iconic or contextual references, it operates as a transhistorical, transcultural, and transmedial study of the image. Aiming for the design of a general iconics,[17] it is, per se, defined as a transnational study.

In sum, it is more than obvious that Boehm and Mitchell's assessments of the pictorial/iconic subscribe to two complementary agendas with regard to the

---

16 In his essay "Pictorial Turn," this correlation comes in the form of an imaginary encounter between Panofsky and Althusser.

17 The main objective of the project of a 'general iconics' is comparable to that of general linguistics as founded by de Saussure. It must be clearly distinguished from the idea of a general image science (*Allgemeine Bildwissenschaft*) as defined by Klaus Sachs-Hombach, since it radically excludes all semiotic and metalinguistic definitions.

transnational study of culture: a modernist agenda, based on self-reflexivity, universality, and the hermeneutics of immanence; and a postmodernist agenda shaped by the global, contemporary constitution of culture and the notion of society as spectacle. There is a human-science interest in studying the iconic as the *conditio sine qua non* of human perception and cognition – and, therefore, a strong incentive to move the study of the image beyond the framework of cultural studies into the direction of a *science* of the image; there is also a socio-cultural, political, and psychological interest in understanding and deconstructing the ideological power of images and visualization mechanisms, be they media-technical or social.

2 Neg(oti)ating Differences: Visual Studies as a Transnational Contact Zone between Visual Culture and *Bildwissenschaft*?

The transatlantic exchange of ideas about the status and meaning of the pictorial/iconic turn has helped raise international awareness of *Bildwissenschaft* as a German-specific visual study approach. In particular, it has familiarized scholars in Anglo-American visual (culture) studies with the conceptual differences of *Bildwissenschaft*. Whereas in the first decade after its emergence, *Bildwissenschaft* remained a transnational German phenomenon, almost unperceived and not received by the international visual studies movement, a new tendency to include *Bildwissenschaft* in global academic discourse on the transnational study of the visual has emerged within recent years. It is best exemplified by Keith Moxey's article "Visual Studies and the Iconic Turn" (2008) which (1) deliberately chooses the term 'iconic turn' to represent the German turn towards *Bildwissenschaft* instead of the term 'pictorial turn,' usually identified with the Anglo-American tradition of visual culture; (2) discusses, for the first time in full breadth, German approaches to *Bildwissenschaft* in comparison to visual studies approaches; and (3) was published in the *Journal of Visual Culture*, a prominent organ for cutting-edge research in North American and international visual culture studies.

Two different readings of this article are possible. Firstly, because the Anglo-American visual studies movement has global reach, as the establishment of new, international study programs evidences, one might interpret the analysis of how visual studies and the iconic turn are connected as an attempt to incorporate the German movement of *Bildwissenschaft* into the scientific program of visual studies and, thus, eliminate conceptual differences in approaching the visual. Secondly, one could read the article as a subtle interpretation of where, and at which points, the pictorial and iconic turns join and how they might produce research synergies. The most remarkable aspect of the discussion of visual studies and the iconic turn is that the author does not set the Anglo-American approach of visual culture/visual studies against German- and French-based image studies. Rather, he identifies a rift between visual studies/*Bildwissenschaft* and visual culture. Moxey acknowledges a difference between the "phenomenological concern for the power of the image to determine its own reception" (Moxey 2008: 131) and the visual culture approach that emphasizes political implications of a culture and society dominated by the power of images. Despite these differences in the conception of the visual as powerful (self-)presentation or reflective *re*presentation, the author is convinced that "the ontological and semiotic perspective on visual objects might in fact be reconcilable" (Moxey 2008: 142).

As convincing as the argument for the transatlantic translatability and alliance between visual studies and *Bildwissenschaft* is, the object giving name to these study approaches is not further problematized. Taking this perspective into account, it might become questionable whether visual studies are identifiable with image studies, if not explicitly equivalent, as Elkins once suggested (Elkins 2003: 7). Whereas visual culture has long since bid farewell to the concept of image, especially to the integrity and historicity of the single picture, *Bildwissenschaft* is focused on the notion of the image as formational force. The French film theoretician Serge Daney was one of the first to point out the difference between the image and visuality. Images do not just render something one has seen but rather the act of seeing. The visual is, for Daney, "the optical operation of the proceedings of powers (technological, political, military, or in advertising) that solely intend to evoke the comment: 'It's all understood!'" (Daney 1997: 610). The visual belongs to the optic nerve, but this does not immediately generate an image. The image cuts across the stream of the visual; it forms itself by stopping, resisting, cutting, and condensing this stream. It forces its way to the surface of the visual information stream and into the depths of time of human consciousness. This makes the image an ally to anthropology – while the visual, on the other hand, is a fellow traveler of technology. On the basis of these reflections, the question is how negotiable the differences between *visual* studies and *image* studies are, especially considering that image studies are often subsumed under the umbrella of visual studies.

3 The Power of Academic and Disciplinary Traditions: Untranslatabilities between the Study of Visual Culture and *Bildwissenschaft* as *Kulturwissenschaft*

Both scientific approaches to the study of the visual were developed in the course of the cultural turn in the humanities. Remarkably, the inter- and cross-disciplinary constellations from which the two visual studies approaches emerged were relatively identical: they arose from a convergence in art history, literary studies, media studies (with a particular focus on film studies), and cultural studies. Only later did the social and natural sciences join the visual studies project. The enormous pressure placed on the humanities in crisis led to different developments and solutions in terms of academic change and institutional restructuring in the U.S. and Germany. In her book *Visual Culture: The Study of the Visual after the Cultural Turn* (2005), Margaret Dikovitskaya has shown that, in the U.S., the emergence of visual studies as a university subject and, later on, autonomous study program was part of the 'culture wars' of the 1980s, the conflict between high art and American mainstream culture, as well as the financial crisis of the 1990s. The institutionalization of visual studies was fostered by two changes: (1) a profound transformation of student population and demands – in the form of resistance to traditional European, elite culture and canonicity combined with increased interest in mass media culture and consumerism; and (2) the new economic need to run universities in a consumer-friendly and business-efficient way. Decreases in funding, which threatened the existence of major study programs and faculty, were countered by cross-disciplinary visual studies.

The establishment of departments for *Kulturwissenschaft(en)* at German universities followed the same pragmatic survival logic in the face of the potential elimination of programs or even entire institutes. In contrast to the American situation, this form of cultural studies turn did not result in exclusively visual culture study programs. For the most part, art history continued on its historical humanities path, thus, driving a wedge between visual art studies and visual culture studies. *Bildwissenschaften*, which included the historical tradition of art history and a new field of historical and contemporaneous image cultures, performed its own cultural turn from 1995 onwards, in the form of what might be classified as a (German) *Sonderweg*. Significantly, the influence of Anglo-American cultural studies was only heralded from afar; it functioned as an actuator for rediscovering *Kulturwissenschaften* and, thus, reoriented art history towards *Bildwissenschaft*.

German philosophy and anthropology of culture, in particular Ernst Cassirer's theory of symbolic forms, played large roles in turning art history into a cultural study of images. Today, there is agreement among leading German image researchers that the Hamburgian art historian Aby Warburg, famous for being a fanatic collector and organizer of images of all kinds, including non-artistic images of popular and technical culture, had initiated a far-reaching paradigm shift in art history towards *Bildwissenschaft* that has only been recognized almost a century later – that is, since the iconic turn seized German academia in the mid-1990s. From today's scholarly perspective, Aby Warburg is considered a '*Bildwissenschaftler avant la lettre.*' The interesting fact is that the German term *Bildwissenschaft*, now covering a new research field in German science, appears early on in his writings. Thomas Hensel has revealed that Aby Warburg defined himself as an "image historian, not art historian,"[18] and that, in a letter from 1925, he speaks of "methodological attempts to proceed from art history to the study of the image (*Wissenschaft vom Bilde*)" (Warburg quoted in Hensel 2007: 131).

By drawing on Aby Warburg and his creation of the *Bilderatlas Mnemosyne*, Hensel explains the cultural-historical roots of the German project of *Bildwissenschaft*: "Warburg's art history became a study of the image not only by the extension of its study objects to non-artistic images, to 'image and word sources of all qualitative levels and medial forms', to life styles, rituals or habitual patterns. The thesis is that it rather developed into a study of the image because in its structure it was essentially coined by visualizing technologies and technical images" (Hensel 2007: 132).[19] This last statement acknowledges the media-theoretical and media-critical dimensions of Warburg's historical *Wissenschaft vom Bilde*. It refers to electronic techniques of image transmission, such as image telegraphy, that shaped Warburg's cultural theory of the image, his notion of images as cultural engrams, and his interest in following the migration of images through different media, historical epochs and cultures. Already in this early stage, the project of *Bildwissenschaft* is riddled by conflicting connotations: the fascination for new visual technology as a transmitter of culture, and the fear that anthropological traditions and values of human culture could be overruled and destroyed by the increased use of visual media technologies.

---

18 Diary entry of February 17, 1917 (cf. Hensel 2007: 131).
19 English translation by the author.

Warburg's turn towards the study of images, born out of the scientific traditions of philosophy and anthropology of culture, prefigured future projects and
branches of German *Bildwissenschaft*. *Bildwissenschaft* has now evolved into
four main approaches:[20] (1) image history (*Historische Bildwissenschaft*) as an
extension and transgression of art history; (2) image anthropology; (3) image
philosophy; and (4) media studies of the image.[21] All of these sprang from the
disciplinary context and scholarship of art history. Due to these roots, image
history has developed into a kind of convergence point where different approaches – usually informed by the concepts of renowned German art historians
such as Hans Belting, Horst Bredekamp, and Gottfried Boehm, and also Martin
Warnke and Martin Kemp – potentially meet and fuse. Bredekamp's approach
most directly connects with the Warburgian (and Panofskian) legacy of image
history and its extension into media-critical art history.

Endeavors to integrate the various German approaches to the study of images – that is, to form and institutionalize a *Bildwissenschaft* in German academia – have been undertaken. Two volumes edited by Klaus Sachs-Hombach
document this joint project and provide evidence of efforts toward the unification of *Bildwissenschaft*. Whereas the first volume proposes launching an interdisciplinary project, inquiring into contributing disciplines, methods, and topics (Sachs-Hombach 2005), the second volume explores the cultural and
anthropological foundations upon which a general *Bildwissenschaft* could be
built (Sachs-Hombach 2009). As ambitious as these two projects have been,
they did not result in the transdisciplinary formation and academic institutionalization of the cultural study of the image (see also Bachmann-Medick 2008:
12). The project of unifying and integrating various *Bildwissenschaft*en into one
overarching *Bildwissenschaft* has failed – in part due to the fact that the diversity of image studies' approaches resisted the uniform, semiotic-based framework
of a General Image Science (*Allgemeine Bildwissenschaft*). Today's situation of
transnational German *Bildwissenschaft*en is characterized by the paradox that
the iconic turn promised to break up disciplinary, scientific-cultural barriers
and implement transdisciplinarity as trans-science but ended up renewing and
reviving existing (multi)disciplinary structures of science. It is a fact that *Bildwissenschaft* was absorbed as a new and challenging research topic by a rich

---

20 For a detailed discussion of the main positions of *Bildwissenschaft*, see Bachmann-Medick
2010: 334–352.
21 I deliberately avoid the common English term 'visual media studies,' since it would be
misleading.

variety of disciplines from the humanities through to the social sciences and life sciences; this process has, meanwhile, turned it into a kind of subdiscipline.

With regard to the initial uneasy relation between *Bildwissenschaft* and art history, it can be stated that, today, *Bildwissenschaft* has become a constituent part of and companion to art history and that it has – in a positive sense – reshaped art-historical studies into culture- and media-critical studies. Due to the etymological relatedness between *Bild* (image) and *Bildung* (education/formation), *Bildwissenschaft* also had a strong impact on pedagogy and graphic design. This has given rise to the proclamation and theorization of visual competence as a highly relevant skill for coping with the visual overkill of today's digital media society in both practical and theoretical terms. James Elkins' lecture "Farewell to Visual Studies" points in the same direction just mentioned: the enforced integration of the visual studies perspective into the framework of existing disciplines, as well as the incorporation of the study of the visual into new multisensory and hypermodal research. It remains to be seen how this turn might affect the international distribution of study programs in visual culture on a global scale.

4 Transcultural Image Studies: The Emergence of Global Art History and World Art Studies

As transnational as the study of the visual has been, a focalization of visual/image studies on inter- and transculturation processes as core elements and main effects of the visual-cultural turn is still largely underrepresented. In both Anglo-American visual culture studies and German *Bildwissenschaften*, conceptual approaches to and case studies of visual transculturality can be found (Mirzoeff 2002; Belting 2001; Mersmann 2004, 2008, 2013). Until now, they remained marginal, representing only one visual study-track among various others. This might have to do with the fact that transculturation is regarded as a 'natural' ingredient of the visual-cultural turn. As a consequence, visual studies have concentrated on acting under the theoretical umbrella of global studies, postcolonial studies, and/or translation studies but have not specifically problematized or theorized visual or iconic transculturality in order to build a prominent branch of transcultural visual/image studies.[22]

---

22 For the difference between studies in visual transculture and transcultural visual studies, see Mersmann 2004.

A relatively recent phenomenon is that art history alone, the traditional discipline of visual/image study, has leapt into the void left by visual/image studies as cultural studies, filling it with new inter- and transcultural conceptualizations. Academic asynchronies and asymmetries, described earlier, are emphasized by the fact that the postcolonial turn has left almost no mark on art history, in particular German art history, as a constituent part of the cultural turn (Schmidt-Linsenhoff 2002). Currently, art history as a discipline of Western/European academic origin and coinage is undergoing an extensive and profound transnational turn that partially involves a postcolonial turn with regard to the self-reflection of its own history as a discipline, i.e. the colonial history of art history.

Two models of art history with global perspectives have emerged as transnational extensions of the classical art-historical scope and canon: world art studies and global art history. Both art-historical reorientations are motivated by the global challenge to surmount the cultural and academic split between Western art history and non-Western art histories, including regional art histories; however, their conceptualizations of how this could and should happen differ tremendously. We are not confronted with a rift between an Anglo-American and German model of art-historical reformation, as in the case of visual culture studies and *Bildwissenschaft*, but rather a split between disciplinary approaches and scientific traditions in addressing and categorizing art-(ifacts) from all over the world. In a nutshell, this rift is determined by a split between art and anthropology/ethnology, traditionally preoccupied with the study of 'foreign' – that is, non-European – artifacts, including the preservation of this visual cultural heritage, on the one hand, and art history as shaped historically and methodologically by the aesthetic analysis of Western-European high art, on the other hand.

As its title signals, world art studies adopts the historical concept of world art that was predominant in Europe around 1900 and tries to redefine it in light of the current globalization of art and the need to globalize art history. The revival of the study of world art was initiated by John Onions, who published the *Atlas of World Art* in 2004. Kitty Zijlmans and Wilfried van Damme (2008) continued to conceptualize world art studies as a new, comprehensive approach to visual art. Based on a critique of West-centrism in traditional art history, world art studies aims to expand the research scope and framework of visual art by including artistic forms of expression from all over the world and throughout the ages. To explore world art as the heritage of mankind, different disciplinary approaches and methods from the fields of anthropology, evolutionary biology, and neurosciences are applied. Kitty Zijlmans emphasizes intercultural perspectives as counter-discourses to Western models and methods in art history. The intercultural approach is intended to apply to both art and art history, thus, allowing for critical assessment of Western art historiography.

Zijlmans' intercultural conceptualization of art (history) is productive to the extent that it seeks – despite its adherence to the somewhat problematic notion of interculturality – to escape binary oppositions of appropriation and othering, inclusion and exclusion, centre and periphery, by stressing the dynamic exchange and circulation involved in intercultural interactions. Zijlmans underlines the fluctuating relationships between center and periphery, Western and non-Western art, by which fixed positions are constantly shifted and cultural syncretisms produced. She, accordingly, discards the idea of a fixed canon of art. As important and pressing as the intercultural perspectivization of world art studies is, it remains questionable to what extent the notion of art is adequate and resilient within this framework. One might ask whether this perspective is not too strongly loaded with values and definitional sovereignties to apply it to works of world 'art,' or, more neutrally formulated, visual artifacts produced worldwide. To come to terms with this inconsistency, an inter- and transcultural critique of art, its diverse concepts, aesthetics and practices in visual cultures around the globe is required.

Global art history, as a newly emerging field of study in both North America and Germany, is shaped by a different orientation. It does not envisage an expansion in terms of global objects of study, as pursued by world art studies. Rather, it projects a global perspective onto art history as an academic discipline and method. While world art studies confronts universalist claims, hegemonies of material culture, and the past and presence of colonial heritage, global art history faces Western disciplinary hegemony – its theories, methods, and historical self-conception. James Elkins' roundtable discussion *Is Art History Global?* – later published as a book under the same title (2007) – was a testing ground for inquiring into the legitimacy and suitability of global art history. It debated the conditions and prerequisites for art history to become a global discipline. The discussion participants all, to greater or lesser extents, agreed that global art history could and should be determined by common research methods and theories. This, however, engenders a dilemma: the unavoidable nature of art history's Western socialization as an academic discipline. Independent of the global nature of the art-historical field, applied methods and theories usually belong to a West-centered art-historical discourse.[23] Due to the

---

[23] From this split situation, Elkins draws the conclusion that a global art history can only be united by a Western model. This view is hegemonic, as it imposes the (still) dominant Western knowledge and science system onto non-European art and art history.

fact that art history originated as a Western/European academic discipline, we face a disciplinary and institutional vacuum in non-European and non-North-American countries. How to accommodate these imbalances?

German academia is among the forerunners in forming art history as a discipline of global scope. The topic of 'global art' and its relation to art history was first introduced by the German art historian Hans Belting. It was defined from a specific focal point, namely, the relation between "Global Art and the Museum."[24] According to Belting's interpretation, global art is a recent contemporary phenomenon, produced by international art festivals and their curators' ambitions. Based on this observation, he argues that global art, due to its inherent contemporaneousness, determinedly forms a counter-concept to modern art – in particular its universal ideals. The introduction of the concept of the 'global contemporary' takes this 'newness' into account. Global art is not only "critical in political terms" but also "in terms of art categories defined by inclusion or exclusion. New art often blurs any kind of border between mainstream art, on the one side, and popular art, on the other, and thus abolishes the old dualism between Western art and ethnographic practice by using indigenous traditions as reference" (Belting and Buddensieg 2009: 40). Based on the notion that global art, as global contemporary art, only came into being twenty years ago, global art history does not encompass the history of global art but is rather a "global extension of today's art history as a method and academic discipline" (Belting and Buddensieg 2009: 45).

One of the main problems is the conflict between the pronounced contemporary definition of global art and the historical dimension of art history as an academic discipline. The approach to global art history pursued by Monica Juneja is laid out to reconcile these differences.[25] On the one hand, she objects to global art history's definition as history of art from around the world, clearly marking it off from world art history/world art studies and their universalistic claim to "compile the history of art comprehensively around the globe or even in one single time frame" (Juneja 2012: 6). By defining global art history as transcultural art history, she not only emphasizes the self-critical revision of art history's Eurocentric methods, theories and subjects but also encourages the transhistorical study of the globalization of art and art history.[26] In this concep-

---

24 See his research project of the same title located at the Centre for Art and Media Technology (ZKM) in Karlsruhe, Germany (cf. Belting et al 2013).

25 Monica Juneja holds a professorship for Global Art History at the Cluster of Excellence Asia and Europe in a Global Context at the Universität Heidelberg, Germany.

26 "Globale Verflechtungsprozesse lassen sich durch fast alle Zeiten hindurch untersuchen – selbstverständlich haben sie je nach historischem Kontext einen anderen Charakter als die

tion, deconstruction plays a key role in inducing the de-westernization (and also decolonization) of art history. It is targeted at debunking the classical binarism between Western and non-Western art (and art history) and the tendency to essentialize identities and indigenize alterities. Fixed art-historical categorizations, be they national, regional or religious, are problematized and questioned by transculturations as processes of entangled art histories. This also involves an art-historical analysis of how the term and idea of art was shaped historically in different regional contexts.

A transculturally designed art history is the conceptual framework for the first study program in global art history in Germany. At the Freie Universität zu Berlin, the MA program Art History in a Global Context (*Kunstgeschichte im globalen Kontext*) was launched in the academic year 2008/2009. It represents the innovative merging of art history and regional studies, among them Asian and African studies, under the departmental roof of History and Cultural Studies. Art history can be studied with a focus on either Europe and America, East Asia, South Asia, or Africa. While the classical continental/regional mapping of cultural studies persists in these specializations, the theoretical program aims at surpassing these allocations, searching for new models and methodologies that surmount regional focuses: "Die Forschergruppe untersucht künstlerische Artefakte als 'Agenten' innerhalb eines transkulturellen Verhandlungsraumes, der sich im Agieren und Interagieren von und mit ihnen erst formiert. In den Teilprojekten soll daher untersucht werden, wie sich künstlerische Artefakte und Praktiken als Reflexionsmedien kultureller Verhandlungsprozesse herausgebildet haben" (Stemmrich 2012: 98).

The transcultural approach proves to be a connective model in German academia that shapes global art history as an academic discipline and a methodology. This might be ascribed to the fact that transculturality was most prominently theorized by the German philosopher Wolfgang Welsch (1994) and has, since its framing, seen vital reconceptualizations in academic discourses on the globalization of culture. As challenging and promising as it seems to utilize the concept of transculturality for global art history, it should be made clear that it is taken seriously as a model that transgresses inter- and multicultural constructions of visual art and culture. If global art history as transcultural art history is

---

moderne Globalisierung. Es gilt also für jeden Bereich und für jeden Zeitraum, nach weiträumigen Beziehungen zwischen Kulturen zu fragen und sie ans Lokale zurückzubinden. Eine transkulturell ausgerichtete Kunstgeschichte hat das Ziel, die vielfältigen Prozesse der Aneignung, Abgrenzung, Rekonfigurierung und Übersetzung in neuen Zusammenhängen herauszuarbeiten, um nach der konstitutiven Rückwirkung dieser Prozesse auf alle daran beteiligten Agenten und visuellen Systeme zu fragen" (Juneja 2012: 7).

not able to exceed the traditional 'modern' framework of writing art history as a history of mutual influences and relations, if it becomes stranded as comparative art history, then it will not fulfill its 'global' claim.

What are the consequences of this global perspectivization and 'transcultural turn' in art-historical studies, from global art history to world art studies? What are its effects on the transnational study of culture, including the study of visual culture and *Bildwissenschaft*? As a matter of fact, globally defined art studies cannot avoid growing into transnational transdisciplines. In order to successfully navigate, negotiate, and translate between different notions, models, and histories of art, as well as bridge the interdisciplinary gap between art history and cultural/regional studies as main scientific actors, they will undergo this transformation process naturally. The fierce battle over which new art-historical approach, world art studies or global art history, is better suited to transnationalize art and art history is of secondary importance. It marks the line of conflict that runs between two distinct fields of interest and worldviews pushed to the forefront by globalization: culture-anthropological versus art-theoretical approach; a historical (including prehistorical and transhistorical) perspective with a focus on human civilization versus a contemporary perspective with an emphasis on the art system, its conceptual and institutional framework. By turning attention to differences, assimilations, and fusions between Western and non-Western art forms and functions in a global context, idiosyncrasies are laid bare.

What surfaces with vivid urgency is the question of the relationship between cultural perception and symbolic form with regard to the sensorial and representational modes of seeing and visualizing. Under these circumstances, the research agenda of visual studies gains top priority for the field of global art studies; if globally oriented art studies aspire to develop into transnational studies of high world impact, they cannot circumvent dealing with the cultural and social construction of vision, the gaze, and visuality. They must, indeed, deal with techniques of seeing and practices of displaying while also exploring their neuroscientific underpinnings. Because the entanglement of the visual in systems of power is highly concentrated in the global art world, globally oriented art studies are obliged to act as a critical iconology in the sense of Mitchell.

Image studies could assume an important role in mediating art studies, visual studies, anthropological studies, and cultural studies to form a new branch of transcultural visual studies. The various approaches and theories put forward by German *Bildwissenschaft*, such as Belting's *Image Anthropology*, Boehm's *Iconic Criticism*, and Bredekamp's *Theory of Image Act*, have the potential to move in this direction, since they (1) do not operate with a fixed notion of art but rather with an open 'image' concept that also includes non-artistic images and visual practices; (2) are characterized less by object access rather than by methodological and theoretical orientations; (3) proceed inter- and transdisciplinarily, thus, facilitating new conceptual syntheses; (4) draw upon forms and functions of seeing, perceiving, and representing and, thereby, (5) help discern cultural differences and transculturations in the fluctuation zone between visual culture, cultural images, and visual art. Due to the fact that they have been (until now) historically and politically unburdened, aesthetically neutral, and approach-oriented, image studies could not only help translate between Western/European and non-European art histories, but they could also facilitate the academic transition from global art studies to transnational cultural studies. By acting as science brokers, image studies might considerably contribute to the development of a new set of methodological tools and theories in the service of shaping global art studies as transcultural studies. In order to be successfully implemented, the transnational study of the visual will also have to integrate non-European concepts and approaches, including indigenous methods.

Reassessing the effects of the iconic turn, it might seem paradoxical that, among the traditional disciplines of the humanities, it is art history alone – one of the most vehement opponents to the visual culture studies movement – that has found new ways to expand and transform itself into transnational cultural studies. *Bildwissenschaft*, until now a German *Sonderweg*, could surf on art history's wave of globalization and potentially grow into a transnational transdiscipline: visual studies.

References

Audric, Lorrain. "Visual Cultural Studies in France." *Imago*.
    http://culturevisuelle.org/imago/archives/13, 2010 (22 July 2013).
Bachmann-Medick, Doris. "Gegen Worte – Was heißt 'Iconic/Visual Turn'?" *Gegenworte. Hefte für den Disput über Wissen* 20 (2008): 10–15.
Bachmann-Medick, Doris. *Cultural Turns. Neuorientierungen in den Kulturwissenschaften.* 4th edition. Reinbek: Rowohlt, 2010 [2006].
Belting, Hans. *Bild-Anthropologie. Entwürfe für eine Bildwissenschaft.* Munich: Fink, 2001.
Belting, Hans. ed. *Bilderfragen. Die Bildwissenschaften im Aufbruch.* Munich: Fink, 2007.
Belting, Hans, and Andrea Buddensieg, eds. *The Global Art World: Audiences, Markets, and Museums.* Ostfildern: Hatje Cantz, 2009.
Belting, Hans, Andrea Buddensieg, and Peter Weibel, eds. *The Global Contemporary and the Rise of New Art Worlds.* Cambridge, MA: MIT Press, 2013.
Boehm, Gottfried. "Die Wiederkehr der Bilder." *Was ist ein Bild?* Ed. Gottfried Boehm. Munich: Fink, 1994. 11–38.

Boehm, Gottfried. *Wie Bilder Sinn erzeugen. Die Macht des Zeigens*. Berlin: Berlin University Press, 2007.

Boehm, Gottfried, ed. *Was ist ein Bild?* Munich: Fink, 2004.

Boehm, Gottfried, and W.J.T. Mitchell. "Pictorial versus Iconic Turn: Two Letters." *The Pictorial Turn*. Ed. Neal Curtis. New York: Routledge, 2010. 8–26.

Bredekamp, Horst. "Drehmomente – Merkmale und Ansprüche des iconic turn." *Iconic Turn. Die neue Macht der Bilder*. Eds. Christa Maar and Hubert Burda. Cologne: DuMont, 2004. 15–26.

Bredekamp, Horst. *Theorie des Bildakts. Über das Lebensrecht des Bildes*, Frankfurt a.M.: Suhrkamp, 2011.

Bruhn, Matthias. *Das Bild. Theorie – Geschichte – Praxis*. Berlin: Akademie Verlag, 2009.

Burda, Hubert, ed. *In medias res. Zehn Kapitel zum Iconic Turn*. Munich, Fink, 2010.

Cassirer, Ernst. *Philosophie der symbolischen Formen*, vol. 1. Darmstadt: WBG, 1964.

Curtis, Neal, ed. *The Pictorial Turn*. London: Routledge, 2010.

Daney, Serge. "Vor und nach dem Bild." *Politics-Poetics. Das Buch zur documenta X*. Ed. Catherine David. Osterfildern: Hatje Cantz, 1997.

Dikovitskaya, Margaret. *Visual Culture: The Study of the Visual after the Cultural Turn*. Cambridge, MA: MIT Press, 2005.

Elkins, James. *Visual Studies: A Skeptical Introduction*. New York/London: Routledge, 2003.

Elkins, James. *Is Art History Global?* New York: Routledge, 2007.

Faßler, Manfred. *Bildlichkeit*. Vienna/Cologne/Weimar: Böhlau, 2002.

Frank, Gustav, and Barbara Lange, eds. *Einführung in die Bildwissenschaft. Bilder in der visuellen Kultur*. Darmstadt: WBG, 2010.

Hensel, Thomas. "'Von der Kunstgeschichte zur Wissenschaft vom Bilde' (Aby Warburg) oder von der Geburt der Bildwissenschaft aus Sendetrommeln, Karoluszellen und Stromschwankungen." *Carte Blanche. Mediale Formate in der Kunst der Moderne*. Ed. Silke Walther. Berlin: Kadmos, 2007.

Hornuff, Daniel. *Bildwissenschaft im Widerstreit. Belting, Boehm, Bredekamp, Burda*. Munich: Fink, 2012.

Imdahl, Max. *Giotto. Arenafresken: Ikonographie-Ikonologie-Ikonik*. Munich: Fink, 1988.

Juneja, Monica. "Kunstgeschichte und kulturelle Differenz. Eine Einleitung." *Kritische Berichte* 2 (2012): 6–12.

Mersmann, Birgit. "Bildkulturwissenschaft als Kultur*Bildwissenschaft*? Von der Notwendigkeit eines inter- und transkulturellen Iconic Turn." *Zeitschrift für Ästhetik und Allgemeine Kunstwissenschaft* 49.1 (2004): 91–109.

Mersmann, Birgit. "(Fern-)Verkehr der Bilder. Mediologie als methodischer Brückenschlag zwischen Bild- und Übersetzungswissenschaft." *Mediologie als Methode*. Eds. Birgit Mersmann and Thomas Weber. Berlin: Avinus, 2008. 149–167.

Mersmann, Birgit. "Global Routes: Transmediation and Transculturation as Key Concepts of Translation Studies." *Transmediality and Transculturality*. Eds. Nadja Gernalzick and Gabriele Pisarz-Ramirez. Heidelberg: Winter, 2013. 405–423.

Mirzoeff, Nicholas. "Visual Colonialism/Visual Transculture." *The Visual Culture Reader*. Ed. Nicholas Mirzoeff. New York: Routledge, 2002. 473–482.

Mitchell, W.J.T. *Picture Theory: Essays on Verbal and Visual Representation*. Chicago: University of Chicago Press, 1994.

Mitchell, W.J.T. *What do Pictures Want?* Chicago: University of Chicago Press, 2004.

Moxey, Keith. "Visual Studies and the Iconic Turn." *Journal of Visual Culture* 7 (2008): 131–145.

Peirce, Charles Sanders. *The Philosophy of Peirce: Selected Writings*. Ed. Justus Buchler. New York: Dover, 1955.

Probst, Jörg, and Jost Philipp Klenner, eds. *Ideengeschichte der Bildwissenschaft*. Frankfurt a.M.: Suhrkamp, 2009.

Sachs-Hombach, Klaus. *Bildtheorien. Anthropologische und kulturelle Grundlagen des Visualistic Turn*. Frankfurt a.M.: Suhrkamp, 2009.

Sachs-Hombach, Klaus, ed. *Bildwissenschaft. Disziplinen, Themen, Methoden*. Frankfurt a.M.: Suhrkamp, 2005.

Schmidt-Linsenhoff, Viktoria. "Warum hat die kritische Kunstgeschichte in Deutschland den postcolonial turn ausgelassen?" *Kunst und Politik. Jahrbuch der Guernica Gesellschaft* 4 (2002): 7–16.

Schulz, Martin. *Ordnungen der Bilder. Einführung in die Bildwissenschaft*. Munich: Fink, 2005.

Stemmrich, Gregor. "Zur Einrichtung der Forschergruppe 'Transkulturelle Verhandlungsräume von Kunst. Komparatistische Perspektiven auf historische Kontexte und aktuelle Konstellationen' (FOR 1703) am Kunsthistorischen Institut der Freien Universität Berlin." *Kritische Berichte* 2 (2012): 97–101.

Welsch, Wolfgang. "Transkulturalität – die veränderte Verfassung heutiger Kulturen." *Sichtweisen. Die Vielheit in der Einheit*. Ed. Freimut Duve. Weimar: Stiftung Weimarer Klassik, 1994. 83–122.

Zijlmans, Kitty, and Wilfried van Damme, eds. *World Art Studies: Exploring Concepts and Approaches*. Amsterdam: Valiz, 2008.

Notes on Contributors

Doris Bachmann-Medick is Permanent Senior Research Fellow at the International Graduate Centre for the Study of Culture (GCSC) of the Justus-Liebig-Universität Giessen. She held numerous appointments as a visiting professor, recently at the universities of Graz, Göttingen, Cincinnati, and the University of California, Irvine. Her main fields of research are cultural theory, *Kulturwissenschaften*, literary anthropology, and translation studies. Her publications include *Die ästhetische Ordnung des Handelns. Moralphilosophie und Ästhetik in der Popularphilosophie des 18. Jahrhunderts* (Metzler, 1989), the edited volumes *Übersetzung als Repräsentation fremder Kulturen* (Erich Schmidt, 1997), *Kultur als Text. Die anthropologische Wende in der Literaturwissenschaft* (Francke, 2004 [1996]), the special issue "The Translational Turn" of the journal *Translation Studies* (2009), and the monograph *Cultural Turns. Neuorientierungen in den Kulturwissenschaften* (Rowohlt, 2014 [2006]) (English translation: De Gruyter, 2016). She serves on the editorial board of *Translation Studies* (since 2008).

Boris Buden is a writer and cultural critic based in Berlin. He received his PhD in cultural theory from the Humboldt-Universität zu Berlin. His essays and articles cover the topics of philosophy, politics, cultural and art criticism. He has participated in various conferences and art projects in Western and Eastern Europe, Asia and the USA, including *Documenta XI*. Buden is a Permanent Research Fellow at the European Institute for Progressive Cultural Policies in Vienna and Visiting Professor in the Faculty of Art and Design, Bauhaus-Universität Weimar. His recent publications include: *Übersetzung. Das Versprechen eines Begriffs* (with S. Nowotny; Turia + Kant, 2008), *Zone des Übergangs. Vom Ende des Postkommunismus* (Suhrkamp, 2009), *Findet Europa. Eine Suche in der Dolmetscherkabine* (Turia + Kant, 2013).

Dipesh Chakrabarty is the Lawrence A. Kimpton Distinguished Service Professor in the Departments of History, South Asian Languages and Civilizations, and the College at the University of Chicago and the former Faculty Director of the University of Chicago Center in Delhi. He is also a Faculty Fellow at the Chicago Center for Contemporary Theory, an Associate Faculty member of the Department of English, and he holds a courtesy appointment at the University of Chicago Law School and a visiting position at the Research School of Humanities at the Australian National University in Canberra. He is a founding member of the editorial collective *Subaltern Studies*, a co-editor of *Critical Inquiry*, and a founding editor of *Postcolonial Studies*. Chakrabarty's current research is focused on three areas: the history of objectivity in history with a focus on the Indian historian Sir Jadunath Sarkar (1870–1958); the implications of the science of climate change for historical and political thinking; and democracy and political thought in South Asia.

Christa Knellwolf King is Senior Researcher at the Universität Wien, where she teaches English and Comparative Literature, and she is an Honorary Professor at the University of Queensland. She has published two monographs on early modern literature, *Representations of the Feminine in the Poetry of Alexander Pope* (Manchester University Press, 1998) and *Faustus and the Promises of the New Science* (Ashgate, 2008), as well as several collections of essays, including *The Cambridge History of Literary Criticism*, vol. 9 (Cambridge University Press, 2001), *The Enlightenment World* (Routledge, 2004), *Frankenstein's Science* (Ashgate, 2009), and *Stories of Empire* (WVT, 2009). She is currently completing a book manuscript entitled *Empire of the Mind*, which explains the role of voyaging literature in the dissemination of imperial ideology.

Andreas Langenohl is Professor of Sociology with a focus on Comparative Studies at Justus-Liebig-Universität Giessen. His research and teaching encompass the following areas: social studies of finance, economic sociology, modernization theory, societal majorities and minorities, transnationalism, and history and epistemology of the social sciences. His recent publications in English include "Modernization, Modernity, and Tradition: Sociological Theory's Promissory Notes" in *Rethinking Cultural Difference: Around the Work of Naoki Sakai* (Routledge, 2010), "Divided Time: Notes on Cosmopolitanism and the Theory of Second Modernity" in *European Cosmopolitanism in Question* (Palgrave Macmillan, 2012) and "Scenes of Voting: Reactions to the Swiss Referendum on the Ban on the Construction of Minarets (2009) in Switzerland and Germany" in *The Meanings of Europe: Changes and Exchanges of a Contested Concept* (Routledge, 2013). A monograph on town twinning as a local transnational practice is scheduled to come out with Palgrave Macmillan in 2014.

Christina Lutter is Professor at the History Department, Universität Wien. Her PhD deals with political communication in the early modern period (Oldenbourg, 1998); her habilitation deals with monastic reform communities in the 12th century (Oldenbourg, 2005). From 1994 to 2007, she worked at the Austrian Ministry of Science and Research in programme management and as Deputy/Head of the Department for Humanities & Social Sciences. She serves on the editorial boards of *Cultural Studies* (Routledge) and *Zeitschrift für Kulturwissenschaften* (transcript) and as Vice President of the Scientific Board of the International Research Centre Kulturwissenschaften (IFK) in Vienna. Her current research focuses on social and cultural communities across medieval religious, urban, and courtly spaces. Recent publications include: "Visions of Community: Comparative Approaches to Medieval Forms of Identity in Europe and Asia" (*History and Anthropology*, 2014), "Übersetzungen" (edited with B. Wagner and H. Lethen; *Zeitschrift für Kulturwissenschaften*, 2012), *Zwischen Hof und Kloster. Kulturelle Gemeinschaften im mittelalterlichen Österreich* (Böhlau, 2010), and *Cultural Studies. Eine Einführung*, 6th edition (with M. Reisenleitner; Löcker, 2008).

Birgit Mersmann is Professor of Non-Western and European Art at the international Jacobs University in Bremen. She studied art history and literature, earning her PhD from Ludwig-Maximilians-Universität, Munich. Before coming to Jacobs University in 2008, she was a Senior Researcher at The National Centre of Competence in Research (NCCR) Iconic Criticism at the Universität Basel in Switzerland. From 1998 to 2002, she taught as DAAD Visiting Professor in the department of German Language and Literature at Seoul National University in South Korea. Her research interests encompass image and media theory; art theory and aesthetics; theory and politics of exhibition; contemporary Western and Asian art; global art history; transculturality; cultural translation; and interrelations between script and image. Recent publications include: "Global Routes. Transmediation and Transculturation as Key Concepts of Translation Studies" in *Transmediality and Transculturality* (C. Winter, 2013), *Bild Macht Schrift. Schriftkulturen in bildkritischer Perspektive* (edited with A. Loprieno and C. Knigge Salis; Velbrück, 2011), *Transmission Image: Visual Translation and Cultural Agency* (edited with A. Schneider; Cambridge Scholars Publishing, 2009), *Movens Bild. Zwischen Affekt und Evidenz* (edited with G. Boehm and C. Spies; Fink, 2008), and *Kulturen des Bildes* (edited with M. Schulz; Fink, 2006).

Matthias Middell is Professor of Global History and the Director of the Global and European Studies Institute at the Universität Leipzig. He became Director of the Graduate Center Social Sciences and Humanities at the Research Academy Leipzig in 2006 and, since 2009, he also serves as Spokesperson of the Center for Area Studies at the Universität Leipzig. He was a visiting fellow and guest professor at the universities of Paris, Rennes, Rouen, Santa Barbara, Stellenbosch, Turin, and Yaoundé. In 2008, he was the Fulbright Distinguished Professor in Transnational History at Duke University and, in 2011, he was a Fellow of the Netherlands Institute for Advanced Study. Since 1991, he serves as an editor of the journal *Comparativ. Zeitschrift für Globalgeschichte* and, since 2004, he edits, together with Michel Espagne, the e-journal *geschichte.transnational*. His main research interests include global history with an emphasis on spatial configurations; cultural transfers between France and Germany as well as the history of historiography in the 19th and 20th centuries. Among his more recent publications are: *Transnational Challenges to National History Writing* (with L. Roura; Palgrave Macmillan, 2013) and *Self-Reflexive Area Studies* (Leipziger Universitätsverlag, 2013).

Ansgar Nünning is Professor of English and American Literature and Cultural Studies at Justus-Liebig-Universität Giessen. He is the founding and managing director of the "Giessener Graduiertenzentrum Kulturwissenschaften" (GGK) established in 2001; the "International Graduate Centre for the Study of Culture" (GCSC) funded by the Excellence Initiative and inaugurated in 2006; and of the European PhD Network "Literary and Cultural Studies." He had published extensively on English and American literature, cultural memory studies, genre theory, narratology, and literary and cultural theory. His most recent English book publications include *Travelling Concepts for the Study of Culture* (edited with B. Neumann; de Gruyter, 2012), *A History of the American Short Story: Genres – Developments – Model Interpretations* (edited with M. Basseler; WVT, 2011), *A History of British Drama: Genres – Developments – Model Interpretations* (edited with S. Baumbach and B. Neumann; WVT, 2011), *Cultural Ways of Worldmaking: Media and Narratives* (edited with V. Nünning and B. Neumann; de Gruyter, 2010), and *A Companion to Cultural Memory Studies* (edited with A. Erll; de Gruyter, 2008). He edited the 5th edition of the *Metzler Lexikon Literatur- und Kulturtheorie* (Metzler, 2013), and he is the editor of the series *Uni Wissen Anglistik/Amerikanistik, Uni Wissen Kernkompetenzen, WVT-Handbücher zum literaturwissenschaftlichen Studium* and *ELCH: English Literary and Cultural History* (both with V. Nünning) as well as *MCM: Media and Cultural Memory/ Medien und kulturelle Erinnerung* (with A. Erll) and *WVT-Handbücher zur Literatur- und Kulturdidaktik* (with W. Hallet).

Jon Solomon currently resides in Lyon, France, where he is Professor at the Institute of Transtextual and Transcultural Studies and Director of the Comparative Cultural Studies international Master's program at Université Jean Moulin (Lyon 3). Born in the United States and trained at Cornell University, he lived in east Asia for 25 years before coming to Europe and is competent in Chinese, Japanese, French and English. His current project is to develop a discussion of 'area' as an essential operation for the governing capacity of the state in parallel to the question of 'population,' a form of the investment of state power within life – what can be called, after Foucault, 'biopower.' These parallel operations of articulation called 'area' and 'population' are required by the state in order to give to itself an image of community called 'nation,' an image that folds back into itself in order to naturalize the modern form of belonging to the nation-state (which is essentially a form of racism), and to create heuristic measuring devices for 'normal' and 'exceptional' positionalities within it. Within this project, an examination of the biopolitics of translation occupies a privileged place for understanding the relations among anthropological difference, geocultural area, and primitive accumulation.

Thomas Weber has been Professor for Media Studies at the Universität Hamburg since October 2011 and Project Leader of "Topics and aesthetics of the documentary film," part of the DFG-project "History of the German documentary film after 1945" (started in 2012). Recent publications include: "Documentary Film in Media Transformation" (*InterDisciplines – Journal of History and Sociology*, 2013), *Mediale Transformationen des Holocausts* (edited with U. von Keitz; Avinus, 2013), *Medialität als Grenzerfahrung. Futurische Medien im Kino der 80er und 90er Jahre* (transcript, 2008), and *Mediologie als Methode* (edited with B. Mersmann; Avinus, 2008).

Rainer Winter is Full Professor of Media and Cultural Theory and Head of the Institute of Media and Communications at the Alpen-Adria-Universität in Klagenfurt at Lake Woerther (Austria). He is Adjunct Professor at the Charles Sturt University in Sydney (Australia). He held numerous appointments as a visiting professor, recently at the Capital Normal University Beijing, the Shanghai International Studies University and the Charles Sturt University in Bathurst (Australia). His publications include *Filmsoziologie. Eine Einführung in das Verhältnis von Film, Kultur und Gesellschaft* (Herbert von Halem, 1992), *Der produktive Zuschauer. Medienaneignung als kultureller und ästhetischer Prozess* (Herbert von Halem 2010 [1995]), *Die Kunst des Eigensinns. Cultural Studies als Kritik der Macht* (Velbrück, 2014 [2001]), and *Widerstand im Netz* (transcript, 2010). He has edited more than ten books: for example, *Global America? The Cultural Consequences of Globalization* (with U. Beck and N. Sznaider; Liverpool University Press, 2003; German translation: transcript, 2003; Chinese translation: Henan University Press, 2012), *Die Zukunft der Cultural Studies* (transcript, 2011) and *Transnationale Serienkulturen* (with S. Eichner and L. Mikos; Springer, 2013). He serves on the editorial boards of *European Journal of Cultural Studies* (since 2006) and *Cultural Studies* (since 2009).

Index

www.ingramcontent.com/pod-product-compliance
Lightning Source LLC
Chambersburg PA
CBHW051956270326
41929CB00015B/2672